Children of a Compassionate God

A Theological Exegesis of Luke 6:20-49

L. John Topel, S.J.

A Michael Glazier Book

THE LITURGICAL PRESS
Collegeville, Minnesota

www.litpress.org

A Michael Glazier Book published by The Liturgical Press

Cover design by David Manahan, O.S.B. Photo by CLEO Photos.

1   2   3   4   5   6   7   8

Library of Congress Cataloging-in-Publication Data

Topel, L. John.
    Children of a compassionate God : a theological exegesis of Luke 6:20-49 /
L. John Topel.
        p. cm.
    "A Michael Glazier book."
    Includes bibliographical references and index.
    ISBN 0-8146-5085-6 (alk. paper)
        1. Sermon on the mount—Commentaries. 2. Bible. N.T. Luke—Theology.
    I. Title.

 BT380.3 .T67 2001
 226.9'07—dc21   2001029591

Contents

Preface

The Subject

Most New Testament monographs begin with an apologia for yet another study of a shop-worn text. I need not apologize, for, although the Lukan Sermon on the Plain is one of the most significant foundations for Christian ethics, there has been, in the entire history of New Testament exegesis, only one brief study of this important text![1] The reasons for such neglect are various,[2] but with the advent of redaction criticism and literary-critical approaches to the NT they long ago lost their validity. The Lukan selection, compression, and rhetorical shaping of the traditional material has transformed it into an eloquent sermon with its own appeal for the contemporary Christian. The work cries out for exposition.

The Method

I was educated in historical-critical exegesis, the diachronic methods culminating in a kind of composition criticism that in the 1960s was forming a bridge between redaction criticism and a synchronic literary/rhetorical

[1] Heinrich Kahlefeld, *Der Jünger: eine Auslegung der Rede Lk 6,20-49* (Frankfurt: Josef Knecht, 1962), whose theological method argues from various passages of the gospel tradition rather than giving a theological exegesis of Luke itself.

[2] One of the reasons may be the Church's preference for the Gospel of Matthew; see Edouard Massaux, *The Influence of the Gospel of Saint Matthew on Christian Literature Before Saint Irenaeus,* translated by Norman J. Belval and Suzanne Hecht; edited and with an introduction and addenda by Arthur J. Bellinzoni. New Gospel Studies 5 (Leuven, Belgium: Peeters ; Macon, Ga.: Mercer, 1990), and his "Le texte du sermon sur la montagne de Mattieu utilisé par saint Justin," *ETL* 28 (1952) 411–48; Heinrich Greeven, "Erwägungen zur synoptischen Textkritik," *NTS* 6 (1959–60) 289. A second reason may be a conviction that the fullness of Matthew's version (107 verses compared to Luke's 30) gives a more complete picture of Jesus' ethical teaching as a whole; see my "The Lukan Version of the Lord's Sermon," *BTB* 11 (1981) 48–53 for further details.

criticism of the text.[3] I found congenial the increasing importance of more literary models of criticism in the 1970s and 1980s, and I have worked my way through structuralist, narrative, reader-response, and socio-critical approaches to NT exegesis. I have utilized the techniques which were helpful, but I have also discovered the internal contradictions of these theories that have led many NT critics to question them.[4] NT exegetical methodology is now more pluralistic than ever.

I seek a method that best brings out the underlying theological intent of the text, for the biblical text is at home not in the academic world but in the believing community.[5] Therefore I am not seeking some newer and better refinement of secular literary analysis as model. Biblical texts, repeatedly read in the believing community, shape and demand a different kind of listener and implied reader.[6] Further, the faith of the biblical reader goes far beyond the willing suspension of disbelief recommended by Co-

---

[3] For the methodology see Quentin Quesnell, *The Mind of Mark*. AnBib 38 (Rome: Biblical Institute Press, 1969) 45–57; William G. Thompson, *Matthew's Advice to a Divided Community*. AnBib 44 (Rome: Biblical Institute Press, 1970) 4–12.

[4] Against the (deconstructionist) hermeneutical principles that rely exclusively on objectification of the text see Paul Ricoeur, "The Hermeneutic Function of Distanciation," *Philosophy Today* 17 (1973) 129–41; *Time and Narrative*.Vol. 1 (Chicago: University of Chicago Press, 1984); V. Polythress, "Philosophical Roots of Phenomenological and Structuralist Literary Criticism," *WJT* 41 (1978–79) 165–71; Dame Helen Louise Gardner, *In Defence of the Imagination* (Oxford: Oxford University Press, 1982); D. S. Greenwood, "Poststructuralism and Biblical Studies: Frank Kermode's *The Genesis of Secrecy*," in R. T. France and David Wenham, eds., *Gospel Perspectives: Studies in Midrash and Historiography III* (Sheffield: JSOT Press, 1983) 263–88. Against a text-bound "reading" of the text, as opposed to an oral/aural "listening" to it, see Walter Ong, "The Writer's Audience is Always a Fiction," in his *Interfaces of the Word: Studies in the Evolution of Consciousness and Culture* (Ithaca: Cornell University Press, 1977); idem, *Orality and Literacy: The Technologizing of the Word* (New York: New Accents, 1982), especially 164–77. Against a literary criticism that fails to do justice to the "ideological" (I would say "theological") character of biblical narrative, see Meir Sternberg, *The Poetics of Biblical Narrative: Ideological Narrative and the Drama of Reading* (Bloomington, Ind.: Indiana University Press, 1985). For a synthetic attack on a host of defects of narrative/reader-response criticism see Stephen D. Moore, "Doing Gospel Criticism as/with a 'Reader,'" *BTB* 19 (1989) 85–93.

[5] Sandra Schneiders, *The Revelatory Text* (San Francisco: HarperSanFrancisco, 1991; new ed. Collegeville: The Liturgical Press, 1999), and Francis Watson, *Text, Church and World* (Grand Rapids: Eerdmans, 1994).

[6] As a Christian, I cannot come at the text as the "virgin reader" implied by most narrative-critical models of analysis. I have heard the text orally since I was a child, I have heard it interpreted by hundreds of preachers, and I have pored over it hundreds of times as a scholar. Further, this familiarity is not accidental to the NT text, since its origin and transmission were such that it has rarely had a Christian virginal reader. Thus the reception history of the text (the world in front of the text) and intertextuality are integral to the reader-response of the gospel text.

leridge or a "religious studies" approach.[7] Although Luke may have been trained in Hellenistic literature and rhetoric, his preface makes clear that he is not writing for literary effect, but to lay secure foundations under the faith of those already catechized in his community. He is, as redaction critics saw, a pastoral theologian.

Consequently, biblical interpretation must find its own method for its own kind of text.[8] At present I find composition criticism (as late-stage redaction criticism) the best available tool for uncovering the theological intent of the implied author. But I do not think naïvely that the author's *explicit intent* is all that resides in the text.[9] And so my composition criticism is enriched by the following approaches:

1. I welcome the shift from diachronic to synchronic methods. I will be interpreting the meaning of the text as a literary artifact interacting with today's reader. Historical questions explored by diachronic methods (the written sources, the oral tradition, the words and deeds of Jesus) are important elements of the whole interpretative process, but they are increasingly hypothetical, and so are better investigated only after one has explored synchronically the meaning of the final, canonical text as the whole literary work its author intended. Consequently, I will use diachronic methods (principally redaction criticism) only to uncover theological interests of the present Lukan text.

2. In synchronic method I begin from the difference in narrative criticism between the real author, the implied author, and the narrator; also between the narratee, the implied reader, and the real reader.[10] Here I wish to specify only one of these terms. The implied reader is the one implied by the text: the text presupposes the kind of reader who can take its directives and put the text together, create the text. The implied reader must be prepared to

[7] The Christian reader's faith and sacramental celebration of life link her to the intent of the author and his immediate readers much more closely than does the continuity in the same language or culture that, according to Gadamer, enables interpretation.

[8] Although I accept and admire Mark Coleridge's asssumption that "content and form, theology and technique, the 'what' and the 'how' of the biblical text, are inseparable" (*The Birth of the Lukan Narrative*. JSNT.SS 88 [Sheffield: Sheffield Academic Press, 1993] 14–20, especially 16), my emphasis will be clearly on the theology of the text.

[9] Again, Coleridge's discussion of the "surplus of meaning" beyond the authorital intent is especially cogent in *Birth of the Lukan Narrative* 19, especially n. 1.

[10] For the classical expositions of these terms see Wayne C. Booth, *The Rhetoric of Fiction* (Chicago: University of Chicago Press, 1961) and Wolfgang Iser, *The Implied Reader* (Baltimore: Johns Hopkins University Press, 1974) and the literature cited in both. For application to NT studies see Norman Petersen, *Literary Criticism for New Testament Critics* (Philadelphia: Fortress, 1978) and Terence J. Keegan, *Interpreting the Bible* (New York: Paulist, 1985).

engage the text in such a way as to enable the act of reading to transform her life. Although each reader brings her individual presuppositions and interests to the text, the more the readers share the preconceptions, world view, and interests of the implied author, the more they will approach the ideal reader who understands fully the meaning communicated by the text.

Still, one cannot shuffle off all the particular interests of the implied reader into a category called the real reader, who is not part of the interpretative process. If the individual real reader shares the major presuppositions of the author (is willing to have his life interpreted by the text) and has the grounds (e.g., faith) for this to happen, then his individual ways of doing this will be part of the implied reader envisaged by the text. Thus my notion of the implied reader emphasizes those aspects of Iser and Resseguie's reader-response criticism that integrate individual interpretation into the implied reader.[11]

In my view, the implied reader of Luke is a person of Christian faith (Luke 1:4), living in a Christian community where there is some controversy over who Jesus is and what discipleship means. She will approach the "ideal reader" if her community is exercised over the meaning of the parousia, the reality of persecution, the problems of poverty and other injustice, the object of prayer, the "reality" of Jesus, and the other themes of the gospel. I expect I will fill the role of the implied reader insofar as I listen to[12]

> (1) how the biblical tradition (text, and community shaped by that text) has already created the Christian person I am, my world-view and aspirations, as well as my heuristic approach to interpreting the text;
>
> (2) how the words, structures, and resonances of the text engage not only my mind's efforts to "put it all together," but also my affections and aspirations to be healed by the good news and live it;[13]
>
> (3) how the good news summons me to Christian orthopraxis in my community and world.[14]

---

[11] Iser, *Implied Reader,* 274–75; James L. Resseguie, "Reader-Response Criticism and the Synoptic Gospels," *JAAR* 52 (1984) 307–24, especially 307–308, and Moore's discussion in "Doing Gospel Criticism," 89–90.

[12] See Moore's cogent criticism of the anachronistic psychocultural assumptions of a typographic culture which underlie reader-response criticism as currently practiced, ibid., 86.

[13] Here I am enriched by, and endorse, Moore's criticism of "the Unfeeling Reader" in ibid., 87–88.

[14] See Bernard Lonergan's demonstration that deliberation and action necessarily follow on knowing in his *Method in Theology* (New York: Herder and Herder, 1972) 34–36. In gospel criticism see again the suggestions of Moore, "Doing Gospel Criticism," 88.

3. Again, in Part I, the narrative of Luke 1:1–6:19, I will attend to some of the following literary elements, which embody the theology of the text:

a. Narrative Style: I will examine point of view (the degree of omniscience of the narrator) and voice (analytically caught in the characterization of the narrator).

b. Plot Analysis: I will examine rising action, complication, climax, anticlimax, subplot, as well as temporal sequence, retrospective and anticipatory breaks in chronological order, and the long or short duration of reporting.

c. Reader Response: I will look at the gaps, ambiguity, redundancy, and patterns of analogy that engage the reader in recreating the text.[15]

4. Finally, since I think that the gospel genre is as much rhetorico-didactic as it is narrative, the techniques of the rhetorical criticism developed by James Muilenburg and by George A. Kennedy will be integral to my reading of Luke 1:1–6:19, and especially of 6:20-49.[16]

Gratitude to Colleagues

I conclude this Preface with an expression of gratitude to those who have made its production possible: to Norbert Lohfink, S.J., Ignace de la Potterie, S.J., and Luis Alonso-Schökel, S.J., who introduced me to historical, redaction, and literary criticism of the Bible at the Pontifical Biblical Institute; to Quentin Quesnell of Marquette University, who impressed on me the theological approach to the text that has informed not only my work but my life; to the Most Reverend Terrence Prendergast, S.J., D.D., who, as dean of St. Mary's College in Toronto, facilitated a sabbatical semester that

[15] My mentors in this kind of criticism have been principally Robert E. Scholes and Robert Kellogg, *The Nature of Narrative* (New York: Oxford University Press, 1966); Wayne C. Booth, *Rhetoric;* Wolfgang Iser, *Implied Reader* and *The Act of Reading: A Theory of Aesthetic Response* (Baltimore: Johns Hopkins University Press, 1978); Gérard Genette, *Narrative Discourse: An Essay in Method,* translated by Jane E. Lewin (Ithaca: Cornell University Press, 1985); Meir Sternberg, *Expositional Modes and Temporal Ordering in Fiction* (Baltimore: Johns Hopkins University Press, 1978) and idem, *Poetics of Biblical Narrative.*

[16] For the foundational idea see James Muilenberg, "Form Criticism and Beyond," *JBL* 88 (1969) 1–18; Jared J. Jackson and Martin Kessler, eds., *Rhetorical Criticism: Essays in Honor of James Muilenburg* (Pittsburgh: Pickwick, 1974), especially ix–xviii; for a more systematic sketch see George A. Kennedy, *New Testament Interpretation through Rhetorical Criticism* (Chapel Hill, N.C.: University of North Carolina Press, 1985), and the literature cited there; Burton L. Mack, *Rhetoric and the New Testament* (Minneapolis: Fortress, 1990.

enabled me to pick up a project that had lain fallow for fifteen years and to write the first two chapters of this book; to William Sullivan, s.j., who appointed me to the Stamper Chair of Catholic Intellectual and Cultural Traditions at Seattle University, which afforded me the time for research needed to complete the manuscript; to Dennis Hamm, s.j., Professor of New Testament at Creighton University for a reading of the penultimate draft that was both critical and encouraging; to Linda Maloney, whose careful editing of the text has purged it of many errors; to Jomar Nacanaynay, my research assistant, for his diligent proofreading and the creation of the biblical index. I thank the University of North Carolina Press for permission to reproduce Gerhard Lenski's illustration in my Appendix B.

Finally, I wish to dedicate this book to my first teachers, upon whose foundation every other bit of my education depends: to my father and mother who taught me to seek the truth, and to the Sisters of the Holy Names of Jesus and Mary, who gave me the tools for learning. Most of those who taught me at St. Joseph's school in Seattle have gone to their reward and some changed their names, but these ring in my memory: Sisters Rebecca Mary, Joanne Marie, Bernard Marie, Elaine Claire, Jeanne Claire, Veronica Maureen, and Imelda Ann. May their tribe increase!

Abbreviations

ABD	David Noel Freedman, ed. *The Anchor Bible Dictionary.* 6 vols. Garden City, N.Y.: Doubleday, 1992.
AnBib	Analecta Biblica
ANET	James Pritchard, ed. *Ancient Near Eastern Texts Relating to the Old Testament.* Princeton, N.J.: Princeton University Press, 1969.
ATANT	Abhandlungen zur Theologie des Alten und Neuen Testaments
AUSS	*Andrews University Seminary Studies*
BAGD	Walter Bauer, William F. Arndt, F. Wilbur Gingrich, and Frederick W. Danker. *A Greek-English Lexicon of the New Testament and Other Early Christian Literature.* Chicago: University of Chicago Press, 1961.
BBB	Bonner Biblische Beiträge
Bib	*Biblica*
BibRes	*Biblical Research*
BiKi	*Bibel und Kirche*
Billerbeck	Hermann L. Strack and Paul Billerbeck, *Kommentar zum Neuen Testament aus Talmud und Midrasch.* 6 vols. in 7. Munich: Beck, 1922–1961.
BTB	*Biblical Theology Bulletin*
BZ	*Biblische Zeitschrift*
BZNW	Beihefte zur *ZNW*
CBQ	*Catholic Biblical Quarterly*
CCER	*Cahiers du Cercle Ernest-Renan*
CTS	College Theology Society
CurTM	*Currents in Theology and Mission*
DBT	Xavier Léon-Dufour, ed. *Dictionary of Biblical Theology.* New York: Seabury, 1973.

EBT	Johannes B. Bauer, ed. *Encyclopedia of Biblical Theology: The Complete Sacramentum Verbi*. New York: Crossroad, 1981.
EDNT	Horst Balz and Gerhard Schneider, eds. *Exegetical Dictionary of the New Testament*. 3 vols. Grand Rapids: Eerdmans, 1990–1993.
ETL	*Ephemerides theologicae lovanienses*
ETS	Erfurter theologische Studien
EvTh	*Evangelische Theologie*
ExpT	*Expository Times*
GB	Max Zerwick. *Graecitas Biblica*. Rome: Biblical Institute Press, 1966.
GL	*Glaube und Lehre*
HTKNT	Herders theologischer Kommentar zum Neuen Testament
HTR	*Harvard Theological Review*
ICC	International Critical Commentary
IndThSt	*Indian Theological Studies*
Int	*Interpretation*
JAAR	*Journal of the American Academy of Religion*
JBL	*Journal of Biblical Literature*
JSNT.SS	Journal for the Study of the New Testament. Supplement Series
JTSA	*Journal of Theology for Southern Africa*
LSJ	H. G. Liddell, Robert Scott, and H. Stuart Jones. *A Greek-English Lexicon*. Oxford: Clarendon Press, 1925.
MSSNTS	Society for New Testament Studies Monograph Series
NIGTC	New International Greek Testament Commentary
NovT	*Novum Testamentum*
NovVet	*Nova et vetera*
NRT	*Nouvelle revue théologique*
NTA	Edgar Hennecke and Wilhelm Schneemelcher, eds. *New Testament Apocrypha*. 2 vols. London: Lutterworth, 1963.
NTS	*New Testament Studies*
OGIS	Wilhelm Dittenberger. *Orientis Graeci Inscriptiones Selectae*. Leipzig: S. Hirzel, 1903–1905.
OTP	James H. Charlesworth, ed. *The Old Testament Pseudepigrapha*. 2 vols. Garden City, N.Y.: Doubleday, 1983, 1985.
OTS	Oudtestamentische studiën
RB	*Revue biblique*
RevCatTeol	*Revista catalana de teologia*

RExp	*Review and Expositor*
RHPR	*Revue d' histoire et de philosophie religieuses*
RivBib	*Rivista biblica*
RSR	*Recherches de science religieuse*
SANT	Studien zum Alten und Neuen Testament
SBLDS	Society of Biblical Literature, Dissertation Series
SBLMS	Society of Biblical Literature Monograph Series
ScrBull	*Scripture Bulletin*
SJT	*Scottish Journal of Theology*
SNTU	Studien zum Neuen Testament und seiner Umwelt
SNVAO	Skrifter utgitt av det Norske Videnskaps-Akademi i Oslo
SUNT	Studien zur Umwelt des Neuen Testaments
TBei	Theologische Beiträge
TDNT	Gerhard Kittel and Gerhard Friedrich, eds. *Theological Dictionary of the New Testament.* 9 vols. Grand Rapids: Eerdmans, 1964–1974.
TDOT	G. Johannes Botterweck and Helmer Ringgren, eds. *Theological Dictionary of the Old Testament.* 10 vols. Grand Rapids: Eerdmans, 1974–.
ThGl	*Theologie und Glaube*
ThQ	*Theologische Quartalschrift*
TLNT	Ceslas Spicq. *Theological Lexicon of the New Testament.* 3 vols. Peabody, Mass.: Hendrickson, 1994.
TS	*Theological Studies*
TTZ	*Trierer theologische Zeitschrift*
TZ	*Theologische Zeitschrift*
WMANT	Wissenschaftliche Monographien zum Alten und Neuen Testament
WuW	*Wort und Wahrheit*
WUNT	Wissenschaftliche Untersuchungen zum Neuen Testament
ZAW	*Zeitschrift für die alttestamentliche Wissenschaft*
ZEE	*Zeitschrift für evangelische Ethik*
ZST	*Zeitschrift für systematische Theologie*
ZTK	*Zeitschrift für Theologie und Kirche*

Part I

The Literary Context of the Sermon

Chapter 1

The Prologue
(Luke 1:1–2:52)

Method

Whether we follow the most coherent statements on redaction-critical method of those educated in historical-critical exegesis, or subscribe to contemporary analysis of the NT works as pieces of narrative literature, we assume that the author puts the work together as a coherent structure "from top to bottom." This seems obvious in an author who can write the most elegant prose in the NT (Luke 1:1-4), and who shows not only in his two prefaces but also in his careful balancing or echoing of one passage by another[1] that he has conceived of each volume of Luke-Acts as a sequenced unit fitting into an integrated whole.[2]

If the work has literary integrity, this means that

1. beginnings (preface, prologue, introductions to pericopae and sections) and endings ("punch-lines," summaries, reflections)[3] are keys to understanding units and the whole work;[4]

---

[1] Jacques Dupont, "La salut des gentiles et la signification théologique du livre des Actes," *NTS* 6 (1959–60) 132–55; A. J. Mattill, Jr., "The Jesus-Paul Parallels and the Purpose of Luke-Acts: H. H. Evans Reconsidered," *NovT* 17 (1975) 15–46; Charles H. Talbert, *Literary Patterns, Theological Themes, and the Genre of Luke-Acts.* SBLMS 20; (Missoula: Scholars, 1974), especially 83–91; Robert C. Tannehill, *The Narrative Unity of Luke-Acts: A Literary Interpretation* (Philadelphia: Fortress, 1986) 1:xiii, *passim.*

[2] For the achievement that justifies the theory see Luke T. Johnson, *The Literary Function of Possessions in Luke Acts.* SBLDS 39 (Missoula: Scholars, 1977); Charles H. Talbert, *Reading Luke* (New York: Crossroad, 1982); Tannehill, *Narrrative Unity.*

[3] See Henry J. Cadbury on Luke's freedom in recomposing openings and closings in *The Style and Literary Method of Luke.* HThS 6 (Cambridge: Harvard University Press, 1920) 105–15.

[4] Neglect of this principle caused Hans Conzelmann's celebrated blunder of excluding the prologue (Luke 1–2) from his *The Theology of St. Luke* (London: Faber, 1961).

2. passages build on each other sequentially, so that what precedes (immediately, proximately, remotely) communicates its meanings, heuristic possibilities, and hermeneutic context to following passages, which then reinforce and comment on those meanings, and in turn set up the context for passages that follow.

Consequently, to interpret the Lukan Sermon we have to read it in its context in the gospel, beginning from 1:1 and reading through to 6:19. We must note the explicit statements of the author's purpose and goals in his preface (1:1-4), the proleptic meanings he gives to Jesus' person and life in the prologue to his career (1:5–2:52),[5] the foreshadowing of that career in his preparation for ministry (3:1–4:13), and its programmatic inauguration in 4:16-30. Finally, we must find the patterns of that incipient ministry that evoke discipleship (4:31–5:7 → 5:8-11; 5:12–6:11 → 6:12-16), and so give meaning and context to his Sermon on his disciples' ethics (6:20-49). Throughout we will be alert to whatever touches on his authority to teach, as well as his style and the content of his teaching.

Within these larger structures we shall find individual words, phrases, idioms, and images that, because of position or repetition as favorite expressions, will manifest cumulatively the mind of Luke. If we can see by separating tradition from redaction that these expressions are Luke's deliberate choices we shall be arriving at the conscious theology of the implied author. Still, words that derive from a tradition can also be unconsciously chosen and carry his theology as well.[6] As present in the text they constitute the narrative world of the author and carry the text's meaning. Finally, we shall look not only for individual expressions but also for the types of structures the author uses to carry forward various themes.

As we look at all these possibilities we cannot undertake a line-by-line commentary on Luke 1–6. Part I will for the most part follow the scholarly consensus for these chapters without even citing much of the relevant literature. What will be new will be our consistent highlighting of

---

[5] Acts 1:21 indicates implicitly that 1:5–2:52 is but prologue to Jesus' career, which really begins with the baptism by John (3:1-20). Jean-Paul Audet, "Autour de la théologie de Luc I-II," *ScEccl* 11 (1959) 409–18 treats Luke 1–2 as a *prooimion* (as in Aristotelian rhetoric), to introduce the themes of the work.

[6] From a host of statements of redaction critics to this effect, just one: "A possibility for reconceiving redaction criticism is to understand Luke holistically . . . and approach his product as an intentional unity. Redaction criticism, then, would not simply concentrate on the editorial activity of Luke, but would range over the entirety of his literary product. In brief . . . approaching Luke's gospel as if we knew nothing about his sources . . ." Joseph B. Tyson, "Source Criticism of the Gospel of Luke," in Charles H. Talbert, ed., *Perspectives on Luke-Acts* (Edinburgh: T. & T. Clark, 1978) 39.

the words, images, themes, and structures that prepare the reader for the Sermon's message.

The Preface (1:1-4)

Upon opening Luke the reader is surprised by language strikingly different from what she is used to hearing in the gospel tradition. One third of the words are those of classical Greek;[7] the sentence structure is a classical period, with the main clause suspended until the third verse.[8] Those who were familiar with "middle-brow" Greek *Fachprosa* of 100 B.C.E. to 100 C.E. would have recognized a style appropriate for prefaces to technical or professional works.[9] What effect did the implied author of this "purple patch" intend in the implied reader?

Perhaps the "listener," Theophilus, will provide a clue.[10] Most probably Theophilus was a Gentile Christian, a member of one of Luke's

---

[7] Ἐπειδήπερ, ἀνατάσσεσθαι, αὐτόπται do not occur anywhere else in the Greek Bible; διήγησις occurs only here in the NT; ἐπιχείρειν, καθεξῆς, and κράτιστος occur only in Luke-Acts, and rarely.

[8] There are four subordinating conjunctions and two participles in function of subordinate clauses, as well as two accurately used perfect participles and an inclusive word order with assimilated antecedent (περὶ ὧν κατηχήθης λόγων) in v. 4. Joseph A. Fitzmyer, in *The Gospel According to Luke I–IX*. AB 28 (Garden City, N. Y.: Doubleday, 1981) 288 notes the balance of the sentence, so that the protasis (vv. 1-2) and the apodosis (vv. 3-4) contain three parallel phrases.

[9] The century-long debate over the literary genre of Luke's preface is succinctly summarized in Loveday Alexander, "Luke's Preface in the Context of Greek Preface-writing," *NovT* 28 (1986) 48–74. Her own identification of the preface as "a *label* with an *address*" occurring most clearly in the professional prose of "the scientific tradition" (medicine, philosophy, engineering, rhetoric, etc.) seems to me best grounded methodologically.

[10] Alfred Plummer, *The Gospel according to Saint Luke*. ICC (Edinburgh: T. & T. Clark, 1901) lists those from Origen on who have maintained that "Lover of God" is only a symbolic name for the Christian reader. Because Theophilos is attested as a proper name in Greek from 250 B.C.E., and was common among the Jews (as Jedidiah), it should be a real person's name. The use of κράτιστε rather than ἀδέλφε, the normal appelative for a Christian, also indicates a definite historical person. Some suggest a wealthy patron who published Luke's work—it is a common title in dedications (BDF #60 [2], 33); others suggest a powerful figure with influence on Roman colonial policy, so that Luke-Acts would be a formal apologia for Christianity as a *religio licita*. Both are possible, but there is no evidence for either position; see the discussion in Fitzmyer, *Luke* 299–300. The appelative κράτιστε is not limited to officials (although Luke uses it of procurators in Acts 23:26; 24:3; 26:25), but probably refers to anyone of equestrian rank: Cadbury, "Commentasry on the Preface of Luke," in F. J. Foakes-Jackson and Kirsopp Lake, eds., *The Beginnings of Christianity* (London: Macmillan, 1926) 2:505–506; Fitzmyer, *Luke* 300. It designates someone with some rank, but not necessarily an official with power to control the Christian community. The gospel itself is not constructed as a formal apologia addressed to officialdom.

communities,[11] one with rank and authority and enough education to recognize from the style of the preface a genre of literature designed to give
a coherent explanation of the history, principles, and practices of the
community he had joined. In short, dedication to "Theophilus" addresses
the gospel to the world of Greek culture.

What, then, can we know of the character and purpose of the gospel
from this preface?

1. It is a final stage of the continuing events of the Christian tradition
"that have been fulfilled among us" (πεπληροφορημένων ἐν ἡμῖν πραγ-
μάτων), from Jesus' birth to his ascension and the outpouring of his Spirit that
carries the saving word to the ends of the earth and even to Luke's writing.

2. It is trustworthy, because it is based on eyewitnesses become ministers of the Word[12] who are not only reliable sources but also a faithful
check on the process of transmission. Its surety (ἀσφάλεια) is also secured by Luke's own process of careful research (παρηκολουθηκότι
ἄνωθεν πᾶσιν ἀκριβῶς καθεξῆς σοι γράψαι) according to the canons of
the scientific tradition designated by the preface.[13] Ultimately, however, it

---

That it has motifs similar to apologetic historiography does not alter the fact that the genre
is a unique form—the Christian gospel—aimed at elaborating and strengthening the faith
of the Christian believer. Richard J. Dillon, *From Eye-witnesses to Ministers of the Word:
Tradition and Composition in Luke 24.* AnBib 82 (Rome: Biblical Institute Press, 1978),
successfully demonstrates this point against the Conzelmann school's assertion that Luke is
apologia rather than kerygma.

[11] Luke 1:4 says that Theophilus has been catechized and is a Christian neophyte. Since
the rest of the gospel contains no asides to explain to an outsider the terms of Christian
practices or beliefs it must be addressed to a member of the community. This means that
Theophilus is, in his singularity, representative of the community as a whole. If Theophilus
was not a member of the community, then he can be the "listener" only of the preface, and
not of the gospel as a whole. The change of language in 1:5 probably indicates that the highlighted role of the "listener" ceases when the gospel proper begins, and all members of the
school are addressed. After the preface the listener becomes simply the implied reader.
There is no consensus on the location of Luke's community. Perhaps Luke writes for a number of local communities with the same *Sitz im Leben* (persecution, struggle with delay of
the parousia, division between rich and poor, Gentile interests); see Robert J. Karris, "Missionary Communities: A New Paradigm for the Study of Luke-Acts," *CBQ* 41 (1979)
80–97, and Luke T. Johnson's argument, "On Finding the Lukan Community, A Cautious
Cautionary Essay," in *SBL Seminar Papers* 16:1 (1979) 87–100.

[12] This is Dillon's argument throughout *Eye-witnesses.*

[13] Meir Sternberg, *The Poetics of Biblical Narrative* (Bloomington, Ind.: Indiana University Press, 1985) 86 finds a conflict between Luke's assertion of empirical method and
his later authorial omniscience which exceeds that method, but, as his own n. 3 implies, that
is putting a modern construction on empirical method. Mark Coleridge's "relative omniscience" reconciles the two more accurately in *The Birth of the Lukan Narrative.* JSNTSS
88 (Sheffield: JSOT Press, 1993) 215–16.

is trustworthy because God has accomplished all these things according to divine plan.[14]

3. Its purpose is to confirm securely[15] in the faith (offer motives of credibility for) what Theophilus (and Luke's community) had already accepted.[16] Luke here offers to do what any gospel does: tell what God has accomplished (note the divine passive of πεπληροφορημένων) in Jesus.[17] Even if Luke emphasizes ἀσφάλεια more explicitly than other gospels, this gospel is not an apologia, especially not one divorced from the gospel's function of *kerygma*.

The preface, then, is an aside from the author designed to build that trust in the authority of the author necessary for successful narrative communication.[18] The "listener" like Theophilus who is educated in Greek rhetoric will recognize from the language and form of the preface that Luke is an insider who has done his homework and knows how to investigate and write a treatise worthy of confidence. The reader implied by the rest of the gospel, raised mostly on the rhetoric of the LXX, will rely on Luke because it is in touch with her tradition, and the "orderly account" makes sense of the Christian catechesis as she is actually living it. Finally, for the reader approaching Luke for the purpose of finding moral guidance the ἀσφάλεια is not only about God's vindication of Jesus as the Christ but also about the vindication of the ethical directives given in the gospel.[19]

---

[14] Michael Dömer, *Das Heil Gottes. Studien zur Theologie des lukanischen Doppelwerkes.* BBB 51 (Köln: P. Hanstein, 1978) 5–14; Beverly Roberts Gaventa, "The Eschatology of Luke-Acts Revisited," *Encounter* 43 (1982) 27–42.

[15] Ἀκριβῶς and καθεξῆς do not guarantee historical or chronological accuracy (modern concepts), but rather promise a theologically ordered account that makes sense of both the catechesis and the problems the community is presently facing.

[16] Richard J. Dillon, "Previewing Luke's Project from His Prologue (Luke 1:1-4)," *CBQ* 43 (1981) 205–27, especially 220–27.

[17] The *indicative* of the Christian message. However, implied in Jesus' actions, and explicit in his summons to discipleship (also part of the πεπληροφορημένων), is the *imperative* that flows from what God accomplished in Jesus.

[18] See Steven M. Sheeley, *Narrative Asides in Luke-Acts.* JSNTSS 72 (Sheffield: Sheffield Academic Press, 1992) 98–119 on the purposes of such asides, especially in establishing the credibility of the author; Shlomith Rimmon-Kenan, *Narrative Fiction: Contemporary Poetics* (London: Methuen, 1983) 100.

[19] Presumably the implied reader, no less than today's contemporary reader, is reading the text not just for information, but also for the transformation of her own life. Assurance is especially needed for those who have committed their lives to Jesus' radical program; Sandra M. Schneiders, *The Revelatory Text: Interpreting the New Testament as Sacred Scripture* (1st ed. San Francisco: HarperSanFrancisco, 1991) 13–17.

Some commentators have expected Luke 1:1-4 to reveal the gospel's theological themes, but that is not the task of a preface.[20] Aristotle (*Rhetoric* III, 14 [1414b-1416a]) indicates that while forensic *exordia* deal with praise, blame, and advice, and ought to render the audience attentive, benevolent, and docile, all *exordia* have the primary aim of indicating the purpose of the writing (1415a, 22-26). In literature the *prologue* introduces the themes of the work (1415a, 18-21). Thus Luke 1:1-4 ought to be called the preface, and 1:5–2:52, which introduces the main themes of the work,[21] ought to be called the prologue. The reader alerted to expect an orderly exposition of the deeper significance of the catechesis now turns to that prologue with an interest in its main themes.

The Prologue (1:5–2:52)

1. *The Annunciation of John's Birth* (1:5-25):[22] With the first words of 1:5 the Christian reader recognizes "his" language—the vocabulary, idioms, and syntax of the Septuagint[23]—and so recognizes the story that corresponds to his catechesis. That it begins in the reign of Herod (in a Jewish

---

[20] The Hellenistic historical prologues adduced as models for Luke 1:1-4 reveal nothing of the situation in which the work was written or any of the themes to be treated. Only Josephus gives a specific purpose for his works—to correct published lies of others which have misrepresented the Jews—and outlines the structural divisions of his work (but not their themes!).

[21] Ancient birth and childhood stories are forecasts of the career of the hero, and so are prologues to their lives. For Greek literature, Plutarch's lives of Coriolanus and Fabius Maximus are cited by Gottfried Erdmann, *Die Vorgeschichten des Lukas- und Matthäus-Evangeliums und Vergils vierte Ekloge*. FRLANT 47 (Göttingen: Vandenhoeck & Ruprecht, 1932) 8. Rudolf Bultmann, *The History of the Synoptic Tradition* (Oxford: Blackwell, 1963) 300–301 cites Herodotus' account of Cyrus, Plutarch's of Alexander, and Philostratus' of Appolonius of Tyana. For OT birth stories see the births of Moses (Exodus 1–2), of Ishmael and Isaac (Genesis 16–22), of Samuel (1 Samuel 1–3); for haggadic midrashim on the birth of Moses see Philo (*Vit. Mos.* I–VI) and Josephus (*Ant.* 2.6-9.205-37). For indications of how Luke 1–2 fulfills this function see Paul S. Minear, "Luke's Use of 'the Birth Stories'" in Leander E. Keck and J. Louis Martyn, eds., *Studies in Luke-Acts; Essays Presented in Honor of Paul Schubert* (Nashville: Abingdon, 1966) 111–30.

[22] There is a consensus in contemporary exegesis that the infancy narrative is structured into two diptychs of the annunciations (1:5-38) and the births (1:56–2:40) of John and Jesus, partly designed to demonstrate the superiority of Jesus. My own structure for this section is similar to that of Fitzmyer in *Luke* 313–15.

[23] E.g., ἐν ταῖς ἡμέραις instead of the genitive absolute of 3:1b, the parataxis in the first sentence, and the Hebrew idiom πορευόμενοι ἐν . . . ἐντολαῖς in 1:6. Alexander, "Luke's Preface," 67, shows that this "scientific tradition" commonly dropped the preface's literary language to take up the vocabulary and style proper to the tradition.

milieu), with a man and woman of striking Jewish piety[24] and a priest of-fering sacrifice in the Jerusalem Temple, says that the forthcoming story is a continuation of the history of the Jews, beginning with Abraham and continuing to the latest prophets (Malachi 3) and most recent political events (Herod). Further, it is a sacred story, beginning in the Temple and ending there (2:41-52; 24:53),[25] in an atmosphere of sacrifice (1:9), of prayer (1:10), and of praise of God (24:53).

The Lord's messenger (1:11) abruptly breaking into the scene seizes our attention: what will God reveal? The annunciation form focuses our attention on the angelic revelation in 1:13-17.[26] The first spoken words in Luke are "Do not be afraid," and the angel goes on to describe the birth of John as a great joy and delight, thematic words for Luke.[27] John's very name, "Yʜᴡʜ is gracious," indicates Yʜᴡʜ's impending act of salvation in him. But the meat of the prediction about John occurs in 1:15-17: he will be a prophet (filled with the Holy Spirit, 1:15)[28] in the manner of the Elijah figure of Mal 3:1, 23-24, going before the just God (1:17)[29] to turn the hearts of fathers toward their children (1:17), and the sons of Israel to-ward their God (1:16), that is, toward the wisdom of the wise (1:17).[30] All of this is to prepare an apt people for the Lord (1:17).[31]

---

[24] The justice, with the age and sterility of Zechariah and Elizabeth, echo the piety, ac-companied by age and sterility, of Abraham and Sarah (Genesis 17–18).

[25] This motif functions also in the heart of the gospel: the Journey to Jerusalem (9:51–19:44) closes with Jesus entering not Jerusalem but the Temple.

[26] Whether one takes the form as an "annunciation of a birth," as in Raymond E. Brown, *The Birth of the Messiah* (Garden City, N.Y.: Doubleday, 1977) 156–59, or as a miraculous birth story, as in Fearghus ó Fearghail, "The Literary Forms of Luke 1,5-25 and 1,26-38," *Marianum* 43 (1981) 321–44, it focuses attention on the angel's message. The messenger announces with divine authority what God is about to do.

[27] Χαρά is used 8x in Luke, more than in any other synoptic gospel, and ἀγαλλίασις occurs 3x in Luke-Acts, making up sixty per cent of total NT usage.

[28] Although in the earliest period prophecy is rarely ascribed to the Spirit of the Lord (1 Sam 10:10; 1 Kings 22:24), in the postexilic prophets the Spirit of God is widespread as the motive force behind prophetic utterance; see John Barton, "Prophecy (Postexilic He-brew)," in *ABD* 5:493 for abundant examples. In 7:26; 9:7-8, 19 Luke expands the tradi-tion's grouping of John with prophets.

[29] Ἐνώπιον αὐτοῦ in 1:17 refers to κύριον τὸν θεὸν of 1:16 as the "before me" of Mal 3:1 refers to the "just God" of Mal 2:17.

[30] These elements of 1:15-17 are picked up again in the canticle celebrating John's birth and career in 1:76-79. The elements of 1:13-15 are also developed later in Luke, for they forecast his career (v. 13 = 1:57-66; v. 14 = 1:24, 58; v. 15a = 7:26-28a; v. 15b = 7:33; v. 15c = 1:41-44).

[31] Although Luke 1:15-17 has many OT resonances, ἐπιστρέψαι καρδίας πατέρων ἐπὶ τέκνα (1:17) is a closer Greek translation of the Hebrew text of Mal 3:24 than that of our LXX. The rest of Luke 1:16-17 is a paraphrase of Mal 3:24 (echoed by a similar

Implicitly Luke here makes four points:

1. God initiates salvation,[32] sending his angel and making the barren fertile.

2. The eschatological[33] age of salvation is beginning:

a. The angel Gabriel's only appearance in the OT was in Daniel's visions of Israel's final deliverance from foreign oppression.[34] There Gabriel's interpretation of Jeremiah's seventy years into seventy weeks of years became an apocalyptic expectation of the end of time, even up to Luke's days.[35]

b. John is the prophet like Elijah, come immediately before the Lord's judgment in Mal 3:1-2, 23. Elijah was known as the precursor of the final days, if not explicitly of the Messiah.[36] If Jews believed that

---

paraphrase in 1:76). Precisely the same ethical task and its explicit coupling with the spirit and power of Elijah in 1:17 make the reference to Mal 3:24 clear.

[32] This is a constant *theologoumenon* of the prologue, as Coleridge, *Birth of the Lukan Narrative,* demonstrates in almost every pericope.

[33] "Eschatology" is so controverted a notion (see the articles by David L. Petersen, George Nickelsburg, and David Aune in *ABD* 2:575–609) that I must define my use here. Eschatology refers to "the last times," when God's intervention will so change the course of history that one can speak of an entirely new state of reality. For Luke the presence of the Spirit in Jesus' conception, call to mission, and baptizing his disciples with that Spirit in Acts 2 has inaugurated that new stage of reality. It will reach its completion when the Son of Man returns in the final judgment. In the meantime all human action is valued and judged by the final judgment that is impending, if not imminent. Thus Luke-Acts embodies both a prophetic and an apocalyptic eschatology. I will argue this case more fully in my commentary on the Reign of God in ch. 3.

[34] Brown, *Birth* 270–71 lists a number of details to show that Luke is consciously alluding to Daniel 8–9—not all equally convincing, but on the whole probative.

[35] Gabriel in Dan 9:2, 24-27 expands by *pesher* Jeremiah's prophecy of seventy years of exile (Jer 25:11-12; 29:10; cf. 2 Chr 36:21) into seventy weeks of years before the Jews will be delivered. This deliverance, after the manner of Jewish apocalyptic literature, is already understood as transcending historical space and time (Dan 8:17 is "for the time of the end"): the 490 years in Dan 9:2, 24-27 are "to bring in *everlasting* righteousness, to seal both vision and prophet, and to anoint a holy place." Since no historical deliverance in the Maccabean time fits 490 years, its expectation of deliverance was extended into Roman times; cf. its different uses in Josephus, *Ant.* X.11.7; 4 Ezra 12:11-12; Hermann L. Strack and Paul Billerbeck, *Kommentar zum Neuen Testament aus Talmud und Midrasch.* 7 vols. in 6 (Munich: Beck, 1922–1961) [= Billerbeck] 4/2:1002–11. First-century prophecy was primarily prediction of the age to come or of the events signaling it: David Aune, *Prophecy in Early Christianity and the Ancient Mediterranean World* (Grand Rapids: Eerdmans, 1983) 124.

[36] Already existing beyond the bounds of space and time (2 Kings 2:9-12) suggests eschatological reality. Further, Sir 48:10 has Elijah as the restorer of the tribes of Jacob at the end of time. Finally, "the day of his coming" (Mal 3:2) and "the great and terrible day of the Lord" (Mal 3:23) increasingly had eschatological resonances throughout Israelite prophecy.

prophecy would return to Israel when the Messiah came, the birth of a prophet would signal the advent of the Messiah.[37]

3. Fulfillment of Mal 3:23-24 begins Luke's scheme of prophecy and fulfillment.[38] On the one hand not only Malachi 3, but the whole sweep of biblical history, suggested by various allusions to the OT in Luke 1:15-17, is coming to fulfillment;[39] on the other hand the angel's promise is itself fulfilled in Elizabeth's conceiving in 1:24, and even more in John's birth in 1:57-66, as is reinforced by the canticle in 1:67-79.

4. Although John is not explicitly called a prophet here (cf. 1:76), the Elijah role is that of a prophet, and so John's ministry will have two characteristics:

a. He will be oriented toward the future—both by his preaching that the Lord is coming[40] and in his preparing a people for the Lord who comes after him.

b. He will have a moral role of converting Israel to the Lord's ways;[41] Luke will highlight this by giving an ethical content to his preaching (3:10-14).

---

[37] Psalm 74:9; 1 Macc 4:43-46; 9:27; 14:41 speak of a period without prophets but do not indicate that it ends at the eschaton or with the Messiah. Later Jewish tradition interprets this as a period without the Holy Spirit: "When Hagg, Zech, and Mal, the latter prophets, were dead, the Holy Spirit departed from Israel, but the heavenly will was made known to them by the *Bat Qol*" (*T. Sota* 13, 2). Numbers Rabbah 15, 25, interpreting Joel 3:1, says that the Spirit returns at the eschaton: Billerbeck 2:134.

[38] Although Luke as narrator only once cites Scripture explicitly, allusions and indirect citations are so abundant that the narrated events are regularly seen as fulfillment of the OT promises; see Coleridge, *Birth of the Lukan Narrative* 217. Though there is considerable disagreement over exactly how Luke handles the scheme, there is a scholarly consensus that Luke develops the theme of (OT) prophecy and fulfillment throughout Luke-Acts; see the key article by Paul Schubert, "The Structure and Significance of Luke 24," in Walther Eltester, ed., *Neutestamentliche Studien für Rudolph Bultmann zu seinem 70. Geburtstag am 20. August 1954* (Berlin: Töpelmann, 1957), especially 176–78, and the discussion of the debate in Darrell L. Bock, *Proclamation From Prophecy and Pattern: Lucan Old Testament Christology.* JSNTSS 12 (Sheffield: Sheffield Academic Press, 1987), ch. 1 and the literature cited there. More recently B. C. Frein has described Luke's fulfillment of internal (literary) prophecies in "Narrative Predictions, Old Testament Prophecies and Luke's Sense of Fulfilment," *NTS* 40 (1994) 22–37.

[39] Coleridge, *Birth of the Lukan Narrative* 35–36.

[40] This is the sense of the prophetic figure in Mal 3:1-2, 23-24, the role John plays in his apocalyptic preaching in Luke 3:3-6, 15-17 and in the gospel as a whole.

[41] Note that John is to turn the disobedient (ἀπειθεῖς, 1:17) to the prudence of the just (φρονήσει δικαίων, 1:17) both terms describing ethical behavior. Whoever is the Messenger of the Covenant in Mal 3:1c, "covenant" bespeaks reform of conduct, either of shoddy cultic practices in the covenant with Levi (Mal 2:4-9) or of the injustice forbidden

Thus the reader now knows that God is eschatologically intervening in human history by sending a prophet, here a prophet who heralds and prepares for God's own arrival as judge. This creates in the reader an anticipation of fulfillment in John's birth and career, just as the sign given to Zechariah looks forward to fulfillment. But Luke seems to postpone that fulfillment, interposing a second scene of annunciation of another's birth; the postponement highlights the fulfillment that eventually follows in the birth of John.

2. *The Annunciation of Jesus' Birth* (1:26-38): What is postponement for the virginal reader is fulfillment of narrative prediction for the regular reader, who recognizes in Jesus' conception the coming of the Lord for whom the Baptist will be preparing. The announcement of Jesus' conception is immediately linked to the preceding by μηνὶ τῷ ἔκτῳ in v. 26 (cf. v. 24, μῆνας πέντε). Its continuity with the annunciation of John's birth is also carried by the literary form itself,[42] by the role of Gabriel as messenger in both scenes, and by the repeated mention of Elizabeth's sixth month in v. 36 as a sign to Mary. But this linkage and the similarity of literary forms really highlight a contrast in which Jesus is shown as superior to John in every way.[43] Finally, Luke has introduced another instance of promise/fulfillment: The conception is the fulfillment of the promise in 2 Samuel 7 and is itself a promise of Jesus' birth and fulfillment of the work of the Messiah in the rest of the gospel.

Again the story's main point is in the angel's proclamation of who Jesus is to be:

a. The Davidic Messiah, receiving the throne of his father David and exercising an everlasting reign. Luke 1:32-33 is the fulfillment of YHWH's

---

by the Sinaitic covenant (Mal 3:5). In any case Malachi 3 predicts an ethical renewal of the people before the Lord can suddenly come to his Temple. This correlation between eschatological prophecy and ethical reform occurs in Jer 25:3-12; Dan 9:2-29, and often in OT prophecy.

[42] Even if one identifies the form as a call narrative, as do Klemens Stock, "Die Berufung Marias (Lk 1,26-38)," *Bib* 61 (1980) 461–65, P. Bellet, "Estructura i forma: annunciació de naixement i forma d'eleccio profètica (Lc 1,26-38)," *RevCatTeol* 7 (1982) 91–130, and Fearghus ó Fearghail, "Literary Forms," the points of similarity indicated by Brown remain constant. I do not judge that the differences Coleridge finds between the two annunciations subvert the overall structure of the diptych.

[43] Brown, *Birth* 300, lists nine ways in which Luke articulates Jesus' superiority to John in both the annunciation and birth scenes. On *synkrisis* as a Hellenistic rhetorical trope that compares lives in order to highlight the superiority of one, see Friedrich Focke, "Synkrisis," *Hermes* 58 (1923) 327–68, and the discussion in Fearghus ó Fearghail, *The Introduction to Luke-Acts*. AnBib 126 (Rome: Biblical Institute Press, 1991) 33–36.

promise of an everlasting kingdom over the house of Jacob for David's son in 2 Sam 7:12-13.[44]

b. "Son of the Most High" (1:32). The title can reinforce his messianic role as ruler of the house of Jacob,[45] but because of the clear connection of his virginal conception with the power of the Holy Spirit (διò, 1:35)[46] the title "Son of God" intimates a special personal relationship of Jesus to God to be developed throughout the gospel.[47] If this is so, then Luke is carrying through the identification of Jesus with the God of justice (Mal 2:17–3:1) for whom John is preparing the people.[48] This is the root of his superiority to John in the prologue and throughout the gospel.

c. Finally, Mary's grace-driven (κεχαριτωμένη) and faith-filled response (1:45) in v. 38 serves as the model of discipleship for which she will be praised indirectly (8:21; 11:28), and prepares for future responses of disciples (5:11, 28) and for the response in the Sermon of all who hear (6:27) Jesus' own words (6:47-49).[49]

---

[44] Brown, *Birth* 310, finds these verses "a free interpretation of 2 Sam 7:8-16" based on the recurring words *great, throne, house, kingdom, forever.* The notion of an everlasting kingdom for Israel is part of the hope of deliverance in Dan 2:44; 7:14, 27, and part of the messianic expectations that derive from Isa 9:7 and Mic 4:7. The more that the messiah is conceived as the divine agent at the end of time (especially as this is connected with a fiery judgment, as in 3:7-9; cf. Mal 3:2-3), the more this figure can be assimilated to the God of justice expected in Mal 3:1.

[45] Although Fitzmyer, *Luke* 206–207, has demonstrated that "Son of God" is not an explicit messianic title in the OT or in the Palestinian Jewish tradition, still the title does refer to the Davidic king (2 Sam 7:14; Pss 2:7; 89:27), and so it may have had messianic resonances for the Jews. Such resonances explain the high priest's question making "Messiah" and "Son of God" appositives in Mark 14:61 // Matt 26:63.

[46] Luke has moved the "christological moment" backward from the resurrection through Jesus' ministry into his infancy: Brown, *Birth* 481.

[47] Cf. 3:21 and the discussion there. This emphasis is in Luke's sources in 3:22; 9:35; 10:22, and in his own redaction in 2:49; 3:23; 4:41, and in 22:67, where Luke removes "Son of God" from its apposition with "the messiah" and affirms it as a separate aspect of Jesus' identity in 22:70. On God's son here see. John J. Kilgallen, "The Conception of Jesus (Luke 1,35)," *Bib* 78 (1997) 225–46.

[48] Indeed, the name Jesus, in its root meaning "YHWH, help," responds to the salvation sought in Mal 2:17, which provoked the oracle in Mal 3:1. The title "Messiah" will find confirmation later in the prologue, in Bethlehem as David's city (2:4) and in the angels' proclamation in 2:11. For the fact that the language here would have evoked OT nationalistic messianic expectations, cf. Lucien Legrand, "The Angel Gabriel and Politics. Messianism and Christology," *IndThSt* 26 (1989) 1–21.

[49] Coleridge gives the best explanation of Mary's question in 1:34: that it is her legitimate question about the "how" of a conception to which she is already on the way in a faith-filled assent (*Birth of the Lukan Narrative* 61–66).

The alert reader now understands that this second annunciation, far from interrupting the fulfillment of John's story in 1:5-15, introduces the subject of his prophecy. This conjunction of the two subjects is now made explicit in the next scene where the mothers of these divine agents reflect on this divine intervention.

3. *The Visitation* (1:39-56) complements the annunciations, joining the mothers of the two children foretold in Luke 1:5-25, 26-38. Mary's encounter with Elizabeth and subsequent Magnificat continue to relate John and Jesus, and make three points about John, Jesus, and Mary, and one point about the character of God's saving acts.

a. *John begins his prophetic role.* His leap in the womb (1:41, 44) fulfills Gabriel's word that he would be filled with the (prophetic) Holy Spirit while still in his mother's womb (1:15), for Elizabeth clearly ascribes (γὰρ, 1:44) her recognition that Mary is the mother of her Lord to John's leaping for joy in her womb. John's role of preparing the way of the Lord has begun.

b. Still, it is Elizabeth who is explicitly filled with the Holy Spirit (1:41) to proclaim that Mary is the mother of her *Lord*. Since Hebrew *ʿādōn* and Aramaic *mārêʾ* and *māryāʾ* were Palestinian terms for YHWH, using κύριος of Jesus meant placing him on the same level as YHWH, which seems to have taken place early in the kerygma.[50] Luke himself makes κύριος his favorite title for Jesus, and retrojects the Christian proclamation of Jesus' status into Jesus' earthly ministry and also into the infancy accounts (2:11). And so the reader who calls Jesus "Lord" sees more deeply why Jesus is superior to John.

c. With *Luke's first makarism* Elizabeth praises Mary for her faith in God's words to her (1:45); this makarism is echoed in Luke 11:28, where Mary is to be praised for hearing the word of God and keeping it. Indeed, this is what makes her mother of the Lord (8:21; 1:38). But Mary praises YHWH (1:47) for what he has done for her in the immediate past of these two conceptions, which will flow into his saving actions in the careers of these two children.[51] This praise shows her to be what she proclaimed, the handmaid of the Lord (1:38).

---

[50] Fitzmyer summarizes his previous exhaustive research in *Luke* 202–203.

[51] The *magnalia Dei* (cf. 1:49a) were ordinarily intended for the establishment and growth of the People of God: Aristide M. Serra, "'Fecit mihi magna' (Lc 1,49a). Una formula communitaria?" *Marianum* 40 (1978) 305–43.

d. *The Magnificat*[52] also articulates in 1:51-53 God's characteristic actions for the poor of Israel in the past, and so the character of the salvation now inaugurated:[53] it will be consistent with all of God's saving activity, in which he reverses "the conditions that human beings create for themselves."[54] This reversal has already been seen in the barren Elizabeth's becoming fruitful (1:6-7, 25) and the virgin Mary's conceiving (1:34-35), which have removed Elizabeth's shame (1:25) and Mary's lowliness (1:48). In the Magnificat the social hopes of Israel and of the Christian *ʾAnawim* come to expression.[55] God has rejected the proud and mighty (v. 51) and has regarded and elevated the lowly (ταπείνωσιν, vv. 48, 52); God has fed the hungry and sent the rich away empty (1:53).[56] This is what God's merciful coming to the aid of Israel (1:54) has meant: the execution of the covenant YHWH had made with Abraham and his descendants (1:55). The reader is being prepared for God's action of reversing human conditions and values throughout the gospel. It is the memory of God's typical way of mercifully saving God's people that grounds the faith of Mary and provides the ἀσφάλεια on which the readers' faith is based.[57] Proleptically the Sermon's beatitudes and woes are embedded in this canticle, which describes more than Mary's role (indeed, only v. 48 refers to

[52] The canticle is a hymn of praise. Brown (*Birth* 346–55) elaborates Benoit's thesis that the prologue's three major canticles (I exclude 2:14) come from a circle of Jewish Christian *ʾAnawim* celebrating YHWH's gift of salvation through the house of David (Jesus) for the poor and oppressed who depend on him.

[53] In Jewish thought what YHWH did in the past continues in the present life of the community (Deut 5:2); the cultic memorial bears this intergenerational continuity (Exod 12:24-27; 13:8). Thus the past tenses in 1:51-55 can refer to all of OT history, and everything done in Mary and her child, now and proleptically of his career.

[54] Fitzmyer, *Luke* 361; Jacques Dupont, "Le Magnificat comme discours sur Dieu," *NRT* 102 (1980) 321–43. This reversal, seen throughout the OT, is expressed most clearly in Hab 3:14.

[55] Although the aorists in vv. 51-54 describe the actions of God throughout Israel's history, it is probable that the Jewish Christian *ʾAnawim* would have understood that they who were poor have now been offered salvation through their king Jesus, triumphant over death and his enemies through his resurrection: Brown, *Birth* 350–54. Luke's readers, mostly poor and oppressed, would have understood the salvation pronounced by Mary as proleptically applying to themselves.

[56] For M. Trèves, "Le magnificat et la Benedictus," *CahCercErn Ren* 27 (1979) 105–10, these canticles celebrate a political liberation of Israel that neither the Baptist nor Jesus realized. For Luise Schottroff, "Das Magnificat und die älteste Tradition über Jesus von Nazareth," *EvTh* 38 (1978) 298–313, they express the Jewish Christian experience of social and political deprivation: this oldest apocalyptic tradition about Jesus embodies a consolation, "the divine equalization of social destinies."

[57] On Luke 1 as the "birth of memory" see Coleridge, *Birth of the Lukan Narrative* 94–95.

Mary). Rather Luke foreshadows the kind of salvation that will emerge in his gospel, a gospel of mercy, eschatological reversal,[58] and joy.

4. *The Birth of John* (1:57-80): the second diptych[59] describes the births of John and Jesus as the first historical fulfillment of the promises in the annunciations.

The scene is divided formally into three units: (1) the narrative of the birth, circumcision, and naming of John (1:57-66); (2) Zechariah's canticle elucidating the theological significance of the name (1:67-79); and (3) the growth refrain (1:80). John's birth is the occasion for revelation: first, it reveals God's mercy to Elizabeth (1:58; cf. 1:25); second, the narrative controversy over naming him John (1:59-63) reveals the fidelity of Zechariah to the words of Gabriel (1:13) and also fulfills them; third, the "miraculous" birth to such old parents and the return of Zechariah's speech set the stage for the following canticle to answer the climactic question, "what, then, will this child be?" (1:66).

The canticle reinforces four previous points:

a. *Prophecy returns* in 1:67,[60] and so the eschaton is breaking in.[61]

b. *Fulfillment of prophecy:* Zechariah uses Gabriel's terms to describe John's identity and mission as the Elijah-like eschatological prophet of Mal 3:1, preceding the LORD to prepare his way (1:76-79). Now with John's birth the prophecy has begun to be fulfilled. Further, Luke portrays this eschatological deliverance as fulfilling the whole of God's faithful saving of Israel, through the covenants with David (1:68-71) and with Abraham (1:72-73),and fulfilling the range of Hebrew prophecy (1:70).

c. *Zechariah proclaims salvation* as God's reversal of the Jews' situation: God has saved those oppressed by their enemies who hate them

---

[58] The classical literary term is περιπέτεια. The reversal motif will arise in explicit phrases like "the last shall be first," "whoever humbles himself will be exalted" (cf. 9:48; 13:30; 14:10-11; 18:14; 22:26). It occurs in those situations where the poor are the saved (6:20-26; 14:33; 16:19-31; 18:18-30; 21:1-4), children are accepted (10:21; 18:17), Jewish outsiders or sinners are saved (2:8-20; 5:8-10, 30-32; 7:47; 10:29-37; 14:21; 15:1-32; 17:16-17; 19:1-10), and where Gentiles are saved instead of Jews (3:8; 4:24-29; 7:9; 10:13-15; 11:31-32; 13:28-29; 14:23; 20:16; Acts 13:46; 18:6; 19:8-9; 28:28).

[59] See n. 22 above.

[60] Not only is Zechariah filled with the Holy Spirit (1:41), but he explicitly prophesies: προφητεύω, here formally used for the first time in Luke, strictly speaking refers only to John's mission in 1:76-79. That Zechariah begins with a hymn of praise in 1:68-75 makes this passage a reprise of 1:39-56, which joined prophecy and praise, as Coleridge demonstrates in *Birth of the Lukan Narrative* 117–18.

[61] See n. 35 above.

(1:68, 71, 74).[62] Here the messiah is a victorious military leader.[63] In that Jewish context the ethical response of the people saved from their foes is to serve YHWH in holiness and justice (1:74-75).[64]

    d. Again *a passage focused on John speaks rather of Jesus.* Even in Zechariah's grateful pride, his canticle praises the salvation coming not from his tribe but from the one for whom John is preparing, the messiah from David's house (1:69-70). Even in the verses that apply to John, the ἀνατολή from on high that visits them (1:78) is Jesus.[65]

    The passage's new element is that John will provide knowledge of God's salvation by the forgiveness of sins (1:77). Although this prophecy refers immediately to John's baptism for the forgiveness of sins (3:3), it also refers to the salvation brought by Jesus Messiah, since forgiveness of sins is Luke's favorite way of describing Jesus' redemptive work.[66]

    As John's annunciation and birth had defined him as pointing to the one who comes after him, so, in Luke's narrative, John's birth story points to the second birth story of the diptych.

    5. *The Birth of Jesus* (2:1-21): Again Luke changes the scene, from the Jewish milieu to that of the Roman empire. In obedience to the Roman decree of Augustus, Jesus comes to be born in Bethlehem, the city of David. Whereas John's mission was to Israel, the circumstances of Jesus'

---

[62] Who are the foes from whom Zechariah expects deliverance? He could be expressing the hope that little Israel, economically poor and without independent self-rule for over 500 years, would receive its king who would liberate it politically from the greatest world power yet known: Legrand, "The Angel." More immediately, the Christian *'Anawim* or Luke's readers hoped that the risen Christ was delivering his little flock from those who persecute and oppress them.

[63] See the demonstration of this in Coleridge, *Birth of the Lukan Narrative* 120.

[64] Λατρεύειν and ὁσιότης, as distinct from δουλεύειν and δικαιοσύνη, originally had religious or cultic meaning, but already in the LXX they came to refer to ethical conduct in fulfilling covenant obligations. In the NT both take on the notion of Christian religious duties, fulfilled by actions of justice in the world: Hermann Strathmann, "λατρεύω," *TDNT* 4:61; Friedrich Hauck, "ὅσιος," *TDNT* 5:491.

[65] However one translates and understands ἀνατολή, it refers to Jesus. As a translation for צֶמַח, as the LXX takes it in Zech 3:8, it refers to the branch of David's line, the Messiah (cf. Isa 11:1). As "the rising" it can refer to Mal 3:20, "the sun of righteousness *shall rise* with healing in its wings," probably referring to the "God of righteousness" under the ancient Near Eastern symbol of the winged sun disk. But since that God of righteousness follows the Elijah figure, and Jesus also follows John as the Elijah figure, ἀνατολή identifies Jesus as that divine judge. See Fitzmyer, *Luke* 387–88.

[66] Coleridge, *Birth of the Lukan Narrative* 121–22, cites Luke 4:18-19; 5:17-26; 7:36-50; 15:1-32; 19:1-10; 23:34b; 24:47; Acts 4:10-12; 5:31-32; 13:38.

birth highlight his relation both to the Jews and to the Gentile nations of the world, οἰκουμένη (2:1; cf. Acts 26:26).

The passage is divided into three parts: Jesus' birth (2:1-7), the angelic proclamation to the shepherds and their response (2:8-20), and the circumcision and naming of Jesus (2:21). These three elements carry four theological points:

a. *The main point is christological,* revealed by the angelic proclamation (2:11) to which the passage builds: Jesus is the savior, messiah, and Lord. The literary form echoes the annunciation scenes—the appearance of a divine messenger (2:9), the assurance, "Do not be afraid" (2:10), the proclamation of tidings of joy (2:10), the sign given of the event (2:12)—and so it emphasizes the *"good news"* of the angel given in 2:11 as central to the passage. The role of messiah (1:32-33), the title of Lord (1:17, 43), and the name of Jesus (1:21) had already been given to Jesus, and so the birth and circumcision are again fulfillment of literary prophecies when on this day[67] he is again proclaimed from heaven as Christ[68] and Lord, but now newly as *savior,* perhaps in contrast to Augustus' being styled the savior of the world.[69]

b. Yet this messiah, Lord, and savior not only appears as a fragile baby (as of course did Augustus), but in very humble circumstances: on the road and homeless (as he would spend his career), and laid in a manger.[70] *The eschatological reversal* enunciated in the canticles of Luke 1 has already come to pass in Jesus' birth.

c. *The birth is of significance for all the world,* for in Luke-Acts Jesus' salvation will reach out to all humans. The birth takes place in the Roman empire, as do all the elements of Jesus' career (Acts 26:26); the message goes out not to the powerful and observant Jews, but to shepherds, a despised class and religiously outcast;[71] the angelic message is

---

[67] Σήμερον is a Lukan formula for the day of eschatological salvation here and in 4:21; 5:26; 13:32-33; 19:5, 9; 23:43.

[68] Jesus' birth in Bethlehem is new verification of his Davidic descent (Mic 5:1).

[69] Note that in 1:47 Mary had hailed God as Savior. The Myra inscription acclaimed Caesar σωτῆρα τοῦ σύμφαντος κόσμου and the Priene inscription, which deified him, called his birthday the beginning of *the good news:* Fitzmyer, *Luke* 394.

[70] For the manger's polysemic range see E. Heck, "Krippenkind—Schmerzensmann. Eine bibeltheologische Betrachtung zu Lukas 2,1-20," *GuL* 61 (1988) 451–59, and Jacques Winandy, "Le signe de la mangeoire et des langes," *NTS* 43 (1997) 140–46. Whether one takes it as a symbol for Christ as food, or for his suffering, or as a sign of poverty (my preference), it marks a reality humiliating enough to constitute a sign to the shepherds (2:12).

[71] The rabbinic tradition considered them sinners, either as ignorant of the Law and non-observant, and/or as thieves; cf. Billerbeck 2:113–14.

for all people (2:10), as in Luke-Acts Israel accepts the nations into its salvation.[72]

d. *The birth of Jesus as Savior-Messiah-Lord is good news* because it brings true peace on earth to those whom God favors, which is the glory of God (2:14). With the angelic host's hymn Luke again challenges his Greco-Roman readers accustomed to think of Augustus as the author of peace (the *Pax Augustana*).

6. *The Presentation of Jesus in the Temple* (2:22-40): For the canticle describing Jesus' career, parallel to that of John (1:67-80), Luke has Jesus' parents take him to the Temple in Jerusalem. This *mise-en-scène* resumes the notions that Jesus' parents are devout Jews, observing the prescriptions of Exod 13:1-2, 11-16 and of Lev 12:8).[73] Jesus too is at home in the Temple (2:41-50). More importantly, the location shows that Jesus is the Lord coming to his Temple prophesied in Mal 3:1.[74] Thus the prophecies about John and Jesus are coming to pass and the eschatological crisis is at hand, now indicated by the Spirit-guided witness of Simeon and Anna.

The proclamations of these two carry the main point of the passage. Both Simeon and Anna are Wisdom figures, because of their age and virtue (2:25, 36-37), and their awaiting God's deliverance.[75] More important, both are vessels of divine revelation: Simeon is endowed with, and recipient of a revelation by, the Holy Spirit (2:25-26); he now comes into the Temple at the instigation of the Spirit (2:27). Anna is described as a prophet (2:36).[76]

---

[72] Jacob Jervell, *Luke and the People of God* (Minneapolis: Augsburg, 1972) 41–74.

[73] That Luke may have confused the rituals is irrelevant to our reading. The passage evokes the presentation of Samuel at the shrine of Shiloh (1 Sam 1:24-28), and so continues the correlation with Hannah's canticle in 1 Sam 2:1-10 introduced by Mary's Magnificat: Brown, *Birth* 447–51.

[74] Malachi 3:1-3 had expected an eschatological judge to come with fire to purify his people (as John expects in Luke 3:6-9). The Jesus who comes to his Temple as the end of his journey to Jerusalem (9:51–19:44) does come as a purifying force (19:45-48), but here he comes in the opposite *Gestalt,* a baby who needs redemption. That this is God's eschatological salvation is the theme of the following prophecies of Simeon and Anna.

[75] Simeon awaits the consolation of Israel, 2:25; Anna associates with those awaiting the redemption of Jerusalem, 2:38. Brown, *Birth* 453–54, 457–59 shows how these words, as well as the images of the *Nunc Dimittis* itself, echo the awaited eschatological deliverance in Isaiah 40–66.

[76] Although Anna is not here described as prophesying, "prophet" lends divine authority to her utterance. For Luke the gift of the last days includes women's prophecy in the divine Spirit (Acts 2:17; cf. Joel 2:28). Such prophesying by women has continued in his community (Acts 21:9).

Simeon's canticle is at the center. He praises God because he has now seen God's salvation (the savior of 2:11 and the messiah of 2:26), as a light of revelation to the Gentiles, for the glory of Israel (2:29-32).[77] Thus the canticle describes salvation as already begun in the reality of the messianic child Jesus, confirming the promise of the angel in 1:32-33 and the Spirit in 2:26. The oracle that follows in 2:34 foretells the divided response Jesus' career will receive, foreshadowing Jesus' own words in 12:51-53. Anna, for her part,[78] implicitly identifies Jesus[79] as the redemption of Jerusalem, by metonymy referring to Israel. Yet in spite of this christological emphasis on Jesus as messiah, salvation of all peoples, the light of revelation, and the glory of Israel, the closing growth refrain (2:39-40, again alluding to 1 Sam 2:26 and completing the births diptych by echoing the refrain of 1:80) affirms Jesus' humanity in the humble town of Nazareth.

In sum, the presentation scene brings divine confirmation that Jesus is the messiah, the eschatological redeemer of Israel, whose revelation will extend also to the Gentiles. For the first time an ominous note of Jesus' rejection by Israel has been struck and Jesus is foreshadowed as the man of sorrows.[80]

7. *The Boy Jesus in the Temple* (2:41-52): This addition to the diptych pattern,[81] foreshadowing in the manner of Hellenistic biography what the child will be as a man,[82] is the climax of the prologue. Gone are interpreting angels and the Holy Spirit. Jesus, speaking as a free human agent, becomes *the* interpreter of his identity.[83] The passage makes four main points about Jesus:

[77] Revelation to the Gentiles is the glory of Israel, as in Isa 2:1-4. The allusion to Isa 49:6, "a light to the nations," is Luke's first hint that Jesus will be a messiah after the manner of the Servant of Deutero-Isaiah, confirmed by reference to his rejection in 2:34.

[78] Why Luke balances men with women throughout Luke-Acts (cf. the list in Helmut Flender, *St Luke, Theologian of Redemptive History* [London: S.P.C.K., 1967] 9–10) is unclear, but it could underscore the role of women as disciples in Luke-Acts.

[79] The περὶ αυτοῦ of 2:38 grammatically should refer to God, but the whole context marks Jesus as the one spoken of.

[80] Darrell L. Bock, *Proclamation* 85–88, notes the ways in which Luke has used Isaian texts to develop a Servant christology.

[81] Although it balances the complementary scene of the first diptych (1:39-56), it does not synthesize its two previous scenes as the Visitation does: Brown, *Birth* 479.

[82] See n. 22, and specifically Marinus de Jonge, "Sonship, Wisdom, Infancy: Luke ii.41-51a," *NTS* 24 (1978) 317–54. Brown, *Birth* 482, shows that Josephus describes his own childhood with the two words σύνησις and ἡλικία, corresponding to Luke's use of σοφία and ἡλικία here of Jesus.

[83] Coleridge, *Birth of the Lukan Narrative* 188–89.

a. *It again locates Jesus within the circles of Jewish piety.* Not only do his parents make the Passover pilgrimage to Jerusalem (2:41), but so does Jesus,[84] before he is so obliged by the Law.[85] He is a pious child, obedient to his parents (2:51).

b. *It foreshadows Jesus' career* not as a miracle worker, as in the apocryphal gospels,[86] but as an original interpreter of the Torah.[87] For not only does he show himself an acute student (listening and questioning, 1:46), but his answers to the lawyers' questions astonish these veterans (1:47). Luke alerts his readers to expect original and dramatically different teaching about the conduct of one's life.

c. *It manifests Jesus as the Son of God in a special way.* Luke builds suspense through the long search for Jesus to his first words in the gospel, which carry the theological freight of the passage and of the whole gospel. Jesus' answer asserts a filial relationship to God,[88] whose uniqueness is emphasized by his parents' lack of understanding (2:49-50). Thus the prologue's climactic title for Jesus is Son of God. This fulfills Gabriel's prophecy that Jesus would be called the Son of God in 1:32, 35, and points forward to the heavenly proclamation of Jesus as Son of God in 3:22 and 9:35, as well as to Jesus' own assertion of his special relationship as Son of God in 10:21-24. However, the christological assertion also implies in δεῖ (2:49) [89] that Jesus must do his Father's will and interpret it for his people.

d. Although his parents of course must have understood that Jesus must be about God's will, the way in which he has done this is *an enigma* to them (2:50). The passage and the prologue end on a note of mystery dominant in Mark but present also in Jesus' enigmatic revelation of God's identity and will in Luke. The prologue ends by having Jesus assert his special mission (2:49) and yet return to Nazareth to be as subject to his

[84] Ἐπορεύοντο (2:41), actually marking Jesus' third trip to Judea (1:39; 2:3-4) will describe Jesus' journey from Galilee to Jerusalem in the Journey Narrative (9:51–19:44).

[85] *Niddah* 5:6 obligates a Jewish boy to observe the Torah at thirteen: Fitzmyer, *Luke* 440–41.

[86] *The Infancy Story of Thomas,* and the other infancy gospels in Edgar Hennecke and Wilhelm Schneemelcher, *New Testament Apocrypha* (London: Lutterworth, 1963) 1:388–417.

[87] John J. Kilgallen, "Luke 2.41-50: Foreshadowing of Jesus, Teacher," *Bib* 66 (1985) 553–59.

[88] This is true whether Jesus means "I had to be in my Father's house" or "I had to be engaged in my Father's business." Brown, *Birth* 475–77; Fitzmyer, *Luke* 437, 443–44.

[89] For δεῖ in Luke-Acts as the necessary fulfillment of God's saving intention see Charles H. Cosgrove, "The Divine ΔEI in Luke-Acts: Investigations into the Understandings of God's Providence," *NovT* 26 (1984), 168–90.

parents as would any twelve-year-old Jewish boy (1:51). Thus Luke asserts that the revelation of the Son of God will be made through the ordinary structures and exigences of his humanity.

Summary of the Infancy Account

If these accounts form Luke's prologue, the reader of the gospel will expect development of these themes:

1. God initiates and carries through human salvation. The human response is faith, and a secondary human initiative carried out in that faith.

2. The eschatological age of salvation is arriving, for (a) prophecy reappears (1:15-17, [41, 44], 67; [2:25], 36); (b) the eschatological prophet like Elijah (Mal 3:23-24) comes to prepare for the arrival of the Lord (1:16-17, 76-79); (c) the messenger of this is Gabriel, the OT messenger of end-time revelation (Dan 9:21-27; Luke 1:19, 26); (d) the Messiah is born (1:32; 2:11).

3. The main emphasis is christological: Jesus is fully human in pregnancy and vulnerable at birth (2:7), growing like any child (2:40, 52) in obedience to parents (2:51), and yet he is (a) already an original interpreter of Torah (2:46-47); (b) the Messiah of David's line (1:32 [35], 69-70; 2:11, 26 with 30); (c) Savior (2:11); (d) the Lord (1:43; 2:11); (e) the Son of God (1:32, 35; 2:49), also obliquely described as the God of justice of Mal 2:17–3:1, for whom John prepares (1:15, 17, 76-77) and who suddenly comes to his Temple (2:22, 26); and yet (f) a sign of contradiction (2:34), foreshadowing his human destiny.

4. The salvation Jesus brings is (a) in continuity with God's covenants with the Jews in the OT (1:55, 68-71, 72-73), especially as Luke expresses this through (1) figures of Jewish piety (1:5-6, 15; 2:25, 36-37), (2) the setting of actions in the Temple (1:9; 2:27, 46), and (3) the observance of Torah (1:9, 59; 2:21, 22, 39, 41); (b) for Israel (1:48, 51-53; 2:10, 32) and for all nations (2:32); (c) a reversal of the oppressed situation of believers (1:48, 51-53; 2:7); (d) comprised of the forgiveness of sins (1:77), joy (1:14, 44, 58), mercy (1:25, 50, 54, 78), and peace (1:79; 2:14).

5. God's saving action demands discipleship as in (a) Mary's obedience to God's word (1:38) in faith (1:45); (b) praising God for God's blessings (1:47-50, 68-75; 2:14, 20); (c) obedience to the Holy Spirit's prompting (1:41, 44; 2:27); (d) Jesus' response to his destiny as Son (δεῖ, 2:49).

The reader now is prepared to begin Luke's account of Jesus' career.

Chapter 2

Beginnings of Ministry
(3:1–6:16)

Inauguration of John's and Jesus' Careers (3:1–4:44)

The prologue's contrasting parallel between John and Jesus has pre-pared the reader to find that parallel in their ministries.[1] This expectation is confirmed by the most "objective" criterion for literary parallelism, ver-bal echoes produced aurally by words of the same Greek stem:

John	Jesus
3:2b ἐγένετο ῥῆμα θεοῦ	3:21-22 ἐγένετο . . . καταβῆναι τὸ πνεῦμα τὸ ἅγιον
ἐπὶ Ἰωάννην	ἐπ᾽ αὐτὸν
τὸν Ζαχαρίου υἱὸν	Σὺ εἶ ὁ υἱός μου (+ 3:23-37)
ἐν τῇ ἐρήμῳ	4:1-13 ἐν τῇ ἐρήμῳ
3:3 ἦλθεν . . . πᾶσαν τὴν περίχωρον	4:14 ἐξῆλθεν καθ᾽ ὅλης τῆς περιχώρου
κηρύσσων	4:15 ἐδίδασκεν
3:4 γέγραπται ἐν βίβλῳ λόγων Ἠσαίου τοῦ προφήτου	4:17 βιβλίον τοῦ προφήτου Ἠσαίου . . . γεγραμμένον
3:6 ὄψεται πᾶσα σὰρξ τὸ σωτήριον	4:24-30 (salvation to the Gentiles)

[1] The context of Luke 3–4 (the formal contrasting parallelism of Luke 1–2) *has* evoked in alert readers an expectation that its parallel would continue: Helmut Flender, *St Luke, Theologian of Redemptive History* (London: S.P.C.K., 1967) 22; Charles H. Talbert, *Literary Patterns, Theological Themes, and the Genre of Luke-Acts*. SBLMS 20; (Missoula: Scholars, 1974) 45–48; Christopher F. Evans, *Saint Luke* (Philadelphia: Trinity Press International, 1990) 228; Robert C. Tannehill, *The Narrative Unity of Luke-Acts: A Literary Interpretation* (Philadelphia: Fortress, 1986) 1:52. Raymond E. Brown, *The Birth of the*

Luke further secures this parallel with echoing literary forms: a prophetic call formula (in classic form for John in 3:2b and in altered form for Jesus in 3:21-22 to show his superiority) and poetic passages from Isaiah to forecast their careers (3:4-6; 4:18-19a). From this contrasting parallel the following sequence emerges: both John and Jesus (1) receive a prophetic call, (2) are in the desert, (3) spread their ministry throughout a whole region, (4) have their ministry forecast by an oracle from Isaiah, (5) inaugurate a mission to all people. This structure will now inform our rapid reading of 3:1–4:30.

1. *The Career of John the Baptist* (3:1-20): The solemn synchronism in 3:1-2a, correlating Roman and Palestinian rulers, depicts what follows as a part of Hellenistic world history (cf. Acts 26:26). The missions of John and Jesus now bring to historical fulfillment what had been prophesied about them in the prologue.

a. God is beginning the eschatological age:

(1) Prophecy, signified by the prophetic call formula for John in 3:2b, returns to Israel.[2] John is the eschatological Elijah come to prepare the people for the return of the just God (Mal 2:17–3:24), and this is shown by citation of Isa 40:3-5 as a consoling message of eschatological deliverance.

(2) But John preaches an apocalyptic message (3:7-9), warning of coming judgment and calling for good fruits to flow from the penitent hearts of those wanting to be ready for the apocalyptic crisis.[3]

Messiah (Garden City, N.Y.: Doubleday, 1977) 250 lists five parallel elements: John and Jesus both are (1) in the desert (3:2; 4:1); (2) written of by Isaiah (3:4-6; 4:17-19); (3) issuing OT warnings (3:7-9; 4:24-27); (4) questioned about their identity (3:15; 4:34); (5) preaching the good news (3:18; 4:43). Fearghus ó Fearghail, *The Introduction to Luke-Acts.* AnBib 126 (Rome: Biblical Institute Press, 1991) 34–35, finds the second half of a *syncrisis* in a contrasting parallel between John and Jesus in Luke 3–4.

[2] Ordinarily the prophetic call formula is ἐγένετο λόγος κυρίου πρὸς (name in accusative) τὸν (υἱον) τοῦ . . . (Ezek 1:3; Hos 1:1; Mic 1:1; Zeph 1:1; Zech 1:1). Use of ῥῆμα and ἐπὶ may allude to Jer 1:1, but ἐπὶ prepares for the echoing preposition in Luke 3:21. Since no other evangelist introduces John by a call formula, Luke emphasizes that John is embarking on the eschatological Elijah role assigned him in the prologue (1:17, 76).

[3] John's speech is not full enough to fit the prophetic forms studied in Claus Westermann, *Basic Forms of Prophetic Speech,* translated by Hugh Clayton White (Philadelphia: Westminster, 1967), but his threat of punishment is thoroughly apocalyptic. The ὀργὴ θεοῦ refers to YHWH's historical punishment of his people (Isa 10:5; 26:20; Jer 42:18), but from the seventh century it can refer to the eschatological Day of the Lord (Zeph 2:2). In the NT ὀργή is used of apocalyptic judgment (cf. 1 Thess 5:9; Rev 19:15). πῦρ is associated with apocalyptic judgment in Isa 66:24; Mal 3:2, 19; Mark 9:43-44, 48; Matt 5:22; 13:40; 2 Thess 1:8; Heb 10:27; 2 Pet 3:7, 12; Rev 10:1; 11:5. Wrath and fire together describe

(3) John identifies the messiah as the one who brings the eschato-logical outpouring of the Spirit (3:17).[4]

b. Christologically, John points to the Stronger One who comes after him:

(1) Not only is John preparing the way for the Lord (Luke 3:4-6), but Luke's extension of the Isaian oracle to Isa 40:5 indicates that his ministry is but the beginning of Jesus' mission, which will bring sal-vation to the Gentiles only in Acts.[5]

(2) John's preaching so effectively draws people from all walks of life (3:7, 10-14) that he must quash expectations that he is the messiah. His christological teaching (3:15-18) identifies the messiah as the stronger one coming after him, who will baptize in the Holy Spirit and fire.[6] Thus John's apocalyptic preaching makes the one coming after him into the apocalyptic judge, separating the wheat from the chaff and punishing the unfruitful with fire (3:16e-17).

c. John's preparation implies an ethical concern:

(1) John proclaims a baptism of repentance for the forgiveness of sins (3:3).[7]

(2) His apocalyptic preaching (3:7-10) identifies this conversion as producing ethical good works as fruits of this repentance.

(3) John's apocalyptic demand for fruits of repentance leads to his listeners' desire to have this spelled out in specific actions. Luke's

---

divine judgment in Isa 30:27-33; 66:15-16; Zeph 1:15–3:8). Ἀξίνη has apocalyptic meaning only here in Luke 3:7, but it is implied in the cutting down of the fig tree in Luke 13:6-9.

[4] The Spirit is eschatological in Isa 32:15; 44:3; Ezek 18:31; 36:25-27; 37:14; 39:29; Joel 2:28-29. The messiah was expected to be a revealer of the Holy Spirit in *CD* 2:12.

[5] Since John does not preach to the Gentiles he begins a process that will culminate in the Spirit's work of incorporating Gentiles in Acts. His admonition that God can raise up from stones children of Abraham (3:8) prefigures the Gentiles' inclusion in reconstituted Israel, a decisive argument against Conzelmann's exclusion of John from the period of salvation.

[6] John probably expected a baptism in the Holy Spirit that would be at once purifica-tion and refinement. Fitzmyer, *The Gospel According to Luke I–IX*. AB 28 (Garden City, N. Y.: Doubleday, 1981) 474, argues this not only from Isa 4:4-5; 32:15; 44:3; Ezek 36:25-26; Mal 3:2b-3, but especially from the remarkable linkage of baptism in water, the holy Spirit, and purification by fire in 1 QS 4:20-21. Luke's own reference is to the baptism in the Spirit with tongues of fire in Acts 1:5; 2:33, which purifies the disciples of cowardice and fires their enthusiasm to evangelize.

[7] The prophetic message ordinarily demanded a μετάνοια, conversion of one's think-ing and acting (Isa 6:10; Ezek 3:19), and so the proclamation effects John's task of prepar-ing the people (Luke 1:76). Forgiveness of sins recalls Zechariah's specification of this preparation in 1:77. It is a favorite Lukan way of expressing the salvation effected by Christ (Luke 24:47 and Acts 2:38; 5:31; 10:43; 13:38; 26:18).

addition of John's ethical instruction (3:10-14)[8] between two pieces
of eschatological teaching (3:7-9, 16-17) begins the relationship between eschatology and ethics in Jesus' message.[9]

Since this ethical teaching is an advance on the material of the prologue and is central to the theme of this book, we will develop John's ethic
here. His teaching is, in summary form, an expansion and application of
the OT command to love the neighbor in Lev 19:18. To the crowds' question, "What should we do (3:10)?" John responds that the one with two
shirts should give the extra to the one with none, and likewise the one with
food.[10] This ethic of sharing with the needy responds closely to a number
of OT ethical demands.[11] However, John's responses to the toll collectors
("exact no more than what has been allotted" 3:13) and to the soldiers
("Don't shake anyone down . . . be content with your wages," 3:14) have
no antecedents in the OT, but rather in Hellenistic prescriptions.[12] As in
most OT covenant commands, John does not indicate reverence toward
God or the work of the cult but rather the demands of interhuman justice
as preparation for God's ultimate judgment. The ethic is not revolutionary,
since John does not ask the toll collectors to give up their sinful profession[13] but to practice it justly.[14] Although his demands for justice and for a
sharing that goes beyond justice (insofar as the needy in v. 11 utter no
claim in justice) meet the highest levels of ethical thinking in most cul-

[8] Luke is the only evangelist to specify John's ethical teaching. Josephus, *Ant.* XVIII,
5, 2 (116-119) describes John as "exhorting the Jews to live upright lives," but does not describe his preaching. The addition points to Luke's answering his own Christian readers' interest in the content of "fruits of repentance."

[9] John's combination of eschatology and an ethic of sharing with the poor reappears
in 16:19-31 when the rich man's appeal to Abraham in his eschatological crisis fails because he had not shared his clothing and food with Lazarus (3:11); cf. Tannehill, *Narrative
Unity* 1:50, in a different context.

[10] The parallel sharing of food shows that this text does not refer to wearing two shirts
against the cold, as in Jos., *Ant.* XVII, 5, 7.

[11] Cf. Exod 22:25-26 = Deut 24:6, 17 on restoring the coat taken as a debtor's pledge;
Job 31:16-20; Isa 58:7; Ezek 18:7; Tob 1:17; 4:16 speak of both clothing and feeding as the
basic Jewish ethic. Thus Walter Grundmann, "καλός," *TDNT* 3:545–48, takes the καρπὸν
καλὸν of 3:9 as an ethic of sharing similar to the works of love *(maʿsîm tôbîm)* taught by the
rabbis.

[12] There are similar instructions to magistrates in the Palmyrene inscription of 137 C.E.
in Wilhelm Dittenberger, *Orientis Graeci Inscriptiones Selectae* (Leipzig: Hirzel,
1903–1905) 629, 14-15; διάσειν occurs in the papyri; see BAGD 188.

[13] Toll collectors were despised throughout the Roman empire; for the later Jewish
judgment on the sinfulness of the occupation itself see Billerbeck 1:378–79.

[14] Limiting the toll collectors to the amount for which they secured the franchise caps
their greed, and asking the soldiers to be content with their wages excludes the extortion
and blackmail that come from armed might and its authority.

tures and religions, Luke is preparing his readers for Jesus' even more demanding ethic in 6:20-49. Thus even John's ethical preaching serves the contrasting parallel between John and Jesus.

John has fulfilled his mission: his apocalyptic threats urging a conversion issuing in fruits of repentance (3:7-9), his specification of the ethics that produce fruits of repentance (3:10-14), and his identification of the messianic agent of his apocalyptic expectation as the one who will baptize in the Holy Spirit and with fire (3:16-17) all prepare his people (and Luke's readers) for the arrival of Jesus on the gospel scene. Luke has John, his work completed, clapped in prison, removed from the scene so that Jesus can make his superior entrance.[15]

2. *The Preparation for Jesus' Ministry* (3:21–4:13):[16]

a. Jesus' Baptism as Prophetic Call (3:21-22): In Luke's contrasting parallel, Jesus now appears without introduction, to be baptized without John doing the baptizing![17] As John had received the Word of God, Jesus now receives the Holy Spirit in a similar formula. Luke highlights the scene by having Jesus at prayer,[18] but his literary form uses the opened heaven[19] to make the heavenly voice proclaiming Jesus as God's Son carry the central meaning of the passage.

---

[15] Neil J. McEleney, "Peter's Denials—How Many? To Whom?" *CBQ* 52 (1990) 469 details the Lukan literary feature of clearing the stage of actors to prepare for the next scene. But if that were the only motive John could be removed less permanently. Involved here is a Lukan polemic against the Baptist's followers (16:16; Acts 13:25; 19:4), which even separates him from the act of baptizing Jesus that was so ambiguous for the earliest church (cf. Matt 3:14 in conjunction with Heb 4:15). For other readactional emphases on the superiority of Jesus see Walter Wink, *John the Baptist in the Gospel Tradition.* MSSNTS 7 (Cambridge: Cambridge University Press, 1968) 55.

[16] Although 3:21–4:44 is a literary unit (see Ulrich Busse, *Das Narareth-Manifest Jesu: eine Einführung in das lukanische Jesusbild nach Lk 4, 16-30.* SBS 91 [Stuttgart: Katholisches Bibelwerk, 1978]) 4:14-44 as the beginning of Jesus' ministry constitutes a second half of that unit.

[17] Jesus is baptized in only two words of a badly constructed genitive absolute (its subject, ἐπ᾽ αὐτὸν, appears in the main clause), a construction generally expressing a subordinate circumstance. Not only has John been removed from the scene (3:19-20), his role in the baptism does not appear later in a flashback or even a reference.

[18] Luke has Jesus pray before significant events of his life (5:16; 6:12; 9:18, 28-29; 11:1; 22:41). The Spirit's descent may be God's answer to a prayer like Isa 63:19.

[19] Ἀνεωχθῆναι is the regular translation for Hebrew verbs describing the opened heavens in Isa 63:19; Ezek 1:1; Gen 7:11; Isa 24:18; Mal 3:10. The opening facilitates a vision or a salvific irruption of a savior, as in Isa 63:19. Since many of the OT uses are apocalyptic (W. D. Davies, *The Setting of the Sermon on the Mount* [Cambridge: Cambridge University Press, 1964] 36 n. 3), the descent of the Spirit is an eschatological gift.

Here Luke makes three points:

(1) Jesus is the Son of God. Divine sonship could refer to his status as king, messiah,[20] but the reader has been prepared by the angelic annunciation of 1:32, 35 and by Jesus' own identification in 2:49 to expect more intimacy with the divine than that of the adoptive royal sonship. Luke will continue to define this sonship.[21]

(2) The Holy Spirit, which had made him Son of God in his conception (1:35), now makes him Son of God in his prophetic ministry (see 4:1, 14, 18). The Holy Spirit empowers and guides his ministry, enabling Jesus to introduce the eschatological age (11:20; Acts 2:17). Possession of the Spirit, which enables Jesus to bestow it, is precisely what distinguishes the ministries of John and Jesus throughout Luke-Acts (Luke 3:16; 24:29; Acts 1:4-5; 18:24-26; 19:1-6).

(3) Jesus is the eschatological prophet of Isa 61:1, since Luke 4:18, 22 refers to this anointing in its identification of Jesus as that prophet.[22] The words ἐν σοὶ εὐδόκησα may allude to YHWH's servant in Isa 42:1.[23] In that case the baptism of Jesus as Son of God is also his call to live out his sonship as the Servant prophet.[24] This prophetic role will also be developed as Jesus' career unfolds.

b. Jesus' Genealogy as Son of God (3:23-38) is placed here, rather than in the prologue (cf. Matt 1:1-16), to clarify that Jesus is not an adopted Son of God, for the ὡς ἐνομίζετο of 3:23 reminds readers that Jesus was Son of God at his conception (1:32, 35). The genealogy ascends to Adam to teach the universality of salvation in Jesus (3:6) and to argue, by analogy

---

[20] For the king as son of God see Jarl E. Fossum, "Son of God," *ABD* 6:128–37. Although "Son of God" may not have been a messianic title (see above, ch. 1 n. 46) the earliest Christians would have considered it so (cf. Mark 14:61); this would explain D's gloss on the text citing the Davidic enthronement, Ps 2:7.

[21] Indeed, M. Wren, "Sonship in Luke: The Advantage of a Literary Approach," *SJT* 37 (1984) 301–11 makes a good case that this sonship is the most characteristic and important aspect of Luke's theology.

[22] Acts 10:38 seems to understand this reception of the Spirit as a prophetic anointing, since preaching of the word (10:36), healing (10:38), and mission to the nations (Acts 10) are works of Isaiah's Servant (cf. Matt 8:17; 12:17). Luke makes this point by having these activities (4:31-44) flow from Jesus' proclamation in 4:18.

[23] since God puts his Spirit upon the Servant in Isa 42:1. But the identification is not as secure as in Luke 9:35, where ἐκλελεγμένος provides a much clearer intimation of the Servant. Still, a majority of scholars think the Servant is alluded to here; see Fitzmyer, *Luke* 486 and I. Howard Marshall, *The Gospel of Luke: A Commentary on the Greek Text.* NIGTC 3 (Grand Rapids: Eerdmans, 1978) 156.

[24] André Feuillet, "Vocation et mission des prophètes. Baptême et mission de Jesus," *NV* 54 (1979) 22–40 relates baptism to prophetic call and mission.

with Adam, that Jesus is the unmediated Son of God.[25] Thus the genealogy, as an appendix to the baptism, legitimates the title Son of God and, through that title in 4:3, 9, bridges to the devil's temptation of Jesus.

c. The Temptation of God's Son in the Desert (4:1-13): Luke now continues his contrasting parallel with John's ministry by having Jesus ἐν τῇ ἐρήμῳ (3:2b//4:1), for both John and Jesus the place of preparation for ministry. The devil's twice addressing him by "if you are the Son of God," (3:22; 4:3, 9) and the Spirit's agency in leading Jesus to this temptation (3:22; 4:1) connect the temptation with Jesus' baptism. Though the temptation seems a challenge to Jesus' just-proclaimed identity as Son of God, it is rooted in his human ability to be tempted and so the temptation has both a christological and a soteriological message.

(1) Israel as God's son had proved disobedient in the desert; Jesus proves himself in the desert to be God's obedient son.[26] Satan tempts him as Son of God to use divine powers to avoid the ordinary conditions of his human life:[27] to provide himself with bread by his miraculous powers,[28] to make himself king of the world by worshiping the devil,[29] and to call attention spectacularly to his status as Son of God by having God pluck him

---

[25] Fitzmyer, *Luke* 504; Christopher F. Evans, *Saint Luke* 253.

[26] This is the common understanding of the temptations since the magisterial studies of Birger Gerhardsson, *The Testing of God's Son (Matt. 4:1-11 & par. An Analysis of an Early Christian Midrash.* CB, NT 2/1 (Lund: Gleerup, 1966), and Jacques Dupont, *Les tentations de Jésus au désert* (Bruges: Desclée de Brouwer, 1968). The forty days of Jesus' fast could be simply a round number, or could refer to Moses' or Elijah's "forty days and forty nights" (Exod 24:18; 34:28; 1 Kings 19:8). In view of Jesus' three citations from Israel's desert experience (Deut 8:3; 6:13, 16), they more likely refer to Israel's forty years in the desert (Deut 8:2).

[27] Jesus' response, "[The human being (ἄνθρωπος)] does not live by bread alone" sets "human being" against "Son of God." "The Son of God does not step out of his human existence by using his Sonship for his needs, but ratifies it by his trusting reception of his life from God." Walter Grundmann, *Das Evangelium nach Lukas.* THKNT 3 (Berlin: Evangelische Verlaganstalt, 1961) 115. Christopher F. Evans' "[the temptation's] motive cannot have been simply to demonstrate the humanity of Jesus (Heb. 2:17; 4:15), since the temptations are not those of common humanity but of the Son of God . . ." (*Saint Luke* 255) misses the point that *these are all*, in one way or another, temptations of humans, even the desire to rule all the nations of the earth.

[28] Jesus has miraculous power to produce bread, but he does so only in service of others (Luke 9:10-17). In the Exodus story the Hebrews got bread (manna) from God but selfishly and disobediently hoarded it (Exod 16:19-20, 27-28). Those events produced Moses' proverb in Deut 8:2-3, which Jesus uses to respond to the devil in 4:4.

[29] This central temptation makes explicit what is fundamental in all three: Jesus is tempted to turn from fidelity to his Father to be directed by the devil. Here Jesus' response alludes to Israel's idolatry in the desert (Deut 6:10-15): Fitzmyer, *Luke* 511.

out of the air.[30] But Jesus will manifest himself as Son of God only by being faithful to his Father's plan announced in Scripture, to overcome human sinfulness through the faithful human life, death, and resurrection of God's servant as messiah (Luke 24:26, 46-47). Jesus' rejection of bread, vanity, and ruling power grounds the critique of material goods, honor, and power in the Sermon.

(2) The temptation is not just preparation for, but also the start of Jesus' saving ministry.[31] Intertestamental literature witnesses to the belief that at the eschaton the evil forces of Satan would be overthrown.[32] This overthrow is associated with the Son of Man in 1 Enoch 69:27-29, with the messiah in 1 QM 11:8; it is often described as the establishment of the reign of God. Implied in this eventual overthrow is the belief that Satan has been given sovereignty over the world and exercises it at the time of Jesus.[33] In Luke 4:6 the devil offers to Jesus the authority he himself has been given (the divine passive), if Jesus will worship him. If Jesus does this he becomes a false prophet, an agent of the devil, and his work as Son of God is finished.[34] But Jesus' insistence on the sovereignty of God over-

---

[30] Luke's reversal of the second and third temptations (Fitzmyer, *Luke* 507) has destroyed the climactic arrangement of temptations in Q, to lead his readers to interpret all the temptations in light of Jesus' journey to Jerusalem and what happens there. On the cross his opponents tempt Jesus to save himself by coming down from the cross so that they might believe he is the Messiah (23:35-37).

[31] The Spirit received at baptism (3:22; 4:1) leads Jesus into the desert to be tempted (4:1b), and so into his ministry (4:14, 18).

[32] *Jub.* 23:29; *1 Enoch* 69:27-29; *T. Mos.* 10:1, *T. Levi* 18:12-13; *T. Zeb.* 9:8-9; 1 QM 1:10-14; 4:9; 11:8; 13:11-16; 14:10-11; 15:2-3, 15-18; 17:5b-6; 18:1, 3, 11. Background for this belief may be found in the myths of the war between YHWH and the chaotic forces of evil: Werner Foerster and Gerhard von Rad, "διαβάλλω, διάβολος," *TDNT* 2:71–81; Bent Noack, *Satanás und Sotería: Untersuchungen zur neutestamentlichen Dämonologie* (Copenhagen: G.E.C. Gads Forlag, 1948); Neil Forsyth, *The Old Enemy: Satan and the Combat Myth* (Princeton: Princeton University Press, 1987); Peggy L. Day, *An Adversary in Heaven: Satan in the Hebrew Bible.* HSM 43 (Atlanta: Scholars, 1988). The NT witnesses this belief that the messiah and the end of the age would bring about Satan's overthrow (John 12:31; Rom 16:20; Rev 20:1-3).

[33] In the intertestamental period there is a movement from seeing Satan as part of the heavenly court to a dualistic absolutizing of his power over against God. Since the dragon of Revelation 12 is the Satan figure, and both the beast from the sea and the beast from the earth receive power from it, Susan Garrett's elegant parallel between Luke 4:5-7 and Rev 13:7b-8 articulates three elements of this abuse of authority: the devil has authority (Rev 13:7b; Luke 4:6), he delegates it to others (Rev 13:2, 12; Luke 4:6), and his goal is worship of himself (Rev 13:4, 8, 12; Luke 4:7): Garrett, *The Demise of the Devil: Magic and the Demonic in Luke's Writings* (Minneapolis: Fortress, 1989) 38–39 and the literature cited in her nn. 8, 9, 13.

[34] Jeffrey B. Gibson, "A Turn on 'Turning Stones to Bread.' A New Understanding of the Devil's Intentions in Q 4:3," *BibRes* 41 (1996) 37–57.

comes the tempter. The devil's withdrawal now is a sign of his having been conquered in principle (10:18),[35] even if the victory continues to be achieved in Jesus' exorcisms (4:31-36, 41; 8:26-39; 11:14-23) and those of his disciples (10:17). Thus Jesus' victory is a realization of his spiritual power (3:22; cf. 4:18), the inauguration of his mission (4:31-44), and a prefiguration of his final triumph over the powers of darkness (4:6, 13; 10:18; 22:3, 53). The reader, aware of the source and outcome of Jesus' power, looks forward to his ministry, which Luke now develops.

3. *The Beginning of Jesus' Mission in Galilee* (4:14-44)[36]

a. A Summary of Jesus' Ministry in Galilee (4:14-15).[37] The synoptics begin Jesus' Galilean career with a summary of his activity (Mark 1:14b-15//Matt 4:13-17//Luke 4:14-15). While Mark and Matthew's summaries describe Jesus' ministry as proclaiming the arrival of the reign of God and demanding repentance, Luke's summary emphasizes four other facets of Jesus' ministry:

(1) It is under the guidance of the Spirit (4:14), as had been his conception (1:35), his baptism (3:22), and even his temptation (4:1). Thus his being, his preparation for ministry, and its inception are of one piece. (2) It is a ministry of teaching (ἐδίδασκεν instead of Mark's κηρύσσων). (3) The proclamation of the reign of God is not its primary object; indeed, the content of the teaching is not specified and so the reader's curiosity about it is aroused.[38] (4) The teaching is popular, since Jesus is glorified by all;

---

[35] Garrett shows that total defeat causes the devil's withdrawal: *Demise* 41–43. The ἀπέστη ἀπ᾽ αὐτοῦ ἄχρι καιροῦ (4:13) does not postpone the cosmic struggle to 22:3 or create a temptation-free time for Jesus' ministry (Hans Conzelmann, *The Theology of St. Luke.* Translated by Geoffrey Buswell [New York: Harper, 1961] 28, 80–81). Rather it points to the climax of the head-to-head conflict in the Passion, where Jesus triumphs not by casting Satan out but by giving his life to overwhelm sin.

[36] O'Fearghail, *Introduction* 24–29, establishes 4:14-44 as a literary unit, but not his thesis that it is only an anticipation of Jesus' ministry. His stress on the formal αὐτοψία of the Twelve (Acts 1:21-22; 10:37-39) ignores eyewitnessing (even by some of the Twelve) in 4:38, and his beginning of discipleship in 5:1-11 cannot square with Acts 1:22 or 10:37, where Jesus' career begins with the baptism of John.

[37] Again note the verbal parallels with John's ministry. As John had gone through the whole region (πᾶσαν περίχωρον, 3:3) of the Jordan, now Jesus' fame spreads through the whole region (καθ᾽ ὅλης τῆς περιχώρου, 4:14) of Galilee.

[38] Possibly, in connection with synagogue worship (if 4:15, 44 are an *inclusio* for the unit), Luke means the kind of homily on the readings to which Jesus is invited in Nazareth: Evans, *Saint Luke* 265. Under the influence of the Spirit he had interpreted Scripture in the desert, and thus might be doing so here (Grundmann, *Lukas* 118). But Luke does not say so, and this piques the reader's curiosity.

δοξαζόνενος in 4:15 echoes the comment on Jesus' reputation in 4:14b and forecasts the reaction to his teaching in the Nazareth synagogue in 4:22. With great artistry Luke develops each of these four elements in the following programmatic sermon at Nazareth.

b. Jesus' Programmatic Sermon in Nazareth (4:16-30).[39] The reader now expects an oracle describing Jesus' ministry, such as she had read about John (3:4-6). Luke this time makes the citation that announces the nature of Jesus' mission the text for a sermon he delivers in his home town. When Jesus announces that he is the eschatological prophet of Isaiah 61 he is at first accepted warmly, but then the townsfolk turn against him, and after Jesus points out that it is Gentiles who receive God's healing they attempt to kill him. The citation, the sermon, and the response to it are all programmatic for the gospel.[40] Our main concern is with the elements that foreshadow the Sermon on the Plain. Luke makes the following six points:

(1) Jesus is the eschatological prophet fulfilling the role of the Isaian prophets.[41] The only clues to the identity of this prophet lie in his anointing[42] and his role, both of which point to a prophet in the line of Isaiah's Servant.[43] As Isaiah 40–55 announced a redemption from the Babylonian captivity conceived as a new and glorious exodus, so Isaiah 60–62 pro-

---

[39] One of Luke's most difficult passages for source and form critics; their discussions are summarized in Marshall, *Luke* 178–80 and Fitzmyer, *Luke* 526–28. Our interest, however, is in the literary questions detailed below in our text.

[40] Although Jesus' terse homily is focused by the congregation's (and so the reader's) hanging on his words (ἀτενίζοντες), Luke's literary structure highlights the citation describing Jesus' mission by artistically framing it in a three-part chiasm: (ἀνέστη . . . ἐπεδόθη . . . ἀναπτύξας . . . [Isaiah] . . . πτύξας . . . ἀποδοὺς . . . ἐκάθισεν).

[41] There are many models of the prophetic role Jesus plays in Luke: the eschatological prophet like Moses (Deut 18:15-19, as in Acts 3:22-23), or like Elijah (Mal 3:23-24, as alluded to by Luke 7:11-17 as a pastiche of 1 Kings 17), or the prophet like YHWH's Servant (Isa 42:1, as reflected in Luke 3:22; 9:35).

[42] There is no indication of the anointing of a prophet in the OT except for Isa 61:1, which may refer to the prophetic Servant's reception of the Spirit in Isa 42:1. Although Elijah is to anoint Elisha as prophet in 1 Kings 19:16, the text does not narrate his doing so. *CD* 2:12; 6:1; 6QD 3:4 do not seem, *pace* Fitzmyer, to give a clear picture of anointed *prophets* in pre-Christian Palestinian Judaism. Because of this, many have maintained that this is a messianic anointing (as in Acts 10:38): Robert L. Brawley, *Luke-Acts and the Jews: Conflict, Apology, and Conciliation.* SBLMS 33 (Atlanta: Scholars, 1987) especially 11–14.

[43] The prophet of Isa 61:1-2 claims to continue the saving work of the whole Isaian line. Preaching good news to the oppressed was the work of Isaiah 40–55, although εὐαγγελίζεσθαι is not used. More striking, Isa 35:5-6; 42:7-9; 61:1 all conceive of YHWH's salvation as recovery of sight for the blind. Further, both 42:7 and 61:1 speak of liberty for captives. Thus it appears that the prophet's role in Isa 61:1 is more specifically a continuation of the Servant's role in Isa 42:1-9.

vides eschatological consolation[44] for the poor and discouraged returnees from Babylon who have found this exodus hardly a glorious triumph. Thus Jesus' use of Isa 61:1 identifies him with the eschatological prophet of Isaiah's whole line, especially with the Servant of YHWH.

(2) Jesus' own work is guided by the Spirit.[45]

(3) His mission, in the Isaian tradition, is to bring salvation and healing to the oppressed. The πτωχοί who receive the good news are the socioeconomically poor who are a prime concern for Luke's Jesus.[46] The

[44] In contrast to Deutero-Isaiah, Trito-Isaiah does not connect the promised new deliverance to any historical figure or event. Further, the atmosphere of Gentile nations coming to feed and serve Israel in Isa 60:5-14 and 62:2-5 echoes the eschatological triumph of Israel in 2:1-4; 26:6-8. Paul D. Hanson judges Trito-Isaiah's eschatology as a beginning of the apocalyptic movement in *The Dawn of Apocalyptic* (Philadephia: Fortress, 1975) especially 46–76, and all of ch. 2.

[45] His ministry is linked remotely to his conception through the Spirit (1:35), proximately to his baptism (3:22) and temptation (4:1) as preparation for the mission, and immediately to his inauguration of the mission (4:14). Luke 10:21 gives a glimpse of the communion in the Spirit that guided his whole ministry; Acts 1:2, 6-8; 2:1-4, 17-21 depict the Pentecostal outpouring of the Spirit as a fulfillment of Jesus' role of baptizer in the Holy Spirit prophesied by John in Luke 3:16.

[46] Although some take the poor as a generic term encompassing all the oppressed specified in 4:18, neither Isa 61:1 nor Luke 4:18 clearly indicate this. There are two basic approaches to identifying the poor here (and throughout Luke-Acts). The first is christological, stressing Jesus' identity and the reaction to him: from a historical-critical approach, Gabriel Kyo-Seon Shin, *Die Ausrufung des endgültigen Jubeljahres durch Jesus in Nazaret: eine historisch-kritische Studie zu Lk 4, 16-30*. EHS, XIII/378 (Bern and New York: Peter Lang, 1989); from a more literary approach, Luke Timothy Johnson, *The Literary Function of Possessions in Luke-Acts*. SBLDS 39 (Missoula: Scholars, 1977), and now S. John Roth, *The Blind, the Lame, and the Poor: Character Types in Luke-Acts*. JSNTSup. 144 (Sheffield: Sheffield Academic Press, 1997) who make the poor, etc. into metaphors corresponding to those who accept Jesus the prophet or into character-types, ministry to whom vindicates Jesus as Messiah. The second looks to the poor, etc. in their socioeconomic condition: Jacques Dupont, "The Poor and Poverty in the Gospel and Acts," in Augustin George, et al., *Gospel Poverty: Essays in Biblical Theology,* translated and with a preface by Michael D. Guinan (Chicago: Franciscan Herald, 1977) 25–52; Richard J. Cassidy, *Jesus, Politics, and Society: A Study of Luke's Gospel* (Maryknoll, N.Y.: Orbis, 1978); Walter E. Pilgrim, *Good News to the Poor: Wealth and Poverty in Luke-Acts* (Minneapolis: Augsburg, 1981); Sharon H. Ringe, *Jesus, Liberation, and the Biblical Jubilee: Images for Ethics and Christology* (Philadelphia: Fortress, 1985). These see as essential to Jesus' messianic and prophetic mission a commitment to the economically poor, with which he charges his followers. In Luke's carefully constructed context of the biblical jubilee the second seems the correct approach to Luke 4:16-30 and subsequent collective uses of the poor, blind, lame, and oppressed in Luke. Rainer Albertz, "Die 'Antrittspredigt' im Lukasevangelium auf ihrem alttestamentlichen Hintergrund," *ZNW* 74 (1983) 182–206, shows that the insertion of Isa 58:6 into the text manifests that the beneficiaries of Isa 61:1-2 are those in socioeconomic need, as are those in Isaiah 58.

identification of the αἰχμαλώται, "captives," is unclear since the word does not recur in Jesus' mission. Although the Lukan usage of ἄφεσιν, which usually means the remission of sins,[47] may make sin or domination by Satan the captivity from which Jesus frees, in Isa 61:1-2 it probably meant those in prison for debt.[48] "Recovery of sight to the blind" is a parallel in Near Eastern literature to "release for the captives,"[49] but Luke 7:19, 21-22 makes physical recovery of sight a sign of the eschatological vision to come (cf. the prophetic role in Isa 35:5-6; 42:7-9). Luke's substitution of Isa 58:6, "setting at liberty those who are shattered" for Isa 61:1's "to heal the broken-hearted" is problematic,[50] but the τεθραυσμένους on any reading would be the marginalized. Finally, the oracle summarizes Jesus' work under the rubric of the Jubilee year release of those socioeconomically oppressed.[51] Eschatological salvation is now present in Jesus' historical mission.[52] This emphasis on rectifying the plight of the oppressed will be very important in understanding all of Jesus' works, his

[47] ἀφιέναι is not a Lukan verb, but fourteen of his thirty-one uses (5:20, 21, 23, 24; 7:47 (2x), 48, 49; 11:4; 12:10 (2x); 17:3, 4; 23:34) deal with the forgiveness of sins. Only once (11:4) does it refer to forgiving debts, but that in synonymous parallelism with the forgiveness of sins (11:4). Ἄφεσις is Lukan (Luke-Acts has ten of seventeen NT uses), and all texts have to do with forgiveness of sins except for the ambiguous two uses in Luke 4:18.

[48] Ordinarily αἰχμαλώτοι would be captives taken in war (BAGD 27) or debtors in prison (Joseph A. Fitzmyer, *Essays on the Semitic Background of the New Testament*. SBS 5 [Missoula: Scholars, 1974] 256–57). Since Isa 61:2 refers to the jubilee year when debts were cancelled, that should be the original meaning of Isa 61:1; cf. James A. Sanders, "From Isaiah 61 to Luke 4," in Jacob Neusner, ed., *Christianity, Judaism and Other Greco-Roman Cults: Studies for Morton Smith at Sixty* (Leiden: Brill, 1975) 75–106, especially 80–88.

[49] Sanders, "From Isaiah 61 to Luke 4," 81–82.

[50] Fitzmyer, *Luke* 533, explains it as a catchword bond with ἄφεσιν. Richard J. Dillon argues that Christian editing conflated Isa 58:6 with 61:1 to expand the notion of Jesus' messianic release to include both forgiveness and release from the devil's power through healings and exorcisms (especially in 4:38-39), in "Easter Revelation and Mission Program in Luke 24:46-48," in Daniel Durken, ed., *Sin, Salvation, and the Spirit : Commemorating the Fiftieth Year of the Liturgical Press* (Collegeville: The Liturgical Press, 1979) 253.

[51] That the ἐνιαυτὸν κυρίου δεκτὸν is the Jubilee year of Lev 25:8-24, see Robert Bryan Sloan, Jr., *The Favorable Year of the Lord: A Study of Jubilary Theology in the Gospel of Luke* (Austin: Schola Press, 1977), the first two chapters, and Ringe, *Jubilee*. Ringe's conservative typology, in which only those texts can be considered jubilary that combine the terms found in Leviticus 25 and Isa 61:1-2 (ἄφεσις in the sense of *derôr*, ευ-'αγγελίζεσθαι in the sense of *bśr* and perhaps *yôbēl*) makes Luke 4:18 the clearest instance of a jubilee year in the NT. As a summary of the eschatological prophet's proclamation, the Jubilee intends a restoration of the prior egalitarian justice of the tribes of Israel; see Christopher J. H. Wright, "Jubilee, Year of," *ABD* 3:1025–30.

[52] Richard Glöckner, *Die Verkündigung des heils beim Evangelisten Lukas*. Walberger Studien 9 (Mainz: Matthias Grünewald, 1975).

teaching of the reign of God, and especially his conception of his disciples' ethics (6:20-49).

(4) As the oracle characterizes Jesus' mission, so does the Nazarenes' response to it programmatically announce the reaction of Israel to the message in Luke-Acts. Luke adumbrates the inexplicable fact that the Jews missed the fulfillment of their centuries-old eschatological expectation.[53]

(5) The Gentiles become the principal beneficiaries of Jesus' restoration of Israel.[54]

(6) Finally, Jesus' own fate is foreshadowed in the desire of his townspeople to cast him from the nearby brow of the hill to kill him.[55] Jesus will live a prophet's mission, and suffer a prophet's fate (Luke 13:31-35).

This is perhaps the most important text for understanding the mission of Jesus in Luke-Acts. Whereas the prologue had called Jesus "Son of God" as Messiah and the baptism made him Son of God as Servant of YHWH, 4:16-30 makes him the Son of God as Isaiah's eschatological prophet gathering the poor into a restored Israel. These marginalized are the subjects of Jesus' healings and of his ethical teaching. The Nazarenes' rejection of the prophet not only opens salvation to the Gentiles but also manifests Jesus' fate as that of a prophet.

c. Jesus' Ministry in Capernaum (4:31-44) flows from the inaugural sermon, and so specifies and explains it.[56]

(1) An exorcism of an unclean spirit (4:31-37) is Jesus' first work after the Sermon. Here Luke makes three points:

[53] It is not Luke's clumsiness in conflating sources but theological mystery that obscures the cause of the transition from the hearers' approval of Jesus (4:22ab) to their rejection of him in 4:22c-30. Surely it is not Jesus who provokes the rejection by his accusation in 4:23 (*pace* Joachim Jeremias, *Jesus' Promise to the Nations*. Translated by S. H. Hooke [London: S.C.M., 1958] 44–45), for Οὐχὶ υἱός ἐστιν Ἰωσὴφ οὗτος; "How can Joseph's boy be this prophet?" (4:22c) is already the Nazarenes' disparaging remark. Note their ignorance of what the reader knows, that Jesus is not really Joseph's son (3:23). In that case Jesus' response in 4:24 has read the situation correctly and foretells the scandal of his rejection by those who had been prepared for him.

[54] In Luke-Acts salvation must first be preached to the Jews; only when they refuse the message does it pass on to the Gentiles (Acts 13:46). But the Gentiles who accept the message still become members of eschatologically reconstituted Israel. Fitzmyer tersely summarizes the discussion in *Luke* 187–92.

[55] Thus Luke presages Jesus' own fate "according to the Scriptures" even earlier than does Mark 3:6.

[56] The material resumes the Markan sequence after the disciples' call: Mark 1:21-28//Luke 4:31-37; Mark 1:29-34//Luke 4:38-41; Mark 1:35-39//Luke 4:42-44. Much of Luke's redaction of his source is to specify the mission of the Nazareth homily.

(a) Jesus' ministry is teaching (ἦν διδάσκων),[57] and even Jesus' exorcism is a λόγος.[58] As the introduction to the pericope (4:32) stressed the authority of his teaching, the conclusion (4:37) also stresses the authority of his word. But the content of his teaching is not mentioned, building suspense in the reader: what is he teaching?

(b) Jesus' ministry continues his eschatological triumph over the forces of Satan begun in 4:1-13. Luke 11:14-22 considers the demons part of Satan's kingdom, and the humans these inhabit as part of the "strong one's possessions."[59] Indeed, the protest of the unclean spirit, "Have you come to destroy us?" (4:34) seems to speak of a wholesale apocalyptic war, not merely the chasing of a single demon.[60]

(c) Since Jesus' ministry flows out of his proclamation of his mission in 4:18, those under the power of the devil may well be the captives Jesus has come to release (4:18d).[61] In that case Jesus begins his ministry with the most wretched of humans, those who had lost human control to the demons who held them captive.

---

[57] Paul J. Achtemeier, "The Lukan Perspective on the Miracles of Jesus: A Preliminary Sketch," *JBL* 94 (1975), 550–59 points out that Luke frequently "attempts to balance Jesus' miraculous activity and his teaching in such a way as to give them equal weight." See also Joel B. Green, "Jesus and a Daughter of Abraham (Luke 13:10-17): Test Case for a Lukan Perspective on Jesus' Miracles," *CBQ* 51 (1989) 646 and ó Fearghail, *Introduction* 145–47. I go a step further: in this section the blocks of material are not held in balance, but the miracles are described as a kind of teaching; note how Luke infuses this healing ministry with teaching even when this seems discordant in the text: διδάσκειν/διδαχή in 4:31, 32; 5:3, 17; 6:6; λόγος in 4:32, 36; 5:1), and preaching (εὐαγγελίζεσθαι in 4:43; κηρύσσειν in 4:44).

[58] Λόγος (4:36) could represent a *dābār* as deed rather than word, but in view of the emphasis on teaching throughout this section, "word" seems preferable.

[59] The notion that the demons were part of Satan's kingdom was popular in first-century Palestine; cf. *Jub.* 10:7-13 and the discussion in Noack, *Satanás und Soteria* 14, 23, 33, 44. Garrett also shows that Luke took the possessed as part of Satan's possessions in *Demise of the Devil* 39, 44–45.

[60] The title the demon gives Jesus, "the holy one of God," may refer to Jesus' divine power in this ultimate victory (cf. Ezek 39:7 where God's triumph over Gog manifests him as the Holy One in Israel). Garrett, *Demise of the Devil* 46–57, argues from Luke 10:1-24 that Jesus' triumph over Satan is accomplished in his resurrection and enthronement at God's right hand; Jesus' vision of Satan's fall (from heaven) in 10:18 is, then, an apocalyptic vision of that triumph in his enthronement as Son of God. The disciples' power over Satan in Acts (8:7; 28:5 in connection with Luke 10:19) is then a mopping-up operation.

[61] Acts 10:38 speaks of Jesus' ministry as healing all those under the domination of the devil. Although 10:38 καταδυναστευομένους is not the same as the αἰχμαλώτοις of Luke 4:18d, its association of ministry with the anointing of the Spirit (Isa 61:1) refers to Jesus' situation in 4:18; Ulrich Busse, *Die Wunder des Propheten Jesus: Die Rezeption, Komposition und Interpretation der Wundertradition im Evangelium des Lukas.* FzB 24 (Stuttgart: Katholisches Bibelwerk, 1979) especially 433; George E. Rice, "Luke 4:31-44: Release for the Captives," *Andrews University Seminary Studies* 20 (1982), 23–28; Tannehill, *Narrative Unity* 65, 83–84; David G. Reese, "Demons, New Testament," *ABD* 2:140–42.

(2) The healings of 4:38-41 continue this conflict with Satan, since Luke 13:16 shows that Luke considered physical sickness to be caused by Satan.[62] Here Luke makes two salient points:

(a) Jesus' healings of physical sickness continue his ministry to captives of Satan. Peter's mother-in-law is συνεχομένη πυρετῷ, not only "seized by," but also "captured by" a fever.[63] Jesus "rebukes" (ἐπετίμησεν) the fever, as if it was personal. Further, by suppressing the demoniacs who were in his source for v. 40 Luke creates the impression that demons are coming out of sick persons, not out of possessed people.[64] Thus physical healings, too, are part of the cosmic war between Belial and the eschatological power of God.

(b) Although the demons proclaim his true identity, Jesus prohibits them from identifying him (4:42). Nevertheless the spirit world has proclaimed to Luke's readers that Jesus is the Son of God and Messiah (4:41). "Son of God" refers Jesus' present ministry to his anointing by the Spirit (3:22; 4:18), and so ties his healings to his mission in 4:18[65] as well as clarifying what Christ means for Luke.[66]

(3) A preaching tour (4:42-44)[67] now summarizes not only Jesus' teaching ministry, but also ties this teaching and healing ministry to the proclamation of the reign of God. Here Luke makes two main points:

---

[62] Biblical tradition connects human suffering with sin. Exodus 20:5 shows God using suffering as punishment for sin. The NT represents this view in John 5:14; 9:2; 1 Cor 11:29-30; perhaps Jas 5:15. An evil spirit is the cause of physical illness in 1QapGen 20:16-29. The analogies of "binding" and "untying" for a crippled woman in 13:12, 15, 16 (2x) suggest that for Luke such physical healing is part of the "release" of the bound captives of 4:18d. This makes Acts 10:38 also susceptible of this interpretation: Tannehill, *Narrative Unity* 65; Garrett, *Demise of the Devil* 129 n. 15.

[63] Helmut Koester, συνέχω, *TDNT* 7:883 and the discussion in Tannehill, *Narrative Unity* 84.

[64] In the parallel passage, Mark 1:32 speaks of the townspeople bringing Jesus their sick and τοὺς δαιμονιζομένους, but Luke 4:40 omits this mention of the possessed. Consequently, when the healing of these sick in 4:40 results in δαιμόνια coming out of many in 4:41, this implies that physical sickness is caused by demons. No wonder Jesus rebukes the fever in 4:39!

[65] The divine power by which he overcomes Satan may well continue the reader's pondering of the special claim embedded in the title in 1:32, 35; 2:49.

[66] There is no "messianic secret" in Luke, but Luke does avoid the political overtones of the title, as in 9:22; 22:67-68 in contrast to Mark 14:62: Fitzmyer, *Luke* 199.

[67] That this is Lukan redaction of Mark 1:35-39 is made clear by Jesus' going to the desert, being sought out, and responding that his mission is to proclaim the reign of God. Luke's substituting the crowds for the disciples as the ones seeking Jesus highlights the success of his mission: although his townsfolk had rejected him, the crowds of Capernaum would constrain him to stay, to continue his healings.

(a) Jesus' mission[68] is to announce the good news of the reign of God. Whereas in Mark 1:15//Matt 4:17 Jesus programmatically proclaims the *imminence* of the reign of God, that is not Luke's emphasis.[69] What could it mean here?

(b) The proclamation of the reign of God includes Jesus' *actions* of healing and exorcising as the overcoming of Satan. In both 4:18 and 4:43 Luke uses ἀποστέλλειν to describe Jesus' mission from God. This makes the infinitive object of that verb in 4:43 (εὐαγγελίσασθαι τὴν βασιλείαν τοῦ θεοῦ)[70] equivalent to its object in 4:18 (κηρύξαι αἰχμαλώτοις ἄφεσιν)—two formulations of one mission. Further, the *inclusio* formed by these two statements of mission indicates that the concrete expression of that preaching of release is the liberating work Jesus had been doing in 4:31-41: the exorcisms and healings are the preaching of the reign of God. This understanding of proclaiming the reign of God as overthrowing the reign of Satan accounts for the orality of Jesus' "works" in 4:35, 36, 39, the use of καὶ in 4:43,[71] and Luke's identification of the casting out of demons with the reign of God in 11:20. The good news of God's reign is that the reign of Satan is over (see n. 60).

Jesus Calls Disciples to His Healing Ministry (5:1–6:16)

We have been introduced to the prophet and the opposition to him. This unit[72] on discipleship and opposition to Jesus introduces the disciples' faith commitment, which the Sermon will demand, and points out,

---

[68] Luke uses δεῖ to designate Jesus' God-given mission and destiny in 2:49; 4:43; 9:22; 13:33; 17:25; 19:5; 21:9; 22:37; 24:7, 26, 44, and 17x in Acts.

[69] Only the disciples in Luke 10:9, 11 proclaim that the reign of God is at hand. The other Lukan proclamations of that reign refer to something already in action or to be completed at the end of time; see the discussion of this reign in 6:20.

[70] Εὐαγγελίζεσθαι is Luke-Acts' favorite verb (4x) for proclaiming the reign of God, followed closely by κηρύσσειν (3x).

[71] "*Also* to the other cities" indicates that Jesus' power over the demons in Capernaum (what formed the crowd's understanding of his mission and their desire to keep him there) *was* preaching God's reign.

[72] The preaching in the synagogues of Luke 4:44 forms an inclusion with 4:14, and so rounds off a unit in 4:14-44. The Sermon in 6:20-49 and its introduction in 6:17-19 seem to form another discrete unit. Does anything mark off 5:1–6:16 as a unit? That Luke found the material united in his source (Mark 2:1–3:6) is immaterial to the implied reader. Although most commentators treat 5:1–6:11 episodically, with no thematic groupings, there are some indicators of a unit. First, the content: the calls of disciples (5:1-11, 27-29; 6:12-16) are interleaved and contrasted with the emergence of his opponents and four controversies with them (5:17-26, 30-39; 6:1-5, 6-11). Second, the first three passages and the last three all begin with Luke's favorite (καὶ) ἐγένετο δὲ ἐν (5:1, 12, 17; 6:1, 6, 12). (Ἐγένετο δὲ is exclusively Lukan in the NT [17x in Luke; 21x in Acts]; ἐγένετο + giving of time + the infinitive is a Lukan Septuagintalism: Joachim Jeremias, *Die Sprache des Lukasevangeliums* [Göttingen: Vandenhoeck & Ruprecht, 1980] 25–29). Commentators attuned to

by means of the controversies, how radically different will be Jesus' ethics in the Sermon.

1. *Jesus Calls Peter and the First Disciples* (5:1-11): As the text stands, a miracle story is so integrated into a call narrative[73] that the miracle provides context and motivation for responding to the call. Luke makes four points:

a. In 5:1, 3 Jesus expands the teaching ministry of 4:14-44 into the fields rather than in synagogues, on workdays rather than on Sabbaths. His teaching ministry has begun in earnest. We still do not know what he is teaching.[74]

b. The call narrative highlights Simon's faith as paradigmatic for those who also respond (v. 10).[75] The first time he appears in the gospel he does the Lord's bidding beyond reasonable expectation (5:5b); this implied act of faith provides the occasion for the miraculous catch of fish.[76] Simon's transition from calling Jesus Ἐπιστάτα (v. 5) to Κύριε (v. 8) adumbrates his growth to post-resurrection faith.

Luke as a literary work often make 5:1–6:11a unit. Eugene LaVerdiere (*Luke*. New Testament Message 5 [Wilmington, Del.: Michael Glazier, 1983]), Josef Ernst (*Das Evangelium nach Lukas*. RNT [6th rev. ed. Regensburg: Pustet, 1993]), and Christopher F. Evans *(Saint Luke)* make the calling of disciples the theme for the unit. But if calling disciples is thematic, the unit should include 6:12-16.

[73] The miraculous catch of fish has remarkable similarities with that of John 21:1-11, and notable dissimilarities; see Fitzmyer (*Luke* 560–61). Possibly an early stage of the oral tradition recorded a miraculous post-resurrection appearance of Jesus, but, as Luke or his source combined the story with the call taken from Mark 1:16-20 the post-resurrection features disappeared.

[74] Could he be teaching about the reign of God, which he had just acknowledged as his mission in 4:43? The content of his teaching in 5:1 is the word of God. But Lukan usage of "word of God" in Luke 5:1; 8:11, 21; 11:28 seems not to indicate the proclamation of the Kingdom so much as the articulation of what the hearers must do. Further, διδάσκειν is more ordinary than εὐαγγελίζεσθαι, and it never takes the reign of God as direct object in Luke-Acts or anywhere else in the gospels.

[75] Peter's prominence here becomes programmatic for his role throughout Luke-Acts. He will be called Simon until 6:14 and Peter after his name is changed symbolically there (except in 22:31; 24:34). He is the leader and spokesman for the disciples in 6:14; 8:45, 51; 9:20, 28, 32-33; 12:41; 18:28; 22:8, 31, 34, 54-61; 24:12, 34 and throughout Acts 1–12. The Lukan *Sondergut* at 22:31-33 foreshadows Peter's role in the community of Acts.

[76] As a professional fisherman Peter knows the conditions of the lake (v. 2), and he has just toiled in vain at optimal time. Perhaps Jesus' miraculous healing of his mother-in-law has led Peter to consider Jesus as "Master" and to believe in an unexpected catch. Ἐπιστάτα is Lukan usage reserved to disciples and people seeking help (Luke T. Johnson, *The Gospel of Luke*. SP 3 [Collegeville: The Liturgical Press, 1991] 88), and so it emphasizes the faith dimension of discipleship.

c. The call narrative highlights discipleship. The miraculous catch evokes discipleship as Simon falls to his knees with a sense of unworthiness in the presence of divine power.[77] Jesus calms this fear, and uses Simon's awe to commission a disciple (cf. Isa 6:5-8) to catch living people. As the miraculous catch (5:4-7) occasions Jesus' promise of a catch of humans for Peter (5:10), so the abundance of the former promises superabundance for that later catch.[78]

d. Peter and his partners leave everything to follow Jesus.[79] Luke mentions the boats, which represent their former means of livelihood, and he explicitly affirms that they left everything (ἀφέντες πάντα), the usual Lukan theme for the cost of discipleship (5:28; 14:33; 18:22-23). This must affect the interpretation of the "poor" in 6:20.

Thus Luke's Jesus has begun to call disciples to help in his liberating work as the Isaian prophet (4:18, 43). Prerequisite for the call is faith, and its concomitant is leaving all to follow. Such discipleship reaps an abundant harvest.

2. *Jesus Cleanses a Leper* (5:12-16). With this simple miracle story Jesus resumes his direct ministry, which he had enunciated in 4:18, and also provokes the opposition he had adumbrated in 4:27-29. Luke makes four main points:

a. Healing of a leper is one of the (messianic) signs Jesus will adduce in Luke 7:22 as evidence that he is the one to come.[80]

---

[77] Karl H. Rengstorf, *Das Evangelium nach Lukas*. NTD 3 (17th ed. Göttingen: Vandenhoeck & Ruprecht, 1978) 74, Marshall, *Luke* 205, and Johnson, *Luke* 88 make the θάμβος explaining his confession (γὰρ in v. 9) one of religious awe before the *mysterium tremendum et fascinans* rather than a sense of special sinfulness.

[78] Tannehill, *Narrative Unity* 1:203–205, beginning from Jean Delorme, "Luc v. 1-11: Analyse Structurale et Histoire de la Redaction," *NTS* 18 (1972) 331–50, asserts that Jesus' superabundant catch prefigures the superabundant catch of people that the disciples themselves will achieve, and shows that the disciples are already a distinctive band by 5:30 and are a large enough group for Jesus to need to select twelve by 6:13, 17. This growth resembles the astonishing growth in the eschatological *Kontrastgleichnisse* of Luke 8:4-8; 13:18-21. This surprising growth implicitly begins the gathering of eschatological Israel.

[79] Ἀκολουθεῖν is the LXX translation for *hālāk 'aḥᵉrei*, used in the OT (1 Kings 19:20-21) and frequently in rabbinic literature to describe becoming a disciple of someone: Gerhard Kittel, 'ακολουθέω, *TDNT* 1:210–14. It denotes not only physical following but the spiritual following of a disciple in the master's footsteps (5:27-28; 9:23, 49, 57, 59, 61; 18:22, 28, 43; 22:39, 54). Peter and the Twelve to be called in 6:12-16 do not take up an active role in Jesus' ministry until 9:1. They are fulfilling the role of witnessing that is so important in the naming of apostles in Acts 1:21-22.

[80] Marshall, *Luke* 207.

b. The leper is sent to the priests so that he might be declared clean and once again be admitted to the community and its functions. Jesus' mission of liberation includes bringing outsiders into community.[81]

c. Luke portrays Jesus as both going beyond Mosaic Law and obeying it. The leper violates Mosaic Law by being within a city, and so his approaching Jesus would be a sign of his desperation and/or his faith in Jesus. According to the Law, Jesus' touching him would render Jesus unclean, but Jesus' will to heal is so great that he does touch him. Rather than Jesus becoming unclean, he cleanses the leper. Still, in spite of this breaking of Mosaic Law, Jesus is still portrayed as observing the Law: in accordance with Lev 14:1-32 he sends the leper to the priests for verification and instructs him to bring the sacrificial animals needed for the rite. His observance here "serves as a foil to the following narratives" in which opponents will object to Jesus' breaking the Law.[82]

d. Finally, when the crowds overwhelmed him Jesus used to retire to deserted places to pray (5:15-16). Ἐρήμοις recalls the Spirit's work in him in the desert (4:1-13) and so reminds the reader that his contact with God is the source of his teaching and healing power. It also evokes a picture of Jesus as a devout Jew regularly communing with God[83] just as we are about to read five episodes in which his opponents will accuse him of being nonobservant and even blasphemous.

3. *Jesus' Healing Shows Authority to Forgive Sins* (5:17-26). Luke has been escalating the difficulty of Jesus' physical healings, from those with fevers (4:39) and diseases (4:40) to instantaneous cure of leprosy (5:13), and now the healing of a crippling paralysis. The emphasis here is not, however, on the healing, but rather on Jesus' power to forgive sins. This the scribes and Phrarisees take as an arrogation of divine power, and the whole becomes a controversy story[84] in which Jesus vanquishes his opponents by manifesting divine power. As Evans[85] puts it so elegantly,

---

[81] Other outsiders whom Jesus addresses, heals, or gathers into his community include tax collectors (5:27-32; 15:1; 18:9-14; 19:1-10), public sinners (7:36-50; 15:1), Gentiles (6:17; 7:1-10; 13:29), Samaritans (17:11-19), women in unaccustomed roles (8:1-3) and with ritual impurities (8:43-48).

[82] Marshall, *Luke* 207.

[83] Frederick W. Danker, *Jesus and the New Age: A Commentary on the Third Gospel* (new ed. Philadelphia: Fortress, 1988) 119. The periphrastic imperfect is iterative: this was Jesus' regular practice.

[84] Tannehill designates this a quest story in *Narrative Unity* 1:111–26. There is not enough unity in his examples given to fix such a literary form, and in any case, in this passage the controversy is more important to Luke's theology than the quest.

[85] *Saint Luke* 296.

deliverance from paralysis by the power of God in response to faith demonstrates deliverance from sin by the authority of the Son of Man in the face of unbelief. Luke makes five points:

a. Jesus' mission continues to be a teaching one, now come openly and publicly to the professionals, the Pharisees and the teachers of the Law,[86] who come from every village of Galilee, Judea, and Jerusalem. The reader still does not know the content of this teaching.

b. Jesus' healing continues his liberating mission of 4:18, for δύναμις θεοῦ (5:17d) refers to πνεῦμα θεοῦ ἐπ᾽ ἐμέ (4:18a).[87] Further, this healing points forward as the second of the signs of his messiahship (χωλοὶ περιπατοῦσιν), which Jesus gives John in 7:22.

c. That Jesus as the Son of Man has divine authority to forgive sins is the main point of the story, focused by the objection of the Pharisees. In v. 20 Jesus proclaims a forgiveness already given by God,[88] thus claiming the power to announce what God has done, a power given only to priests in their performance of the sacrificial ritual. But in v. 21 the Pharisees and scribes change the claim by asserting that Jesus arrogates power to forgive sins, a power belonging to God alone.[89] This arrogation of divine power forms the basis for their charge of blasphemy. In v. 24 Jesus accepts their charge and claims as Son of Man the (divinely delegated)[90] power to forgive sins, and he demonstrates[91] this by the healing of the paralytic.[92]

---

[86] Νομοδιδάσκαλοι, almost exclusively Lukan and rare, heightens the professionalism.

[87] Evans (*Saint Luke* 300) shows Luke's correlation of the power of God and the Spirit of God in 1:35; 4:14; 24:49 (referring to Acts 2); Acts 10:38. Luke 4:14 and Acts 10:38 make the Spirit received in baptism the power of God out of which Jesus does his teaching and miracles.

[88] Note the perfect tense and the divine passive. Why Jesus begins with the forgiveness proclamation is undiscoverable in this passage, but it may depend on a connection between paralysis and sin.

[89] If Luke or his tradition knew of a human power to remit sins for God such as Fitzmyer (*Luke* 585) discovers in 4Q Pr Nab 1-3:4, it was irrelevant to this story.

[90] The Son of Man *receives* authority in the originating vision (Dan 7:14, 18, 27), as well as in the NT (Matt 28:18).

[91] Jesus assumes in 5:23-24 that it is easier to say "your sins are forgiven" because the statement cannot be empirically verified, while "rise and walk" has a visible control of its truth. Therefore doing the more difficult thing proves that he has power to do the easier thing. The Pharisees, however, consider forgiving sins to be the more difficult thing. Actually, both things are impossible for humans, and so whichever he does proves that he has divine power (v. 17) and authority (v. 24): Heinz Schürmann, *Das Lukasevangelium: Kommentar zu Kap. 1,1-9, 50*. HThKNT 3/1 (2nd rev. ed. Freiburg: Herder, 1994) 1:283. Jesus accomplishes the healing effortlessly (with a word, σοὶ λέγω) and instantaneously (παραχρῆμα).

[92] Not only his walking, but also his δοξάζων τὸν θεὸν witnesses to the forgiveness of sins: Walter Grundmann, *Das Evangelium nach Lukas*. Edited by Friedrich Hauck. THKNT 3 ([3rd ed.] Berlin: Evangelische Verlagsanstalt, 1964) 132.

d. This is the first indication that salvation in Luke is first of all the forgiveness of sins. Whether or not the ἀφέωνταί σοι αἱ ἁμαρτίαι (5:20) identifies the captives of αἰχμαλώταις ἄφεσιν (4:18) as those captivated by the devil, forgiveness of sins does release humans from subjection to evil. It is also one of the most strikingly gratuitous signs and effects of the good news of God's reign.

e. This is the first of Jesus' series of five controversies with the Pharisees leading up to the Sermon's command to love one's enemies (5:21-26, 30-32, 33-39; 6:2-5, 7-11). The Pharisees will continue to be his principal opponents,[93] and so Luke has begun the battle that will lead to Jesus' death in Jerusalem.

4. *Jesus Calls Levi* (5:27-32). Luke continues the account of the calling of disciples (5:1-11; 6:12-16) and the increasing strife with the Pharisees and scribes (5:17-26).[94] He makes three main points:

a. Jesus continues to call disciples. Parallel with the call of Peter (5:1-11), discipleship is distinguished by following Jesus (ἀκολουθεῖν in 5:11, 27), and by giving up all possessions (5:11, ἀφέντες πάντα; 5:28, καταλιπὼν πάντα). In neither case does Jesus demand abandonment of profession or possessions, but discipleship seems to mean following Jesus on his journey, and so implies such renunciation.[95]

---

[93] In 7:30, 36-50; 11:37-44; 12:1; 14:1-6; 15:2-3; 16:14-18; 18:9-14; 19:39-40; the scribes and the lawyers will oppose him in 7:30; 10:25-37; 11:45-53; 14:1-6; 15:2-3. The Pharisees are not the opponents in Jerusalem who bring him to death; that work belongs to the scribes (9:22; 19:47; 20:1, 19, 46-47; 22:2, 66-71; 23:10), the elders (9:22; 20:1; 22:52), and the high priests (9:22; 19:47; 20:1, 19; chs. 22–23 *passim*). But in Luke's narrative the Pharisees as the principal opponents of his ministry are in solidarity with those who will have him condemned.

[94] The form is complex, joining a kind of call narrative (5:27-28) with a controversy (5:29-32), which itself may have originally been an apophthegm. Lukan redaction makes them read smoothly as a unit: the pronouncement about forgiveness of sins in 5:23 provides the background to Jesus' association with sinners here (Fitzmyer, *Luke* 587), and Tannehill points to redactional omissions that tighten the connection between the healing of the paralytic and the call of Levi, and between the call of Levi and the meal he hosts *(Narrative Unity* 1:104–105).

[95] The Twelve (5:10-11; 6:12-16) are summoned to a preaching career (9:1-10); their identification with the apostles (ἀποστέλλω, "send out") in 6:13 reinforces their missionary role. They remain on the road with Jesus to Jerusalem (8:1; 17:5; 18:31; 22:14; 24:9-10, 33). But other disciples, too, seem to follow on the road: the volunteer of 9:57 receives for discipleship Jesus' model of homelessness. The member of the crowd whom Jesus calls to follow him in 9:59 is asked to leave his father unburied (an unheard-of request) to proclaim the reign of God. But these may also be called to preach, since 10:1-17 follows immediately upon their call. Nevertheless, other disciples (μαθηταί) follow (5:30; 6:1, 13, 17,

b. At the meal Levi then provides, the Pharisees and their scribes continue their attack on Jesus by objecting to table-fellowship with tax collectors and sinners.[96] This attack enunciates their notion of salvation by segregation[97] and evokes Jesus' teaching of salvation by association.[98] Jesus himself answers their objection to the disciples' practice, thus giving authoritative affirmation of the Lukan community's incorporation of outcasts and sinners in its membership.[99] He does so first (5:31) by employing a Hellenistic proverb about the sick needing physicians,[100] who run the risk of direct contact with disease. Jesus' actions with the leper had already constituted a direct attack on any separatist spirituality.

c. His second response (5:32) reaffirms Jesus' larger mission[101] to outcasts.[102] That mission was identified as one to the poor, imprisoned,

---

passim) with no indication that they preach. Gerd Theissen's distinction, in *Sociology of Early Palestinian Christianity,* translated by John Bowden (Philadelphia: Fortress, 1978), between wandering charismatics who preach in poverty and disciples who are settled in the local communities is not clear in Luke, but it appears in Acts, and undoubtedly Luke's reader's would have interpreted renunciation in terms of it.

[96] For dining as an institution of social bonding, uniting one with the intentions and qualities of one's companions at table, see the summary by Dennis Smith in *ABD* 6:302–304. For direct taxes τελῶνες were public officials in the lands of Jesus' ministry and during the formation of the gospel tradition. Indirect taxes, principally toll collections for the transport of goods, were usually subcontracted out to "tax farmers." The Pharisees' association of them with (public and ostracized) sinners (Luke 7:34; 15:1-2; 19:7) was probably due not so much to their collaboration with an occupying power as to the exaction of more than was allotted to them either as public officials or as tax farmers (Luke 3:12-13; 19:8); see John Donahue in *ABD* 6:337–38.

[97] The Pharisees, by all accounts, were separatists, basing their practice on Lev 10:10 (Fitzmyer, *Luke* 589). Early sources on the Pharisees are scant; for the ways of interpreting the data see Anthony Saldarini, *Pharisees, Scribes, and Sadduccees in Palestinian Society* (Wilmington, Del.: Michael Glazier, 1988), and his shorter study in *ABD* 5:289–303. For a brief sketch of their politics of holiness see Marcus Borg, *Jesus: A New Vision* (San Francisco: Harper, 1987) 86–90.

[98] William Manson, *Luke.* MNTC (New York: Harper, 1930) 55. This is "the first of several occasions in Luke when Jesus teaches from the position of a guest at a meal (7:36-50; 10:38-42; 11:37-52; 14:1-25)": Evans, *Saint Luke* 305.

[99] Perhaps the plural ἐσθίετε reveals the original *Sitz im Leben* of the passage; it is the church that is being attacked for its practice of openness.

[100] The parallels were noted as early as Jacob Wettstein, Ἡ Καινὴ Διαθήκη: *Novum Testamentum Graecum* (Amsterdam: Blaev, 1751) 1:358; Johnson, *Luke* 97, connects the proverb to Hellenistic imagery equating the moral philosopher's curing of ignorance and vice with the doctor's healing.

[101] Luke uses "come" with the infinitive to express Jesus' purpose in 7:34; 12:49, 51; 19:10; cf. the comparable expression in 4:43. Evans, *Saint Luke* 308, points out that "I have come to" has no background in the OT or parallels in Hellenistic religion.

[102] For the Jewish community sinners were the chief outcasts. Luke makes the forgiveness of sins one of the primary fruits of the gospel: 1:77; 3:3; 5:20-24; 7:47-49; 11:4;

blind, and oppressed in 4:18, one accepted by Gentiles in 4:24-27, and one that relies on sinners in 5:11. It includes sinners here, and the poor, the mourners, the hungry, and the persecuted in 6:20-26, as well as the blind, lame, lepers, deaf, dead, and the poor in 7:22 and 14:13, 21.

5. *Controversy over Fasting* (5:33-39).[103] Next the Pharisees object directly to Jesus about the disciples' lack of fasting and formal prayers, standard religious practices of John and the Pharisees.[104] Lukan redaction stresses two main points:

a. Jesus is the bridegroom. The figure in 5:34 does not have to refer to Jesus: the metaphor simply says that there is no fasting on an occasion of such great joy as a wedding feast. The introduction of the christological notion of the bridegroom being taken away (5:35) applies the figure to

---

12:10; 17:3-4; 23:34; 24:47; Acts 2:38; 5:31; 10:43; 13:38; 26:18. Often this forgiveness is linked to repentance: 3:3; 5:32; 15:7, 10; 17:3-4; 24:47; Acts 2:38; 5:31; 8:22. Evans (*Saint Luke* 309) notes that the parallel statement in Mark 2:17 has Jesus calling sinners without reference to repentance, thus provoking the Pharisees' scandal. Luke's addition of calling sinners "to repentance" is, then, an innocuous statement, one to which any Jew would subscribe. But this misses the point: Levi's fellow tax collectors, come to enjoy his retirement party, have not repented, and yet Jesus is eating with them. *The party is the summons:* this scandalous association is the means by which Jesus' healing begins, before human response.

[103] Luke omits Mark's description of fasting, thus making Jesus' antagonists (οἱ δὲ) and the place of the controversy the same as those at Levi's feast. And so Johnson, following the tradition of older commentators such as Alfred Plummer, J. M. Creed, and Walter Grundmann, takes 5:27-39 as a unit with three commonalities: the audience and interlocutors, the theme of eating and drinking, and the replacement of old observances by new ones (*Luke* 98). As in 5:30, the accusation about the disciples' practice may witness to an apologia for the early church's practice (cf. 5:35). Again Jesus justifies their practice. But the early church's fast was not for mourning or repentance but was joined with prayer as part of a discernment process for mission in Acts 13:2, 3; 14:23.

[104] Although Luke 18:12 speaks of Pharisees fasting twice a week, fasting was not as important to them as were the other topics of these controversies: avoidance of blasphemy (5:17-26), separation from sinners (5:27-32), and Sabbath observance (6:1-11). Both blasphemy and violation of the Sabbath were public offenses punishable by stoning: Raymond Westbrook, "Punishments and Crimes," *ABD* 5:546–56. In Mosaic law the only prescribed public fast was on the Day of Atonement (Lev 16:29-31). After the exile Zech 8:19 specifies four fast days, but since these commemorate God's reversal of disasters surrounding the destruction of the Temple, the fasts look like occasions of joy. The intertestamental period witnessed an increase in Jewish asceticism; cf. Tob 12:8, which links fasting, prayer, and almsgiving. The Essenes and some others fasted regularly. Evans, *Saint Luke* 310, points out that for Tacitus, *Hist.* V, 4 fasting was "for some Gentiles the hallmark of the Jew." In Luke the verb is used only four times; the noun is used only of Anna's life (2:37). Fasting neither creates nor maintains the social boundaries of Jewish identity as effectively as do rules for table fellowship or Sabbath observance; see Marcus Borg, *Conflict, Holiness and Politics in the Teaching of Jesus* (Lewiston, N.Y.: Edwin Mellen, 1984) 73–95, 145–48.

Jesus.[105] We have no evidence of Jewish expectation of a bridegroom to come (as a sort of messianic figure),[106] but the early Christian community understood Jesus as the bridegroom, probably based on the image of the wedding feast of the Son as symbol of the eschatological banquet (Matt 22:1-14; 25:1-13; John 3:29; Rev 19:7-9). The metaphor carries the notion of fulfillment (the long time of betrothal ends), of newness (the marriage is a new reality), and of joy (represented by the wedding banquet and the expectation of progeny for the people).[107] The continuation of the argument in 5:36-39 depends on Jesus' embodiment of this fulfillment, joy, and, especially, newness.

b. This newness introduces an incompatibility between the forms of Jewish piety and the practices of Christian faith.[108] Jesus' response is complex:

(1) The Lukan introduction of παραβολή in 5:36 (unrepeated at 5:37, 39) applies it not only to the question of fasting (5:36-39), but to the whole series of controversies over Jewish and Christian practices in 5:17–6:11.[109]

(2) The first parable (v. 36) stretches the reader's imagination. Ordinarily one sews a patch from a used piece of cloth onto a used garment. Cutting a new garment to patch an old one is bizarre, and that is precisely the point: it is absurd to cut up (destroy) this new dispensation of Jesus to patch an older dispensation that could not tolerate it.[110] Jesus accuses the Pharisees of not recognizing the perfection of who he is and the radical newness of what he proclaims.

(3) The next figure (5:37-38) describes more usual behavior. Young wine continuing to ferment in the wineskins ruptures weakened old skins,

---

[105] Nothing in bridegroom imagery prepares for the bridegroom being taken away. This intimation of Jesus' death and departure from this earth compares with the nobleman going away to receive a kingdom in Luke 19:12.

[106] YHWH is, by his covenant with Israel, her bridegroom in the Torah (YHWH is the jealous God in Exod 20:5, and Israel's apostasy is whoring in Exod 34:15-16), and in the prophets (Hos 2:16-23; Jer 2:2; 3:1-3; 16:9; Ezekiel 16; Isa 61:10; 62:5; Mal 2:14).

[107] This joy of fulfillment constitutes Jesus' *joie de vivre,* and makes it look to the Pharisees as if he and his disciples are always partying; cf. 7:34, where eating with sinners and feasting instead of fasting are brought together as a reproach by John's disciples (7:18-19) and the Pharisees (7:30).

[108] This passage exaggerates the discontinuity between (Pharisaic) Judaism and Christianity. There is no real opposition between Jewish and Christian fasting, as the church later practices it (5:35; Acts 13:2-3; 14:23). Fitzmyer (*Luke* 178) points out that Luke ordinarily stresses the continuity between Judaism and Christianity.

[109] Tannehill, *Narrative Unity* 1:174.

[110] The bizarreness is emphasized by the destruction of both garments. Jesus' joyful eschatological dispensation would not destroy Judaism, but purge it of Pharisaic obsessive legalism and the social boundaries their practices maintained.

and so should be poured into new skins. Jesus' figure stresses the incompatibility of newness (and vitality) with old forms of piety.

(4) The final figure is a proverb explaining the preceding figures. Why do the Pharisees not see the radical discontinuity to which Jesus is pointing, and keep harassing him with these objections? Those satisfied with old wine have no interest in the new; the old is good enough.[111] The Pharisees are so satisfied with their later Jewish moral practices and forms of piety that they will not taste the newness and joy of Jesus' wine of eschatological fulfillment. This newness and its joyful fulfillment will come to a climax when Jesus reveals in a coherent way his new Christian morality in the Sermon of 6:20-49.

6. *Controversies over Sabbath Observance* (6:1-11).[112] Jesus had already healed on a Sabbath (4:31-37), which had provoked no controversy. But the report of it had spread (4:37) and prepared the Pharisees to argue with him over this violation of the Sabbath (6:1-5), and gather evidence for a formal accusation (6:7c), for they expect him to heal on this Sabbbath (6:7a).

Beyond the general prohibition of work on the Sabbath, the OT gives little specification of what is actually forbidden.[113] Probably the Pharisees and scribes had traditions that on a Sabbath forbade eating anything from a field (*CD* X, 23), reaping and threshing (*b. Šabb.* 7,2), straightening a deformed child's body or setting a broken limb (*b. Šabb.* 22,6). They may have understood that these prohibitions gave way for someone in danger of death (*m. Yoma* 8,6). When neither the disciples' "harvesting" of grain (6:1-5) nor Jesus' healing of a withered hand (6:6-11) responds to the danger of death, the Pharisees and their scribes pounce. In his treatment of these two stories Luke makes four main points:

---

[111] Wine is the perfect example, since the ancients (cf. Lucian, *De merc. cond.* 26) also knew that aging improves wine. Those who take χρηστός as superlative (see the MSS variants and Johnson, *Luke* 99) miss the point: these people are so satisfied that they do not even recognize the new so as to compare it.

[112] We read the fourth and fifth controversies of 5:17–6:11 together since, on a different day, they feature the same adversaries—the Pharisees (6:2, together with the scribes, 6:7), deal with the same subject (Sabbath observance), and are introduced in parallel by ἐγένετο δὲ ἐν σαββάτῳ. This formula not only connects 6:1-5, 6-11 with 6:12-16, but unites these passages with 5:1-11, 12-16, 17-26, which used the same formula.

[113] The prophets imply that no business could be conducted on the Sabbath (Amos 8:5; Jer 17:21-22). Evidence in the Bible and in extrabiblical literature that Israel lost Lachish and Jerusalem by refusing to defend itself on the Sabbath indicates that the prohibition of Sabbath work must have been seriously observed. The Zadokite Document (*CD* X,14–XII,5) contains a long series of activities prohibited on the Sabbath. The Mishnah codifies thirty-nine classes of work prohibited on the Sabbath; the Pharisees must have been at the origin of some of these prohibitions: Gerhard F. Hasel, "Sabbath," *ABD* 5:849–56. Still, the Mishnah itself comments wryly on Sabbath legislation, "The rules about the Sabbath . . . are as mountains hanging by a hair, for Scripture is scanty and the rules many" (*m. Hag.* 1:8).

a. In Jesus' new dispensation, human concerns supersede the Sabbath regulations so central to the Pharisees' politics of holiness. Jesus' defense of his disciples' "threshing" (ψώχοντες) is not based on the nature of the Sabbath, but on the nature of law, which cedes to human need, in this case hunger. Because neither his example from Scripture[114] nor the disciples' situation speaks of danger of death, Jesus is stressing the humanitarian nature of divine law. In 6:6-11 Jesus argues not from Scripture but from human experience. Having the man stand before his opponents, Jesus appeals to their compassion, especially on the Sabbath. Jesus argues that to refuse to do good is to do evil,[115] a strange observance of the Sabbath, which is designed as an opportunity to reflect the creative goodness of God and to relieve creatures of their burden! Jesus' interpretation of the Sabbath reestablishes the divine intention of the Sabbath law.[116] It reinforces its humanitarian character, especially as articulated in Deut 5:12-15, and its congruence with God's own creative activity on the Sabbath.[117]

b. Jesus' solution to the controversy is again rooted in Luke's christology: Jesus, as Son of Man, is Lord of the Sabbath (6:5). The argument from David's experience in 6:3-4 is open to the objection, "but that was (only) for David."[118] Jesus argues that his authority as Son of Man is greater than that of David. At the least the title "Lord of the Sabbath" points to authority to decide when Sabbath regulations must be set aside (13:10-17; 14:1-6).[119] However, it is probable that the lordship claimed

---

[114] First Samuel 21:1-6 recounts not a Sabbath incident, but the priest's giving hungry men the showbread, which the Law permitted only to priests. The priest responded to human need. Hunger is not mentioned in Luke 6:1-5, but it must be the implied middle term between the disciples' situation and that of David.

[115] See Fitzmyer's analysis of the argument, *Luke* 611. Since the man is not dying, asking them whether it is lawful to save life on the Sabbath is rhetoric reinforcing Jesus' argument that the Sabbath is for life. Note that the scribes' and Pharisees' entrapment of Jesus is itself doing evil on the Sabbath!

[116] "The spirit of the sabbath ordinance is that people should be preserved from exploitation by others and have the opportunity to ponder the goodness of God" (Danker, *New Age* 133). The Sabbath is to produce delight (Isa 58:13).

[117] Before Luke, Philo had argued for Hellenistic Jews that God's rest on the seventh day need not mean inactivity, since God works with absolute ease and without toil or suffering: Evans, *Saint Luke* 313. Cf. the later gospel tradition of God's working on the Sabbath and Jesus' divine authority to do so in John 5:17-18.

[118] "Any actions or words which went beyond the boundaries of legitimate discussion of what was implied by sabbath law would raise acutely the question of his authority" (Evans, *Saint Luke* 313).

[119] Tannehill, *Narrative Unity* 1:174. Luke, who shows so little interest in Jewish law, has more passages in which Jesus violates the Sabbath than any other gospel.

partakes somehow of the divine Lordship.[120] The miraculous healing of Luke 6:6-11 demonstrates Jesus' assertion in 6:5.[121]

c. The healing continues the release that was Jesus' announced mission in 4:18. Here the release is from those imprisoned in an oppressive interpretation of law.

d. Jesus' message and identity are here rejected just as they were in 4:23-30.[122] Though the Pharisees do not implement their plan to formally accuse him of breaking the Sabbath, they are seized by a frenzy[123] making them even more determined to do something against him.[124]

In these two passages, too, Jesus is portrayed as a teacher (6:6) and we still do not know what his message is. But the reader's curiosity is about to be answered.

7. *Jesus Chooses the Twelve Apostles* (6:12-16): This is a bridge passage,[125] closing out the section that intersperses the calling of disciples with controversies (5:1–6:16), and opening the section on the Sermon on the Plain (6:12-49).[126] This passage climaxes the callings, since the call

---

[120] See Fitzmyer, *Luke* 606, who adds, "His 'lordship' is now added to his 'power' (4:14, 36; 5:17) and his 'authority' (4:32, 36; 5:24); and he is 'lord' precisely as 'the Son of Man.'" It is God who established the Sabbath (Gen 2:2; Exod 20:11; Deut 5:12) and the Sabbath belongs to God (Exod 20:10; Isa 56:4). See Fitzmyer's vindication of the use of *mar* ("Lord") for Yʜᴡʜ in pre-Christian Palestine, and his discussion of Luke's use of κύριος for Jesus even in his earthly ministry (*Luke* 200–203).

[121] It does so just as the healing of the paralytic had demonstrated Jesus' claim to forgive sins as Son of Man in 5:24. In both passages Jesus has the power to know the thoughts of his adversaries, thus fulfilling Simeon's prediction in 2:35; cf. also 9:47; 11:17. In 5:22 the knowledge could have come from the whispers of his adversaries (5:21), but in 6:8 the thoughts seem to be entirely internal, verging on the divine cardiagnosis of John. This knowledge may reveal divine power in Jesus (5:21; 6:5).

[122] Note the same elements: Jesus teaches on the Sabbath, proclaims his identity, and is rejected by his compatriots.

[123] If ἄνοια is a reaction to the healing it probably means "frenzy"; if it is the author's reflection on the Pharisees' imperceptiveness from 5:17 to 6:11 (or to the end of the gospel, as in Acts 3:17; 13:27) or to the end of Acts (as in 28:26-27) it might be translated as "folly" or "stupidity": Tannehill, *Narrative Unity* 1:176.

[124] The Lukan formulation is less dramatic than the formal adumbration of the Passion in Mark 3:6, but the opposition to Jesus is no less permanently engaged.

[125] A bridge passage contains rhetorical structures, themes, characters, and scenes in common with the section that precedes it and the section that follows it. As such it forms a transition from one section to another while belonging to both. Luke is especially fond of the device.

[126] It is part of 5:1–6:16 since it contains the third of the ἐγένετο δὲ ἐν introductions, which respond to 5:1, 12, 17, and it continues the theme of calling disciples (5:1-11, 27-32; 6:12-16). It is part of 6:20-49 because the disciples are called to hear the Sermon.

results from divine inspiration (6:12-13) and the Twelve are the central group of Jesus' disciples. Most often called "the Twelve" in Luke and "the Apostles" in Acts 1–6, they accompany Jesus, especially at significant moments (8:1; 9:1-12; 17:5; 18:31; 22:3, 14; 24:10; Acts 1:1-12). In Acts 1–15 they are the central authority in the early constitution of the Christian community. As Twelve, they symbolize eschatological Israel and are portrayed mostly as faithful to Jesus (Luke 22:28-30).[127] As principally fishermen unlettered in the Law they are the counter to Jesus' learned opponents, who cannot see the new dispensation. Their real role here is to hear the Sermon, and so their calling will be discussed in the next chapter.

Summary of Luke 3:1–6:16 as Setting of the Sermon

1. *John and Jesus Fulfill Prologue Themes:*

a. The eschatological age of salvation arrives:

(1) The Elijah-like prophet has come, preparing a people for the Lord by a baptism of repentance, apocalyptic preaching, and pointing to the Messiah (3:1-20).

(2) The reign of Satan is overthrown (4:1-13), manifestly in exorcisms (4:31-41).

(3) Jesus is the eschatological prophet of Isa 61:1-2, the Son of Man (6:5), and the Bridegroom (5:34).

(4) Jesus' ministry is so new that Jewish forms do not fit it (5:33-39).

(5) Jesus forms eschatological Israel on the Twelve Apostles (6:12-16).

b. Jesus' identity is central to his mission:

(1) His humanity is shown in his temptation (4:1-13) and his prayer (3:21; 4:42; 6:12).

(2) He reinterprets OT law and custom (6: 1-5, 9).

(3) He is the Messiah (4:41) and the Lord (5:8; 6:5).

(4) More, the Spirit makes him Son of God in his ministry, and he is proclaimed such (directly, 3:22; 4:41; obliquely, 3:23, 38; 4:3, 9).

---

[127] The literature on the Twelve is extensive, much of it on whether Jesus or the Church created it; see now John Meier, "The Circle of the Twelve: Did it Exist during Jesus' Public Ministry?" *JBL* 116 (1997) 635–72. A concise summary of their role and theological use by the evangelists is Raymond F. Collins, "Twelve, The," *ABD* 6:67–71. For their role as eschatological Israel in Luke-Acts see Gerhard Lohfink, *Die Sammlung Israels. Eine Untersuchung zur lukanischen Ekklesiologie.* SANT 39 (München: Kösel, 1975).

2. The Ministries Add other Themes to the Prologue:

a. John's teaching has an ethical component, emphasizing conversion (3:8), expressed in an ethics of sharing (3:10-14).

b. Jesus proclaims a present reign of God, a liberation from oppression (4:18), manifested in exorcisms and healings (4:31-43; 5:17-26; 6:6-11).

c. Jesus' mission is to outcasts, the poor, captives, blind, oppressed (4:18), lepers (5:12-16), the lame (5:17-26); as Son of Man he has authority to bring divine forgiveness of sins (5:20-26) and associates with sinners (5:29-32); he restores the outcasts to community (5:12-16, 29-32).

d. Jesus summons to discipleship, described as helping him in his mission (5:10-11), following him (5:11, 27-28), radical dispossession (5:10, 28), in his own model of filial obedience (4:1-13).

e. Jesus is a teacher (4:14, 31, 44; 5:3, 17; 6:6), but his teaching is not described.

In sum, Luke 1–6 has presented Jesus as a teacher with divine authority whose mission is to deliver the marginalized and oppressed. Since the Baptist had prepared a people fit for the Lord (1:17), an ethical people (3:7-14), the reader should presume from the continued contrasting parallelism with the Baptist that Jesus must be summoning to conversion, a summons that begs for ethical teaching (as in 3:10-14). The reader, teased by Luke's refusal to describe the content of this preaching, is now about to have her curiosity satisfied.

Part II

Exegesis of the Sermon on the Plain

Chapter 3

Blessed Are the Poor
(6:20)

Luke has been introducing *his* audience (the implied readers) to Jesus as the messiah, come as the Son of God with a special relationship with his Father. Jesus formally introduced himself as the eschatological prophet sent to proclaim the year of release for the oppressed, which he then effected by overcoming Satan with exorcisms and healings. This irruption of divine liberation into their regular religious world provoked opposition from the Pharisees and scribes, but also provided the basis for the whole-hearted response of a few disciples. Through Luke 1–6 Jesus has taught, but Luke has concealed the content of this teaching. The Sermon on the Plain now breaks this silence and reveals the message that accompanies his liberating activity.

The Audience of the Sermon

In Chapter 2 the naming of the twelve apostles (6:12-16) is the conclusion of the unit on discipleship and opposition. But it is also a bridge passage, serving as the first gathering of the audience for the coming Sermon.[1] In 6:17 Jesus descends with the Twelve[2] to a plain[3] where they are

---

[1] Source criticism indicates Luke's redactional intent: he has been following the order of Mark 1:14–3:6. As he inverted the order of Mark 1:16-20 and 1:22-39 for a theological purpose (see n. 56, p. 35), so he now inverts the order of the healings (Mark 3:7-12//Luke 6:17-19) and the calling of the Twelve (Mark 3:13-19//Luke 6:12-16). The revised order brings the crowds into place to hear the Sermon that immediately follows, while including the disciples, who mingle with the crowds (6:17), as its audience. Johannes Beutler, "Lk 6,16: Punkt oder Komma?" *BZ* 35 (1991) 231–33 shows how 6:12-19 is a unit introducing the Sermon.

[2] Although the μετ' αὐτῶν could refer to both the Twelve and the disciples from whom he chose the Twelve, ordinarily αὐτός would refer to the last-named persons. Luke's accent here is on the Twelve as those who accompany Jesus.

[3] Hans Conzelmann (*The Theology of St. Luke* [New York: Harper & Row, 1960] 44) sees the mountain, where God is present, as the place of revelation and prayer in Luke

joined by a great crowd of his disciples,[4] and along with them a great
throng of people—from all Judea and Jerusalem, even from the coastal
cities of Tyre and Sidon.[5] They have come to hear Jesus and to be healed
of their diseases (6:18).[6] They are not disappointed: the divine δύναμις
(6:19), which had previously been expressed in his speech, now is so pal-
pable in his healing that the unfortunate reach out to touch him, to be
saved by the very touch.[7] This divine power in speech and healing limns
Jesus as he opens his mouth in the Sermon.[8]

(6:12; 9:28); Jesus descends from the mountain to meet the people. Although Luke does not
have the developed Moses/Jesus typology of Matthew, there is something to Heinz Schürmann's contention (*Das Lukasevangelium* [Freiburg: Herder, 1969] 1:320) that as Moses
goes up and comes down to the foot of Mount Sinai to communicate God's will to the
people (at least five times in Exodus 19:20–34:29), so does Jesus here. Jesus' descent breaks
the mountain contact with God, but insofar as 6:12-16 sets the scene for the Sermon, something of the divine communication on the mountain extends to the content of the Sermon
and the reverence with which it is heard.

    [4] Where did this crowd come from? We have heard only of the calls of Levi (5:27-28)
and of Peter, James, and John (5:1-12—or did others of their μετόχοι also beach their boats
to follow?). By 5:33 and 6:1-2 the number of disciples is large enough to be attacked, but
that could still be a number not much larger than the Twelve (6:13). Dennis Hamm (*The Beatitudes in Context* [Wilmington, Del.: Michael Glazier, 1990] 38–40), following the lead
of Siegfried Schulz, Hans Joachim Degenhardt, and Heinz Schürmann (see the bibliography in Schürmann, *Lukasevangelium* 321), gives the best solution: only in 6:13 and in 19:37
does μαθηταί refer to a group larger than the Twelve, while in Acts it refers to all believers. In the contexts of 6:17 and 19:37 μαθηταί appears to be Luke's proleptic reference to
the whole post-Easter community. Then the Sermon is addressed to all Jesus' disciples over
the centuries.

    [5] Πλῆθος πολὺ τοῦ λαοῦ refers to the people of Israel, which Luke has shown await-
ing messianic redemption in 1:17, 53-55, 67, 80; 2:10, 25, 32, 38; Hamm, *Beatitudes*
38–39. As opposed to the disciples, they are not believers. Their many homelands show
Jesus' message reaching to all the people, even those in Gentile lands, a proleptic description of the spread of the gospel in Acts.

    [6] Here, as in 5:15, the crowd has come both to hear and to be delivered from what op-
presses them. This double intention resumes the coupling of the word and healing in 4:31-
44, but, in view of the coming Sermon, the emphasis now will be on Jesus' teaching as a
word of liberation.

    [7] In 1:17 the Baptizer is to come in the spirit and power of Elijah, who not only
preached, but worked wonders and healed. John's power was only in his prophetic word
gathering and purifying the people. Jesus, however, has preached and healed. Luke here and
elsewhere portrays Jesus' power as so substantial that touch can convey it (8:46); the notion
is carried further in Acts, where Peter's shadow (5:15) and cloths touched to Paul (19:11-
12) have healing power.

    [8] Jesus' healing power functions rhetorically as a prior "external proof " of the Sermon
to follow; George A. Kennedy, *New Testament Interpretation through Rhetorical Criticism*
(Chapel Hill: University of North Carolina Press, 1984) 40, 42.

The mixed character of the audience Luke has assembled for the Sermon is reinforced by the Sermon itself, when Jesus first looks on his *disciples* as he speaks (6:20), and yet at the end is said to have spoken to *all the people* (7:1).[9] This shift of hearers may be imperceptible to the virginal implied reader, but it affects Christian readers' interpretation of the meaning of the Sermon.

The Tradition of the Sermon

The following table of the Sermon's contents and order reveals that Luke did not create his Sermon from scattered teachings of Jesus, but that it had already existed in a source utilized by both Matthew and Luke:

Luke	Matthew	Content
6:20-23	5:3, 6, 11	Beatitudes
6:27-28	5:43-44	Love of enemies
6:29-30	5:39-40, 42	On nonretaliation
6:31	7:12	The so-called Golden Rule
6:32-33	5:46-47	Christian retribution
6:35b, 36	5:45, 48	Imitation of the Father
6:37a, 38b	7:1, 2b	Not judging and its rewards
6:41-42	7:3-5	Trope on not judging
(6:43-44)	(7:16-17)	(trees and fruit)
6:46-49	7:21, 24-27	Exhortation, parable of house builders[10]

[9] Note the same ambiguity about the audience in Matthew's Sermon: in 5:1 Jesus moves from the crowds to the mountain, where his *disciples* come to him and he addresses them directly (5:2). Yet at the end of that Sermon the *crowds* are astonished by his teaching! It is possible that the double audience served a theological motive in Q, but it certainly does in each gospel (see below, Chapter 8). Cf. also Mark 13:37, "What I say to you I say to all."

[10] Thus of the material in Luke's Sermon only vv. 24-26 (woes), 34 (loans), 35a (repetition of loving enemies), 37b-38a (not judging, giving, forgiving), 39-40 (proverbs on the blind leading the blind, disciple and master), 45 (good person producing good) have no correlative in Matthew's Sermon. That some of this material stood in their common source can be assumed from the use of correlatives to Luke 6:39, 40, 45 in Matt 15:14; 10:24-25; 12:35, respectively. I follow the scholarly consensus that the common source of both sermons was Q, and I explain the differences between the sermons not by the methodologically uncontrollable hypothesis of two different recensions of Q, but by the redactional interests of the two evangelists. I do not utilize source criticism to separate tradition from redaction, as I consider this, in view of the divergent results of its foremost practitioners, a fruitless enterprise (see my article, "The Lukan Version of the Lord's Sermon," *BTB* 11 [1981] 48–49).

Not only is the material common to both sermons, but so is its general sequence.[11] But our interest is not in the tradition as it came to Luke, but in the whole Sermon the implied author now addresses to the implied readers of his community.

The Rhetoric of the Sermon

1. *The Structure of the Sermon* is less controverted than are its sources: all agree that 6:20-26 forms the initial unit of the Sermon, but there is considerable disagreement about the following "units."[12] Accordingly, I will here give the structure of the Beatitudes and Woes as the exordium of the Sermon, and postpone to Chapter 5 the controversies over the structure of the love command.[13]

Μακάριοι οἱ πτωχοί,	20b
ὅτι ὑμετέρα ἐστὶν ἡ βασιλεία τοῦ θεοῦ.	20c
μακάριοι οἱ πεινῶντες νῦν,	21a
ὅτι χορτασθήσεσθε.	21b
μακάριοι οἱ κλαίοντες νῦν,	21c
ὅτι γελάσετε.	21d
μακάριοί ἐστε	22a
ὅταν[14] μισήσωσιν ὑμᾶς οἱ ἄνθρωποι	22b
καὶ ὅταν[15] ἀφορίσωσιν ὑμᾶς	22c
καὶ ὀνειδίσωσιν	22d
καὶ ἐκβάλωσιν τὸ ὄνομα ὑμῶν ὡς πονηρὸν	22e
ἕνεκα τοῦ υἱοῦ τοῦ ἀνθρώπου ·	22f
χάρητε[16] ἐν ἐκείνῃ τῇ ἡμέρᾳ	23a

[11] Both sermons begin with the beatitudes and end with the exhortation and parable of the housebuilders, and, except for the place of the love command and the golden rule, the material follows the same sequence in each.

[12] The chief differences are whether the material on the love commandment breaks at v. 36 or v. 38, and whether 6:43-45 is a unit with what precedes it; see the survey in "Lukan Version," 49–50.

[13] A grammatical analysis, in which structure is determined by whether a clause is independent or subordinate (adverbial, adjectival, or nominal) does not aid exegesis as much as a rhetorical one, in which clauses are arranged according to their parallel and contrasting functions. The following structure, then, is rhetorical, with footnoted cautions derived from a more grammatical analysis.

[14] As adverbial, this clause should be moved right, parallel to the ὅτι clauses, but rhetorically it functions adjectivally, as οἱ μισησούμενοι parallel to οἱ πτωχοί.

[15] Grammatically these next three ὅταν clauses are parallel to the one in 22b, but rhetorically they are subordinate to that one, defining how the disciples are hated.

[16] Since χάρητε is either the beginning of a new sentence or an independent clause asyndetically joined to the previous one, grammatically it should be diagrammed as far left

καὶ σκιρτήσατε,   23b

    ἰδοὺ γὰρ[17] ὁ μισθὸς ὑμῶν πολὺς ἐν τῷ οὐρανῷ   23c

    κατὰ τὰ αὐτὰ γὰρ ἐποίουν τοῖς προφήταις   23d
        οἱ πατέρες αὐτῶν.

Πλὴν οὐαὶ ὑμῖν τοῖς πλουσίοις,   24a

    ὅτι ἀπέχετε τὴν παράκλησιν ὑμῶν.   24b

οὐαὶ ὑμῖν, οἱ[18] ἐμπεπλησμένοι νῦν,   25a

    ὅτι πεινάσετε.   25b

οὐαὶ, οἱ γελῶντες νῦν,   25c

    ὅτι πενθήσετε   25d

    καὶ κλαύσετε.   25e

οὐαὶ ὅταν ὑμᾶς καλῶς εἴπωσιν πάντες οἱ ἄνθρωποι ·   26a

    κατὰ τὰ αὐτὰ γὰρ ἐποίουν τοῖς ψευδοπροφήταις   26b
        οἱ πατέρες αὐτῶν.

2. *The Rhetoric of the Sermon:* From the above structure emerges the artistry of the Sermon, marked by three striking features:

a. Symmetry:

1. The four beatitudes in one strophe (6:20-23) are balanced by four woes in the following strophe (6:24-26).[19]

2. The content of each woe is a negative reprise of the content of its corresponding beatitude.

3. In each strophe the pattern is 3 + 1, i. e., (a) *in the first three cola* the adjective (μακάριοι) or interjection (οὐαὶ) + noun or noun clause denoting the subject is followed by a subordinate clause introduced by ὅτι, giving the reason for the description; (b) *in the fourth colon* the adjective or interjection + ὅταν giving the actions by others that affect the subjects is followed by a reason (γὰρ) drawn from past example that is predictive of future beatitude or woe.

---

as μακάριοι. The present rhetorical diagram shows that its joy is still in function of the conditions of the fourth macarism, and not applicable in the first instance to all the beatitudes (as v. 23d makes clear).

[17] Although strictly γάρ is a coordinating conjunction, still there is a nuance of subordination (as opposed to καὶ), and so it is slightly indented here.

[18] Since it is not in the dative, the participial phrase grammatically represents an adjectival clause (and so should be subordinated diagrammatically to ὑμῖν), but rhetorically it functions as if it were dative, an appositive parallel to τοῖς πλουσίοις in v. 24a. Note that in v. 25c the pronoun in the dative is dispensed with, as a variant of the same construction.

[19] The balance is unmistakable because the key word (μακάριοι, οὐαὶ) is placed at the beginning of each clause and echoes the others in series.

4. The length of the fourth element is almost as long as or longer than the prior three of the series, and so "balances" them and forms a conclusion to each strophe.

This carefully crafted structure is not just an aesthetic exordium to evoke the *pathos* of the audience, but a structure interpreting Jesus' teaching. The echoing strophes enable the exegete to interpret the first beatitude by the other three in its strophe, as well as by contrast with its corresponding woe in the next strophe.

b. Variety:

Luke does not like mechanical repetition of vocabulary or syntax,[20] and so within this general symmetry there is considerable artistic variation:

1. The conclusions of the first beatitude and first woe are longer than those of the two that follow; thus each initial element functions as a generalized statement that the following two elaborate.

2. The subjects of the first beatitude and woe are simple substantivized adjectives, while the subjects of the next two beatitudes and woes are substantivized participles. Indeed, the variation in subjects of the woes is particularly subtle.[21]

3. The γελάσετε of the third beatitude is contrasted with a double verb, πενθήσετε καὶ κλαύσετε, in the third woe for a rhetorical fullness that ends the series in 6:25.

4. The νῦνs that relate the four cola of two verses (21a, 21c, 25a, 25c) also cause these verses to vary from the first and last member of each strophe; indeed, they highlight the fact that the reward of the first beatitude and woe are in the present, while the rewards in 21b, 21d, 25b, 25d are rewards in an eschatological future.

5. The fourth beatitude shares the same structure as the fourth woe, but added descriptions of the actions of adversaries make it half again as long as that woe, which then can be shorter because the actions of that

---

[20] Henry J. Cadbury, *The Style and Literary Method of Luke* (Cambridge, Mass.: Harvard University Press, 1920) 83–84; it was a sign of good Greek rhetoric not to be mechanical in repetition.

[21] Οὐαὶ followed by the personal pronoun in the dative, with the substantivized adjective in apposition (6:24a); again ὑμῖν, but now the substantivized participle is not in the dative but in the nominative, as if it were the subject of a relative clause (οἱ ἐμπεπλησμένοι εἰσιν; 6:25b); the personal pronoun has now been suppressed and so the substantivized participle in the nominative functions either as a relative clause where the pronoun has assimilated its antecedent or has turned the οὐαὶ into a predicative adjective analogous to μακάριοι (6:25c).

long beatitude are carried by the structure into the understanding of the fourth woe.

6. The two imperatives in 23a,b are not repeated in the corresponding fourth woe.

c. Sound and tone:

Two features are immediately striking:

1. There is a kind of music in the repetition of the same words at the beginning of each colon: μακάριοι οἱ . . . ὅτι, μακάριοι οἱ . . . ὅτι, μακάριοι οἱ . . . ὅτι, μακάριοι . . . ὅταν . . . καὶ ὅταν. When this was read aloud among Luke's community the very music must have touched the *pathos* of the audience.

2. Μακάριοι, as the initial word of the Sermon repeated three times in a refrain, sets a theme of consolation and spontaneous joy that rings throughout the proemium, but also throughout the sermon of which it is the exordium. From the outset the Sermon is marked by a theme of happiness that is characteristic of the reign of God. On the other hand, the οὐαὶ that follows in v. 24 is also repeated three times and adds its somber note of warning to the Sermon's tone. The Sermon summons to choice,[22] and this persistent alternation between living the divine ethic and living the world's wisdom (6:20-23<—>24-26, 27-31<—>32-34, 37-38<—>41-42, 45a<—>45b, 47-48<—>49) intones the struggle between the promises of Jesus and human intransigence.

So much for the overall rhetoric of the Sermon; for the specific details of our rhetorical analysis we now turn to exegesis of the beatitudes and woes.

Exegesis of the First Beatitude

6:20a: Καὶ αὐτὸς ἐπάρας τοὺς ὀφθαλμοὺς αὐτοῦ εἰς τοὺς μαθητὰς αὐτοῦ ἔλεγεν, "And lifting his eyes to his disciples, he said" specifies those to whom Luke's Jesus primarily addresses the Sermon: the disciples of his own community, whose experience is here described and whose symbolic universe enables them to understand the ethic of the Sermon.

6:20b: Μακάριοι οἱ πτωχοί, "Blessed the poor." The first words of the Sermon are winning: the Lord speaks immediately about the blessings and joy that come to those affected by his "program." The address in the second person plural[23] seizes those who are listening and the joyful proclamation renders them benevolent.

---

[22] Hence it contains deliberative rhetoric: Kennedy, *Rhetorical Criticism* 19.

[23] Formally, Luke's macarism retains the third-person formulation; it is not until the ὅτι clause of the first three beatitudes that the second person plural transforms the beatitude

Μακάριος is the usual LXX translation of אַשְׁרֵי.[24] In contrast to εὐλογητός, (בָּרוּךְ), *'ashrei* does not confer a blessing, but recognizes an existing state of happiness.[25] Among the Greeks μακάριος referred to the happy state of the gods; when it began to apply to humans in the Hellenistic age it referred to those beyond normal human cares, those happy as the gods.[26] In the LXX a macarism congratulates a human for a God-given state of happiness, and implicitly for the present relationship with God that effects it. The motive for the praise or congratulation is to persuade the reader to value and imitate the values being praised.[27]

The form occurs almost entirely in Wisdom literature and the Psalms. There it commonly expresses practical desires for daily life (prosperity, honor, a good wife, etc.: Sir 25:8; 26:1) as God grants these to one who observes the Law. The highest possession for which this literature counts one blessed is wisdom (Prov 3:13; Sir 14:20).[28] Isaiah is the only prophet to use this Wisdom form, mostly to stress material abundance and prosperity coming to the holy people, but Isa 30:18 counts as blessed those

---

to direct address of the hearer. Virtually all translations introduce this second person into the beatitude itself (Dennis Hamm, *Beatitudes* 15, 18). If, as most exegetes think, the second-person form is due to Luke's redactional activity, then Luke himself underlines the immediacy of the beatitude for his readers. For Luke's readers the macarism comes as no surprise: the opening lines of the Jesus story had spoken of blessings (1:45, 48). Ernst Bammel points out that the poor are never directly addressed as a class in the OT, and only once in Judaism (*T. Isaac* 8:12): "πτωχός," *TDNT* 6:888–95, especially n. 82.

[24] The bibliography on the macarism is extensive. A fairly comprehensive view of this scholarship can be found in Friedrich Hauck and Georg Bertram, "μακάριος," *TDNT* 4:362–70; Raymond F. Collins, "Beatitudes," *ABD* 1:629–31, with its selective bibliography; and Dennis Hamm, *Beatitudes*.

[25] Εὐλογητός is most properly used of God. When it is predicated of humans it is an invocation of God's blessing, a wish that one be granted divine favors.

[26] The form is usually μακάριος ὅστις, and the person is judged blessed mostly for possession of earthly goods or pious sons. At its most exalted μακάριος refers to those who have fame, honor, ἀρετή. See Friedrich Hauck in *TDNT* 4:362–64.

[27] The beatitude "has the social function of promoting those values and behaviors which the community holds dear" (Hamm, *Beatitudes* 12). The beatitude thus functions as a kind of epideictic rhetoric; see George A. Kennedy, *Rhetorical Criticism* 19.

[28] Sometimes the very possession of these things, however, pales in relation to the supreme blessing of the sage's personal communion with God: in Psalm 1 the sage delighting in the Law is clearly in love with his law-giving God. But this relationship is not consciously expressed as the reason for one's beatitude. I include in the category of religious Wisdom beatitudes those of 4Q525. The four (or five) beatitudes of column 2 bear a superficial resemblance to some of the Matthaean beatitudes (Emile Puech, "4Q525 et les péricopes des béatitudes en Ben Sira et Matthieu," *RB* 98 [1991] 80–106), but not to anything in the Lukan forms. I agree with Robert H. Eisenman and Michael Wise, *The Dead Sea Scrolls Uncovered* (Rockport, Mass.: Element, 1992) 168–69 that "Beatitudes Scroll" is "a misnomer."

who wait for the Lord. This motive is expanded in apocalyptic literature, beginning with Dan 12:12 where hope for an eschatological deliverance by Yhwh is the "cause" of the beatitude.[29] Nevertheless, the overwhelming use of the macarism is platitudinous, expressing common wisdom in which those who are near to God already share divine favors and prosperity. It is not a form to express the striking paradoxes of the Sermon's beatitudes, and Jesus' first listeners must have been amazed at the content of these beatitudes.

NT usage refers to the distinctive religious joy of persons sharing the salvation of the reign of God. The normal wisdom form[30] then carries expectations which exceed material human desires, and so participates in the paradoxical character of the reign that Jesus proclaims.

Luke uses μακάριος more than any other NT author.[31] A brief survey of his eleven beatitudes outside of the Sermon may reveal some interpretative keys to the Sermon's macarisms.

1:45: καὶ μακαρία ἡ πιστεύσασα ὅτι ἔσται τελείωσις τοῖς λελαλημένοις αὐτῇ παρὰ κυρίου, "And blessed is she who believed that what the Lord spoke would be fulfilled in her,"[32] could be a normal religious beatitude, praising anyone who believes that God will accomplish what

[29] Scholars often distinguish on the basis of *content* between Wisdom beatitudes and apocalyptic beatitudes. "*Wisdom* beatitudes focus on attitudes and behavior valuable for one's personal well-being in the here and now. *Apocalyptic* beatitudes . . . focus on attitudes and behaviors which find their reward in God's future intervention into history" (Hamm, *Beatitudes* 11). I count some 37 beatitudes in the apocalyptic literature (including Dan 12:12), most of these in 1 and 2 Enoch. Even where the motive for present beatitude is not eschatological hope, the apocalyptic beatitudes more commonly stress what we would call religious sentiments, such as 2 Enoch 52:1, "Blessed is he who opens his heart for praise, and praises the Lord."

[30] The form has μακάριοι first in the sentence and used predicatively. Then comes the subject, either the proper name or an article with a common noun or adjective, and then the reason for the beatitude, usually expressed in a subordinate clause. Although the OT almost always uses the third person for the beatitudes, the NT often has the second person.

[31] Fifteen times in the Gospel and twice in Acts (as opposed to thirteen for Matthew, none for Mark, two for John, and seven for the rest of the NT): thirty-four per cent of fifty NT uses. Μακάριόν ἐστιν μᾶλλον διδόναι ἢ λαμβάνειν (Acts 20:35) is not a beatitude. The impersonal usage removes it from the category of praise or congratulation, and makes μακάριόν a synonym for μειζόν; the motive or ground is lacking either in a ὅτι clause or in a context for the agraphon itself.

[32] It is impossible to know whether ὅτι introduces a noun clause as the object of believing or a causal clause giving the reason for blessedness. I take it as "believes that what the Lord spoke to her will be fulfilled" because the original annunciation scene stressed Mary's belief in its fulfillment (1:38, in contrast to 1:20) and because Elizabeth's own utterances in the immediate context of the beatitude also stress that the τελείωσις has begun (1:43-44), which is more consonant with Mary's belief than a cause that would stress the futurity of the action.

he promises her. But the context refers the beatitude to Mary's blessedness in believing in the miraculous arrival of the Messiah/Lord (1:43). Mary is blessed for belief in the imminent eschatological deliverance now to be effected by Jesus. This sense of salvation being already under way is confirmed by Mary's canticle, which reflects on her blessedness as deriving from God's already having done great things for her (1:47-55, especially 48-49).

7:23: καὶ μακάριός ἐστιν ὃς ἐὰν μὴ σκανδαλισθῇ ἐν ἐμοί, "And blessed is whoever is not scandalized at me." The whole passage (7:18-35) manifests Jesus as "the one to come" (7:19), proved by his eschatological works for the poor and oppressed (7:22 reflects on 4:18-44). Consequently the beatitude praises those who accept Jesus as the eschatological prophet/healer now at work.

10:23: Μακάριοι οἱ ὀφθαλμοὶ οἱ βλέποντες ἃ βλέπετε, "Blessed the eyes that see what you see." The context of this beatitude is one of eschatological power and reward: the disciples collaborate in Jesus' apocalyptic triumph over Satan (10:17-19), although their greater joy is that their names are inscribed in the heavens (10:20). Further, as "little ones," they now receive the unique revelation of the Father by the Son (10:21-22). So Jesus' beatitude for them must identify the things that they see (ἃ βλέπετε) as his present eschatological work (not only 10:1-23, but what they have been witnessing in 4:30–10:23) and the Father's unique revelation of the identity and works of Jesus. Consequently, the disciples are congratulated for being right now in the right spot at the eschatological time that prophets and kings have longed to see.

11:27-28: Μακαρία ἡ κοιλία ἡ βαστάσασά σε καὶ μαστοὶ οὓς ἐθήλασας. . . . μενοῦν μακάριοι οἱ ἀκούοντες τὸν λόγον τοῦ θεοῦ καὶ φυλάσσοντες, "Blessed the womb that bore you and the breasts that nursed you . . . . rather blessed are they who hear the word of God and keep it." These two linked beatitudes arise from Jesus' casting out of a demon (11:14) as the sign that the eschatological Reign of God had arrived in this work (11:20). Further, the assertion of this eschatological power occasions Jesus' speech about his cosmic struggle with Satan and the fact that humans must choose sides in that struggle (11:21-23). Not choosing Jesus' side leads to a worse state of being under Satan's control (11:24-26). Consequently, the woman's beatitude for Mary, which could be a Jewish woman's praise for any good man's mother, now becomes praise because she has brought eschatological salvation to birth in the present world. Responding in that context, Jesus' common religious beatitude praising those who hear and keep God's word now becomes eschatological: blessed are those who accept God's word as it now comes to pass in Jesus' words and works.[33]

[33] Luke T. Johnson (*The Gospel of Luke.* SP 3 [Collegeville: The Liturgical Press, 1991] 132, 185) points out that Jesus' sowing of the Word of God infuses a new meaning

12:37-38: Μακάριοι οἱ δοῦλοι ἐκεῖνοι, οὓς ἐλθὼν ὁ κύριος εὑρήσει γρηγοροῦντας· . . . κἂν ἐν τῇ δευτέρᾳ κἂν ἐν τῇ τρίτῃ φυλακῇ ἔλθῃ . . . μακάριοί εἰσιν ἐκεῖνοι. At the beginning of a long passage on eschatological readiness (12:35–13:9) Jesus uses a similitude (12:35-39) to exhort his disciples (12:22) to be ready for the return of the apocalyptic Son of Man (12:40). Disciples found awake and watching will receive the extraordinary favor of having their Lord serve them (12:37). Both beatitudes have subtle tense usage. The one in 12:37 has, as usual, no linking verb in the main clause, but the future tense, εὑρήσει, in the subordinate clause may imply a future notion in the suppressed verb in the main clause: "Blessed (will be) those servants whom the master *will find* watching when he comes." The beatitude in 12:38 has ἐὰν + aorist subjunctives (ἔλθῃ, εὕρῃ) in the main clause, which approximate a future tense,[34] but has an expressed linking verb in the present tense (εἰσιν) in the beatitude: "Blessed are you, if the master should come in the second or third watch and find you waiting." Thus the first beatitude is final eschatology: those found waiting at the time of the apocalyptic Son of Man's visitation will then be blessed. The second beatitude is mixed: blessed are you now, whose present continued state of readiness for the Son of Man's delayed return will then reap its reward. Blessed are those who are living this age as continuous with that of the return of the apocalyptic judge.

12:43: Μακάριος ὁ δοῦλος ἐκεῖνος ὃν ἐλθὼν ὁ κύριος αὐτοῦ εὑρήσει ποιοῦντα οὕτως, "Blessed that servant whom the Lord on his arrival . . . will find so acting." The next similitude is linked to the former (12:41), and its beatitude stresses the future, as does that of 12:37. The servant who in this time feeds those in his charge will be blessed because he will in the future judgment be placed in charge of all the Lord's possessions. Yet 12:45-48 makes the same argument as 12:38 in its context: if one is not serving one's fellows now, the Son of Man will come at an unexpected time and the one who is not so serving will be slashed up and dispossessed. One's future beatitude so depends on one's present action that the blessedness to come already influences one's present state of blessedness.

14:14: Καὶ μακάριος ἔσῃ, ὅτι οὐκ ἔχουσιν ἀνταποδοῦναί σοι, ἀνταποδοθήσεται γάρ σοι ἐν τῇ ἀναστάσει τῶν δικαίων, "And blessed will you be because they have no resources to repay you, for you will be repaid at the resurrection of the just." Here both the beatitude and the reward

---

of hearing the word of God into 8:21 and 11:28. Joseph A. Fitzmyer (*The Gospel According to Luke.* 2 vols. AB 28, 28A [Garden City, N.Y.: Doubleday, 1981, 1985] 929), writes: "Jesus' beatitude echoes that of Elizabeth in 1:42" and, I add, even more than in 1:45.

[34] The aorist subjunctive can be used for what is general, what is impending, or (rarely) what is past (BDF #373). The context here surely implies a less vivid future.

have future tenses, and so the beatitude expresses final eschatology. Jesus expressly excludes present reward from those invited to one's banquet, and places not only God's reward of such behavior, but also the blessing of such behavior in the most future time of all, the resurrection of the dead.

14:15: Μακάριος ὅστις φάγεται ἄρτον ἐν τῇ βασιλείᾳ τοῦ θεοῦ, "Blessed whoever eats bread in the Reign of God." One of those at the Pharisee's meal understood that Jesus had been speaking of the eschatological banquet (Isa 25:6-8), and called down a beatitude on those who will participate in that meal. The whole context speaks so strongly of eschatological reward that even the present verb of the beatitude is invested with future meaning.[35]

23:29: Μακάριαι αἱ στεῖραι καὶ αἱ κοιλίαι αἳ οὐκ ἐγέννησαν καὶ μαστοὶ οἳ οὐκ ἔθρεψαν, "Blessed the barren, and the wombs that did not bear and the breasts that did not nurse." To those women who bewail his way of the cross Jesus speaks a paradoxical macarism which says that their historical state[36] will be worse than his—so bad that sterility (the cause of a woman's dishonor and social dislocation)[37] will be more prized than fertility.[38] This beatitude most approaches a sapiential beatitude bearing on the vicissitudes of this life, but the paradox is so severe that it escapes that category. Rather it alone echoes the kind of paradox found in the four beatitudes of the Lukan Sermon.

In sum, these are the characteristics of the macarism as Luke uses it:

1. Luke does not use sapiential macarisms pragmatically, describing normal human happiness; the two closest to this genre are so transformed by their eschatological context (11:27) and their bitter paradox (23:29) that they exceed it.

---

[35] BDF #323 speaks of the present used with future meaning "in confident assertions regarding the future." Although the grammar fails to adduce this as an example, it certainly fits: the whole point of Jesus' parable in rejoinder (14:15-24) is to undermine the false confidence with which the (presumably Jewish) speaker speaks.

[36] "Days are coming" refers to the situation indicated by the same phrase in 19:43, the Roman sack of Jerusalem. Luke does not assign the sack any eschatological weight: 21:20-24 omits Mark's reference to the abomination of desolation, with its eschatological resonances in Daniel, and historicizes the subsequent time of the Gentiles.

[37] Bruce J. Malina and Richard Rohrbach, *Social-Science Commentary on the Synoptic Gospels* (Minneapolis: Fortress, 1992) 287.

[38] Fitzmyer has the meaning of the paradox: those without children will be spared the added torture of seeing them put to death, a notion found in classical literature (*Luke* 1498). His reference to Isa 54:1, however, contradicts his point: in Isaiah 54 the barren are blessed because God will make them fruitful, whereas in Luke 23:29 the barren are blessed because of their sterility.

2. All but 23:29 have explicitly religious subjects or motives deriving from their relation to God or from God's action in Jesus on their behalf.

3. These other ten are all, in one way or another, eschatological. The state of blessedness is due to God's unique and definitive intervention in history through Jesus of Nazareth. These beatitudes praise

(a) a present state of blessedness, because God's eschatological action is already present (1:45; 7:23; 10:23; 11:27, 28) or because God will finally reward a present action that is continuous in time with its reward (12:38);

(b) a future state of blessedness when the reward of their action is given (12:37, 43; 14:14, 15).

Conclusion: Μακάριος, as it came to Luke from Greek culture, the LXX, Jesus' usage, and that of his sources, is a plastic word. Under the strain of expressing the realities of the Reign of God it has been transformed from a platitudinous to a paradoxical expression. All but one of Luke's beatitudes refer to religious blessedness and eschatological reward, but they are very diversely rooted in the eschatological action of God in the present and in the apocalyptic age. Thus in order to find out what state Jesus is praising and when the blessedness will occur, we must turn to the content of each beatitude itself.

Οἱ πτωχοί. No other word in the beatitudes has provoked more diverse interpretation. *Hermeneutically* its interpretation seems strongly influenced by the subjective experience and perceptions of the interpreter. *Exegetically* the words "poor" and "rich" are mostly economic and social terms for a modern reader, but in the Bible they refer to a mixture of social, economic, political, and religious dimensions. Hence discussion of πτωχοί will be long and complex: we must survey the biblical terms for *poor,* analyze OT usage and interpretation, examine in the Ancient Near East and Israel the role of the king *vis à vis* poverty, see how this relationship functions in eschatological expectation, and finally examine πτωχοί in Luke-Acts before we can determine its meaning in this beatitude and in the Sermon's rhetorical structure.

1. *Semantic Overview:* Greek has principally two words for poor: πένης, one who has to toil in difficult circumstances to eke out a living (artisans, peasants—the common people), and πτωχός, the beggar, the wretch who is incapable of eking out a living.[39] The πένης has nothing superfluous;

---

[39] LSJ, *ad loc;* Friedrich Hauck, *TDNT* 6:885–87; Dupont, *Béatitudes* 2:20–25. Etymologically, πένης derives from πένομαι, to toil, labor; πτωχός from πτώσσω, to shrink, cringe, cower—the position of a beggar.

the πτωχός lacks even what is necessary. Πένης is more commonly used in Greek literature, but appears only once in the NT (2 Cor 9:9, citing the LXX of Ps 112:9). Πτωχός occurs thirty-four times in the NT. Of its twenty-four Gospel uses, fifteen refer to those who receive alms, and three other uses denote persons clearly belonging to the beggar class. The other six uses describe privileged beneficiaries of the reign of God.[40] Possibly the NT dominance of πτωχός is due to increased numbers of the dispossessed,[41] or to extension of its meaning to include the category of laborers. In any case LXX usage must have influenced Luke's use, and so we must now investigate that usage.[42]

2. *Old Testament Terms:* There are six word stems in the Hebrew Bible that mean poor, oppressed, afflicted, weak, humble: *'ānî* (used 80x)/*'anāwîm* (24x), *'ebyôn* (61x), *dāl* (48x)/*dallāh* (5x), *rāš* (22x), *maḥsor* (13x), *misken* (4x).[43]

עָנִי *('ānî)* is not only the most commonly used Hebrew word for "poor," but also the one πτωχός most frequently translates (38x).[44] It generally means one who is oppressed, who has to submit because he or she is incapable of resisting.[45] In the prophetic literature (25x) it is used to de-

---

[40] Dupont, *Béatitudes* 2:23, n. 1 provides the relevant texts and interpretations.

[41] Wolfgang Stegemann, *The Gospel and the Poor* (Philadelphia: Fortress, 1984) 19–20 gives these causes for an increase of the destitute: (1) Pompey's radical reorganization of Palestine removed from the Jewish state the coastal plain and the cities of the Decapolis, thus increasing the number of dispossessed farmers and reducing trade; (2) Herod the Great's expropriation of large stretches of farmlands (to be sold to wealthy landowners) concentrated lands in the hands of a few and created a large class of tenant farmers; (3) the crushing burden of taxes (over thirty per cent) from Rome and the Herods forced peasant and tenant farmers into debt; (4) periodic crop failures ruined small farmers and tenant farmers. All of these changes also impoverished the artisans dependent on farming economy in the rural areas.

[42] S. John Roth, *The Blind, the Lame, and the Poor: Character Types in Luke-Acts* (Sheffield: Sheffield Academic Press, 1997) 80–94 shows that the LXX is Luke's primary intertext.

[43] Since πτωχός does not translate *maḥsor* and *misken,* they do not affect our investigation of its meaning. The statistics and my general argument follow closely J. David Pleins, "Poor, Poverty," *ABD* 5:402–14, whose treatment of the words is based not only on etymology but on context and usage. Πτωχός is used sparingly in the deutero-canonical books; its twenty-three occurrences in Sirach do not diverge from that of the Tanakh, and so are not treated separately here.

[44] Almost forty-eight per cent of the time *'ānî* is translated by πτωοχός, but it is also translated twelve times by πένης, ten times by ταπεινός, eight times by ἀδικία, and four times by πραΰς.

[45] It most probably comes from *'ānāh* (as its *niphal*), meaning to be bowed down, afflicted, oppressed; thus etymologically it is a good match with πτωχός. In its *pi'el* form (its most common usage), *'ānāh* means to oppress, abuse, rape (BDB 776).

note economic oppression (Isa 3:15), unjust treatment in the law courts (Isa 10:2), and victimization through oppression (Isa 32:7). Its concrete meaning is reinforced by frequent pairing with *'ebyôn*.[46] In the Psalms it is used 31x, mostly in psalms of lament. Here it is usually paired poetically with *'ebyôn,* and it always refers to economic injustice, as it does in Wisdom literature and in the legal texts of Exodus 22 and Deuteronomy 15 and 24, which prohibit lending at interest to the poor. In his exhaustive study of words for the poor in the Hebrew Bible, J. David Pleins cannot find a single use of *'ānî,* including the references to the pleader of the psalms of lament, that carries a spiritual meaning ("humble, relying on God"). Its translation by πτωχός indicates that by the third century B.C.E. it had come to describe one so destitute and wretched as to be powerless and vulnerable to any oppression. This state is an appeal for help, which the person in need could expect from covenant partners, but ultimately only from God.[47]

A related term, עֲנָוִים *('anāwîm),*[48] occurs 24x in the Hebrew Bible. It occurs 13x in the Psalms, mostly in psalms of lament. As is the case with *'ānî* in these psalms, few texts give the concrete circumstances of the *'anāwîm*. Where they do, they speak of those who lack food (22:27), are landless (37:11) and in pain (69:33)—in fact, the use of *'anāwîm* in the Psalms is hardly distinguishable from that of *'ānî*.[49] The same is true of its scattered usage in the prophetic literature, with the exception of Zeph 2:3, to be discussed below. Πτωχός translates *'anāwîm* only 4x; it is usually translated by πραΰς (8x, 7x in the Psalms) and ταπεινός (5x).

---

[46] Isaiah 40–66 uses *'ānî* exclusively for the poor. Although it sometimes refers metaphorically to the exiles' sufferings, it is always grounded in the terrible economic and political oppression of the exiles, which YHWH has noted and from which he will deliver them.

[47] Walter E. Pilgrim, *Good News to the Poor: Wealth and Poverty in Luke-Acts* (Minneapolis: Augsburg, 1981) 45 lists the various Jewish practices that aided the beggarly poor: the poor tax of the tithe of produce in the third and sixth years, the sabbath year and annual practice of leaving the leftovers of the fields for the poor, the almsgiving enjoined in rabbinic teaching, and the practice of synagogal care for the poor in the form of shelter, clothing, and food. Although these practices derive from YHWH's commands and concern for the poor, they can have been only sporadically practiced. Ultimately the poor had to rely on some divine intervention, for which they prayed.

[48] Many scholars have conjectured that there is a singular form *'ānāw* that underlies this plural, and indeed a singular occurs once, in the *kethib* of Num 12:3. For the uncertain meanings this unusual form produces see Pleins, "Poor," 412–13.

[49] This is one of the principal reasons for Pleins' considering *'anāwîm* as a dialectical and spelling variant of *'ānîyyîm*; see the other reasons in "Poor," 412–13.

אֶבְיוֹן *('ebyôn)* denotes "poor, needy, powerless." Of its 61 uses it is translated by πτωχός only 11x, and by πένης 30x.[50] It occurs in the prophetic literature (17x) and in the Psalms (23x) in a variety of meanings referring always to social dislocation, economic exploitation, and legal victimization. Pleins calls the *'ebyônîm* the "beggarly poor."[51]

דַּל *(dāl)* is used 48x, and its cognate, דַּלָּה *(dallāh)* 5x in the Hebrew Bible, preponderantly in the Wisdom literature. It probably refers primarily to the poor peasant farmer.[52] Since πτωχός translates *dāl* 21x and *dallāh* 2x, this notion of the beleaguered peasant lies closest, after *'ānî,* to the third-century understanding of πρωχός.

רָשׁ *(rāš)* occurs 22x in the Hebrew Bible, almost exclusively in Wisdom literature, where the educated elite view poverty as resulting from laziness or profligacy. The regular connotation of *rāš* is a bum's poverty (Prov 10:4). Nevertheless, Proverbs still enjoins respect for such persons, and indicates that even the *rāš* is better than the liar and the stupid (19:1, 22). Only in Qoh 5:7 does it refer to one oppressed by the social structures.[53] Consequently, πτωχός translates *rāš* only 9x.

Thus Pleins' contextual survey of the Hebrew words for poverty shows "diverging notions about poverty" that derive from the divergent ideologies of the authors of various streams of tradition. Nevertheless, in all streams the concrete circumstances of socioeconomic and political poverty permeate even the most abstract and metaphorical uses of these words.

Finally, we notice that πτωχός is the one word that translates the five major Hebrew words denoting poverty: *'ānî* (38x), *dāl* (23x), *'ebyôn* (11x), *rāš* (9x), and *'anāwîm* (4x). Although the above frequency shows a marked preference for terms that unambiguously speak of socioeconomic poverty, the range of use indicates the potential to convey all the shades of mean-

---

[50] The LXX translates it also by ἀδύνατος (4x), ἐνδεής (5x), and once or twice each by seven other Greek words, mostly meaning "helpless." Its frequent pairing with *'ānî* (30x) shows their shared meaning of beggarly destitution, but the pairing severely limits the occasions in which it can be translated by πτωχός, which almost always translates the parallel *'ānî.*

[51] Pleins, "Poor," 403.

[52] "The mention of severe grain taxes (Amos 5:11) and lack of sufficient grazing and farmland (Isa 14:30; Jer 39:10) suggests [its] agricultural background ... confirmed by uses of the word *dāl* elsewhere in the Hebrew Bible," Pleins, "Poor," 405. In Wisdom literature *dāl* is transformed by that elite's view of poverty as brought on by the subject's own laziness.

[53] In 1 Sam 18:23 and 2 Sam 12:1-4 it refers to the politically and economically inferior. These are among the very few uses of words for "poor" in the Deuteronomic narratives, whose authors seem more interested in a critique of the kingship and of foreign oppressors than in a critique of poverty in Israel.

ing that the Hebrew Bible attached to this notion. Therefore we must look a little more deeply at this range of usage.

3. *Old Testament Conception of Poverty:*

a. Poverty is evil. The basic Hebrew notion is that YHWH creates abundance for humans (Genesis 1–2) and wants it for all people. Abraham is called to a land in which he will prosper (Gen 12:1-3), and so he does (13:2), as do his descendants (26:13; 30:43; 41:40). Moses is to lead his people into a land flowing with milk and honey (Exod 3:8), and those who live by their covenant with YHWH are promised abundance of material possessions (Deut 28:1-14). The laws of that covenant are summarized in Lev 19:18, "You shall love your neighbor as yourself"—the Hebrews are enjoined in the Law to practice strict justice with one another (Deut 16:20; Exodus 21–23)[54] and give special care to their poor and oppressed (Exod 22:21-27; Deut 15:1-11; 24:12-15, 19-22). To overcome the socioeconomic dislocations that build up over time, a jubilee year would redress inequitable distribution of lands and the loss of freedom (Leviticus 25). Thus YHWH intends a land without any poor (Deut 15:4-6).

Conversely, then, poverty is not what YHWH wills, and is seen as evil throughout the Bible. In the covenant theology of retribution, poverty is one of God's punishments, designed to lead God's people to live in accord with the covenant (Deut 28:15-24; Lev 26:14-26) and so to find prosperity. The causes of poverty in the Bible, then, are human sin, in two ways: (1) Violation of God's covenant.[55] The prophets rail against the greed and dishonest business practices that defraud the poor and strip them of their lands and means of subsistence. The poor described especially by *ʿānî, ʾebyôn, dāl, rāš*, and translated by πτωχός, are not evil; their bad state results from unjust oppression by the rich. When this injustice is rife, it calls down God's punishment to purify his people. (2) Sinful laziness on the part of the poor. This notion is limited to the elite traditions of Wisdom literature (Proverbs 10–29, but not in Job). The special word for this poverty, *maḥsor,* connotes evil in the poor themselves, and so it is not translated by πτωχός in the LXX.

b. The poor are virtuous. Against this overwhelmingly negative view of poverty in the Bible, for over 140 years scholars have argued that in the

---

[54] For a simple survey of how the covenants protect the poor see Pilgrim, *Good News* 21–24 and my *The Way to Peace* (Maryknoll, N.Y.: Orbis, 1979) 22–32.

[55] The covenant theology of retribution often portrays this as infidelity to a jealous God, who then punishes by foreign oppression or poverty. Underneath these images, however, lies a developing theology that idolatry is turning toward the prosperity of fertility gods and away from that authentic Hebrew religion that demands the interhuman justice from which true human prosperity issues: Topel, *The Way* 59–61.

Psalms, and in Zeph 2:3; 3:12, terms for the poor (especially *ʿanāwîm*) take on a spiritual meaning, so that "poor" means "humble, piously locating one's hopes in God."[56] Pleins rejects this view, but there are still some sensitive points in the argument: (1) In the more than forty of the 150 psalms in which the psalmist calls himself poor or praises YHWH as the deliverer of the poor, he usually gives no concrete details of his affliction and so evokes the suspicion that "poor" is a metaphor for any hard-pressed Jew, even the rich, who humbly calls out for deliverance by Israel's God. (2) Often the psalmist gives his poverty and affliction as a reason for YHWH's coming to his aid, and from this some have inferred that the psalmist equates poverty with piety. Some examples adduced, however, are a mixed bag (Pss 25:16, 18; 109:22).[57] In other psalms an equation of piety with poverty is more explicit: for example Psalm 69:

רָאוּ עֲנָוִים יִשְׂמֶחוּ דֹּרְשֵׁי אֱלֹהִים וִיחִי לְבַבְכֶם :33

כִּי־שֹׁמֵעַ אֶל־אֶבְיוֹנִים יְהוָה וְאֶת־אֲסִירָיו לֹא בָזֶה :34

"Let the oppressed see it and be glad; you who seek God, let your hearts revive. For the Lord hears the needy, and does not despise his own that are in bonds" (RSV).

Note that in the synonymous parallelism of the two cola of v. 33 the *ʿanāwîm* (πτωχοί) in 33a are those who seek God in 33b; in the two cola of v. 34 the *ʾebyônîm* of 33a are "his own" in 34b. Further, the piety of the psalmist is revealed in the next verse where he praises YHWH as his deliverer (69:35). Yet even here the concrete affliction of the psalmist reveals real poverty: he is falsely accused of stealing, and the punishment will be to give up his possessions (69:4). This psalm was well known to those who wrote the New Testament,[58] including Luke (Ps 69:21 is cited in Luke 23:36), and so his use of πτωχοί for the pious *ʿanāwîm* is certainly possible.

The parade example of the equation of the poor with the pious is

וְהִשְׁאַרְתִּי בְקִרְבֵּךְ עַם עָנִי וָדָל :Zeph 3:12

LXX: καὶ ὑπολείψομαι ἐν σοὶ λαὸν πραῢν καὶ ταπεινόν,

"For I will leave in the midst of you a people humble and lowly" (RSV).

---

[56] For a thorough review of the course of the discussion see Norbert Lohfink, "Von der 'Anawim-partei' zur 'Kirche der Armen,'" *Bib* 67 (1986) 153–76 and the various *Forschungsberichte* given in his bibliography. Appendix A (p. 266) gives a shorter summary of that scholarly debate.

[57] In both cases one can discover in the argument of the psalmist an underlying situation of poverty, such as seizure of his goods so that his children must beg after he has been killed (Ps 109:8-11).

[58] Various verses of the psalm are explicitly quoted in John 2:17; 15:25; Acts 1:20; Rom 11:9-10; all four evangelists refer to 69:21 in their Passion accounts.

Here Zephaniah prophesies that the remnant will be oppressed and poor (*'ānî wādāl*). Probably because of the contrast with the proud to be removed in v. 11, the LXX translates *'ānî wādāl* by πραῢν καὶ ταπεινόν. The LXX use of πραῢν rather than πτωχόν seems to indicate that the internal attitude of dependence on God characterizes those who will be delivered.[59]

What conclusions can we draw from this debate over the notions of poverty in the Hebrew Bible and its Greek translation? I note five:

(1) The investigations of Jan van der Ploeg and J. David Pleins demonstrate that Hebrew words for poverty (even *'anāwîm*) connote socioeconomic poverty, referring to those who are unjustly oppressed, and so are hungry, naked, and in danger of death. *'Ānî* especially contains the notion of being *economically* exploited and destitute. Both *'ānî* and πτωχός regularly refer to those at the bottom of society's socioeconomic scale, which constitutes the state of the "oppressed poor."[60]

(2) Even where the psalmist's lament is not concretely described, the text often gives clues that his oppression has social and economic causes. Even in psalms where the psalmist gives poverty as a reason for YHWH's intervention, he is in a state of real poverty or oppression, so one cannot simply conclude to "piety" as principal grounds for YHWH's response.

(3) Jacques Dupont, investigating the kinds of people called blessed in the first three beatitudes, has discovered the same triads (the poor, the afflicted, and the hungry) being promised salvation in the OT.[61] He concludes that the poor, afflicted, and hungry form such a unity that to speak of one is to evoke the other two, that not only does the OT mean these terms in their socioeconomic realism, but so do the Gospels, and that to speak of the poor in strongly spiritual terms is not to do justice to the promises of God as they are expressed in the OT and NT.[62]

(4) Zephaniah 3:12 does identify humility with *'ānî*. I explain this exception as I do the attitude to the poor in Proverbs 10–29. Zephaniah's

---

[59] Note a comparable attitude in Psalm 37 (especially vv. 14-17): the Lord takes care of those who trust in him. Psalm 49:13 points out the obverse: those who foolishly trust in their own powers die. This virtue of humble trust in the Lord occurs in Judaism's apocalyptic literature (1 Enoch 94–96; Ps Sol 1:4-8; 5:2-6; 10:6-8) and in Qumran (4QPs 37; 1 QM 11:9-14; 1QH 5:13), although each of these texts bears its own ambiguities.

[60] Dupont, *Béatitudes* 2:29.

[61] Isaiah 61:1, οἱ πτωχοί, συντετριμμένοι τῇ καρδίᾳ, αἰχμαλώτοι/τυφλοί; other texts grouping those to be saved are Isa 29:18-19; 35:3-6; 49:9-10, 13; Jer 31:8-9; Ezek 34:11-29. Those whom the Jews themselves are to succor fall into the same classes of the afflicted; see Isa 58:6-7, 9-10; Job 22:6-9; 24:2-11; 29:15-17; Sir 1–4, 8–10; Dupont, *Béatitudes* 2:39–48.

[62] Dupont, *Béatitudes* 2:40–52.

identification with the royal family (1:1) effects that lack of concern for the poor that characterizes those royal circles that hardly mentioned the poor in the historical books. One ought not to conclude to too much from this isolated text.

(5) Still, one cannot ignore the fact that by the third century B.C.E. the LXX translators were distinguishing between ʿānî (normally translated by πτωχός) and ʿanāwîm (rarely πτωχός).[63] Further, this distinction becomes firmer in post-biblical Hebrew, where ʿanāwîm often emphasizes the interiority of the poor crying out to God.[64] But there is no indication that these poor were not economically poor and oppressed, and there is no indication that their poverty was a virtue that claimed a response from God. In any case, the LXX translators have chosen not to express this nuance by πτωχός, and this determines NT use.

4. *The Protector of the Poor:* Why, then, did the poor cry out to the Lord? Because YHWH had designated himself as their protector.[65] The Ancient Near Eastern god himself is the shepherd of the people and the protector of the oppressed and poor.[66] The king, as the god's son or vicegerent, fills this function, and so as shepherd of the people has the obligation to care for the vulnerable and the poor.[67] Close to Lukan concerns is Assurbanipal's being called the liberator of prisoners, healer of the sick, feeder of the hungry, clother of the naked.[68] In short, the gods in religious texts and the kings and government in secular ones have an essential duty to protect the poor and rectify their oppressed condition in this life.

This commonplace is intensified in Israel, where YHWH's very nature is to do justice to the poor. Since YHWH is king of Israel,[69] his actions are those of the protector of the oppressed. In Deut 10:17-19 he is described

---

[63] J. P. M. van der Ploeg's attempt to divorce ʿanāwîm as the religiously humble so radically from ʿānîyyîm as the oppressed poor does not seem to attend adequately enough to the fact that the two words derive from the same root and share the notion of poverty.

[64] Ragnar Leivestad, "*tapeinos-tapeinophron,*" *NovT* 8 (1966) 36–47.

[65] A thorough but succinct exposition of this material is in Dupont, *Béatitudes* 2, ch. II, "Les Protégès du Roi," 54–90; further study can be done in the secondary literature he cites.

[66] See "The Hymn to Shamash," iii, 20-30, in *ANET* 389.

[67] In Mesopotamia, Hammurabi is anointed by Enlil precisely to protect the weak (the prologue and epilogue to the Code; *ANET* 164, 178). In Ugarit, Yassib accuses his father Keret of being unworthy of kingship because he does not protect the widow and the poor (Keret C, *ANET* 149). In Egypt the εὐαγγέλλιον at the accession of Ramses IV dwells on the joy of the hungry, the naked, widows, prisoners (*ANET* 378–79); a fellah calls a royal official "father of the orphan, husband of the widow" ("The Protests of the Eloquent Peasant," *ANET* 408).

[68] "A Happy Reign," *ANET* 626–27.

[69] Judges 8:23; 1 Sam 8:6-9; 10:17-19, and in the royal psalms. Unlike the practice of the Ancient Near East, in Israel the king is not called the shepherd of the people (though

as a judge passing sentence favorable to the orphan, the widow, and the alien (all without legal protectors). Psalm 68:5-6 describes him as "Father of the fatherless, protector of widows" who "leads out the prisoners to prosperity." Psalm 146:7-8 describes his actions in terms familiar to Luke:

> who executes justice for the oppressed (ἀδικουμένοις);
>
> who gives food to the hungry (πεινῶσιν);
>
> The Lord sets the prisoners (πεπεδημένους) free;
>
> The Lord opens the eyes of the blind (τυφλοὺς);
>
> The Lord lifts up those who are bowed down (κατερραγμένους).

YHWH's response is concrete liberation, feeding the poor, freeing prisoners, executing justice on this earth. This view of YHWH persists into Jewish apocalyptic literature (Ps Sol 5:2, 13) and at Qumran (1 QH 5:16-22).

Further, YHWH sees to it that others do justice to the poor.[70] The Law itself gave all the people directions for doing YHWH's justice, including special care for the vulnerable (Exod 22:21-27).[71] All who have power are to exercise it in favor of the weak (Ps 72:1-2; Jer 22:3-22, especially vv. 3, 15-16; Amos 2:6-7; 8:4; Isa 10:1-2). Again, the most transcendent king, the Messiah, has the task of administering concrete justice to the oppressed (Isa 9:6-7; 11:3-5; Ps Sol 17:23-38).

In all of these texts there is no sense that it is because of some special virtue of the poor that they are to be protected. Rather kings were expected to defend the poor simply because it was one of their essential functions as the god's vicegerent. This notion is intensified in Israel because YHWH's nature is to provide abundance and respond to the outcry of the oppressed (Ps 103:6), as he had shown himself in his first revelation to Israel (Exod 2:23).[72] His people are to be like Him,[73] and if they are, there will be no poor in the land (Deut 15:4).[74]

YHWH refers to them as his sheep in Ezekiel 36); only YHWH is Israel's shepherd. (The single exception is David, who was literally a shepherd before he was a king.)

[70] The Ancient Near Eastern texts do not contain laws on caring for the poor, but Israel's law codes do; Norbert Lohfink, "Poverty in the Laws of the Ancient Near East and of the Bible," *TS* 52 (1991) 34–50.

[71] Aliens, widows, orphans, and especially the poor. The Sabbath legislation (Deut 15:1-11) and the Jubilee year (Leviticus 25) have the same object of release for the oppressed.

[72] YHWH's response to the outcry (ṣā'āq/zā'āq) of the oppressed occurs in all strata of the OT tradition: the mythic (Gen 4:10), the narrative (Exod 3:7; 1 Sam 9:16; 2 Chr 20:9), the legal (Exod 22:23), the prophetic (Hos 8:2; Isa 5:7), the Psalms (9:13; 107:6, 28), the Wisdom literature (Job 34:28; 35:9)

[73] The refrain in the Holiness Code "I am the Lord" (Lev 18:5, and *passim*) together with "You shall be holy for I the Lord your God am holy" (19:2) shows the law commanding YHWH's own liberating action for his people.

[74] Norbert Lohfink, "The Laws of Deuteronomy: A Utopian Project for a World Without Any Poor," *ScrBull* 26 (1996) 2–19.

Finally, YHWH's eschatological deliverance was expected to be just as concrete as was his protection in Israel's history. The obverse of the day of the Lord's vengeance on the nations will be the return of the exiles to a land of abundance (Isa 35:4-6). Eschatological exuberance still expresses itself in terms of concrete human benefits in Isa 61:1-7, where the reason for concrete reversal of fortunes is that the Lord loves justice, and hates robbery and wrong (61:8; cf. Ps 132:14-18; Ezek 4:15-29).

Therefore Jesus' eschatological message of the Reign of God cannot speak of a promise of happiness to be achieved only in the world to come, while the unjust conditions of this world remain unchanged. Rather, in line with his tradition, Jesus speaks of real liberation here and now, the cause of the rejoicing that permeates Luke-Acts. The Isaiah texts on πτωχός, which form the background of Jesus' teaching in Luke 4:18 and 7:22,[75] confirm this emphasis.

5. *Isaiah's Use of* πτωχός: Isaiah uses πτωχός eight times.[76] The texts seem to fall into two kinds of usage: (1) YHWH will judge those who oppress the socioeconomically poor (no trace of piety here);[77] the texts imply that the oppressors will be removed so that the poor will no longer be oppressed. (2) In an oracle of eschatological deliverance (29:17-24) those delivered are similar to those of Deutero-Isaiah: the deaf, the blind, the poor. In 29:19 πτωχοί translates *'anāwîm*, paralleled by *'ebyônîm*—the socioeconomically poor, victims of the ruthless evildoers to be removed in v. 20. Thus First Isaiah uses πτωχός only to express real economic poverty.

Exegetes often find in Deutero- and Trito-Isaiah a spiritual sense of poverty translated as "the people as a whole in need of salvation" or as

---

[75] We saw (p. 73) that Dupont had already found the background for Jesus' beatitudes for the poor, the hungry, and those lamenting in similar Isaian triads. This Isaian background for Luke is made explicit in Jesus' identifying himself with the prophet of Isa 61:1-2 and the eschatological works of Isa 29:18-19; 35:5-6; 42:6-7; 49:9-10. Dennis Hamm (*Beatitudes* 45) notes that 6:20 stands halfway between the two citations of Isaiah in 4:18 and 7:22 .

[76] Πτωχός in Isa 24:6 (without a correlative in the MT) and 25:3 (translating *'ām-'āz*) are translations of corrupt texts; it is difficult to assign any specific meaning to the kind of poverty specified in these passages of the Isaian apocalypse.

[77] Not surprising in the prophet who, with Amos, most condemns socioeconomic injustice in Israel, and so understands poverty as a man-made evil to be overcome (1:15-26; 3:12-24; 5:8-23; 10:1-4; 32:1-20; 35:5-10. In 3:14, 15 πτωχός translates *'ānî* in a situation where social anarchy promotes economic exploitation of the poor robbed of their possessions; in 10:2 it translates *dāllîm,* where judges are castigated for defrauding the needy in legal decisions; in 14:30 the concrete situation is not so clear, but the parallel of *dāllîm* and *'ebyônîm* (both translated by πτωχοί) and the evocation of YHWH as the King protector of the poor point strongly to concrete economic poverty.

"those knowing their need for God."[78] But the evidence is against such interpretations. The authors of Isaiah 40–66 do expand their favorite term for poverty (*ʿānî*)[79] to refer to the entire nation of Israel, politically oppressed by Babylon and economically floundering after the return. But their "notion of *ʿānî*, while somewhat more general than previous prophetic usage, continues to refer to socioeconomic poverty. This is not a theology of humility in the more detached or spiritualized sense."[80]

The use of πτωχός in Isaiah 40–66 is, in fact, quite clear. Deutero-Isaiah uses it only once (41:17), and, although the giving of water is an idealization of the Exodus events, the poor and needy are the politically oppressed in need of historical deliverance. Trito-Isaiah uses it only twice. In 58:7 the fast that YHWH wants from his people is "to share your bread with the hungry and bring the homeless poor into your house." The hungry and the homeless poor are the desperately poor returnees from exile at the end of the sixth century B.C.E., and the passage has a moral meaning rather than an eschatological one:[81] The other use of πτωχός is in the oracle of Isa 61:1-3,[82] which Jesus proclaimed as fulfilled in himself (Luke 4:18). The terms of its liberation are good news for the poor, healing for the wounded, release for prisoners—in short, the Jubilee year. As Jubilees were intended for the socioeconomically bound, so this one is addressed to the concrete social and economic oppressions of the returnees. The text goes on past the end of the citation in Luke 4:18 to speak of concrete liberation for precisely the other people mentioned in the first three beatitudes: the mourners (61:2b-3) and the hungry (61:6b).

[78] David P. Seccombe, *Possessions and the Poor in Luke-Acts.* SNTU, ser. B, 6 (Linz: A. Fuchs, 1982) 24–69; Hamm, *Beatitudes* 47.

[79] This term for concrete socioeconomic oppression is used in all but two of their references to the poor: in 41:17 it is combined with *ʿebyôn*; in 61:1 the word is the cognate *ʿanāwîm*.

[80] J. David Pleins, "Poor," 408–409. It is true, however, that the LXX frequently translates such uses of *ʿānî* by ταπεινός (49:13; 54:11; 66:2). However, ταπεινός also has the meaning of being concretely "laid low, oppressed, afflicted" (Walter Grundmann, "ταπεινός," *TDNT* 8:6–12), and such may be the meaning here. We must be careful of the preconceptions that cause us automatically to translate it as "humble." Even 66:2, the place where ταπεινός most likely means "humble, obedient," could, Pleins asserts, profitably retain its meaning of "politically oppressed."

[81] Responding to the poor people's laments, the oracle charges that it is their own concrete injustice that impedes YHWH's deliverance. Before that deliverance they must do justice to the poor, and *then* (note the sequence of "if . . . if . . . then" in 58:5-10, 13-14) YHWH can bring justice to perfection. Cf. the same theology of impedance and reform preceding divine deliverance in Mal 2:17–3:2.

[82] The oracles of salvation of Isaiah 60–62 are written in the style of the Book of Consolation (chs. 40–55). The exultant poetry may have been composed at the beginning of the exile, before the concrete problems of the return emerged. In any case they are now placed

Thus in all of Isaiah, when the text speaks of Israel's own moral obligations or of Yhwh's delivering the poor from oppression, those liberated are the concrete poor in a historical deliverance.

6. *Socioeconomic Analysis of* οἱ πτωχοί: For thirty years exegetes have been turning to social-science models of pre-industrial Mediterranean societies to gain insight into the concrete meanings of socioeconomic terms in the NT.[83] Gerhard Lenski has provided a particularly useful model of the distribution of wealth in pre-industrial agrarian societies.[84] As best I can extrapolate his model for the agrarian society that was the first-century Roman empire, the top five classes would have constituted twelve per cent of the population, but would have controlled eighty-five per cent of the wealth, an inequitable distribution far surpassing that of preceding horticultural or hunting/gathering societies.[85] The peasant, artisan, unclean/degraded, and expendable classes would have accounted for about eighty-eight per cent of the population with about fifteen per cent of the wealth. My rough reckoning for the πτωχοί, then, would include all of the expendable and degraded classes (about thirteen per cent of the population, with no share in the wealth), the lowest segment of the artisan class, and the section of the peasant class teetering on the brink of foreclosure for debt (about another twelve

---

after Isaiah 58–59, for a people supposed to have initiated the reforms mandated in 58–59. If that is so, then 61:1-3 announces the concrete measures by which the age of ecstatic joy is introduced. (Note how the Spirit of 61:1 resumes the themes of the Spirit in 59:20-21.)

[83] Exegetes have used models taken from the cultural anthropology of Clifford Geertz and Mary Douglas, the sociology of Max Weber and Talcott Parsons, the political science of S. N. Eisenstadt, the economics of Karl Polanyi. Early pioneers were John Gager, *Kingdom and Community* (Englewood Cliffs, N.J.: Prentice-Hall, 1975); Gerd Theissen, *Sociology of Early Palestinian Christianity* (Philadelphia: Fortress, 1978); one of the clearest expositions of these methods can be found in Bruce J. Malina, *The New Testament World: Insights from Cultural Anthropology* (Atlanta: John Knox, 1981 [rev. ed., 1993]), with summaries and bibliographies. Popularizations of an enormous body of work, some reaching back into the nineteenth century, can be found in Carolyn Osiek, *What are They Saying about the Social Setting of the New Testament?* (New York: Paulist, 1992); in John H. Elliott, *What is Social Scientific Criticism?* (Minneapolis: Fortress, 1993); and in K. C. Hanson and Douglas E. Oakman, *Palestine in the Time of Jesus* (Minneapolis: Fortress, 1998).

[84] Gerhard E. Lenski, *Power and Privilege: A Theory of Social Stratification* (Chapel Hill: University of North Carolina Press, 1984) 189–290; his graphic diagram on p. 284 is reproduced in Appendix B (p. 270).

[85] This maldistribution is not nearly so acute as that of a contemporary industrial society, such as the United States, in which the top one per cent of the population controls almost half (forty-six per cent) of the country's financial assets and the top ten per cent controls eighty-two per cent. These calculations are based on 1992 statistics of the Federal Reserve Board by Steve Brouwer, *Sharing the Pie* (New York: Henry Holt, 1998) 11–15; the disparity can only have been increased sharply by the market boom of the 1990s.

per cent of the population, with perhaps two to three per cent of the wealth). Thus I would designate roughly the bottom twenty-five per cent of Palestinian society as the πτωχοί, unable to provide the necessities of life. The next thirty per cent of the population (encompassing the rest of the artisan class, the poorest third of the merchant class, and half of the remaining peasant class) would be the πένεις, scraping by with the bare necessities. In my extrapolation of Lenski's model, Luke's Jesus would be referring to the bottom twenty-five per cent of Palestinian society as the πτωχοί.

7. *Lukan Usage of* πτωχός: The evangelist who uses Isaiah to describe the meaning of the ministries of John and of Jesus also adopts the Isaian meaning for πτωχός. A count of the Lukan uses of the word suggests that it is a Lukan theme. Luke describes only two concrete persons as poor. Lazarus is the classic picture of the πτωχός : a beggar at the gates of a rich man's residence, starving and covered with sores, totally without resources (16:21). The poor widow of 21:2-3 is the classic picture of the *ʿānāw:* her total possessions are a meager two lepta[86] and yet, full of trust in her God, she throws it all into the Temple treasury. These two images of stark poverty must guide our understanding of Luke's other uses of πτωχοί as a literary type,[87] where we construe his meaning from association and context. Apart from 6:20, how does Luke describe the πτωχοί?

4:18: Isaiah 61:1-3 consoles the wretched postexilic community of Trito-Isaiah: the Jubilee year of deliverance is at hand. Jesus avers in 4:22 that this redemption is now fulfilled in his presence and work. The πτωχοί here are not described as humble or spiritual; they are the economically poor whom the eschatological prophet associates with

(1) αἰχμαλώτοι, in Isaiah 61 those in prison for debt, to be forgiven in the Jubilee year. This was probably the original meaning for Jesus at Nazareth, but we have seen from 4:31-41 that Luke may have understood it in a transferred sense of those bound by Satan. In either case, their concrete captivity is described;

---

[86] Experts do not hazard a guess about the value of Greco-Roman coinage in today's currency. The lepton was the smallest unit of currency in use. Reckoned by the depressed agricultural economy of Palestine, the widow's whole fortune would amount to less than a dollar in a Third-World economy.

[87] More recent literary critics of Luke-Acts, such as Luke T. Johnson, *The Literary Function of Possessions in Luke-Acts.* SBLDS 39 (Missoula: Scholars, 1977); David P. Seccombe, *Possessions and the Poor;* S. John Roth, *The Blind,* have taken the poor, etc. as literary types. Although they usually insist that the socioeconomically poor are meant, they are more interested in the symbolic meanings of the type. Roth, *The Blind* 73–79 persuasively shows that in Luke oi πτωχοί are types, without any distinguishing personal characteristics, and without the resources to be responsible actors in their own lives (which constitutes character in ancient literature).

(2) τυφλοί, totally dependent on family or on a beggar's alms;[88]

(3) τεθραυσμένοι, those shattered by oppression.[89]

It is clear by association that πτωχοί here means the destitute poor who are to be liberated by Jesus' Jubilee proclamation *now,* σήμερον (4:22).

7:22: John performs his last Elijah function of preparing for the Lord by asking Jesus if he is ὁ ἐρχόμενος.[90] Luke hastens to show Jesus now raising people from the dead (7:11-17), healing and exorcising (7:21a), and, just now, healing the blind (7:21b), so that Jesus' historical career might vindicate the role of the one coming to introduce the eschatological age: the blind see (7:21), the lame walk (5:25), lepers are purified (5:13), the deaf hear (not to be accomplished until 11:14), the dead are raised (7:14-15), and the poor have the good news proclaimed to them (6:20!). Again, the poor are by association the economically poor, lumped in with those who cannot work (the blind, lepers), those with impoverishing disabilities (the lame, deaf), and those without life itself. None of these is described as pious or welcoming of Jesus. Jesus reverses these unfortunates' fortunes right now, in his eschatological time of messianic healing.[91]

While Jesus has reversed the physical malady of all these afflicted, he has not made the poor rich, but rather has preached the good news to them. Why? Jesus cannot say that the poor have become rich here, or anywhere else in Luke, because for Luke πλούσιος is a bad category, the subject not of beatitude but of woe (6:24). The consolation of the poor is, however, not

---

[88] In the ancient world, without Braille, seeing-eye dogs, or sidewalks and curbs that guide a cane, the blind are doomed to dependency. If they are not among the few who have adequate means or special talents to become musicians, seers, or philosophers, they become beggars. Although both the OT and NT use τυφλός in a transferred sense, when they are lumped together with other physically disabled the meaning of dependent poor is stressed; Wolfgang Schrage, "τυφλός," *TDNT* 8:270–94.

[89] Not only are they lumped together with other unfortunates in 4:18, they were also so categorized in the original Isa 58:6 (with the hungry, homeless, and naked). Indeed, it is probably because they need liberation (ἄφεσις) that Luke has introduced them into his oracle in 4:18.

[90] Along with most commentators I take the title to refer to the Messiah. Fitzmyer's identification of it with *Elijah redivivus* is attractive but seems unlikely when Jesus refers to John as Elijah in the same pericope (7:27). Further, John the Baptist, unlike the implied author, has restricted vision: his sense of ἐρχόμενος corresponds to his pointing to Jesus as the stronger one who is coming (ἔρχεται) in 3:17. That usage was in direct response to messianic expectation (3:15), and so John here, as there, must be thinking of the Messiah as ὁ ἐρχόμενος.

[91] Note that the misfortunes listed here correlate with the list of those to be delivered in the time of eschatological visitation in Isa 29:18-19 (the deaf, blind, poor); 35:5-7 (the blind, deaf, lame, the mute), Isa 42:7 (the blind and prisoners), Isa 61:1 (the poor).

simply hope of eschatological reward. Luke has shown, however subtly, the poor being fed (5:6-7; 6:1-5). This theme will be made explicit throughout the rest of Luke (cf. 9:12-17) and in Acts, where the good news to the poor is that there are no needy in Luke's community (Acts 2:44-45; 4:32-35). Luke makes this concrete in the next passage in which he uses πτωχός.

14:13: In the middle of the so-called "Lukan symposium" Jesus advises the wealthy to invite not those who can repay them with an invitation to their own banquet, but rather the πτωχούς, ἀναπείρους, χωλούς, τυφλούς.[92] The poor are described by their company, and also as those who, by the rule of Greco-Roman reciprocity, will never partake of a banquet. They are not described as pious. Jesus' reversal of the Greco-Roman reciprocity rules expects its reward not on this earth but in the eschatological resurrection of the just (14:14), and this provides the ultimate ground for calling such a bizarre host μακάριος (14:14).[93] Note, however, that the remedy for the poor is not postponed to the resurrection; they attend the banquet now. This, then is an essential object of preaching of the good news to the poor: they are to be fed *now*.

14:21 balances that immediately: the same tetrad will also eat the eschatological banquet promised by Jesus' good news. And so Jesus' good news for the poor is not an either/or: they will, in the fulfillment of Jesus' designs, be the recipients not only of adequate food in this historical age (14:13), but also of the eschatological banquet of perfect and permanent reward described in the parable (14:16-24).

16:20, 22: In this parable (16:19-30) Lazarus is called πτωχός, graphically described as so poor that he is starving, so malnourished that his sores will not heal, so weak that he cannot ward off the dogs that lick them. Nowhere does the parable mention his pious dependence on God or speak of the pride or godlessness of the rich man. This poor man, however, will be rewarded eschatologically in the bosom of Abraham,[94] while the rich man will be forever in torment. The reason is given starkly: the rich

---

[92] The lame and the blind among the sons of Aaron were excluded from the altar (Lev 21:17-23) and among the Qumran sectaries they were excluded from the community (1 QSa 2:5-6), perhaps as unfit for the eschatological war (1 QM 7:4). Since ἀναπείροι is a synonym for χωλοί, we have three of the six categories mentioned in Luke 7:22, and previously designated by Isaiah for eschatological deliverance—the blind (Isa 29:18; 35:5; 42:7; 62:1), the lame (35:6), and the poor (29:19; 61:1).

[93] Note that the host *will be* blessed (μακάριος ἔσῃ), indicating that Luke does use the future when he means that the beatitude will be in the future. The rules for reciprocity will be taken up in exegesis of 6:32-34.

[94] This, together with 12:20 and 23:42-43, are the principal texts witnessing to an eschatological reward upon an individual's death in Luke; see Jacques Dupont, "L'Après-mort dans l'oeuvre de Luc," *RTL* 3 (1972) 3–21.

have had their "reward" on this earth; those who are poor now will be rich later (16:25). There could be no more exact illustration of the bald beatitude and woe of 6:20, 24.[95] The good news to the poor is that they will ultimately share an eternal reward. But Luke implies the other face of the good news for the poor: if the rich listened to Moses and the prophets (16:29), or to John the Baptist (3:10-11), or to Jesus (6:20; 14:13), they would share their riches with the poor, thus alleviating their poverty already, in this life.[96]

18:22 verifies this thesis. Against the background of an eschatological discourse (17:20-37) in which the reign of God is proclaimed as already present in Jesus' person and work (17:21), and yet the days of the Son of Man are proclaimed as part of an indefinite future (17:22-37), salvation comes to the marginalized (a widow in 18:1-8, a tax collector in 18:9-14, infants in 18:15-17). But it does not come to the ordinary model of Jewish piety, the rich ruler who has observed all the commandments from his youth (18:18, 21). The reason is that he cannot distribute what he has to the poor (18:22-23). That he is in the same situation as the rich man of the Lazarus story is indicated by the starkness of the figure of the camel and the needle's eye by which Jesus proclaims that it is impossible for a rich man to enter the reign of God (18:24-25).[97] The poor to whom the rich ruler is to distribute his goods are not described as pious; they are not described at all, except as recipients of alms (the root meaning of πτωχός). The correlative of the rich inheriting eternal life is that the poor will, here and now, receive of their riches. In this passage there is no intimation of eschatological reward for the poor. Correlatively, those who leave all to follow Jesus (18:28-29) will not be poor, but will receive a manifold return already in this life (18:30), the sharing intimated in Acts 2:44-45; 4:32-35. The present rectification of the plight of the poor *now* could not be more clearly articulated.

19:8 answers the question implied in 18:25-27: how can the rich be saved? Zacchaeus is a chief tax collector, rich (19:2). But the Lord who has come to call sinners to repentance (5:32, in the context of association with tax collectors) comes to his house. Thereupon Zacchaeus undergoes the

---

[95] No reason is given for this baldness. One can only guess that in a limited-goods economy in an intimate village society being rich is not having shared with the poor, perhaps because of the hidden greed in Luke 12:15. Perhaps this will be clarified when we come to the woe to the rich.

[96] That the majority of the commentators miss or reject this point shows how much the exegete's hermeneutical stance colors his or her vision. The whole chapter speaks of the proper use of money. Walter E. Pilgrim, *Good News* 116–19 lays out the meaning of "Moses and the prophets."

[97] The camel is one of the largest objects in the Jew's ken, and the needle's eye one of the smallest.

μετάνοια to which Jesus calls sinners, and announces he is giving half of his possessions to the poor and making quadruple restitution to any he has defrauded.[98] Again Jesus gives the present distribution of riches to the poor as the means by which the rich enter God's Reign. The poor again are not described as deserving poor—they are simply those who need alms, and the presence of God's Reign means that they receive alms *now* in this life.

21:3: Luke places the story of the widow's mite immediately after Jesus condemns the scribes for their external show and for devouring the houses of widows (20:45-47). The widow is described as utterly poor (see n. 86) and commended for her generosity. But the one pious πτωχός in Luke-Acts is not shown as receiving salvation or a reward on account of her piety. She gives rather than receives. Even the πτωχοί give, in implied contrast with the scribes (20:45-47) and in explicit contrast with the rich in 21:3.

8. *Other Lukan References to Poverty:* Luke can speak of poverty other than by explicit use of πτωχός. Jesus' parents are implicitly described as poor when they offer "a pair of turtledoves, or two young pigeons" (2:24; Lev 12:8). Jesus himself is portrayed as one of the homeless poor when he is laid in a manger (2:7). Others described as poor in Dennis Hamm's summary of Lukan usage are:[99]

- the needy to whom John the Baptist exhorts the crowds to give their extra tunic or their surplus food (3:10);
- those reduced to borrowing or stealing (6:29-30);
- the sick, maimed, blind, lame who, if they were not supported by family, were reduced to begging (e.g., 18:35-43; Acts 3:1-10);
- widows without that culture's necessary male support (7:11-12; 18:1-8; Acts 6:1-6);
- those among the Jerusalem community whose needs were met through benefactions distributed by the apostles (Acts 4:34-35).

Although not designated as πτωχοί, these belong to the category that poverty describes—the *protegés du roi*—widows, beggars, the oppressed, the starving.[100]

---

[98] That Zacchaeus is not stating past or present practice, but rather how he intends to respond to Jesus' summons has been decisively demonstrated by Dennis Hamm in two articles: "Luke 19:8 Once Again: Does Zacchaeus Defend or Resolve?" *JBL* 107 (1988) 431–37; "Zacchaeus Revisited Once More: a Story of Vindication or of Conversion?" *Bib* 72 (1991) 249–52.

[99] Hamm, *Beatitudes* 46.

[100] Unfortunately Hamm, *Beatitudes* 46–47 describes "social outcasts" as the Lukan poor. This is a serious confusion of terminology. Some of these so described were poor (prostitutes, the lame, the blind). But to call a wealthy woman who is infertile "poor" is to

Jesus himself is described as poor from the time of his embarking upon his proclamation of the Reign of God.[101] When he takes up the wandering life of the prophet he is without family for support (8:19-21; 15:25-26), homeless (9:58), dependent on others for food, clothing, shelter (8:1-3), often not shown hospitality (8:37; 9:53). Since the life of master and disciple were shared (6:40), we can see his own life in that of his apostles (9:1-5) and disciples (10:1-12) who followed him to preach in poverty—without staff, sandals, bag, bread, money, or change of clothes. It was a life totally dependent on others for food, clothing, shelter—that of the πτωχός.[102] It is striking that when the disciples leave all to follow him (5:11, 28), or when discipleship means selling all that one has to distribute to the poor (14:33; 18:22), those who follow him do not bring the proceeds from their sale into the group. They remain dependent on the hospitality of those whom they evangelize.[103]

Summary: Luke's explicit use of πτωχός shows these features:

a. The πτωχοί are always desperately poor. The two characters called poor are a beggar who is starving and ulcerated (16:20-22) and a widow without a dollar to her name (21:2-4). The collective noun οἱ πτωχοί is associated with those who receive alms (18:22; 19:8) or cannot provide for themselves (4:18; 7:22; 14:13, 21).[104]

b. There is no indication that the poor's piety or reception of Jesus is a factor in their receiving God's favor or a reason for their receiving alms.

---

subvert Luke's usage. The same is true of his subsequent category of "poor in the Isaian sense"; there is no indication that Luke would call Zacchaeus, or any who know their need for God, poor. Our study of πτωχός argues decisively the opposite. In Luke Jesus saves these people, but not because they are poor.

[101] From Luke we know nothing of Joseph's or Jesus' occupation as a craftsman. This undermines the argument that as a craftsman Jesus would not have been πτωχός.

[102] This would be true, except that the missionaries *are* cared for. Hamm, *Beatitudes* 48, calls this "not poverty, but prophetic strategy." But it is clearly poverty: the poverty is what signalizes the prophetic strategy!

[103] Some who support him seem to be wealthy (8:3, and this will be taken up in our exegesis of 6:24), but they also share the dependence of the wandering preachers. Hamm, *Beatitudes* 48–49 points out that the introduction in 10:7 of the rationale for their traveling light, "the laborer is worth his wages," creates "a new set of reciprocal relationships based on the Kingdom of God" that is not really indigence. This will lead to Acts' settled communities, which support the wandering charismatics. The indigence of Jesus and the apostles is what evokes the alms which they receive as "wages."

[104] No Lukan πτωχός has possessions tempered by spiritual freedom from them (i.e., "poor in spirit"). The woe to the rich (6:24) in Luke's contrasting rhetoric will confirm this description of the poor.

The reason for this unmerited care seems to be YHWH's concern for the poor as his protegés, but that needs to be confirmed in Luke itself.

c. Jesus' summons to discipleship in Luke means taking on some form of poverty, either because of commitment to God's work in the Kingdom or because of the need to share with the poor. Thus Jesus' summons expresses what is possible to humans (18:27) in the eschatological in-breaking of Jesus' Spirit in God's Reign.

d. The poor will, as a last resort, receive their reward in the age to come (14:21; 16:22, 25), but the emphasis in most of Luke's nine uses of the word is on the alleviation of their plight in the present historical dispensation of the Reign of God. That there are no πτωχοί in Acts may indicate that the good news of the Reign of God abolishes poverty through the sharing of this world's goods. If that is the case, the good news to the poor demands an ethic of sharing greater than that of the OT and of John the Baptist (Luke 3:10-14). In that sense, too, the first beatitude is an exordium to the whole of the Sermon that follows.

9. *Who are the* πτωχοί? We have specified *what* the πτωχοί are, but *who* are the poor Jesus addresses? Some exegetes, arguing from ἐπάρας τοὺς ὀφθαλμοὺς αὐτοῦ εἰς τοὺς μαθητὰς, think that all of Jesus' disciples were poor, others that Jesus addresses the poor among the disciples.[105] In Luke the disciples addressed are his community, for whom Luke-Acts was written. These include the Twelve, poor because they have left all to follow Jesus on the road (5:11, 28), and other disciples who do the same (8:1-2; 9:57-62; 10:1-12). The frequency of πτωχός in Luke witnesses to the presence and interests of the poor in his community.[106] At the same time there are wealthy in the community (1:3; 8:3; 19:2; Acts 1:1; 8:9-24, 26-39; 10:1-48; 13:7-12), which accounts for the frequency of the exhortations to the rich to get unattached from their wealth (Luke 12:13-21,

---

[105] A direct second-person address, μακάριοι ὑμεῖς πτωχοί, would address all the disciples as poor, or the poor among the disciples. The ostensible third-person form with the article (probably nominative instead of vocative) opens up more ambiguity in the addressees. We cannot know the number of poor among the historical Jesus' disciples, but a preacher of general reciprocity always attracts a number of poor. The poor figure prominently in all communities of the early Church.

[106] Reasons for the assumption of poverty in the disciples can be many: the disciples' practice of leaving all (5:11, 28), the Lord's command to sell all and distribute to the poor (14:33), the mendicancy of the wandering charismatic preachers (9:1-7; 10:1-12); the response to the Lord's command to share with the needy (6:29-35; Acts 2:43-45; 4:32-37), the persecutions that dispossess both Jewish and Gentile Christians (12:11, 49-53; 21:12-19). Whatever the explanation, most of the disciples of Christ are materially poor.

22-34; 14:33; 18:24-25), to share it with the poor (14:16-24; 18:22).[107]
Thus, in Luke's careful three-part description of the audience of the Sermon, his Jesus addresses not just the poor among them but all the disciples, reminding the poor that their needs will be addressed and exhorting
the rich to take care of those needs. That his church's sharing resulted in
no needy among them shows the success of Jesus' program for the poor,
but his message has to be constantly preached for conversion of those who
live in the world.[108]

But if poverty is to be taken in its strict economic sense, then the beatitude turns out not to be a platitudinous Wisdom form, but a paradoxical
one. "Happy are the poor" made no sense to Jesus' Jewish listeners or
Luke's Greco-Roman readers. The ὅτι clause now tells us how this outrageous statement can be accepted in faith.

6:20c: ὅτι ὑμετέρα ἐστὶν ἡ βασιλεία τοῦ θεοῦ, "for the reign of
God is yours."

῾Υμετέρα: Though a beatitude normally is expressed in the third person, Luke's beatitudes and woes are in the second person,[109] indicating that
the blessed poor are those just directly addressed (6:20a), the disciples themselves. The direct address has greater impact on the hearer than does a third
person *Tugendkatalog.* ῎Εστιν is the only present tense among the verbs explaining why the disciples are blessed.[110] The corresponding woe (6:24) is
the only one of that set of four to be expressed by a present tense. This
strongly suggests that the present possession of the Reign of God is the

---

[107] Robert J. Karris, "Poor and Rich: the Lukan *Sitz im Leben*," in Charles Talbert, ed., *Perspectives on Luke-Acts* (Edinburgh: T & T Clark, 1978) 112–25. Rodney Stark, *The Rise of
Christianity* (Princeton: Princeton University Press, 1996) argues that early Christianity grew
because of extensive networking, and those with such extensive networks are the well-to-do.

[108] The beatitudes turn out to be healing not only for the disciples, but for the whole
world (7:1); for a similar understanding of the audience see François Bovon, *Das Evangelium nach Lukas.* 2 vols. to date. EKK 31/1-2 (Zürich: Benziger; Neukirchen-Vluyn:
Neukirchener Verlag, 1989, 1996) 1:298.

[109] Even Luke ordinarily uses the third person: of the eleven beatitudes outside of the
Sermon only one (14:14) uses the second person. Since woes are usually expressed in the
second person some have conjectured that the second-person beatitude is not a Wisdom
form, but derives from the prophetic *Wehruf* (Isa 33:1) as this gained currency in apocalyptic literature (1 Enoch 9:7-8; 98:9-15); Eduard Schweizer, "Formgeschichtliches zu den
Seligpreisungen Jesu," *NTS* 19 (1972–73) 121–26, especially 123. Debate over whether
Luke's or Matthew's form was found in the source seems inconclusive (as Georg Strecker
also concludes in "Die Makarismen der Bergpredigt," *NTS* (1970–71) 257 n. 1); in any case,
it is irrelevant for us who are concerned with the rhetorical impact of the present text.

[110] Matthew 5:3 also has only the one present tense, explaining the cause of this one beatitude. This similarity, probably from the source, underlines the force of this present tense.

source of present beatitude for the poor.[111] But the Reign of God ordinarily has future reference, too, and so we must interpret the present tense in this beatitude in the light of Luke's whole understanding of the Reign of God.

Ἡ βασιλεία τοῦ θεοῦ: The literature on the Kingdom of God is immense,[112] partially because it is a rare and ill-defined notion throughout the Bible and early Judaism. Here we can only sketch its Jewish background and develop an overview of Luke's conception of it.

1. *The Reign of God in the Old Testament and in Judaism:* The "kingdom of God" is not found in the Hebrew Testament. It does occur in Wis 10:10, where it possibly means God's heavenly dwelling, a transcendent kingdom of wisdom and righteousness for the virtuous ones granted immortality. "Kingdom of YHWH" occurs in 1 Chr 28:5; 2 Chr 13:8 in conjunction with Davidic kingship, and similar expressions in OT literature refer to the fact that YHWH rules (1 Chr 17:14; 29:11; Ps 22:28; 103:19; 145:11-13; Obadiah 21). Thus there is a widespread but unfocused notion that YHWH rules here and now; his kingdom is described as sometimes over all nature,[113] and sometimes over historical Israel (Exod 15:1-18; Isa 44:6-7; 52:7; Psalm 98). In all cases the underlying conviction is that

---

[111] Luke 14:14 shows Luke uses futures for beatitude and reward when he means that. Still, the corresponding woe asserts that the rich have no future reward, which could imply that this beatitude should express a future reward (cf. the poor receiving their reward in the next life in 16:25).

[112] For the OT and Jewish backgrounds see both exposition and bibliographies in Gerhard von Rad and K. G. Kuhn in "βασιλεία," *TDNT* 1:565–76; Kurt Galling in *RGG* 5:912–18; Claus Westermann in *BHH* 3:1573–75; J. Alberto Soggin, *Das Königtum in Israel.* BZAW 104 (Berlin: A. Töpelmann, 1967). For the NT discussion and bibliographies see Ulrich Luz in *EWNT* 1:481–91; Rudolf Schnackenburg, *God's Rule and Kingdom* (New York: Herder & Herder, 1963); Norman Perrin, *The Kingdom of God in the Teaching of Jesus* (Philadelphia: Westminster, 1963), and idem, *Jesus and the Language of the Kingdom* (Philadelphia: Fortress, 1976); Wendell Willis, ed., *The Kingdom of God in 20th-Century Interpretation* (Peabody, Mass.: Hendrickson, 1987); Dennis C. Duling, "Kingdom of God, Kingdom of Heaven," *ABD* 4:49–69. For the Reign of God in Luke see Bent Noack, *Das Gottesreich bei Lukas. Eine Studie zu Luk 17,20-24.* SyBu 10 (Lund: Gleerup, 1948); Martin Völkel, "Zur Deutung des 'Reiches Gottes' bei Lukas," *ZNW* 65 (1974) 57–70; Otto Merk, "Das Reich Gotttes in den lukanischen Schriften," in E. Earle Ellis and Erich Grässer, eds., *Jesus und Paulus. Festschrift für Werner G. Kümmel zum 70. Geburtstag* (Göttingen: Vandenhoeck & Ruprecht, 1975) 201–20.

[113] Some have derived this notion from a nature myth among ancient Near Eastern peoples: in creating the world YHWH became a sacral king who defeated opposing powers, and Israel celebrated his triumph in the "enthronement Psalms" (Pss 47; 93; 96–99). Some have associated the idea of kingship over nature with the Mount Zion traditions, others with a (postulated) annual New Year's festival relating the reigning king of Israel with the sacral power of YHWH as cosmic king.

when God's rule is obeyed, justice and peace ensue. Probably the idea developed from a close equation of YHWH's rule with David's kingship, then to an idealized Davidic kingship when the kings of Judah proved venal and oppressive, to an anticipated arrival of a Messiah when there was no Davidic kingship, to an apocalyptic notion of a final triumph of God's kingship in Israel over the nations at the end of time.

This progression of ideas leading to the gospel usage and to that of Jewish apocalyptic occurs already in Isaiah. The oracle in Isa 31:4-5 proclaims that at the time of Sennacherib's seige of Jerusalem YHWH will come down to fight upon Mount Zion for Jersualem and will deliver it. Thus YHWH does battle where the Temple and the Davidic king's palace symbolize his royal presence. Shortly after the fall of Babylon in 539, Deutero-Isaiah in a series of oracles deliriously celebrates YHWH's triumph over the oppressors of his people. In 40:9-11 the prophet exhorts the messenger of good news to climb a high mountain to summon all the cities of Judah to "Behold your God!" YHWH then comes with might to rule and tenderly shepherd his people, a frequent image of the Ancient Near Eastern ruler. The image of YHWH's reign over Judah is sharper in Isa 52:7: "How beautiful upon the mountains/ are the feet of him who . . . says to Zion, 'Your God reigns.'"[114] The prophet celebrates the good news that God is arriving (52:8) to be again King in Jerusalem, and the Gentile world will see the salvation of God (52:10). In these four verses the prophet has united four elements that belong to the gospel tradition of the Kingdom: the proclamation of good news, peace and salvation in the reign of God over Judah, which the Gentiles recognize. Finally, in an apocalyptic oracle of unspecified date[115] Isa 24:23 speaks of YHWH's reign on Mount Zion and in Jerusalem, to the consternation of the cosmic deities humbled by his triumph. In this final stage, then, the Reign of God is an apocalyptic phenomenon of universal significance.

Jewish apocalyptic expects YHWH's definitive intervention to extend his rule through Israel over all the nations of the earth. Descriptions of this intervention incorporate OT and Judaism's notions of the Day of YHWH as God's judgment on the nations and his opponents, sometimes conceived as a fire of punishment (1 Enoch 90:37; 2 Bar 48:39; 1QS 4:12-13); the

---

[114] Jacques Dupont, *Béatitudes* 2:99–104 finds Isa 52:7 at the base of gospel usage, noting that Acts 10:36-38 had already joined it to 61:1; Rom 10:15 had also used Isa 52:7 to describe the role of evangelizing.

[115] No historical events can fix the dates of the Isaian Apocalypse (Isaiah 24–27), precisely because its imagery is apocalyptic: universal judgment as devastation of the country (24:1-13), eschatological banquet (25:6-8), cosmic signs (24:17-20, 23; 27:1), the ingathering of Israel (24:14-16, 23).

transformation of the cosmos (1 Enoch 91:16-17; *Jub* 1:29), also expressed by the overthrow of Satan and the Gentile nations (*Ass. Mos.* 10), the outpouring of the Spirit on all Israel (Ezek 36:26-27; *T. Jud.* 24:3), and by the resurrection of the dead to eternal life (Dan 12:1-3; 2 Maccabees 7); and the definitive rule of YHWH over the nations (Zech 14:9). Sometimes YHWH rules through a definitive reign of Israel, which in Ps Sol 17:1-38 is brought about through a historical Messiah of David's line. Sometimes the Messiah is conceived more apocalyptically:

> And it will happen that after he [the Messiah of 2 Bar 72:2 who will spare and kill all nations] has brought low everything that is in the world, and has sat down in Eternal peace on the throne of the kingdom, then joy will be revealed and rest will appear (2 Bar 73:1).

The apocalyptic kingdom is sometimes given the Son of Man. In Dan 2:44; 7:1-18 four worldly kingdoms are replaced by an everlasting (apocalyptic) kingdom that God will set up.[116] In 7:18 this is established by the Son of Man as "the Saints of the Most High," Israel.[117] This national notion resides in the rest of apocalyptic literature where the notion of Kingdom of God is most at home (1 Enoch 63:4; 46:4-5; 48:4-5; 62–63; *T. Mos.* 10:1, 3). At the same time, the everlasting reign of God is portrayed as superior to any human kingdom (Dan 4:25). This apocalyptic kingdom of God is the ultimate vindication of the alienated "elect" who are persecuted by the (Gentile) kingdoms of this world.

The Qumran sectarians expected God to establish an eschatological kingdom of Israel in Jerusalem, with a renewed covenant that would effect justice and peace for the poor and oppressed (1QM 12:3, 7-16; 19:8; 1QSb 3–5). The rabbinic literature (whose references may be later than the first century C.E.) transformed the notion into a moral one: to "take upon oneself the yoke of the Kingdom of Heaven" meant to confess the God of the *Shemaʿ* and consequently observe the demands of Torah, thus making the reign of God a visible present reality.[118]

---

[116] While Dan 2:44 probably refers to an earthly kingdom, Dan 7:14's kingdom seems beyond time, as is usually true of the following references to Kingdom of God in the apocalyptic literature.

[117] Although some take the "Saints of the Most High" as a sect of pious Jews (*ḥasidîm*; cf. 11:33-35) and others think of angels in the likeness of human beings (8:13), the identification of Israel makes most sense for apocalyptic (persecution) literature.

[118] Jewish piety, with its roots in the first century, prayed for the coming of God's reign as a future and eschatological reality, in the *Kaddish,* "May he establish his kingdom during your life . . . and during the life of all the house of Israel," and in the Eighteen Benedictions, "Bring back our judges as at first . . . and be Thou King over us, O Lord . . . ."

2. *The Reign of God in Luke-Acts:* If one adds the occurrences of ἡ βασιλεία that refer to the Reign of God to the explicit uses of ἡ βασιλεία τοῦ θεοῦ, the totals in the gospels and Acts are: Matthew 50, Mark 12, Luke 41, John 2, Acts 8.[119] In Mark 1:15 Jesus first appears as an apocalyptic preacher of the imminent Reign of God: πεπλήρωται ὁ καιρὸς καὶ ἤγγικεν ἡ βασιλεία τοῦ θεοῦ, "The time has been fulfilled and the Reign of God has drawn near."[120] This emphasis on the imminence of the reign of God dominates Mark,[121] and modern exegetes have made it characteristic for the vision of the historical Jesus and for the synoptic tradition as a whole (Appendix C).

There is, however, in the synoptic tradition prior to Luke a more varied view of the Kingdom, which conceives of it as coming in three stages:

(1) already present in Jesus: Mark 4:1-9, 26-29, 30-32 and *parr.*; Q 11:20;

(2) coming soon (imminent): Mark 1:15//Matt 4:17; Mark 9:1//Matt 16:28//Luke 9:27; Q 10:9;

(3) coming at the end of time: Q 13:29. Consequently, a wider variety of meanings lies open to our investigation of what Luke meant by the Reign of God.

We cannot here investigate all forty-nine uses of "Reign of God" in Luke-Acts. Our method will be to concentrate on the uses Luke has highlighted by the place he has given them in his structure and to investigate his distinctive usage there.

4:43: Luke does not portray Jesus programmatically announcing the imminence of the Reign, as do Mark 1:15//Matt 4:17. He displays Jesus as the eschatological prophet whose anointing by the Spirit enables him to proclaim the Jubilee year of release for the bound, the oppressed, the blind: good news for the poor (4:18, 22). After he has exercised this ministry by freeing those under Satan's bondage (4:31-41) he describes just this work as proclaiming the Reign of God (4:43).[122] Thus Luke's first use

---

[119] I also count Luke 19:12, 15 and Acts 1:6; 20:25 as instances of the Kingdom of God.

[120] The perfect tense of ἐγγίζω signifies not only that the reign of God has drawn near, but that it is affecting the present. But the opinion of C. H. Dodd, *The Parables of the Kingdom* (New York: Scribners, 1961) 29 that ἤγγικεν is equivalent to ἔφθασεν, "has arrived" (as in Luke 11:20) has not gathered many adherents.

[121] Cf. also 9:1; 11:10; 14:25, and probably 15:43. There is no suggestion that the Reign will arrive much later, at some remove from Jesus' own time or that of Mark's community. Nor does Mark say that the reign of God is present in Jesus' work, although the "growth parables" of the reign of God (4:3-9 [cf. v. 11], 26-29, 30-32) describe it as a reality that begins with Jesus and matures over time. Only recently have exegetes begun to question the dominance of Mark 1:15 in Mark's theology: Burton Mack, "The Kingdom Sayings in Mark," *Foundations and Facets Forum* 3 (1987) 3–47.

[122] The καὶ, εὐαγγελίσασθαι, and ἀπεστάλην of 4:43 indisputably link the Reign of God with the work of the *Heilsprophet* in 4:18. Consequently, Luke has (*pace* Fitzmyer, *Luke* 557) described what he means by the Reign of God.

of the term portrays the Reign as a present reality: Jesus' eschatological overthrow of Satan's reign by healing and exorcising in his ministry. This first description carries two of Luke's principal themes of the Reign of God:

1. It effects healings and exorcisms as the Jubilee release from the power of Satan:

9:12: the disciples' mission is a conjoined proclamation of the Reign of God and healing of the sick; cf. the same combination in Acts 8:5-12;

10:9: the seventy-two are to heal and proclaim that the Reign has drawn near;[123]

11:20: exorcism shows that the Reign of God has arrived and is operative in Jesus' ministry.

2. It is a present reality (as well as a future one):[124]

11:20: Exorcisms demonstrates that the Reign of God has already arrived;[125]

16:16: in the new era after John the Baptist, the Reign of God is not only preached, but is a present reality that people are constrained to enter;[126]

17:21: to the Pharisees' question about the coming of the Reign, Jesus replies that the Reign is "among you," present and active in their own history.[127]

A second emphatic place characterizing Luke's notion of the Reign of God is at the very beginning of Acts. In Acts 1:3 Jesus, as part of his commissioning of his apostles, spends forty days λέγων τὰ περὶ τῆς βασιλείας τοῦ θεοῦ, "speaking of the things about the Reign of God."

---

[123] The "older" preaching of the *imminence* (ἤγγικεν) of the Reign of God is tied to healings, and yet Luke 10:17 portrays the seventy-two as having subjugated the demons (by exorcisms), which Jesus in 10:18 links to the eschatological and final overthrow of Satan. Jesus' present power of the Reign seeps even into Luke's proclamation of the imminence of the Reign of God.

[124] C. H. Dodd, "The Kingdom of God has Come," *ExpT* 48 (1936–37) 138–42; Werner G. Kümmel, *Promise and Fulfillment, The Eschatological Message of Jesus* (London: S.C.M., 1961) 105–109; Theodor Lorenzmeier, "Zum Logion Mt 12;18; Lk 11:20," in Hans-Dieter Betz and Luise Schottroff, eds., *Neues Testament und christliche Existenz. Festschrift für Herbert Braun zum 70. Geburtstag* (Tübingen: Mohr, 1973) 289–304; Erich Grässer, "Zum Verständnis des Gottesherrschaft," *ZNW* 65 (1974) 3–26; see the bibliography and discussion, especially of the "timeless aorist," in Fitzmyer, *Luke* 922–23.

[125] The parable immediately following (11:21-26) confirms this interpretation, even though vv. 24-26 make the present action not as finally determinative as the Reign at the end of time; Johnson discusses this link of 11:14-20 with 11:21-26 in *Luke* 180–84.

[126] Conzelmann, *Theology of St. Luke* 12–17 shows this preaching inaugurating a new stage of history; 16:16c also defines this Reign as a present reality that all are pressed to enter; Fitzmyer, *Luke* 1117–18.

[127] See Fitzmyer's excellent discussion of the controversial ἐντὸς ὑμῶν in *Luke* 1161. Answering the question about the arrival of the Reign, Jesus affirms it has arrived and is present in his ministry, "in your midst." This usage, rather than "within your grasp," coheres with Lukan usage in 11:20; 16:16, and with rejection of an apocalyptic expectation marked by cosmological signs (17:20-37).

This is not proclamation of the Reign's arrival; there is now a *content* (τὰ περί)[128] of the Reign that is being taught. There are no clues to this content,[129] and so we must scrutinize similar intimations of a content in other Reign of God passages in Acts:

> **8:12:** When the Samaritans believe Philip εὐαγγελιζομένῳ περὶ τῆς βασιλείας τοῦ θεοῦ, they are baptized. Again περί gives a content. In 8:5 Philip was proclaiming Christ, exorcising, curing the paralyzed or lame.[130] The content of the evangelization about the Reign made enough sense of the proclamation and the healings to ground a faith that led to baptism.

> **19:8:** Paul in the synagogue at Ephesus speaks boldly,[131] arguing,[132] and πείθων [τὰ] περὶ τῆς βασιλείας τοῦ θεοῦ. Reading τὰ with B, D, Ψ, 1175, 1891 gives the same phrase as in Acts 1:3. When the Jews refuse his message, Paul leaves for the school of Tyrannos, where he *continues* his teaching of "the word about the Lord" (19:9-10). Thus τὰ περὶ τῆς βασιλείας = the word about the Lord, probably the content of the kerygma to be proved and accepted. Further, three other passages in Acts associate the proclamation of this Reign with extensive teaching about Jesus:

> **20:25:** In his farewell address to the elders at Ephesus Paul says that his mission among them had been κηρύσσων τὴν βασιλείαν, which the next verses (20:26-27) identify as telling them the whole of God's plan (presumably as traced in the Scriptures; Luke 24:25-27).

> **28:23b:** In Rome Paul is διαμαρτυρόμενος[133] τὴν βασιλείαν τοῦ θεοῦ, which is immediately (23c) identified with πείθων . . . περὶ τοῦ Ἰησοῦ

---

[128] The τὰ indicates a series of discrete elements. Most commentators on Acts have missed this point; they treat this teaching as simply continuous with what Jesus had been proclaiming in any synoptic gospel, and so miss a characteristic of Luke's Reign, not only in Acts, but also in Luke.

[129] It could be the content of Jesus' post-resurrection teaching in Luke: that the Christ according to Scripture had to suffer and so enter into his glory (24:25-27 [N.b. τὰ περὶ ἑαυτοῦ]); or that the Reign is Jesus as *bearer of the Spirit* and the works that flow from his anointing (as in 4:18); or τὰ μυστήρια of the Kingdom (8:10); or the disciples' conduct in the Reign (22:30).

[130] Note the parallel with Luke 4:16-44, where proclamation of the Christ's identity + his exorcisms and healings = proclamation of the Reign of God.

[131] Παρρησιάζεσθαι occurs 9x in Acts; otherwise only in 1 Thess 2:2 ; Eph 6:20. In Acts 9:27-28; 13:46; 14:3; 18:26; 26:26 the content of the preaching is not clear, but παρρησία describes fearless preaching to unbelievers of the things about Christ necessary to lead people to commit themselves to him and be baptized into the community of his disciples. The content is the Christian kerygma.

[132] Διαλέγεσθαι (0/1/0/0/10 + 2) is used almost exclusively from Acts 17–24 to describe Paul's disputes with the Jews demonstrating from the Scriptures that Jesus is the Christ.

[133] This Lukan word (ten of 15 NT uses) describes Paul's witnessing to the whole gospel of grace (Acts 20:24), beginning from Galilee (10:37) to the last judgment (10:42).

from Moses and the prophets. Again, this is demonstration of a doctrine: Jesus is the fulfillment of the whole Scripture.

In **28:31** Luke concludes his two-volume work with Paul κηρύσσων τὴν βασιλείαν τοῦ θεοῦ, which is associated with διδάσκων τὰ περὶ τοῦ κυρίου Ἰησοῦ Χριστοῦ.

Thus throughout Acts speaking about the Kingdom is talking about the content of Jesus' mission and its appeal to conversion. The emphasis is on the Reign as it has been embodied in Jesus and received by his disciples. Although Acts represents the terminus of Luke's thinking, his gospel, written a scant ten years earlier, reflects this new conception of the Reign of God. This is clear where Luke (alone among the evangelists) makes the Reign of God the direct object of the verbs εὐαγγελίζεσθαι and κηρύσσειν (4:43; 8:1; 9:2, 11, 60; 10:9; 16:16). This usage coheres with that of Luke 4:43, and so the Reign in Luke often functions as a short description of the work of Jesus as the eschatological prophet who heals and brings liberation through the Spirit by which he has been anointed. Although this Reign retains characteristics of the synoptic tradition, referring to a reality inaugurated by Jesus, coming soon, and finally determinative of one's ultimate state at the end of time, Luke has already modified many of these traditional formulations:

1. The imminent arrival of the apocalyptic Reign of God begins to refer to the arrival of the Kingdom in the Pentecostal outpouring of the Spirit.[134] Luke 9:27 may have expressed the historical Jesus' conviction that the apocalyptic Reign would break forth in his own generation. But since Luke has dropped the "reign come with power" of Mark 9:1, it is probable that the Reign Luke foresees is not that of the end of time. Since in Luke-Acts the Kingdom is so connected with the power of the Spirit to heal, it is probable that the Reign Jesus refers to in 9:27 and 22:30 is that possession of the Spirit in which the community will be baptized in Acts 2, and through which Peter and Paul will do the same works as Jesus did. That baptism, called "the last days" (Acts 2:17), does come in the lifetime of Jesus' hearers. The disciples' preaching that the Reign is at hand in 10:9, 11 could retain the earliest tradition's expectation of the imminent Reign, now reminding Luke's community that, as an analogous reality, it is still and always imminent. But the conjunction of this preaching with healing (and exorcism) rather points to the healing power of the Spirit as the Reign present in Jesus and coming to the community in the baptism of Pentecost. The prayer for the coming of the kingdom, so clearly apocalyptic in Matthew's version of the Our Father, seems in Luke 11:2 to refer

---

[134] Fred O. Francis, "Eschatology and History in Luke-Acts," *JAAR* 37 (1969) 49–63.

to a coming in the imminent future.[135] In fact, the application of the accompanying parable (11:5-10) and figures (11:11-12) speaks of God's granting the Spirit, precisely the realization of the Kingdom of which we have been speaking (11:13).[136]

2. *The apocalyptic Reign* is no longer imminent. Although Luke associates it with the *parousia* of the Son of Man (17:20-22; 21:31 with vv. 25-28) at some undetermined end of time, this Reign still determines the final success or failure of human life.[137] Jesus tells a parable of final reckoning in response to the crowd's expectation of the Reign of God (19:11-27).[138] This Reign is described as the eschatological banquet in 13:28-29[139] and 14:15.[140]

---

[135] Luke does not have Matthew's petition to be delivered from the eschatological test (Matt 6:13); his present imperative ἐλθέτω, which most text critics prefer, speaks of a general or continual arrival of the kingdom, rather than the singular apocalyptic arrival signaled by Matthew's aorist.

[136] Also in this category would be the eucharistic words about the Reign. Jesus' saying he would not eat of the Passover again until it was fulfilled in the Reign of God (22:16) or drink of the fruit of the vine until the Reign had come (22:18) can have two explanations. First, as with the Passover Hagaddah, the meal is not just a memorial of the ancient Passover or of Jesus' sacrificial offering of himself (ὑπὲρ ὑμῶν, vv. 19, 20) but also an anticipation of full eschatological deliverance. Second, the community's Eucharist celebrates the arrival of the Reign of God in which Jesus will be present (22:30-31, 35; Acts 10:41; 2:41-47). See Joachim Jeremias, *The Eucharistic Words of Jesus* (London: S.C.M., 1966) 207–18; Fitzmyer, *Luke* 1390–92 with notes and bibliography; Johnson, *Luke* 337–38. Either way, the Reign is anticipated as imminent.

[137] Conzelmann showed (*Theology of St. Luke* 125–31) how Luke has reworked the synoptic apocalypse so that the destruction of Jerusalem (21:5-24) is separated from the coming of the Son of Man as apocalyptic judge (21:25-36) by the era of the Gentiles (21:24c). Then this *parousia* of the Son of Man as judge is equated with the arrival of the Reign of God in 21:31. Note, however, that even though the Reign of God has been pushed off to a distant future the disciples are still to be on the lookout, for they do not know when it is arriving (21:34-36); compare the Lukan texts in which the Son of Man's arrival as judge is unexpected but determinative (12:35-40, 41-48; 17:21-37).

[138] In the parable the nobleman going to receive his kingdom is Jesus (19:12, 37-38), and so the Reign of God the crowd expects as imminent (19:11) is identified with this king's final reckoning.

[139] The context of salvation and judgment (13:23, 25) prepares for an eschatological meaning of the Reign of God, symbolized by reclining with the patriarchs at the eschatological banquet. There is no time given for this event, but it is determinative of one's being saved.

[140] The beatitude pronounced on the generous host, to be rewarded in the apocalyptic resurrection of the dead (14:14), provokes his guest to call blessed those who eat in the Reign of God (14:15). Thus Jesus' parable of the judgment that takes place at the time of the great banquet associates the Reign with that judgment. The time is indeterminate, but the outcome is not.

In Summary, Luke has transformed the Kingdom of God into a many-splendored notion. *Primarily* it refers to the healing presence of Jesus as the eschatological *Heilsprophet* anointed in the Spirit to proclaim and effect the Jubilee year of release from oppression and bondage to Satan's reign (4:16-43). Jesus' ministry of healing and exorcising is the Reign of God already present (11:20; 16:16; 17:21), and a sign that he is the Messiah (7:19-23 in light of 3:15-16; Acts 10:36-38). Proclamations of the imminence of the Reign of God (9:27; 10:9, 11) are then transformed into statements that the Reign of God will enter a new stage with his gift of the promised Spirit (24:49; Acts 1:3-5), which will enable his disciples to do the same works of the Reign that he had done.[141] In this second stage, Luke's own time, preaching or teaching about the Reign of God is explaining from the Scriptures that this Jesus as Spirit-bringer is the Messiah, whose dying and rising inaugurates a second stage of the Reign into which hearers are persuaded to enter (16:16; Acts 1:3; 8:12; 19:8; 28:23, 31), and on account of which they leave all to follow Jesus (18:29). And yet, even though life in this Kingdom feeds the poor so that there are no needy among the disciples (14:33; 18:22; Acts 2:43-47; 4:32-37) the perfect and final Reign of God will occur only when the Son of Man reappears for the apocalyptic judgment (17:20-22; 21:25-31; Acts 1:11) and at that time one will enter the final Reign or be dismissed from it (11:2; 13:28-29; 14:15; 19:11-27; 21:31). Here Luke's thought is similar to that of Jas 2:5, whose poor are "rich in faith and heirs of the Reign." But this time of the Son of Man is in an undetermined future, after the time of the Gentiles (21:24); in the meantime, disciples live the Way of Jesus (Acts 9:2; 19:9, 23; 22:4; 24:22) doing his works in the Reign of God, and at their death enter into some other condition of it (Luke 23:42-43; cf. 12:20).

Conclusion

So how does the Reign of God belong to the poor?

1. Jesus' disciples are the economically oppressed who are God's clients, poor not only because of the inequities of the agrarian system but

---

[141] As Jesus had been baptized in the Spirit (3:21-22), cast out demons (4:33-41; 8:26-39; 11:14-23), healed the lame (5:17-26), raised from the dead (7:11-17; 8:49-56), so are the disciples baptized (Acts 1:5; 2:1-13; 9:18), and Peter, Philip, and Paul cast out demons (Acts 5:16; 8:7; 16:18; 19:11), heal the lame (3:1-10; 8:7; 9:32-35; 14:8-11) and raise from the dead (9:36-42; 20:9-12). It seems, then, as though the power that the seventy-two have over demons in Luke 10:17-18 is a proleptic exercise of powers over Satan that the disciples will have after Pentecost.

also because they sell their goods and distribute to the poor (Luke 12:33; 14:33; 18:22), thus being rich toward God (12:21).[142]

2. Jesus' disciples are happy because they have the Reign of God, which means that

(a) God is *now* removing their poverty in his Reign. The rich, hearing that riches jeopardize their life (6:24; 16:25; 18:24-25) and that the only way God can accomplish their salvation is by converting them to give their wealth to the poor (19:8-9), now distribute their goods to the poor (12:33; 14:33; 18:22, 30; Acts 2:44-45; 4:32-37), becoming voluntarily poor with them—but through their sharing *they are not poor* (Acts 4:34, and the absence of πτωχοί in Acts).[143]

(b) But even when they remain poor in the still developing Reign of God, they are also blessed because by putting their trust in God and not in goods they seek the Reign of God (12:22-31) and are even now in the process of receiving their reward in the fullness of God's Reign (16:22-25; 18:30).

This conclusion can now be tested by its congruence with Luke's rhetorical structure of synthetic and antithetic parallels in the rest of the beatitudes and woes.

---

[142] Luke 12:33-34 is the explanation of what it means to be εἰς θεὸν πλουτῶν (12:21), since the passages are linked by Luke's rare use of θησαυρ– compounds.

[143] Luise Schottroff and Wolfgang Stegemann, *Jesus von Nazareth: Hoffnung der Armen* (Stuttgart: Kohlhammer, 1978) 102–104. Probably at the time of Luke himself this picture had become an idealization used to bring the wealthy in his community to share wealth with the needy; cf. ibid. 108–13.

Chapter 4

Beatitudes and Woes

(6:21-26)

The Beatitudes (6:21-23)

Besides the various triads of the oppressed as clients of God found in the OT (see p. 73), Jacques Dupont finds a LXX background for Q's first three beatitudes in Isa 61:1-6:

61:1b to bring good tidings to the poor (πτωχοῖς)

61:2c to comfort all who mourn (παρακαλῆσαι . . . πενθοῦντας)

61:6c you shall eat the wealth of nations (κατέδεσθε).[1]

In any case, the obvious link between poverty and hunger was common in the OT and Judaism (Isa 32:6-7; 58:6-10; Job 24:4-11; Tob 4:7, 16; Pss 22:26; 132:15; Prov 25:21; Sir 4:1-2; *T. Jos.* 1:5.[2] Many commentators think the three remaining beatitudes specify what is meant by the poor of the first beatitude. As our exegesis will show, these three beatitudes rather intensify the degree of poverty, so that the index of misery rises as one proceeds through the series.

1. *The Second Beatitude* (6:21ab)

6:21ab: Μακάριοι οἱ πεινῶντες νῦν, ὅτι χορτασθήσεσθε. "Blessed the hungry now, for you will be stuffed." Πεινᾶν is the ordinary LXX

---

[1] The promised deliverance from post-exilic poverty and hunger is concrete and historically real. Evidence that Judaism linked these subjects of YHWH's liberation may be found in 1QH 18:12-15, describing the psalmist's task as bringing good news to the ʿanāwîm and joy to those who mourn.

[2] For the linking of the poor, the naked, the hungry, the mourning as one group see not only Isa 61:1-6, but also Job 24:2-12. Poverty is associated with other forms of misery, especially nakedness, in Ezek 18:7, 16; Job 22:7; Tob 1:17; 4:16; *T. Jud.* 25:5.

translation for *rᶜb,* "to be hungry, starving,"³ sometimes in the metaphorical sense, "avidly desiring." Hunger most often results from drought and war as divine punishment for godlessness (Deut 32:24; 2 Sam 24:13; Ezek 5:15-16). Hunger and thirst are considered the worst forms of lack.⁴ In times of hunger Israel learned that YHWH was its deliverer (Exod 16:3-12; Pss 17:14; 37:19; 132:15), and that he took up the cause of the dispossessed hungry (1 Sam 2:5; Pss 107:9, 36-38; 146:7; Isa 65:13). The exilic prophets' extravagant description of abundant food for restored Israel (Isa 49:10; 55:1-2; Jer 31:12; Ezek 34:29; 39:17-20) led to images of a rich eschatological feast for Israel and all nations in Isa 25:6-8 and in subsequent apocalyptic literature.⁵

Further, YHWH demands from his people a corresponding commitment to allay the hunger of their fellows: Isa 58:7, 10 continues the prophetic critique of empty cult practiced without works of justice: the fast YHWH wants is "to share your bread with the hungry" . . . "pour yourself out for the hungry." In the new conception of individual responsibility, the righteous one is described as one who, among other acts of compassion, "gives his bread to the hungry" (Ezek 18:7, 16). Two OT texts are especially relevant for the Sermon: Tob 4:15-16 links the Golden Rule with "give your bread to the hungry . . . all your surplus to charity;" Prov 25:21 extends even to enemies this demand to feed the hungry!

Hunger (especially to starvation), then, is a direr form of poverty, and so the second beatitude intensifies the first. Although πεινᾶν is not a Lukan word (five of twenty-three NT uses), Luke shows this connection between poverty and hunger in 15:14-16; 16:20-21. Four of Luke's five uses of πεινᾶν designate physical hunger: 4:2 (Jesus' hunger after a forty-day fast); 6:3 (the disciples' mild hunger walking through the fields); 6:21a, (where the hunger is as real in this life as the poverty and the wailing);⁶ 1:53 (Mary proclaims that in her conception of Jesus the poor have been fed).

---

³ How severe is the hunger πεινᾶν expresses as the regular translation of *rᶜb* may be indicated by the fact that the noun *rᶜb* is not translated by πεῖνα, but rather by λιμός, famine (Leonhard Goppelt, "πεινάω," *TDNT* 6:14). Jacques Dupont, *Les Béatitudes* (Paris: Gabalda, 1969) 2:38, shows how πεινᾶν in the LXX takes its meaning from the most desperate meaning of starving in *rᶜb.*

⁴ Even Philo calls hunger "the most unbearable of all evils," *Spec. Leg.* 2, 201.

⁵ 1 Enoch 62:12-14; *T. Isaac* 6:13, where those who partake are those who shared their bread with the hungry in this life; 2 Bar 29:1-8, which associates this banquet with the revelation of the Messiah. On sacred (divine) foods and the celebration of YHWH's cosmic triumph over dragons, alien nations, and death see Dennis E. Smith's lucid summary, "Messianic Banquet," in *ABD* 4:788–91 and his bibliographical references, especially to the works of Paul Hanson and Adela Yarbro Collins.

⁶ This beatitude in the Gospel of Thomas (69b) expects a this-worldly reward: "Blessed are the hungry, for the belly of him who desires shall be filled."

Νῦν here and in 6:21c sets up a contrast between present misery and future reversal in the respective ὅτι clauses giving the reasons for these two beatitudes. Χορτάζειν, derived from χόρτος, "pasture, hay, fodder," is used in Greek literature properly of animals, "to feed, fatten" (LSJ 1999–2000).[7] The LXX uses it only thirteen times, always to translate *śbʿ*, "to satisfy, fill" concrete hunger. The OT is full of references to God feeding his people (Isa 49:9-10; 65:13; Ezek 34:29; Pss 17:14; 37:19; 107:9; 132:15; 146:7). This divine agency is expressed by the passive voice in both ὅτι clauses of 6:21.[8]

In the gospels χορτάζειν (4/4/4/1) is used almost exclusively for those satisfied by the multiplication of the loaves.[9] But Luke also uses the word in its gross sense of "to stuff, wolf down" in 15:16 and 16:21, where the Prodigal and Lazarus are so famished they will devour anything. In all cases, "to be satisfied" or "be filled" is too pallid a translation for χορτάζειν.

Luke's one narrative of the multiplication of the loaves (9:10-17)[10] sheds the most light on the usage in the beatitude. It occurs in a christological section (9:7-36),[11] and so the primary meaning of the passage is that Jesus "stuffs" the multitude in the desert. The use of χορτάζειν makes this a narrative fulfillment of the beatitude in 6:21 (and of 1:53), even if the people are not explicitly described as hungry.[12] Jesus exercises divine

---

[7] Χορτάζειν describes the feeding of both animals and humans in Ps Sol 5:8-11. Classical Greek for "to fill with food, satisfy" would be ἀρέσκειν, πιμπλῆναι, πληροῦν, ἀρκεῖν; for "to feed," τρέφειν, νέμειν, βόσκειν, σιτίζειν, πιαίνειν.

[8] The "divine passive" is common terminology since Gustaf Dalman, *Die Worte Jesu; mit Berücksichtigung des nachkanonischen jüdischen Schrifttums und der aramäischen Sprache* (Leipzig : J. C. Hinrichs, 1898); see the discussion and bibliography in Joachim Jeremias, *New Testament Theology* (New York: Scribner's, 1971) 9–14.

[9] Matthew 5:6 also uses it of this beatitude (//Luke 6:21a).

[10] Joseph A. Fitzmyer, *The Gospel According to Luke.* 2 vols. AB 28, 28A (Garden City, N.Y.: Doubleday, 1981, 1985) 762 convincingly shows this passage is an editorial reworking (perhaps with some alternative source material) of Mark 6:32-44; there is no need to study the relation of this passage to Mark 8:1-10 or to John 6:1-15, or even to ask why Luke has omitted a second synoptic account.

[11] Again Fitzmyer has seen this unit most clearly in "The Composition of Luke, Chapter 9," in Charles Talbert, ed., *Perspectives on Luke-Acts,* (Edinburgh: T & T Clark, 1978) 139–52. It begins with Herod's "But who is this?" (9:9), answered by Jesus' nature miracle (9:10-17), Peter's profession that Jesus is the Messiah (9:18-20), and Jesus' instruction that he is the Son of Man in the model of the Suffering Servant (9:21-27). This last identification is confirmed by the climax of this section, the Transfiguration (9:28-36), proclaiming that Jesus is the Son of God (9:35) about to fulfill his exodus in Jerusalem (9:31), and that the disciples must listen (9:35) to his authoritative description of who he is (9:21-22) and how the cross is central for their own lives (9:23-27).

[12] Luke T. Johnson, *The Gospel of Luke.* SP 3 (Collegeville: The Liturgical Press, 1991) 147. Luke 9:12 implies the hunger of those who have spent a day listening to Jesus

power to accomplish what God does in the OT: feed his people. The passage identifies Jesus through OT types. The notions of desert and being filled recall the manna in the desert (Exod 16:4-36), thus making Jesus the prophet like Moses (9:31, 35; Acts 3:22-23; 7:37). He is also a prophet like Elisha, telling his servant to feed the hungry with what he miraculously provides (2 Kings 4:42-44). The five verbs describing Jesus' actions in 9:16 point forward to Jesus' feeding of his disciples at his last supper (22:19), and the subsequent Christian practice of the Eucharist,[13] the eschatological banquet now realized sacramentally in the time of the Church.[14]

This raises the question of the meaning of the future tense of χορτασθήσεσθε: are the hungry to be fed in the immediate future (like the poor) or in the eschaton? Luke's emphasis on food and meals may help answer this question.

> **5:29-32:** the feast in Levi's house (5:29) is depicted as the result of his having left all things to become a disciple (5:28). Gospel renunciation leads to feasting *now.*

> **5:33-35:** Jesus and his disciples eat and drink (cf. 7:34) because the eschatological time of the bridegroom is *now,* in Jesus' ministry.

> **8:54:** upon raising Jairus' daughter, Jesus orders her to be given something to eat; cf. Jesus' own eating after his resurrection from the dead (surely an eschatological event!) in 24:30, 41-42.

> **14:1-24:** the burden of the Lukan symposium is that the poor, lame, crippled, and blind must be fed *now* (14:13), and the reward of that hospitality to outcasts will be eating at the banquet of the Reign of God (14:14-15).

> **16:19-31** does not speak of feeding or satiety, but only of the fact that the poor and hungry Lazarus will be consoled with good things in the bosom of Abraham (16:23, 25). Here the reward for the hungry is purely otherworldly.

---

speaking of the Reign of God. Even 2 Kings 4:42-44, to which the miracle is frequently compared, does not speak of the hunger of those who eat, though there is a famine in the land (4:38). Fitzmyer, *Luke* 764 thinks that the omission of ἐσπλαγχνίσθη in 9:11 means that compassion cannot be Jesus' motive for feeding, but the compassion omitted had referred to the people's lack of instruction (Mark 6:34) or sickness (Matt 14:14), not hunger.

[13] Luke 24:29-30; Acts 2:42, 46; 20:7, 11; Lucien Cerfaux, "La section des pains (Mc VI,31–VIII,26; Mt XIV,13–XVI,12)" in *Synoptische Studien: Alfred Wikenhauser zum siebzigsten Geburtstag am 22. Februar 1953 dargebracht von Freunden, Kollegen und Schülern* (Munich: K. Zink, 1953) 75–76; see Heinz Schürmann, *Das Lukasevangelium* (Freiburg: Herder, 1969) 518–20 and the range of exegetes cited in n. 161.

[14] Isaiah 25:6-8; 1 Enoch 62:14, and the passages cited above in n. 5. One indicator of this eschatological resonance is that Peter in the next passage professes that Jesus is the Messiah. In the logic of the narrative, has the multiplication of loaves produced this identification? Although there are no OT or Jewish expectations of the messiah as one who produces food, the eschatological banquet is loosely associated with messianic times.

22:14-23: the memorial of himself (22:19) that Jesus gives his community is a meal that proleptically celebrates the eschatological banquet of the Reign of God (22:16, 18, 19-30), a meal Luke's community eats *now*, each day (Acts 2:46).

This survey demonstrates how difficult it is to separate the time of Jesus and that of the church from eschatological time. Rather in Luke's conception, the Reign of God has arrived in Jesus (11:20; 17:21) and the last days have arrived in the outpouring of the Spirit (Acts 2:17). The hungry are fed in Jesus' own time (9:10-17), and through the commands he gives his disciples (14:13), because God's will is always that the hungry be fed. But this feeding for some hungry will come only in his final eschatological reign (16:25). In that sense, 6:21a, in spite of its future tense, carries the same combination of temporal/eschatological reward as does 6:20, because the Reign of God is present and active.

2. *The Third Beatitude* (6:21cd)

6:21cd: Μακάριοι οἱ κλαίοντες νῦν, ὅτι γελάσετε. "Blessed those who mourn now, for you will laugh." Those who derive the first three beatitudes from Isa 61:1-6 judge μακάριοι οἱ πενθοῦντες ὅτι παρακληθήσονται of Matt 5:4 to have been the original reading of Q.[15] All the more attention, then, should be paid to κλαίειν as Luke's conscious choice. Κλαίειν translates *bkh* in all but eight of its 145 OT uses, and so takes on its varied meanings: weeping with excitement and joy, wailing over a profound loss or calamity, or grief for the dead. It always describes intense expression of emotion. The wailing characteristic of funeral rites is its most characteristic use, but *bkh* also expresses individual and collective laments for a variety of personal, civil, and religious events, including acts of repentance.[16] In the Jewish experience of life in distress, weeping characterizes those who belong to God and will see their tears turned into joy in personal deliverance, in restoration from the exile, and in the apocalyptic new creation (Isa 35:10; 60:20; 61:3; 65:17-25; Jer 31:13; Job 30:25;

---

[15] Isaiah 61:2 reads παρακαλέσαι πάντας τοὺς πενθοῦντας. Πενθεῖν translates *ʾbl* in all but ten of its sixty-seven uses; the noun, πένθος, strongly favors the same root. Hebrew *ʾbl* means "to dry up, languish; to mourn, lament." In other Semitic languages and in Israel the primary meaning is mourning for the dead, referring more to the external rites of mourning than to inner disposition. This meaning underlies the mourning in oracles of judgment, even when the verb applies to nature and vegetation; Arnulf Baumann, "*ʾābhāl*," *TDOT* 1:44–48.

[16] Vinzenz Hamp, *bacah, TDOT* 2:116–20; *bch*, like κλαίειν, comes from the mouth and voice [throat], while *dmʿ*, "shedding tears," comes from the eyes.

Pss 126:1-6; 137:1). The beatitude's resolution of κλαίειν into γελᾶν or rejoicing is found in Ps 126:1-6; Qoh 3:4.

Κλαίειν (38x) occurs much more often than πενθεῖν (10x) in the NT;[17] among the evangelists it is a Lukan word (2/4/11/8/2). Outside of 6:20-26 Luke uses it primarily to express wailing at someone's death (7:13, 32; 8:52a,b; 23:28b; Acts 9:39; 21:13).[18] It also describes wailing for personal sins in the presence of Jesus (7:38; 22:62) and for the impending destruction of Jerusalem (19:41; 23:28c). Given this variety, it is best to interpret κλαίειν from its context.

Those who are destitute and starving are those who die, and whose mourners are not professionals, but the immediate family. Jesus here addresses the same group who need Jubilee liberation from powers that are oppressing them in this world—those unjustly exploited by the rich, those in constant hunger, those whose malnutrition brings early death. Thus the beatitudes have reached a deeper stage in those who lament: the pain of the poor and the hungry is so intense that they cannot suffer in silence, but break into heart-rending cries of grief.

Jesus may also be addressing those whose empathy for the poor brings them to reach out to them and weep for their plight; precisely this action is attested in Job 30:25; Sir 7:34; Tob 13:14; *T. Zeb.* 7:4.[19] The beatitude, then, could also address those so alive to God's concern for the afflicted that they weep for them and act in solidarity with them. This interpretation corresponds to Paul's paraenesis to "wail with those who wail" in his exposition of the Christian ethics of the Sermon in Rom 12:14-21.[20] In that case the compassion of Christians for those who weep, and the action that flows from that compassion, would bring to laughter here and hereafter those whom God liberates.

---

[17] English readers might suppose that "mourning," as a more general and less extroverted expression than "wailing," might be more common in the LXX. But in fact πενθεῖν occurs only 67x in the LXX, compared to 145x for κλαίειν.

[18] In view of this frequency, Hans Dieter Betz's gratuitous assertion in *The Sermon on the Mount: A Commentary on the Sermon on the Mount, Including the Sermon on the Plain (Matthew 5:3–7:27 and Luke 6:20-49)*, ed. Adela Yarbro Collins. Hermeneia (Minneapolis: Fortress, 1995) 577 that the κλαίειν of the beatitude cannot mean lamenting for the dead is strange.

[19] Solidarity with humans in need is praised in Philo, *Jos.* 94; *T. Iss.* 7:7; *T. Zeb.* 6:5; 7:3; *T. Jos.* 17:7. For examples from later rabbinic writers see Billerbeck 3:298. Modern psychology finds those who weep healthy, since they can enter into painful realities of human life, their own and others'.

[20] Paul expects that when one member of Christ's body suffers, all suffer (1 Cor 12:26//Rom 12:4-8). Dale Allison, "The Pauline Epistles and the Synoptic Gospels: The Pattern of the Parallels," *NTS* 28 (1982) 11–12 demonstrates the relationship of the chief part of this paraenesis to the central section of the Sermon on the Plain (12:14//Luke 6:28; 12:17//Luke 6:27-36; 12:21//Luke 6:27-36).

Γελάσετε likewise is the powerful expression of intense emotion. Classical Greek has only two main verbs for "to laugh," γελᾶν and καχάζειν, both usually used in the sense of "to laugh at scornfully; to deride, jeer at." Only γελᾶν occurs in the LXX (just 18x, and the noun γέλως 21x), to translate either *ṣḥq* or *śḥq*. In most of these cases the laughter is scornful and derisive (Jer 20:7-8; Lam 3:14; Ezek 23:32; Job 17:6; 22:19; Ps 2:4), especially over a fallen enemy (Jer 48:26, 39; Lam 1:7; Ps 52:6; Job 8:21; 22:19), or at least sharply ironical (Gen 17:17; 18:12, 13, 15).[21] Some exegetes find this sense coherent with the woe in 6:25, but not with the beatitude.

But other OT uses express only the beatitude's intense joy of deliverance. When the Lord restored the fortunes of Zion, "then our mouth was filled with laughter,[22] and our tongue with shouts of joy" (Ps 126:2). Qoheleth 3:4 expresses the very dyad the beatitude expresses: "a time to wail and a time to laugh."[23] And so again Lukan use in context will be our best guide.

Luke 6:21, 25 are the only two instances of γελᾶν in the NT.[24] If one were to interpret γελάσετε in context with the Reign of God and the being filled of 6:20, 21, then it could only mean the explosion of mirth and joy of one delivered from a miserable situation into a place where all is harmonious, peaceful, and pleasurable.[25] In that case, as κλαίειν expresses a response to intense misery, γελᾶν expresses not vaunting triumph but the mirthful and joyous consolation of those who follow Jesus' way of the cross through death to resurrection.

3. *The Fourth Beatitude* (6:22-23)

6:22a: Μακάριοί ἐστε ὅταν μισήσωσιν ὑμᾶς οἱ ἄνθρωποι. "Blessed are you when people hate you." This beatitude's different form reveals a different *Sitz im Leben* from the other three,[26] probably the early

---

[21] At least since Freud researchers have found that a great deal of mirth in most societies is built on paradox or irony which is at the expense of someone or some group.

[22] RSV: the Hebrew text has *śᵉhôq,* translated by χαρᾶς in the LXX.

[23] Other non-derisive uses of laughter: Gen 21:6; Job 29:24; 1 Esdr 4:31; perhaps Dan 14:7, 19.

[24] James 4:9 has the single use of γέλως in the NT, and it seems to carry the notion of the scornful (or at least heedless) laughter of the wicked.

[25] Schürmann, *Lukasevangelium* 332 sees here an explosive release of surprised laughter at the moment of liberation.

[26] In both Matt 5:11-12 and Luke 6:22-23 the form is much longer, with χάρητε instead of the short causal form with ὅτι, and the full second-person direct address μακάριοί ἐστε. This similarity between Matthew and Luke indicates that this separate beatitude was probably added to the other three before or in the process of the redaction of Q. For the separate *Sitz im Leben* of this beatitude see Rudolf Bultmann, *The History of the Synoptic*

church's experience of rejection and persecution by outsiders, ἄνθρωποι.[27] Ὅταν + subjunctive, "whenever," refers to actions that may be done frequently; both Matt 5:11 and Luke 6:22 have the aorist subjunctive, referring to individual acts.

Μισεῖν· Although the syntax and phraseology of Luke 6:22//Matt 5:11 are very similar, only ὀνειδίσωσιν of the four verbs in Luke 6:22 is found in Matt 5:11. Both evangelists have considerably reworked the original text, and so μισεῖν must be interpreted in the light of Luke's own structure, especially in view of its upcoming use in 6:27. In Greek literature it signifies the opposite of loving.[28] In the LXX μισεῖν translates six different Hebrew roots, predominantly *snʾ*, signifying human aversion and hostility. Particularly significant for us are the notions that (1) God hates various things, such as idol worship (Deut 12:31), empty cult (Amos 5:21), wickedness in all its forms (Prov 8:13) and all who do it (Prov 6:16-19; Sir 12:6); (2) the righteous hate what God hates (Ps 97:10; Amos 5:15), in the sense of loving the good and avoiding evil (Mic 3:2); (3) the wicked hate God (Pss 68:1; 83:2) and those who follow his ways (Pss 18:17; 25:19; 35:19; Isa 66:5).

Use (3) lies closest to the meaning of Luke 6:22. Throughout biblical history the godless one hates the just and attacks them as enemies: Abel (Gen 4:4-8), Joseph (Gen 37:12-18), the Israelites (Ps 105:24-25), the prophets (1 Kings 22:8), YHWH's anointed king (Pss 18:17; 21:8), the just ones of the Psalms (Pss 18:17; 25:19; 35:19; 38:18-20). The psalmist accepts rebuke from the just but prays not to be anointed by the wicked (Ps 141:5). Closest linguistically to the beatitude's own usage is Isa 66:5, in which YHWH's punishment will come upon those "observant" ones (66:3) whom YHWH describes as "Your brethren who *hate you* and *cast you out for my name's sake* (MT)."[29] This enmity of the unjust for the righteous finds classical expression in Wis 2:12-20, where the godless exploiters kill the son of God (2:13, 16) because his virtuous way of life reproves their

---

Tradition (New York: Harper & Row, 1963) 110, 127; T. W. Manson, *The Sayings of Jesus* (London: S.C.M., 1937) 49; Schürmann, *Lukasevangelium* 335–36.

[27] Ἄνθρωποι here signifies those outside of the community, whether Gentile or Jew, and in this case hostile; Alexander Sand, "*anthrōpos,*" *EDNT* 1:101–102; see the notes and explanation on 6:23.

[28] In Greek thought the gods can hate one either for doing evil or because of blind fate. By the Hellenistic era Epictetus teaches that human hatred can and should be overcome (*Diss.* I, 18,9; II, 22,34); Otto Michel, "μισέω," *TDNT* 4:683–84.

[29] The LXX may have a different *Vorlage.* Claus Westermann sees two factions within post-exilic Israel, perhaps even neighbors in the same villages, in *Isaiah 40–66* (Philadelphia: Westminster, 1966) 416. As in the beatitude, the reason for the hatred and the effect of the expulsion are not clear.

own (2:14-15), and he reproaches them for sins against the Law (2:12-13). The same idea is expressed differently in Isa 52:13–53:12; Psalm 22.

Lukan usage is quite varied. In 1:71 Zechariah expects the new age to achieve Israel's redemption from enemies who hate them (1:71).[30] Luke twice uses "hatred" in the peculiar Semitic sense of not choosing, preferring something else (14:26; 16:13).[31] The closest uses to Luke 6:22, 27 are 19:14, where Jesus' parable depicts those who hate him and reject his rule over them, and 21:17 where Jesus speaks of the persecutions his disciples will undergo from Jews and Gentiles before the destruction of the Temple. They can be hated because they are of God's people (1:71), because they are of Christ (19:14), or especially because they are destined for persecution by their allegiance to Christ (21:17). A more precise meaning of μισεῖν will depend on the context, the other verbs associated with the disciples' being hated in 6:22b-23.

6:22b: ὅταν ἀφορίσωσιν ὑμᾶς καὶ ὀνειδίσωσιν καὶ ἐκβάλωσιν τὸ ὄνομα ὑμῶν ὡς πονηρὸν ἕνεκα τοῦ υἱοῦ τοῦ ἀνθρώπου, "when they shun and revile you, and defame you because of the Son of Man." Luke now adds three verbs in a parallel ὅταν clause to specify this hatred. Ἀφορίζειν has no appropriate Greek, OT, or NT clarification of its meaning. In the OT its primary use is for ritual separation for purity: in Ezra 6:21 the community returned from exile separated itself from the impure, and this separation from the lawless for ritual purity is dominant in the OT and Qumran literature.[32] Closer to our beatitude is Isa 66:5, which speaks of the wicked *hating* the good and *ostracizing* them, though this separation is probably not a formal act of excommunication.[33] The verb *ndi* becomes a *terminus technicus* for formal discipline in rabbinic literature,[34] but this stem is never translated in the LXX by ἀφορίζειν.

---

[30] This canticle most probably refers to liberation from all the forms of hostility suffered by Israel throughout history; in Luke this includes hope for the community's liberation from its persecutors.

[31] Otto Michel, *TDNT* 4:690–91 and the explanation of Deut 21:15 on 685.

[32] Isaiah 52:11 (cited in 2 Cor 6:17); 56:3; *Jub.* 22:16, etc.; 1QS 5:1, 10, 18; 8:11, 13; 9:5, 9, 20; CD 6:14; 7:3, etc. Note how far apart are the inclusiveness for the foreigner and *mutilé* of Isa 56:3 and the ritual separation of Ezra 6:21.

[33] John L. McKenzie, *Second Isaiah*. AB 20 (Garden City, N.Y.: Doubleday, 1968) 208–209 finds no evidence of a formal split. The prophet seems to have considered the leaders of the people an impious lot who have made life miserable for those who hear his word. Such divisions in the post-exilic community occur also in Zech 7:8-14; Mal 3:5-18, but they do not issue in ostracism.

[34] Douglas R. A. Hare, *The Theme of Jewish Persecution of Christians in the Gospel according to St. Matthew* (Cambridge: Cambridge University Press, 1967) 49–53, thinks *nidduy* was a measure aimed at achieving uniformity of doctrine among the Pharisees rather than a ban levied on members of the community.

In the NT ἀφορίζειν primarily means to set persons apart for missionary work (Acts 13:2; Rom 1:1; Gal 1:15); it also means to separate oneself from an impure environment (Gal 2:12; 2 Cor 6:17; perhaps Acts 19:9, without cultic overtones). Although there is no use of ἀφορίζειν meaning "excommunicate" in the NT, scholars used to refer to the ἀποσυνάγωγος of John 9:22; 12:42; 16:2 as an instance of the synagogue ban of the *Birkath-ha-minim*.[35] In light of closer historical investigation this now seems unlikely.[36] It is possible that families excluded or disowned members who converted to Christianity, but Luke 12:49-53 seems rather to speak of continuing strife *within* the family. Thus Jesus in 6:22 probably means exclusion as the worldwide informal process of shunning people for a position or virtue not commonly held or considered threatening to the unity of any given community. Such alienation from one's family, tribe, neighbors, and roots is a far greater attack on the integrity of the first-century dyadic personality than it is on the individuals of contemporary society.[37]

Ὀνειδίσωσιν, from a root meaning "to revile," means "to blame, disgrace, abuse;" its correlative noun ὀνειδισμός means "object of shame, disgrace, reproach." In the LXX both the verb and the noun translate five different Hebrew roots, mostly *ḥrp*, "to reproach" for sin. God reproaches humans for sin, and the sinner's disobedience reviles God.[38] Most relevant to 6:22 is the OT description of the shame heaped on the good, the individuals who observe God's laws (Pss 22:7; 42:10; 69:6-9; 102:8; 119:42; Jer 24:9; 25:9; 51:51) and Israel, whose punishment by God makes it an object of reproach by the nations (Pss 44:13-16; 74:10, 18; 79:12; 89:51;

---

[35] In Judaism one can speak of separation from synagogue worship and/or separation from the social community; François Bovon, *Das Evangelium nach Lukas*. 2 vols. to date. EKK 31/1-2 (Zürich: Benziger; Neukirchen-Vluyn: Neukirchener Verlag, 1989, 1996) 1:303, and the bibliography cited there. Commentators such as M.-J. Lagrange and Alfred Loisy favor an informal shunning process.

[36] Evidence that Jews levied this ban against Christians is indirect; see Ronald R. Kimelman, "*Birkat Ha-Minim* and the Lack of Evidence for an Anti-Christian Jewish Prayer in Late Antiquity," in E. P. Sanders, ed., *Jewish and Christian Self-Definition*. 2 vols. (Philadelphia: Fortress, 1981), vol. 2, *Aspects of Judaism in the Graeco-Roman Period* 226–44, especially 234–36. Even William Horbury, who argues for the existence of such an exclusionary prayer in "The Benediction of the Minim and Early Jewish-Christian Controversy," *JTS* 33 (1982) 19–61, thinks that Luke 6:22 refers only to a generally expected exclusion. In any case, if such a *Birkat Ha-Minim* took effect ca. 85 C.E. it would not have been early enough to have influenced this beatitude already formulated in Q.

[37] On the dyadic personality in the pre-industrial world, see Bruce J. Malina, *The New Testament World: Insights from Cultural Anthropology* (Atlanta: John Knox, 1981; rev. ed. 1993) 51–60.

[38] Johannes Schneider, "ὄνειδος," *TDNT* 4:238–39.

Isa 52:7; Tob 3:1-6). Ultimately the prophets offer the most striking example of this revilement (Jer 15:15; 20:8), although ὀνειδίζεσθαι is rarely used of them.[39]

In the NT Jesus is reviled and despised in his Passion (Mark 15:32//Matt 27:44; Rom 15:3, citing Ps 69:9).[40] His disciples experienced the same fate (Heb 10:33). Especially apposite is the paraenesis in 1 Pet 4:14, where the author, explicitly arguing that if Christ suffered in this way, so must the brethren (4:1,13), joins ὀνειδίζεσθε and μακάριοι, and has ἐν ὀνόματι Χριστοῦ, functionally equivalent to ἕνεκα τοῦ υἱοῦ τοῦ ἀνθρώπου (Matt 5:11, ἐμοῦ), just as does Luke 6:22//Matt 5:11.[41] Acts 5:41 expressed the same notion by ἀτιμασθῆναι: the apostles rejoice (χαίροντες) that they have been dishonored for the Name. These "face to face insults"[42] seem to be a regular part of disciples' fate, as living the word of YHWH exposed the people of God and its prophets to mockery and scorn in the OT. Again, we need to remember how devastating is such reviling in an honor-shame culture.

The awkwardness of ἐκβάλλειν τὸ ὄνομα ὡς πονηρὸν was formerly thought to be due to an Aramaic substrate,[43] but the verbal phrase is found in classical Greek texts (BAGD 237) meaning "to repudiate your name as evil."[44] Luke gives no clues to the meaning of this singular clause. James 2:7 speaks of the wealthy and powerful reviling the good (Christian) name, but this is not an adversarial process. In short, we do not know to what action this expression refers.[45] It is part of the general shaming process so far described.

---

[39] Ὀνειδίζω as a *Geschickverb* is used to describe the fate of the prophets in 1 Enoch 103:4; 108:10; 1 QpHab 10:13; Odil Hannes Steck, *Israel und das gewaltsame Geschick der Propheten.* WMANT 23 (Neukirchen-Vluyn: Neukirchener Verlag, 1967) 258 n. 1.

[40] Luke 23:39 substitutes ἐβλασφήμει for ὀνειδίζων; Luke also omits the mocking of Jesus at the crowning with thorns.

[41] Note that the χάρητε of Luke 6:23//Matt 5:12 is also echoed by χαίρετε in 1 Pet 4:13. Probably Peter has received some form of the Q beatitudes; this is confirmed by the resemblance between 1 Pet 3:14 and Matt 5:10; see Paul J. Achtemeier, *1 Peter.* Hermeneia (Minneapolis: Fortress, 1996) 308 for a discerning discussion.

[42] Douglas R. A. Hare, *Persecution* 118.

[43] הוֹצִיא שֵׁם רַע = "to publish an evil name concerning, to defame" (Deut 22:14; *m. Sota* 3:5); Julius Wellhausen, *Das Evangelium Lucae* (Berlin: Reimer, 1904) 24; Matthew Black, *An Aramaic Approach to the Gospels and Acts* (London: Oxford, 1967) 135–36; Jacques Dupont, *Beatitudes* 1:232–36. According to them the Lukan phrase, as the *lectio difficilior,* would have been originally in Q, and Matt 5:11 εἴπωσιν πᾶν πονηρὸν καθ' ὑμῶν would be a simplification.

[44] Similar phrases occur in Num 14:36-37; Deut 22:19. For the translation of πονηρός as (morally) evil see the comment on 6:45b.

[45] Some think of making one's name into a formal curse word (Billerbeck 2:159), but they adduce no evidence; others think of an exorcism formula (Johnson, *Luke* 107), also without evidence.

In the Bible, ὄνομα signifies one's personal identity.[46] But the name counted as evil is not the individual names of the disciples (which would then have been in the plural), but their common name "Christian" (Acts 11:26).[47] This seems confirmed by the following phrase ἕνεκα τοῦ υἱοῦ τοῦ ἀνθρώπου,[48] the name Jesus uses for himself twenty-five times in Luke.[49] Insofar as it is used in descriptions and predictions of Jesus' suffering and resurrection (9:22, 44; 17:24-25; 18:31), the disciples in this beatitude may be reviled for proclaiming and living the life of death and resurrection that all the beatitudes imply and the following love command entails. In any case, this phrase roots the cause of the persecution in the Christian's faith.[50]

What, then, do being hated, excluded, reproached, and reviled mean to Luke's community? In Appendix D I have surveyed the words for persecution used in the NT itself. No single expression or combination of terms describes an official persecution of the church, either by Romans or by Jews. What seems described is the reaction of groups[51] to the preaching

---

[46] Hans Bietenhard, "ὄνομα," *TDNT* 5:242-83.

[47] We have some evidence of the bad reputation of Christians as "haters of the human race" (Tacitus, Ann. 15.44), "atheists" (Dio Cass., 67.14), given to a mischievous superstition (Suetonius, *Nero* XVI, 2). In Acts 19:9 the evil reputation is ascribed to the Way.

[48] Paul Schanz, *Commentar über das Evangelium des heiligen Lukas* (Tübingen: Franz Fues, 1883) 222, and other commentators. But the argument is not conclusive, for one's own personal name could be vilified because of one's identification with the (hated) Christians.

[49] It is used especially in his rejection, or at least in his historical life on earth (Fitzmyer, *Luke* 635). I prescind from the controverted question of whether and how the historical Jesus used the "title," except to agree with I. Howard Marshall, "The Synoptic Son of Man Sayings in Recent Discussion," *NTS* 12 (1964) 327–51 that the positions taken by historical critics have depended almost entirely upon their presuppositions. For the meaning of the title see the exhaustive article by Carsten Colpe, "ὁ υἱὸς τοῦ ἀνθρώπου," *TDNT* 8:400–77. As to Luke's literary use of the title, I agree with the two principal points of Jack Dean Kingsbury's "Excursus: Jesus' use of "the Son of Man," in his *Conflict in Luke* (Minneapolis: Fortress, 1991) 73–78: "Son of Man" applies only to Jesus in Luke, and is a mysterious title whose meaning only Jesus reveals and reflects on as the gospel story unfolds. However, his assumption that there was no "content" or background significance for the title deriving from Daniel 7 cannot be correct. "Son of Man" in Luke-Acts means not only "this man," but also has resonances of the apocalyptic judge of Daniel 7 (Acts 7:56; Luke 11:30; 12:8, 40; 17:22-30; 18:8; 21:27, 36; 22:69), also in his human ministry (Luke 5:24; 6:5; 7:34; 9:58; 22:48) and in his suffering, dying, and rising as the Servant of YHWH (Luke 9:22, 44; 18:31; 22:22; 24:7).

[50] This might be true of the preceding three beatitudes: not every poor, hungry, mourning, and persecuted person is blessed, but rather those who are so because of their faith in the Son of Man, and the actions they take based on that faith.

[51] Acts 19:23-34 shows that for Luke it was not only Jews who took hostile action against the Christian preachers.

of the Gospel as a disturbing of the established order, or as the promotion of a heterodox opinion. The reaction was violent, and it sometimes used the institutions of the state (imprisonment, beatings, formal accusations, even execution), but it was essentially *ad hoc*. The terms Jesus uses in 6:22, except for the occasional use of the generic μισεῖν and ὀνειδίζειν, do not recur in the rest of the NT to describe the hostilities Christians endure. So, rather than see any of them as *termini technici* for persecution that forms the condition of the beatitude I see them as indicators of the obloquy, hostility, and disenfranchisement suffered by those who live the authentic Christian life in an evil world. Thus the index of misery reaches its climax in social isolation, which makes real and intensifies the preceding three miserable conditions of the disciples. The next verse will enable us to check this tentative conclusion.

6:23a: χάρητε ἐν ἐκείνῃ τῇ ἡμέρᾳ καὶ σκιρτήσατε, "rejoice on that day and leap for joy." Two imperatives now dramatically reinforce the μακάριοι of 6:22a. "Rejoice!" sums up the response not only to this beatitude, but possibly also to the preceding three.

Χαίρειν, "to rejoice, exult" is used only 116x in the LXX, but 140x in the NT. In the LXX it translates *šmḥ,* a term originally used in the Canaanite cult.[52] It is used in the Hebrew cult (Pss 33; 95; 1 Sam 6:13; 2 Sam 6:12, etc.), but its main usage is in response to YHWH's saving work (Pss 5:11; 9:2; 16:9; 33:1; 40:16, etc.), including the Law (Ps 119:14) and the Word of God (Jer 15:16). It is especially at home in the oracles of salvation. Deutero-Isaiah expresses the joy of the return from exile in eschatological terms (Isa 35:10; 51:11; 65:18) and χαίρειν is often used of the joy of the eschaton (Pss 14:7 [= 53:6]; 126:2, 5-6; Isa 9:3; 25:9; 65:17-19; 66:14; Zeph 3:14-17; 1QS 4:7; 1QH 18:15). Joy is also the reward for human fidelity to the Law in Isa 65:13-14; Prov 10:28, both of which have strong resonances with the beatitudes. The OT has no instance of joy *in* suffering, but the theme is developed in intertestamental Judaism (2 Macc 6:28-30; 4 Macc 10:20; 2 Bar 52:5-7).[53]

In the NT the verb sometimes has the secular meaning "Greetings" (Jas 1:1); otherwise it expresses joy in God's salvific work, as does the noun χάρα. In Luke-Acts the verb has the meaning of "greetings" or secular joy only in Luke 22:5; 23:8; Acts 15:23; 23:36. It describes the human response to God's saving work in Luke 1:14, 28 (the conceptions of John

---

[52] Paul Humbert, "'Laetari et exultare' dans le vocabulaire religieux de l'Ancien Testament," *RHPR* 22 (1942) 185–214. Perhaps for that reason, εὐφραίνειν is used approximately four times as frequently as χαίρειν in the LXX.

[53] See these and perhaps less convincing citations in W. Nauch, "Freude im Leiden: Zum Problem in der urchristlichen Verfolgungstradition," *ZNW* 46 (1955) especially 73–76.

and Jesus) and 10:20 (cf. 10:17); 13:17 (the miraculous works of the disciples and Jesus). The parabolic joy over finding the lost (15:5, 32) refers to the same divine salvation as Zacchaeus' joy in hosting Jesus (19:6). The joy of messianic fulfillment underlies the disciples' joy over the entry of their king into Jerusalem (Luke 19:37) and Jesus explicitly tells his disciples that real joy is having their names inscribed in heaven (10:20). In Acts the word usually refers to joy that the Gentiles receive salvation (8:39; 11:23; 13:48; 15:23, 31). However, in Acts 5:41 the disciples rejoice at suffering *dishonor* for *the name,* and the same idea occurs in different words in 16:25; 21:13-14.[54] Against this background χάρητε in 6:23 must refer to joy at God's being present in the suffering, as is indicated by the aorist imperative[55] and the ἐν ἐκείνῃ τῇ ἡμέρᾳ. "On that day" throughout the prophets refers to the eschatological Day of the Lord, and so it does in Luke 10:12; 17:31; 21:34.[56] But the clear present temporal reference again reinforces the eschatological depths of the present in Luke-Acts.

Σκιρτήσατε, "to leap with joy" occurs only seven times in the LXX, mostly of mountains and animals (Ps 114:4, 6; Mal 4:2)! In the NT it occurs only in Luke 1:41, 44 (= Gen 25:22); 6:23.[57] It is as strongly expressive of exuberant emotion as κλαίειν is of distressed emotion.[58] Given its LXX background of leaping animals and mountains, σκιρτήσατε may well depict graphically the disciples' dancing participation in the salvific joy of animals and the whole cosmos.

6:23b: ἰδοὺ γὰρ ὁ μισθὸς ὑμῶν πολὺς ἐν τῷ οὐρανῷ, "for behold, your reward is great in heaven." Ἰδοὺ γάρ is graphic,[59] stronger than ὅτι,

---

[54] Joy in suffering is itself a NT theme; see Edward G. Selwyn, *The First Epistle of St. Peter* (London: Macmillan, 1947) 439–58, who finds a persecution fragment or persecution form in Matt 5:11-12//Luke 6:22-23; 1 Pet 1:4-6; 4:13-14; Jas 1:2, 12; Heb 10:32-36. Even if one does not find a catechetical or paraenetic *oral form* here, the theme recurs in a regular *Gestalt.*

[55] Matthew 5:12 has a present imperative. All but one of the uses of χαίρειν in Luke-Acts refer to joy *now,* as God's eschatological salvation at work now; this is the present experience of the disciples who suffer for Christ in Acts 5:21; 16:25; 21:13-14.

[56] And so Betz, *Sermon* 582, among others, opts for its apocalyptic meaning here and throughout the beatitudes; contrary Fitzmyer, *Luke* 625.

[57] Betz, *Sermon* 583 notes that since the *skirtoi* were satyrs whose bizarre dances were depicted on vases and walls, Luke's readers would have been vastly amused by this reference. I doubt Luke's readers were so sophisticated. Closer, but still speculative, is Jeremias' reference to the leaping of the men's dance after a feast; see the citations in Schürmann, *Lukasevangelium* 334.

[58] As Erich Klostermann points out (*Das Lukasevangelium.* HNT 2:1 [Tübingen: J.C.B. Mohr (Paul Siebeck), 1919] 79), it is more graphic than the ἀγαλλίασθε of Matt 5:12. I think it too graphic for hendiadys, or rhetorical fullness.

[59] Ἰδοὺ enlivens a narrative by alerting readers and by calling them to think; BAGD 370–71.

conveying an element of surprise proportionate to the paradoxical nature of the beatitudes. Still, the γάρ, no less than ὅτι, gives the reason for the preceding commands.

Μισθός is reward for work, a fee, payment. The notion of God as the rewarder of good and the punisher of evil occurs in Greek literature from the time of Homer, but in the OT it is much more deeply rooted in the justice of God. With the development in apocalyptic literature of a notion of an afterlife, reward for human fidelity is often eschatologically awaited ἐν οὐρανῷ (*Tg. Num.* 23:23). Nowhere, however, is this idea so fully and regularly expressed as in Jesus' own teaching and the subsequent NT writings.[60] In NT usage μισθός has both secular and religious uses. In Luke 10:32 the seventy-two are called worthy of their wages (= their daily upkeep); in Acts 1:18 Judas' thirty pieces of silver are the reward of his wickedness; but in Luke 6:35 Jesus promises a great reward to the disciples who love their enemies. Beyond the use of μισθός itself, the concept of divine reward for the disciples' faith is frequently implied, always disproportionate to human expectation of exchange.[61]

Ἐν τῷ οὐρανῷ:[62] In the NT οὐρανός refers to the whole range of its OT uses. Of Luke's eighteen instances only four occur in the plural (10:20; 12:33; 18:22; 21:26) and the first three of these speak of treasure or reward in heaven. Besides referring simply to the sky or to the God of heaven and earth, in Luke it denotes the place of angels (2:13, 15; 10:18), of apocalyptic revelation (3:21-22), the abode of God (9:16, 54; 11:2, 16; 15:7; 18:13), and so the place of reward for the good (6:23; 10:20; 12:33; 18:22; 19:38; 24:51).

In the context of repeated acts of enmity, which include hatred, ostracism, and slander, the disciples are not offered hope of peace on this earth as a reward for their constancy in discipleship. Rather, the shadow of the cross hangs over them too (9:23-26; 21:12-19), and so the reward Jesus offers them is the reward he experiences in Luke-Acts, the resurrection to

---

[60] Reward has been little researched by exegetes. One of the best surveys is still the excursus "Der Lohngedanke im Judentum und in der Lehre Jesu," in Josef Schmid, *Das Evangelium nach Matthäus* (Regensburg: Pustet, 1959) 287–94. See also Morton Smith, *Tannaitic Parallels to the Gospels*. JBLMS 6 (Philadelphia: S.B.L., 1968) 49–73.

[61] Luke 5:6, 24-26; 6:35, 38; 7:41; 8:8; 10:20-24; 11:13; 12:22-34, 37-38, 44; 13:18-21; 14:14; 18:14, 29-30; 19:17; 21:28; 22:28-30; 23:34, 39-43.

[62] In Greek literature οὐρανός occurs only in the singular, referring to the sky; in mythological thought it is the abode of the gods. The OT develops the notion of heaven as the abode of God and the place of salvation. Of its 667 uses in the LXX, only 51 are in the plural, probably representing the plural form of *šāmayîm;* cf. Hellmut Traub and Gerhard von Rad, "οὐρανός," *TDNT* 5:497–511.

eternal life (9:22, 24; 18:33; 24:7, 26, 46) that is ascension to the heaven (24:51; Acts 1:9-11) where their treasure is (10:20; 12:33; 18:22).[63]

6:23c: κατὰ τὰ αὐτὰ γὰρ ἐποίουν τοῖς προφήταις οἱ πατέρες αὐτῶν, "for their ancestors treated the prophets in the same way." The γὰρ now explains how they can be sure of this great reward. Their being mistreated even by Jewish leaders does not mean they are wrong or bad: their Jewish ancestors treated the God-sent prophets just the same way.[64] Jesus implies that the just God has greatly rewarded those mistreated prophets. Κατὰ τὰ αὐτὰ ἐποίουν is Lukan style (6:26; 17:30; Acts 14:1) meaning "just the same way," equivalent to οὕτως in Matt 5:12. Οἱ πατέρες αὐτῶν is confusing: the αὐτῶν could refer to the prophets or to οἱ ἄνθρωποι of 6:22a. But it was not the prophets' ancestors (οἱ πατέρες αὐτῶν), but their contemporaries, who mistreated them. If the pronoun refers to all humans, then Luke's Jesus is saying that all nations persecute their own prophets. In the flow of thought οἱ ἄνθρωποι (6:22a) leaves the identity of the persecutors open to both Jew and Gentile, as was the experience of Luke's community, but the experience of the Jewish prophets was better known to his readers and served as a clearer example of the persecutors being wrong and the persecuted being right.

Τοῖς προφήταις: Especially in the deuteronomistic history the fate of the prophets is persecution, even death.[65] The specific actions against the prophets are that their words are ignored (2 Kings 17:14; Jer 18:18; Ezek 33:31-32; Zech 7:8-14); they are despised and scoffed at (2 Chr 36:15-16; Isa 50:6; Jer 20:7-8), persecuted (1 Kings 19:10, 14; Jer 15:15; 17:18), formally denounced (Jer 20:10), their life sought (1 Kings 18:4, 13; 19:10, 14; Jer 11:9; 18:23), beaten (1 Kings 22:24; Isa 50:6; *Lev. R.* 10:2), imprisoned (1 Kings 22:27), killed (2 Chr 24:19-22; Neh 9:26; Jer 2:30; 26:20-24; Lam 2:20; Jos., Ant. 9.13,2; *Pes. R.* 138a). Luke has this before his eyes in Acts 7:52: τίνα τῶν προφητῶν οὐκ ἐδίωξαν οἱ πατέρες ὑμῶν;

---

[63] Ernest F. Tittle has it right: those who are true disciples of Jesus must suffer his prophetic fate in an evil world; *The Gospel According to Luke* (New York: Harper, 1951) 63.

[64] Frederick W. Danker, *Jesus and the New Age* (rev. ed. Philadelphia: Fortress, 1988) points out the situation: the Pharisees would surely claim that the disciples' poverty and other sufferings were merely the consequences of their breaking faith with Israel.

[65] The classic exposition is that of Steck, *Geschick,* who finds a fourfold pattern explaining the disobedience of Israel as the cause of the historical judgments of 722 and 586: (1) Israel's constant disobedience evokes (2) God's patience in sending the prophets to warn them; (3) Israel mistreats the prophets and rejects their message, which (4) calls down divine punishment on Israel. Steck finds the origin of the pattern in Neh 9:26, and its tradents in the Levitic traditions of the northern kingdom, and argues that it has influenced Palestinian Judaism, the NT, the rabbinic tradition, and the Qu'ran.

"which of the prophets did your ancestors not persecute?" Indeed, only Luke has all the synoptic passages in which Jesus sees this theme of opposition to the prophet fulfilled in his own person:

> **4:24** (//Mark 6:4; Matt 13:57; John 4:44), the prophet without honor;
>
> **11:47-48** (//Matt 23:29-31), the scribes building the tombs of the slain prophets;
>
> **11:49-51** (//Matt 23:34-36), this generation climaxes all the killings of prophets;
>
> **13:13b**, no prophet dies outside Jerusalem;
>
> **13:34-35** (//Matt 23:37-39), Jerusalem is reproached for killing the prophets.[66]

In all these passages opposition to the prophets is depicted as sinful opposition to God's will, and so the opposition of religious leaders to Jesus is portrayed as part of a pattern of sin, which the prophet Jesus is sent to overcome.

Consequently, the fourth beatitude conceives of the disciples as part of the prophetic movement that Jesus inaugurates. (Indeed, they are poor, hungry, and wailing partly because of this unsystematic opposition to their words and actions.) The beatitude speaks of the constant opposition Christians must bear if they take up the way of life proclaimed by the beatitudes and the rest of the Sermon. This way of life is a prophetic word against the world wherever Christians find themselves, and they will reap the same reward as did the Son of Man on whose account they suffer these attacks. The reward promised them is the joy of eschatological salvation (χάρητε) and cosmic exuberance (σκιρτήσατε), which Jesus is already experiencing in heaven and which is promised those who walk in his steps.

Jesus now turns to those who provide such opposition: the rich, the satiated, the merrymakers, whether these be outsiders or among the disciples themselves.

The Woes (6:24-26)

If the Sermon was originally addressed to both disciples and outsiders (Luke 6:17-19), it is possible that the woes were directed more to the outsiders. But Luke gives no indication that they were addressed to a different audience than that of the beatitudes.[67] In Luke's own situation the rich are "why the immediate enjoyment of the blessings that were promised

---

[66] The theme occurs also in 1 Thess 2:15; Rom 11:3; Jas 5:10; Heb 11:35-38.

[67] Many of the modern commentators, perceiving in the Ἀλλὰ ὑμῖν λέγω τοῖς ἀκούουσιν of 6:27 a shift back to the disciples as audience of 6:20-23, think of the rich, etc. of the woes as absent, addressed in an apostrophe that clarifies for the disciples the dangers

for the New Age (see 1:46-55 and 68-70 [6:20-23]) has not been realized in anticipated measure."[68] Since the woes correlate with the language and structure of the beatitudes,[69] our exegesis can now proceed more swiftly.

1. *The First Woe* (6:24a): Πλὴν οὐαὶ ὑμῖν τοῖς πλουσίοις, "But woe to you rich."

Πλὴν, an adversative conjunction, "but, nevertheless,"[70] is Lukan (sixty-one per cent of NT usage), probably due here to Lukan redaction. When it begins a sentence in Luke it strongly reverses, rather than modifies, the previous sentence or block of material.[71] Since it always joins to the preceding thought, it is unlikely that Jesus here addresses a different audience with different subject matter. The interjection οὐαὶ, "alas for, woe to," is an emphatic prophetic form, an *Unheilsankündigung* that serves as a warning, threat, last appeal to those who (already) stand under divine judgment.[72] It often occurs in series of woes (Isa 5:8-23; Hab 2:6-19; 1 Enoch 98:9–99:2, 11-16), and often in combination with blessings (Qoh 10:16-17; Tob 13:12-14; 1 Enoch 99:10-16; 2 Bar 10:6-7).

In the NT οὐαὶ is fairly common. By using the form, Jesus stamps himself as a prophet, warning cities (Matt 11:21//Luke 10:13), the world (Matt 18:7), individuals (Matt 18:7b//Luke 17:1), scribes and Pharisees (Matt 23:23-36//Luke 11:42-52). In all but one (21:23) of Luke's uses Jesus addresses a religious warning to those in danger of losing their religious selves, mostly for their opposition to his person and teaching. Seven times the warning is to his opponents, but twice outside of these uses in the Sermon Jesus addresses a woe to disciples (17:1; 22:22). Therefore Jesus appears in Luke 6:24-26 to be addressing disciples who are not living

---

from which they have been rescued. As Alfred Loisy, *L'Evangile selon Luc* (Paris: E. Noury, 1924) 201 and C. G. Montefiore, *The Synoptic Gospels,* 2 vols. (2nd rev. ed. New York: Ktav, 1968) 2:414 had pointed out, 6:26 raises contradictions to this position. Since there is no indication of such a shift in the text, I take 6:20-23, 24-26, 27-49 as addressed to one audience, the mixed crowd of disciples and crowds named in 6:17-19.

[68] Danker, *New Age* 142.

[69] Even Schürmann (*Lukasevangelium* 339–41), who maintains that the woes were in QMt, thinks their source lies in the early church's attempt to clarify the beatitudes for its own situations.

[70] Especially at the beginning of a sentence πλήν is used colloquially as a conjunction, BAGD 669. In Acts it is exclusively an improper preposition.

[71] The clearest exception is 10:14; 19:27 probably indicates a change of subject more than a reversal of thought; 13:33 could be a coordinating conjunction within the sentence.

[72] In the LXX it occurs 69x, translating *hôi* or *'ôi* or other words deriving from roots meaning "to howl." It occurs mostly in the prophets: Amos 5:18; 6:1; Hos 7:13; Isa 1:4-5; 10:5; 30:1; 33:1; Jer 23:1; Ezek 24:6, etc.; Erhard Gerstenberger, "The Woe-Oracles of the Prophets," *JBL* 81 (1962) 249–63.

out his teaching, and so are in danger of losing their religious selves. This is confirmed by the Sermon's concluding parable in 6:46-49.

Τοῖς πλουσίοις: As πτωχοί in 6:20 meant the economically poor, one expects its antithesis in the woe to refer to the economically wealthy. Both LXX and Lukan usage bear this out. Πλούσιος, πλοῦτος, πλουτεῖν, and πλουτίζειν occur some 180x in the LXX, translating a variety of Hebrew roots, but mostly *ʿšr*. In the OT, especially under the influence of the prophetic/covenant theology of retribution, wealth is a blessing of God bestowed on those who obey God's will (which is for prosperity for God's people).[73] So in times of social dislocation the prophets attack the rich for impoverishing the many. Wisdom literature reflects a more worldly attitude toward wealth: it is a blessing, coming from hard work and frugality, but it is also deceptive and can turn one from God. The views of later Judaism range from almost unqualified acceptance of it to ascetic rejection of it, depending on the variety of Judaism represented.[74] Πλούσιος itself is used about 53x in the LXX, almost always to translate *ʿašîr*. Whether the attitude to the rich is approving or condemnatory, the word always refers to the economically rich; there is no LXX usage of πλούσιος meaning "spiritually wealthy," nor does the adjective refer to God's enemies without reference to economic status.

Luke uses the word group oftener than all the evangelists, especially πλούσιος (thirty-nine per cent of NT usage). Many exegetes have claimed that the attitude of Luke-Acts toward the rich is mixed: while Jesus condemned the rich in the gospel, still, as he associated with the rich in his ministry, so did the community of Acts incorporate the rich, who continued to hold their private possessions.[75] While the centurion of Luke 7:1-10 is rich enough to build a synagogue and yet be praised for his faith, and Joseph of Arimathea can own a tomb and buy linen (23:50-54), these are all in the process of sharing their wealth. Jesus was frequently the guest of the well-to-do in Luke (5:29-32; 14:1-24; 19:5; 22:11, 14-38).[76] Luke's

---

[73] Abraham is the model of this (Gen 12:1-3; 13:2); the Deuteronomic tradition establishes it in the blessings and curses of the covenant (Deuteronomy 28) and traces it in the Deuteronomic History (see especially Judg 2:11-23); it occurs *passim* in the pre-exilic prophets.

[74] See the survey of Friedrich Hauck and Wilhelm Kasch, "πλοῦτος," *TDNT* 6:318–32.

[75] David P. Seccombe, *Possessions and the Poor in Luke-Acts*. SNTU, ser. B, 6 (Linz: A. Fuchs, 1982) not only argues the position but surveys others who hold it; see Luke T. Johnson, *Sharing Possessions: Mandate and Symbol of Faith* (Philadelphia: Fortress, 1981), whose first chapter points up all the *aporiae* in Luke-Acts' teaching on possessions.

[76] We have no idea of the wealth of the Pharisee who hosted him in 7:36, or of the wealth of Martha and Mary (10:38-42).

Jesus has no aversion to the rich; it is out of his love for them that he warns them of the peril presented by their riches. For the simple fact is that in Luke, riches always represent a bad thing, an obstacle to the Reign of God.

This basic attitude is clearly enunciated in Mary's canticle celebrating what her conception means: πεινῶντας ἐνέπλησεν ἀγαθῶν καὶ πλουτοῦντας ἐξαπέστειλεν κενούς (1:53),[77] exactly what Jesus proclaims here in 6:20, 24! The parable of the rich fool in 12:16-21 is a lesson against greed (12:15), hidden in the case of the young man who requests his help in 12:13, but quite obvious in Jesus' parable of the farmer whose only concern is to amass more wealth for his own ease in 12:17-21. Indeed, being rich toward God (εἰς θεὸν πλουτῶν) in 12:21 is interpreted in 12:33 as using one's wealth for the poor.[78]

In 14:12 Jesus suggests not using one's wealth to invite rich neighbors who can return the favor, but inviting the poor, so as to allow God to provide one's reward in the resurrection of the just (6:35b, 38d). The reciprocal circulation of wealth among the few rich is condemned. Again, the rich man in 16:1, if he represents God,[79] is one who wants debts forgiven (16:5-8a; cf. 6:30b, 34-35) and the goods of this world shared with the poor (16:9; cf. 6:30). Riches hoarded (μαμωνᾶ τῆς ἀδικίας) oppose God (16:13).

The parable of the rich man and Lazarus (16:19-31), thrice describing the man as πλούσιος, perfectly illustrates our woe. Nowhere does Abraham, speaking for Jesus in the parable, accuse the rich man of injustice. He is condemned simply because he had wealth in this world (16:25); in the next, the poor man is consoled (παρακαλεῖται), but the rich man is in pain. The woe is perfectly mirrored: οὐαὶ ὑμῖν τοῖς πλουσίοις, ὅτι ἀπέχετε τὴν παράκλησιν ὑμῶν!

Again in 18:23, 25 Jesus asserts that wealth is an insurmountable obstacle to entering the Reign of God.[80] For those who think that somehow God can bring a rich man into this Reign (18:27), Luke immediately provides an

---

[77] I take the aorists of 1:50-55 to describe what God has done in the conception of Jesus (1:49) and, from the standpoint of the evangelist, in his career.

[78] The middle term linking the giving of alms in 12:33 with being rich toward God in 12:21 is the use of θησαυρίζων in 12:21 and θησαυρός in 12:33, 34. These three of only five θησαυρός uses in Luke-Acts form an inclusion around a section that has to do with ascetical freedom from cares about one's food and clothing. Possession of the Kingdom (12:31-32) transmutes this concern into generous almsgiving (12:33), which makes permanent treasure, as opposed to private hoarding (12:21).

[79] L. John Topel, "On the Injustice of the Unjust Steward: Lk 16:1-13," *CBQ* 37 (1975) 216–27.

[80] "The largest of Palestinian animals is compared with the tiniest of commonly known openings" (Fitzmyer, *Luke* 1204). Fitzmyer rightly rejects attempts to reduce the impossiblity conveyed by the hyperbole.

example: Zacchaeus is the only rich man saved in Luke (19:1-10), and in the process he gives away his wealth (19:8), so as no longer to be rich.[81]

Finally, in 21:1 Jesus shows that the offerings of the rich are of little worth in comparison with the tiny offering of the poor widow. Thus Luke is perfectly consistent: no rich person is saved in the gospel,[82] and wealth is a positive hindrance to entering the Reign of God. That Luke does not explain the baldness of this equation has led commentators to adduce some reason for it. Our position is that the rich are not to become beggars (poverty is what Jesus' Reign of God removes), but so to share their wealth that there are no poor in the land.

6:24b: ὅτι ἀπέχετε τὴν παράκλησιν ὑμῶν,"because you have received your reward" gives the reason for the woe: the rich have had all the consolation they wanted. Ἀπέχειν, used in business transactions, indicates that one had received full payment of a debt, and so had no further claims on the debtor.[83] The rich, then, have concluded their bargain with God, comfort in this life; they have nothing more to claim.

Τὴν παράκλησιν: παρακαλεῖν in classical, LXX, and Koinē Greek means "to request, exhort, comfort." When the LXX translates a Hebrew original, the sense of *nhm,* "comfort," predominates; when there is no Hebrew original, "exhort, ask" are the meanings.[84] Especially relevant OT usage is God's consolation of Israel after the exile (Isa 40:1-2; 49:13; 51:3; 57:18), and the promise of eschatological consolation (Zech 1:13; Isa 61:1-2; 2 Bar 44:7).

---

[81] A recent exchange of articles recapitulates previous discussion and joins the main issues: Dennis Hamm, "Luke 19:8 Once Again: Does Zacchaeus Defend or Resolve?" *JBL* 107 (1988) 431–37; A. Mitchell, "Zacchaeus Revisited: Luke 19,8 as a Defense," *Bib* 71 (1990) 153–76; Dennis Hamm, "Zacchaeus Revisited Once More: A Story of Vindication or of Conversion?" *Bib* 72 (1991) 249–52. Hamm has clearly demonstrated that Zacchaeus expresses his resolve upon experiencing the healing grace of Jesus' presence. He will soon be poor if he enacts his resolve of fourfold restitution found in Pentateuchal legislation or Roman law (Fitzmyer, *Luke* 1225), which was so steep that it had to be modified in later Jewish law (to twenty per cent of annual income, according to Billerbeck 4/1:546–51).

[82] Commentators (e.g., Alfred Plummer, *A Critical and Exegetical Commentary on the Gospel according to St. Luke* [Edinburgh: T & T Clark, 1896]) often adduce Joseph of Arimathea, living for the Reign of God (23:51), as a rich man who is saved in Luke. But they fail to note that Luke has redactionally removed all the evidences of his wealth that occur in Mark 15:43 (εὐσχήμων) and in Matt 27:57 (πλούσιος). In Luke he is not a rich man, though he does have the position of a councilor, and can afford to buy a tomb and linens in which to wrap Jesus.

[83] The verb increasingly assumes this meaning in Hellenistic times, which is well-attested in the NT: Matt 6:2, 5, 16; Phil 4:18; perhaps Mark 14:41; BAGD 84.

[84] Otto Schmitz and Gustav Stählin, "παρακαλέω," *TDNT* 5:773–88.

In the NT παρακαλεῖν is common in all its LXX meanings, but connection to the salvation offered in Jesus almost always underlies its use. Luke uses the verb four times as a request for Jesus' help (7:4; 8:31, 32, 41), twice for exhortation (3:18; 15:28), and once, in a passage exactly correlative to this woe, to describe the eschatological consolation of the poor (16:25). Παράκλησις is much rarer and always means either exhortation or comfort. Even where it means exhortation, the notion of comfort is almost always perceptible in the exhortation (Acts 13:15; 15:31). Luke 2:25 has Simeon awaiting the eschatological consolation of Israel, which is equated with the Messiah (2:26, 29-30).[85] Thus Jesus in 6:24b uses the word ironically, contradicting all the eschatological and divine resonances of the word in the NT. The rich in this world have turned their riches into their Consoler, and so in the world to come they lack the consolation of the Reign of God. The future is the final eschatological future: riches, as a treasure that fails (12:33), do not follow the person into the next world (Luke 12:20).[86]

What is the meaning or purpose of such a strong rejection of what the OT had always considered God's blessing? There are three possibilities: First, the poor, who put all their hope in the Lord as their only protector, are the pious ones, whom God will certainly and ultimately care for. The rich have put their security in their wealth and so are the impious, without God. Here being poor corresponds to an ascetic motive: riches clog and divert the spirit, and so divesting oneself places God at the center of one's life and eschatological expectation.[87] Such a motive is rare in the NT and in Luke, perhaps intimated in Luke 12:22-34; 14:33.[88]

---

[85] Billerbeck 2:124–26 gives rabbinic citations in which "the consolation of Israel" means "the Messiah."

[86] Not only have they lost the Reign of God, but also their wealth and the various joys that it brought; Loisy, *Luc* 201.

[87] The Hellenistic moralists' asceticism, oriented to self-perfection, is absent from the Bible. The Jews hardly differentiated between spirit and matter, and so the dualistic Greek ἄσκησις, which rid itself of matter so as to liberate the spirit, had no place in Judaism. Prayer, fasting, and almsgiving were practiced after the exile, yet their goal was not human self-mastery, but union with God. In the NT the verb ἀσκεῖν occurs only in Acts 24:16, where Paul says that he strives to have a clear conscience. Although Luke's Paul there speaks of the Law, his striving is for union with God in worship, faith, and hope (24:14-15). Paul's own description of his self-discipline in 1 Cor 9:25-27 refers to the attainment of the flexibility that enables him to be all things to all humans for their salvation (9:19-24). Other expressions of fighting against the flesh and its weaknesses (Rom 8:12-13; Eph 4:22; 6:8) are likewise in service of union with Christ, just as self-denial in following Jesus is the asceticism of the synoptic gospels. Consequently, an ascetical view whose aim is self-mastery is foreign to the NT. Simple divestment of wealth, no matter how accomplished, as a means of union with God is also rare.

[88] Still, it is the motive adduced by a large number of commentators. Classic examples are M.-J. Lagrange, for whom absorption in the pleasures that wealth provides allows

Second, in Hellenistic rhetoric and moral philosophy a teacher's opponents were often described as the rich, as a result of selling their wisdom or alliance with oppressive forces.[89]

Third, the Lord promises the reign of God to the poor, which means food for the hungry and laughter for those who weep, and all this *now*. But the rich, in an enclosed agrarian society, make it impossible for the poor to have these God-given goods. Since in the pre-industrial agrarian society there is negligible expansion of capital, one person's accumulation of wealth means subtraction of it from another. Possessions are a limited good: the very fact that there are rich means that they have acquired their wealth from the poor, usually through unjust schemes of taxation, pricing, etc.[90] To the discerning eye of Luke's Jesus, wealth was on loan from the poor, to be restored in the Jubilee year (Luke 4:19). The rich who refused to redistribute it were obstacles to God's promise of abundance for the poor. In this view one's divestment of goods must be to the poor, from whom they came in the economic history of the country. The motives for such divestment, then, are justice and charity, the reason we have seen most clearly adduced in Luke-Acts.[91] This explanation makes sense also out of the bald statement of eschatological reversal in 16:25: it is not as if the rich man deliberately ignored Lazarus at his gate; being rich means that he had to have ignored the poor everywhere. Jesus' warning to the rich that they will have no heavenly consolation is at the same time the exhortation for them to feed the poor from their substance (21:3) that effects the care of the reign of God now for the poor, the hungry, and the mourning.

Note, then, that while the beatitudes concentrate on what God is doing in Jesus' introduction of the Reign of God, the woe to the rich has a strongly implied ethic for the reader: give to the poor now, while there is time!

---

no room to desire the Reign of God (*Evangile selon Saiint Luc* [Paris: Gabalda, 1921] 191); more recently Nolland, for whom riches ensnare the soul in a false set of values and loyalties which obliterate desire for the Reign of God (*Luke 1–9:20*. WBC 35A [Dallas, Tex.: Word Books, 1989] 287).

[89] Appendix A, especially the works cited by Betz, *Sermon* 572–73, excursus "Poor and Rich."

[90] That the rich have become so by oppressing the poor, see Jas 5:1-6. For the notion of limited good see Bruce J. Malina, *New Testament World* 71–93 and Halvor Moxnes, *The Economy of the Kingdom: Social Conflict and Economic Relations in Luke's Gospel* (Philadelphia: Fortress, 1988), especially 22–98.

[91] Luke 11:41; 12:33; 14:12-14; 18:22; Acts 2:43-47; 4:32-33. This view is represented elsewhere in the NT (Mark 10:21//Matt 19:21; Matt 5:42; Gal 2:10; 2 Corinthians 8–9; Rom 15:25-29; Jas 2:14-17; 1 John 3:17-18).

2. *The Second Woe* (6:25ab)

6:25a: Οὐαὶ ὑμῖν οἱ ἐμπεπλησμένοι νῦν, "Woe to you who are sated now." As the first beatitude provided the base for the next three, so the first woe has provided the base from which the next three woes develop. In this case, satiety means the rich person is not a miser, but spends to overindulge his or her appetite.

Ἐμπι(μ)πλᾶναι:[92] "to fill, satisfy." In the Bible being filled can refer to the fullness of God's gifts or the sinful satisfaction of the greedy. The LXX prefers the compound forms to the simple πι(μ)πλῆναι, and so they occur some 150x, translating six different Hebrew stems, mostly *ml'* and *śb'*. Ἐμπιμπλᾶν means filling one's belly in Ps 107:9; Deut 31:20; the rich filling their bellies is common in the OT, expressed by other verbs in Job 20:23; Ps 17:14; Jer 51:34; Sir 31:3, etc.[93] Ezekiel 16:49 is most relevant to our woe: Sodom is used as a warning to Israel because it was sated with food but did not aid the poor and needy.

The NT frequently uses πιμπλᾶναι[94] and πληροῦν in contrast with ἐμπιπλᾶναι (sixty per cent of NT usage), so that the compound form assumes its more emphatic tone, "to be filled up, stuffed, gorged."[95] This is the meaning in 1:53, where the contrast between the hungry being filled and the rich being sent away empty prefigures 6:21, 25. This woe, which could refer to any human satisfaction in this life (νῦν), because of the contrast with πεινῶντες in 6:21 and the following 6:25b, speaks of those who are already filled with food, those who are "stuffed" in a world of hunger.[96]

---

[92] The LXX and NT use the alternate forms ἐμπιπλᾶν and ἐμπιμπλᾶναι, indistinguishably.

[93] The idea is also common in Hellenistic literature: Hans Dieter Betz, *Lukian von Samosata und das Neue Testament; religionsgeschichtliche und paränetische Parallelen. Ein Beitrag zum Corpus Hellenisticum Novi Testamenti.* Texte und Untersuchungen zur Geschichte der altchristlichen Literatur 5th ser. 21 (Berlin: Akademie-Verlag, 1961) 84–86, and the literature cited in Betz, *Sermon* 586 n. 138. In both Jewish and Greek literature tales of the underworld have the glutton suffering from hunger and thirst; Betz, *Sermon* 587 n. 140.

[94] The verb is a Lukan favorite, used primarily to mean "to be filled with the Holy Spirit," but also to be physically filled, and "to complete" an allotted time. In both Luke and Acts, πληροῦν is more likely to mean "to fulfill" the Scriptures, etc., although it, too, has a range of meanings.

[95] See this notion of fullness in Acts 14:17; Rom 15:24. The notion of completeness in ἐμπιπλᾶναι allows Luke to substitute it for χορτάζειν, probably to avoid mechanical repetition.

[96] Again, note the relevance of Luke 16:19-31, where the rich man's table was so abounding in food that Lazarus could have lived off the crumbs; in the other world he thirsts (16:24).

6:25b: ὅτι πεινάσατε, "because you will hunger." The concrete denotation of physical hunger in πεινᾶν (see comments on 6:21a) is now connoted in the image of the eschatological banquet of the Reign of God. The same eschatological reversal at work in 6:24 is at work here: those who have eaten richly in a world of hunger have had their consolation, and they will hunger in the world to come. Compare this same reversal in Isa 65:13.

3. *The Third Woe* (6:25cd)

6:25c: Οὐαὶ οἱ γελῶντες νῦν, "Woe to you who laugh now." Some think that γελᾶν indicates that scornful, disdainful laughter now is the reason for the woe.[97] But Luke is rather thinking antithetically of the beatitude in 6:21d, of those whose needs are satisfied and who spend their days in laughter at how good things are.[98] The utmost wealth is now described as not having a care in the world. Inevitably there is a sense of indifference to the needs of others in such self-satisfied joy. Compare Luke 12:19 (φάγε, πίε, εὐφραίνου) with Amos 6:4-6.

6:25d: ὅτι πενθήσετε καὶ κλαύσετε, "Because you will weep and wail." Πενθεῖν, "to mourn, grieve, be sad" is more general and subdued than κλαίειν. Luke had preferred the more dramatic κλαίοντες to πενθοῦντες in 6:21, but now he retrieves πενθεῖν from his source to supply oratorical fullness (hendiadys) with κλαύσετε.[99] Καὶ κλαύσετε speaks of weeping, wailing as the lot of those who have their fortunes reversed in the life to come.[100] This notion occurs in Matthew's κλαυθμός καὶ βρυγμός ὀδόντων, "wailing and gnashing of teeth" (Matt 8:12; 13:42, 50; 22:13; 24:51; 25:30) and Luke's same usage (13:28). Since most of Luke's uses of κλαίειν are in connection with death (7:13, 32; 8:52; 19:41; 23:28), it is a fitting verb to express an eternal loss of life as the opposite of the satiety expressed in γελῶντες.

4. *The Fourth Woe* (6:26)

6:26a: Οὐαὶ ὅταν ὑμᾶς καλῶς εἴπωσιν πάντες οἱ ἄνθρωποι, "Woe to you when all speak well of you." Ὅταν echoes the construction of the

---

[97] I. Howard Marshall, *The Gospel of Luke* (Exeter: Paternoster, 1978) 256 and, more decisively, Betz, *Sermon* 587.

[98] Plummer, *Luke* 183; Fitzmyer, *Luke* 636.

[99] For the use of the two as hendiadys see 2 Sam 19:2; Neh 1:4; 8:9; Sir 7:34; 1 Macc 9:20; Mark 16:10; Jas 4:9; Rev 18:11, 15, 19. They are used in close proximity in many other passages; see Betz, *Sermon* 587–88 n. 149. The hendiadys also breaks up a mechanical repetition of the formulation of the corresponding beatitude.

[100] The wicked wailing at the intervention of the Lord occurs in Isa 13:6; 65:13-14; Joel 1:8-10; Ezek 22:14-31, but these do not clearly refer to the world to come.

correlative beatitude (6:22), and here indicates that a perilous situation is present "whenever" the disciples are praised. While 6:22 had a general attitude (μισήσωσιν) specified by three actions—ostracism, reproach, slander—καλῶς εἴπωσιν expressly resumes only the two verbs that describe speech. Still, by force of its antithetical position and the very generality of its expression it implies all four verbs. The commentators who think the woes are addressed to rich non-disciples take καλῶς εἴπωσιν as flattery for the rich.[101] But its use in Luke's contrasting rhetoric rather indicates the world's approval and acceptance of these "disciples" because theirs is the easier way of life—not living and urging the Son of Man's way of the cross (6:22d, ἕνεκα τοῦ υἱοῦ τοῦ ἀνθρώπου). They are praised because they do not embody the righteous one's way, which challenges and so evokes opposition from the wicked.

6:26b: κατὰ τὰ αὐτὰ γὰρ ἐποίουν τοῖς ψευδοπροφήταις οἱ πατέρες αὐτῶν, "for their ancestors treated the false prophets in the same way." As the disciples' distress at being attacked was ameliorated by the realization that the true prophets were treated the same way (6:23), so the praised disciples should be discomfited by awareness that the false prophets were praised. Ψευδοπροφήται: The Hebrew Bible has no single expression for the false prophet, speaking in Deut 13:2 of *nābî' 'ô* (that prophet) in apposition to the *ḥolēm ḥalôm* (dreamer of dreams); both lead the people to other gods. Deuteronomy 18:20; Jer 14:14-16 condemn the prophet who speaks *yāzîd,* presumptuously (in YHWH's name, but without his authorization).[102] The LXX translates *nābî'* pejoratively by ψευδοπροφήτης in Jer 6:13; 33:7, 8, 11, 16; 34:9; 35:1; 36:1, 8; Zech 13:2.[103] Isaiah 30:10-11; Amos 7:10-13; Mic 2:11; Jer 5:31; 6:14; 23:16-17 show prophets cutting their prophetic message to fit the pleasure of the people; none of these passages shows these false prophets actually being praised.[104]

Ψευδοπροφήτης seems instead to be a NT notion. Linguistically, the ψευδο- can refer to the object (prophesying *lies*) or the subject (one who

---

[101] Betz, *Sermon,* takes it as flattery (synonymous with κολακεία), a common affliction of the rich, and adduces a number of examples on p. 588. This interpretation is as old as John Calvin, *A Harmony of the Gospels 1: Matthew, Mark, and Luke.* Calvin's commentaries, 3 vols. (Edinburgh: St. Andrew Press, 1972) 1:174–75; see also Plummer, *Luke* 183; Walter Grundmann, *Das Evangelium nach Lukas* (Berlin: Evangelische Verlagsanstalt, 1961) 145.

[102] Since Deut 13:2-5 and 18:20-22 are the passages that offer criteria for the true and false prophets one would expect technical terms here, if there were any.

[103] In Jer 33 (26):7-16 the false prophets lead the prosecution of Jeremiah; in all the rest of the texts (except possibly 35 [28]:1) YHWH condemns them.

[104] The literature of middle Judaism contains scattered incidents of false prophets, in particular connected with messianic or apocalyptic movements; Rudolf Meyer, "προφήτης," *TDNT* 6:812–28.

falsely claims to be a prophet, a *phony* prophet). In Mark 13:22//Matt 24:24 the claim is what is false; in 1 John 4:1 and 2 Pet 2:1 both the claim and the utterance are false. The term refers to false Christian teachers (2 Pet 2:1; 2 John 7),[105] but it can refer to OT prophets (Luke 6:26; 2 Pet 2:1), to deceivers at the end-time (Matt 24:11, 24//Mark 13:22), and to the Roman government (Rev 16:13; 19:20; 20:10). Luke's only other use, of a magus who is a Jewish false prophet (Acts 13:6), gives no clue to its use here. The term means what Luke wants it to mean in context.[106]

The concept is to be interpreted in relation to the fate of the true prophets in 6:23 and at the end of the series of woes to the rich, the sated, the merrymakers, and those praised (6:24-25). These last are disciples who have neither listened to (6:27) nor lived out (6:46) the message of the Sermon. They fit into the world as it is, especially the economically distorted world that has produced the poor, the hungry, the lamenting, and the persecuted. Praise of them is praise for those who have cut Jesus' message to fit the contours of this world and so curried its favor. In contrast to the true disciples who challenge the power of the rich and the sated and are condemned by them, these false prophets are praised and pointed to as the authentic interpreters of the Jesus tradition. Alas for them, for they will inherit the condemnation that YHWH directed against the false prophets.

Summary of the Beatitudes and Woes

1. The Sermon reveals Jesus' ethical teaching, primarily to disciples but also to outsiders who are eager to hear him. His first word, μακάριοι, sets a theme of rejoicing for the content of the Sermon as a whole. The reward offered in the first beatitude, ἡ βασιλεία τοῦ θεοῦ, supplies not only the final, but also the efficient cause for all the beatitudes. Thus Jesus transforms the platitudinous OT Wisdom form into paradoxical proclamations of the reversed conditions of the eschatological Reign of God, which he has ushered in. He proclaims blessed those deemed the most wretched in his society, the poor. In Luke the poor are always the desperately poor. They may rely on God to save them, but Jesus never adduces their piety as the ground for God's help or the motive for human generosity to them. Jesus' disciples always are called to real solidarity with the poor, usually by sharing their wealth with them.

---

[105] Schürmann, *Lukasevangelium*, 1:338–39 thinks that Christian false teachers are alluded to here and in Luke 6:37-45, but οἱ πατέρες clearly refers to an OT pattern.

[106] Marshall, *Luke* 257 argues from James' knowledge of the woes (5:1) that the ψευδοπροφῆται were associated with the rich in the church or rich persecutors outside of the church. Perhaps.

This distribution is made possible by the present inbreaking of the eschatological Reign of God. In Luke, Jesus proclaims that this Reign has already arrived in his healing and exorcisms, and in his task of proclaiming good news to the poor and release to the oppressed. He communicates the power of this Reign to his disciples, who are anointed in his Spirit to do his liberating works. And yet the Reign of God remains also an apocalyptic notion, so that what is not yet accomplished in its historical form will come to completion in the Reign ushered in by Jesus as the apocalyptic Son of Man. This future Reign also exercises transforming motivational power on the historical existence of those who vibrantly hope for it.

Thus the poor are proclaimed happy because the rich are summoned by eschatological judgment to distribute their wealth to the poor now. The poor who receive such distribution ideally are no longer needy, and so blessed. The disciples who make such distribution are happy because such distribution makes them eschatologically rich toward God. When such distribution is not complete, the poor at least know that by seeking the Reign of God they are now in the process of receiving their reward in the perfect eschatological Reign of the apocalyptic Son of Man.

2. The next two beatitudes likewise proclaim happy those neglected or despised in Luke's society. Hunger is a consequence of poverty and always in Luke-Acts refers to physical hunger for adequate food. Jesus addresses this hunger in the gospel, and satisfies it with food in 9:10-17. Further, he commands his disciples to feed the hungry in 14:13. Consequently, the blessed state of the hungry arises from their being fed in the present Reign of God (immediately future to Jesus' Sermon) and knowing they will be satisfied in the eschatological meal of God's Reign.

Those who are destitute and starving are going to die; wailing for the dead is the chief meaning of κλαίοντες. Consequently, Jesus proclaims a beatitude to those who weep for the plight of the poor, the hungry, and those in any way oppressed. They will laugh, possibly in the present Reign of God, but the sparse use of γελᾶν in Luke probably indicates a laughter that springs from joy in the full eschatological possession of justice. (As will appear from the rest of the Sermon, any true disciple who carries the cross through to the resurrection will weep.)

3. The different form of the concluding beatitude reveals its formulation in the church's experience of persecution for discipleship of its crucified Lord. Jesus proclaims blessed those who are hated by ἄνθρωποι (Gentiles and Jews) for their commitment to the way of the Son of Man. The generic "hated" probably is to be understood as the hostile rejection of the good by the evil and godless, as Jesus uses the example of Jewish opposition to the God-sent prophets to demonstrate the beatitude. The

specifying verbs "exclude, reproach, revile" are not technical terms describing a formal or legal process of persecution, but rather describe the kind of labeling, shunning, and disenfranchisement everywhere used to discredit and discourage those who disturb the declining mores of the status quo. Jesus himself spoke of his rejection as a prophet, and promised his disciples that as members of his prophetic movement they would suffer the same. (Indeed, they may be poor, hungry, and weeping precisely because of this ostracism.) Nowhere in Luke-Acts does Jesus say that such persecution will end. The disciples will rejoice and leap for joy only in the perfect peace of the eschatological Reign of God. Thus the beatitudes end by stressing eschatological reward as the source of Christians' beatitude.

4. The woe is a prophetic form; Jesus' abundant use of it stamps him as a prophet. Here the woes present the converse of the beatitudes, to reinforce and give their unmistakable interpretation. Jesus names the states and activities that human societies call good and pronounces a condemnation on them. As the state of poverty implies hunger and bewailing one's state, so wealth implies being well-fed and blissfully ignorant of the state of the wretched who surround one. The rich are inevitably exploiters in the first-century economy, and they can enjoy their feasts and entertainments only at the expense of the vast majority of society. They have chosen to live for this world, and they have already had their reward. In the world to come they will starve and lament. In the woes final judgment hangs over the heads of the rich, the fat, and the mirthful, and so they are an implied call to ethical conversion of the reader.

5. The final woe also springs from the experience of the early church: false teachers have arisen in the community who teach a way of salvation not founded on the cross of Christ (Gal 4:3; Col 2:8; 1 Tim 3:3; 6:3; 2 Pet 1:16). They are praised (presumably both by Christians and others) for offering an easier way of life that condones the injustice and hatred seething in their world. They have abandoned the prophetic way of Jesus and his true disciples to curry the favor of this world. Alas for them, they will suffer the same fate as did the Jewish false prophets. Thus the final woe, concluding the Sermon's exordium, performs two rhetorical functions: (1) It summarizes the exordium's message: Jesus' way, in which the cross reverses the condition of the oppressed, radically challenges the powerful and so is opposed by them. It will provoke persecution of the true disciples who share his prophetic message and fate, but who nevertheless will triumph in the eschatological Reign of God. (2) It foreshadows the coming passages that summon disciples to listen to (6:27) and live out (6:46) the Sermon's message.

6. That Jesus' beatitudes and woes so attend to the material conditions of his disciples shows how far he is from preaching a "spirituality"

divorced from the ordinary world created by God and humans.[107] Instead, the spirituality of Jesus' disciples finds God in the midst of the struggle to sustain life and to share it with others: that is the meaning of the Reign of God on earth.

Conclusion

Jesus has singled out the most miserable people of his society to pronounce happy, and has pronounced gloom and defeat on those whom his society takes not only to be happy but good. Each of these embodies a paradox that must be pondered, and yet Jesus has issued them in a rapid-fire order that allows no time for comprehension. Certainly the hearers of his own time and the readers of Luke's community must have been as bewildered at Jesus' opening of his Sermon as are those who sit in the pew and hear them in twenty-first-century America. All these paradoxes, coming at the reader so rapidly, cry out for explanation!

[107] Heinrich Kahlefeld, *Der Jünger, eine Auslegung der Rede Lk 6,20-49* (Frankfurt: J. Knecht, 1962) 35.

Chapter 5

The Love Command

(6:27-36)

Jesus has come, the divine Messiah as eschatological prophet, to overthrow Satan's rule over this world by liberating acts of healing and teaching. His inaugural sermon to disciples and crowds has begun with a revolutionary call to a prophetic life-style. States hitherto seen in the covenant theology of retribution as signs of divine rejection—poverty, hunger, mourning, hatred, and ostracism—are now proclaimed as signs of God's blessing, as sharing in the Reign of God, both as an eschatological reward and as a present liberation in this renewed world. In this eschatologically charged world the rewards of ordinary life—riches, satiety, heedless joy, a good reputation among wrong-thinking people—are seen as "missing the boat" of God's Reign. With these staccato paradoxical warnings still sounding in his hearers' ears, Jesus now turns to the concrete actions that will qualify his disciples for the promises of the beatitudes. They turn out to be as paradoxical and counter-cultural as were the beatitudes and woes.

The Structure of the Sermon's Central Section[1]

1. *The Thematic Division*

The most common division of the Sermon attends to three introductory comments at 6:20, 27, 39, and so divides it into three sections:

> 6:20-26, the prophetic section: the virtues of the subjects of the Reign of God;
>
> 6:27-38, the gnomic section: the distinctive ethic of Jesus' disciples;

---

[1] Although it is obvious to even the superficial reader that Luke 6:27-36 contains material common to Matthew's last two antitheses (Matt 5:38-48) plus the Golden Rule (Matt 7:12), there is no agreement on a reconstruction of the written source (probably Q). Consequently, I proceed simply with the literary text of Luke as he intended it for his readers.

6:39-49, the parabolic section: concluding figurative language calling for action.[2]

A second group of exegetes takes 6:36, "Be merciful," as the conclusion of the Love commands and 6:37, "Judge not," as opening a new section on not judging.[3] A third group ends the middle section at 6:35, "Love your enemies," and takes 6:36, "Be merciful," as opening the section on not judging, which is variously described and divided.[4] A small group holds 6:27-45 together as a unit.[5] Others so atomize the text as to confirm Fitzmyer's judgment, "the Lukan Sermon is loose and rambling."[6]

I hold with I. Howard Marshall and Frederick W. Danker that Luke's use of hinge passages militates against the formation of watertight compartments in the Sermon's structure. Still, the exegete must approach the text with the presumption that there is a pattern in the sequence of materials. In view of the above divergence of opinion we should not expect the pattern to emerge from clear aural and formal indicators in the text, but rather in the bunching of subjects or themes that subtly shade one into another. It will help to take an overview of the themes and their relations:

A. General principle of open-ended loving, like God's
B. General principle specifically—loving one's enemies
C. General principle specifically concrete—doing good to those who do harm
D. Most specifically—giving and lending without hope of return
E. Notion of superabundant reward
F. Not judging others as act of mercy

[2] So formulated by C. F. Georg Heinrici, *Die Bergpredigt (Matth 5–7, Luk 6,20-49)* (Leipzig: Dürr, 1900), 43 on the (dubious) basis of the tripartite ordering of the Shepherd of Hermas into visions, commands, and similitudes. This division also attends to the different moods expressed in each section. Commentaries following this division include Georg Ludwig Hahn, Burton Scott Easton, Friedrich Hauck, Ernest Tinsley, E. Earle Ellis, Josef Ernst, I. Howard Marshall, Charles H. Talbert, David Tiede, John Nolland, Hans-Dieter Betz. Others dividing the text at v. 38 but further subdividing the material after 6:38 into various smaller divisions: Paul Schanz, Karl H. Rengstorf, George B. Caird, Frederick W. Danker, Christopher F. Evans. Walter Grundmann and Michael Goulder divide the Sermon into two parts, 6:20-38, 39-49. For a fuller survey of the competing divisions of the text, see L. John Topel, "The Lukan Version of the Lord's Sermon," *BTB* 11 (1981) 49–50.

[3] This division accounts for the clear relation between 6:39-42 and the material on not judging in 6:37-38. Those dividing the text at 6:36 (Claude G. Montefiore, T. W. Manson, Eduard Schweizer, Wilfrid J. Harrington, Joseph Fitzmyer, Gerhard Schneider, Jacob Kremer, Jan Lambrecht, Fred Craddock) rarely agree on a subsequent division of the text from 6:37 on.

[4] Erich Klostermann, John Martin Creed, Luke T. Johnson, who has a unique two-part division (6:17-35, 36-49).

[5] Alfred Plummer, Marie-Joseph Lagrange, Heinz Schürmann, Jacob Kremer.

[6] Joseph A. Fitzmyer, *The Gospel According to Luke*. 2 vols. AB 28, 28A (Garden City, N.Y.: Doubleday, 1981, 1985) 625. Julius Wellhausen, for example, divides the text into seven units; others, e.g., Luke T. Johnson, have hardly any units after 6:20-26.

Thematic Analysis of Luke 6:27-42

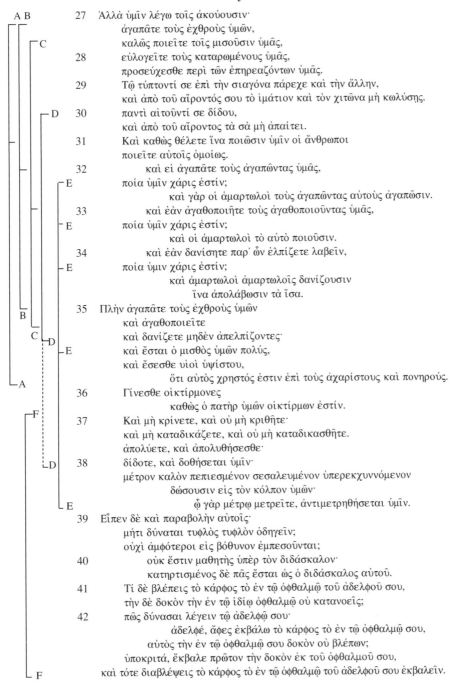

27 Ἀλλὰ ὑμῖν λέγω τοῖς ἀκούουσιν·
ἀγαπᾶτε τοὺς ἐχθροὺς ὑμῶν,
καλῶς ποιεῖτε τοῖς μισοῦσιν ὑμᾶς,
28 εὐλογεῖτε τοὺς καταρωμένους ὑμᾶς,
προσεύχεσθε περὶ τῶν ἐπηρεαζόντων ὑμᾶς.
29 Τῷ τύπτοντί σε ἐπὶ τὴν σιαγόνα πάρεχε καὶ τὴν ἄλλην,
καὶ ἀπὸ τοῦ αἴροντός σου τὸ ἱμάτιον καὶ τὸν χιτῶνα μὴ κωλύσῃς.
30 παντὶ αἰτοῦντί σε δίδου,
καὶ ἀπὸ τοῦ αἴροντος τὰ σὰ μὴ ἀπαίτει.
31 Καὶ καθὼς θέλετε ἵνα ποιῶσιν ὑμῖν οἱ ἄνθρωποι
ποιεῖτε αὐτοῖς ὁμοίως.
32 καὶ εἰ ἀγαπᾶτε τοὺς ἀγαπῶντας ὑμᾶς,
ποία ὑμῖν χάρις ἐστίν;
καὶ γὰρ οἱ ἁμαρτωλοὶ τοὺς ἀγαπῶντας αὐτοὺς ἀγαπῶσιν.
33 καὶ ἐὰν ἀγαθοποιῆτε τοὺς ἀγαθοποιοῦντας ὑμᾶς,
ποία ὑμῖν χάρις ἐστίν;
καὶ οἱ ἁμαρτωλοὶ τὸ αὐτὸ ποιοῦσιν.
34 καὶ ἐὰν δανίσητε παρ᾽ ὧν ἐλπίζετε λαβεῖν,
ποία ὑμιν χάρις ἐστίν;
καὶ ἁμαρτωλοὶ ἁμαρτωλοῖς δανίζουσιν
ἵνα ἀπολάβωσιν τὰ ἴσα.
35 Πλὴν ἀγαπᾶτε τοὺς ἐχθροὺς ὑμῶν
καὶ ἀγαθοποιεῖτε
καὶ δανίζετε μηδὲν ἀπελπίζοντες·
καὶ ἔσται ὁ μισθὸς ὑμῶν πολύς,
καὶ ἔσεσθε υἱοὶ ὑψίστου,
ὅτι αὐτὸς χρηστός ἐστιν ἐπὶ τοὺς ἀχαρίστους καὶ πονηρούς.
36 Γίνεσθε οἰκτίρμονες
καθὼς ὁ πατὴρ ὑμῶν οἰκτίρμων ἐστίν.
37 Καὶ μὴ κρίνετε, καὶ οὐ μὴ κριθῆτε·
καὶ μὴ καταδικάζετε, καὶ οὐ μὴ καταδικασθῆτε.
ἀπολύετε, καὶ ἀπολυθήσεσθε·
38 δίδοτε, καὶ δοθήσεται ὑμῖν·
μέτρον καλὸν πεπιεσμένον σεσαλευμένον ὑπερεκχυννόμενον
δώσουσιν εἰς τὸν κόλπον ὑμῶν·
ᾧ γὰρ μέτρῳ μετρεῖτε, ἀντιμετρηθήσεται ὑμῖν.
39 Εἶπεν δὲ καὶ παραβολὴν αὐτοῖς·
μήτι δύναται τυφλὸς τυφλὸν ὁδηγεῖν;
οὐχὶ ἀμφότεροι εἰς βόθυνον ἐμπεσοῦνται;
40 οὐκ ἔστιν μαθητὴς ὑπὲρ τὸν διδάσκαλον·
κατηρτισμένος δὲ πᾶς ἔσται ὡς ὁ διδάσκαλος αὐτοῦ.
41 Τί δὲ βλέπεις τὸ κάρφος τὸ ἐν τῷ ὀφθαλμῷ τοῦ ἀδελφοῦ σου,
τὴν δὲ δοκὸν τὴν ἐν τῷ ἰδίῳ ὀφθαλμῷ οὐ κατανοεῖς;
42 πῶς δύνασαι λέγειν τῷ ἀδελφῷ σου·
ἀδελφέ, ἄφες ἐκβάλω τὸ κάρφος τὸ ἐν τῷ ὀφθαλμῷ σου,
αὐτὸς τὴν ἐν τῷ ὀφθαλμῷ σου δοκὸν οὐ βλέπων;
ὑποκριτά, ἔκβαλε πρῶτον τὴν δοκὸν ἐκ τοῦ ὀφθαλμοῦ σου,
καὶ τότε διαβλέψεις τὸ κάρφος τὸ ἐν τῷ ὀφθαλμῷ τοῦ ἀδελφοῦ σου ἐκβαλεῖν.

This structure makes clear that only two themes of 6:27-36 recur in 6:37-38: unlimited giving/lending (6:30, 34, 35, 38) and superabundant reward (6:35, 38, which permeates the Sermon in 6:20-26, 32-34, 35, 38, 48). These must function as a hinge or transition from the love commandment to a new section on not judging, because, on the contrary, 6:27-36 contains a tightly integrated triple sequence of themes—loving enemies, doing good to those who do harm, and unlimited giving/lending to those who will not return—which do *not* recur in 6:37-49.[7]

Interspersed with these specific commands are two general commands highlighting the open-ended character of the love being commanded: the Golden Rule of 6:31 and the command to be compassionate as God is (infinitely) compassionate of 6:36. I therefore structure the Sermon:

> 6:27-36 The love command
>
> 6:37-42 The critique of judgment (with 37-38 as the hinge)
> 6:43-49 On the necessity of doing the commands of the Sermon.

Further evidence of this structure will emerge from the exegesis itself.

2. *The Rhetorical Structure of* Luke 6:27-36

Pace the critics, 6:27-36 is an elegantly organized ring structure:

A *6:27b-30 contain two strophes of imperatives in a four-beat rhythm.* Luke varies the striking uniformity of the eight cola with slight changes of syntax and tone: 27b-28ab begin with present plural imperatives followed by the objects of the verbs; then 29-30 begin with the indirect objects followed by present singular imperatives.[8]

> *6:31 is a general principle explaining the previous injunctions.*

> **B** *6:32-34 negatively repeat the injunctions in three-beat conditional rhetorical questions,* starkly contrasting Jesus' ethic with Greco-Roman reciprocity. Luke varies this repetitive structure by

---

[7] They are organized in a ring structure, in which a positive statement of these commands (6:27-30) is followed by a refutation of the opposite practices (6:32-34), and then is reinforced by the identical positive commands (6:35). Taking 6:36 with 6:27-35, rather than with its two following verses, is crucial; John Nolland argues strongly for our division in *Luke 1-9:20* (Dallas, Tex.: Word, 1989) 300.

[8] Luke 6:29 has an aorist prohibitive subjunctive. Note that the first strophe deals with personal injury in a series that moves towards interiority (prayer); the second strophe begins with bodily injury, but the last three injunctions deal with property loss. Attempts to differentiate the sources by use of singular and plural have been as unsuccessful in the Sermon as they have been in Deuteronomy from the time of Willy Staerk, *Das Deuteronomium: sein Inhalt und seine literarische Form* (Leipzig: J. C. Hinrichs, 1894).

variations in the introductory conditional clauses and in the causal clauses.

A' *6:35 repeats the injunctions positively and adds the motive of reward.* The three verbs of 6:32-34 are now repeated as imperatives in the sense of 6:27-30, and the motive clause goes beyond the general principle of 6:31: God's own unconditional love becomes the disciples' standard of conduct. This motive forms the transition to

> *6:36, the deeper Christian general principle explaining the whole passage.* Taking God's compassion as the standard of Christian conduct explains and concludes the whole series.[9]

Exegesis of the Love Commandment (6:27-36)

1. The Command to Love One's Enemies (6:27-30):

6:27a: Ἀλλὰ ὑμῖν λέγω τοῖς ἀκούουσιν, "But I say to you who are listening" has been ascribed to Luke's source,[10] or to his maladroit redaction.[11] The insertion has been taken to mark Jesus' return to his disciples, the audience of the beatitudes, as opposed to the absent or fictive audience of the woes;[12] the larger crowd mentioned in 6:18;[13] or those who are listening in the sense of obeying.[14] But the problem cannot be solved if one presumes that Luke is distinguishing Jesus' historical audiences.

The language is Lukan,[15] and in this light the redaction may not be so maladroit. When the mixed audience of 6:12-19 is primarily conceived as

---

[9] The general principle at 6:31 makes possible another general principle at 6:36. At the same time, as many have seen, οἰκτίρμων provides a transition to the *new* theme of not judging in 6:37-42.

[10] Heinz Schürmann, *Das Lukasevangelium* (Freiburg: Herder, 1969) 340–46, 243 n. 4, and Béda Rigaux, *Témoignage de l'Évangile de Luc* (Bruges and Paris: Desclée de Brouwer, 1970) 168, both referring to the parallel in Matt 5:44, ἐγὼ δὲ λέγω ὑμῖν, find the source in Q. Earlier Friedrich Rehkopf, *Die lukanische Sonderquelle*. WUNT 5 (Tübingen: Mohr, 1959) 97 and his mentor, Joachim Jeremias, had ascribed ὑμῖν λέγω to L, Luke's special source.

[11] Alfred Loisy, *L'Evangile selon Luc* (Paris: E. Noury, 1924) 203.

[12] The majority opinion among commentaries from Euthymius Zigabenus and Hugo Grotius to Hans-Dieter Betz. Sometimes they consider the audience of the woes not as absent (addressed by apostrophe), but as the bystanders who are not committed to the virtues of the Sermon, e.g. Brian E. Beck, *Christian Character in the Gospel of Luke* (London: Epworth, 1989) 17.

[13] Johann Albrecht Bengel, Theodor Zahn, Eduard Schweizer, Josef Ernst, Joseph Fitzmyer, Eugene LaVerdiere, Christopher F. Evans, Michael Goulder, *Paradigm* 1:360.

[14] Euthymius Zigabenus, Paul Schanz, Alfred Plummer.

[15] Both the position of ὑμῖν in ὑμῖν λέγω and the participle with article as a substantive are Lukan style: Jacques Dupont, *Les Béatitudes*. 3 vols. (Paris: Gabalda, 1958–73) 3:34–37.

Luke's own implied readers one can arrive at some clarity about who is being addressed in various sections of the Sermon:

1. The Twelve represent wandering Christian preachers of Luke's time, poor and persecuted because they have responded in faith to Jesus' call to sell what they have, give to the poor, and follow him (5:10-11, 27-28; 8:3; 14:33; 18:22; 19:8-9; 21:1-3; Acts 2:44-45; 3:6; 4:32-37).

2. The larger group of disciples represent Luke's settled Christians, some of whom cling to their resources and reputation in the world (12:13-21, 22-34, 41-48; 14:12-14; 16:1-31; 22:3-6; Acts 5:1-5) and so have compromised their faith response to Jesus' summons.[16]

3. The large crowd of the Jewish people represent non-Christians who read the gospel because they have come to hear and be cured (6:18; 7:7; 8:47; 9:2, 11, 42; 17:15; Acts 28:8).[17]

Luke knew these groups were not completely distinct: those who have left all still feel the pull of riches (12:22-34; 18:26-28); those persecuted want to escape (9:23-26, 45; 18:34; 22:54-62). Those less committed and those not Christians still feel the tug of the good news (18:23). Every reader is addressed as actually or potentially both the poor disciple and also the disciple who falls away under enticement from the devil or the cares of the world (8:11-15). This existential understanding of his readers blurs the gospel's ideal distinctions of his hearers.[18]

---

[16] In spite of the cautions of Luke T. Johnson, Robert J. Karris, "Poor and Rich: the Lukan *Sitz im Leben*," in Charles H. Talbert, ed., *Perspectives on Luke-Acts* (Edinburgh: T & T Clark, 1978) 112–25 is generally correct in seeing Luke as addressing the rich within his community. The NT is replete with reflections on the tepidity of the early Christians who were regularly catechized by the Gospel; most germane to the woes would be Jas 2:1-9 and his "woe" in 5:1-6. Even granted the stylization of such attacks on the rich as a class, James was attacking rich Christians in his own community; see James B. Adamson, *James: The Man and His Message* (Grand Rapids: Eerdmans, 1989) 228–58 and the literature he cites.

[17] For a similar approach to Luke's readership of the Sermon see David L. Tiede, *Luke.* ACNT (Minneapolis: Augsburg, 1988) 140.

[18] In the present case it means that the beatitudes are addressed as a consolation to those who are poor, hungry, mourning, persecuted, and as a promise to those weak disciples and non-Christians who feel the tug of the gospel but have not yet responded authentically to its summons. The woes are addressed not only to tepid disciples as a warning of the consequences of their not practicing what they have professed, and to the outsiders whose commitment to the goods of this world is condemned, but also to the close disciples themselves, lest they fall away. The love commandment is addressed primarily to those who have internalized Jesus' own nonviolent and self-giving life, but it is also addressed to the world as its true hope for peace and justice. The proof of this pudding is in the eating: I appeal to the experience of every Christian reader of the gospel.

But Luke has distinguished the audiences in his text, and we must attempt to understand what τοῖς ἀκούουσιν means in 6:27a. It should refer to the disciples who are addressed by the beatitudes and woes.[19] Luke would then be varying his expression, using οἱ ἀκούοντες as a synonym for the μαθηταί of 6:20. Although ἀκούειν is not used in the sense of discipleship in Luke-Acts generally,[20] exegesis of 6:47-49, the concluding paraenesis summarizing the teaching of the Sermon, will reveal that it is the first step leading to full discipleship. True disciples hear, profess, and do as Jesus commands; other disciples hear and profess, but do not do; outsiders come to hear (6:17), but do not profess and do. With this understanding, in the context of 6:20-26, and especially in contrast to 6:24-26, the τοῖς ἀκούουσιν of 6:27 refers primarily to true disciples who hear, profess, and do. But it is also addressed secondarily to disciples who are rich, fat, mirthful, and praised by this world, and to outsiders come to hear—all who need and want this good news.

Thus the hearers in 6:27a are the larger audience that Luke so carefully gathered to hear the Sermon (6:12-19).[21] The Twelve and other disciples are in the best position to understand what Jesus is saying because they have already seen the effects of his teaching and authority over demons, and have accepted this authority over their own lives. But through the gathering of the crowds (6:17c) Luke signals that Jesus' words are sought for their healing power by the whole world, essential to the life of every human.

We can now interpret the elements of 6:27a: ἀλλὰ signals not a change of audience, but a change of thought and tone, from threats to those not living the life of the beatitudes to the commands to love one's enemies for those who do. Ὑμῖν λέγω is a Lukan reversal of word order emphasizing what follows.[22] Τοῖς ἀκούουσιν are the whole of Luke's

---

[19] The text provides no grounds for distinguishing these hearers: Luke makes no distinction at 6:24 between the hearers of the beatitudes and woes. After Paul S. Minear's decisive argument from the discipleship character of the fourth beatitude and the fourth woe in "Jesus' Audiences according to Luke," *NovT* 16 (1974) 103–109, one can no longer separate the hearers of the beatitudes from those of the woes. The woes are a warning to Luke's Christian readers, the devoted and the failing.

[20] Ἀκούειν in the sense of πείθασθαι (BAGD 32, §4) is rare in the NT, in Luke-Acts only in Acts 28:28.

[21] Minear, "Audiences," 103-109.

[22] On the redactional character of the reversed word order see Wilhelm Ott, *Gebet und Heil: Die Bedeutung der Gebetsparänese in der lukanischen Theologie.* SANT 12 (Munich: Kösel, 1965) 100. Neither in Luke 11:9 nor in 16:9 does the reversed pronoun indicate a change of audience; rather Luke uses the reversal to emphasize what follows, as in English "I tell you." Ὑμῖν λέγω is not as emphatic as the ἐγὼ δὲ λέγω ὑμῖν in Matt 5:44 (reinforced by the antitheses of 5:21-48), but it still emphasizes the authority of Jesus, as Theodor Hahn, Walter Grundmann, and I. Howard Marshall have seen.

readers who come to hear and be healed (6:18), now alerted by this clause to something important for their Christian or human lives.

6:27b: ἀγαπᾶτε τοὺς ἐχθροὺς ὑμῶν, "love your enemies." While Matthew builds to the command to love enemies as the climax and summary of his antitheses (5:44), Luke makes it the first of Jesus' commands, the topic sentence that the rest of his commands exemplify and explain. Its identical wording in Matthew and Luke manifests its currency from earliest traditions as Jesus' fundamental ethical teaching.[23] The love command counters the basic human tendency of revenge and even the principle of reciprocity enshrined in the law of ancient (and modern) civilizations. To catch its counter-cultural character, we will take an overview of love of neighbor and enemy in Judaism and in Hellenism and then interpret the individual words.

a. *In Israel,* as in the ancient world generally, enemies are forever,[24] to be repaid by personal and judical counterviolence. Unbounded tribal vengeance is attested as early as Gen 4:15-24, and the *gôʾēl,* the blood avenger, was a tribal instrument for restoring right order.[25] This tribal restorative retaliation against an enemy was gradually modified by the *lex talionis,* which made the reprisal proportionate to the offense (Exod 21:23-24; Lev 24:20).[26] But in this basic notion the enemy always remains an opponent to be punished for his offense. Considering one's enemies as God's enemies (a not infrequent transposition based on the notions under-

---

[23] It was most probably in Q. Hans-Dieter Betz shows how the rest of the NT takes love of enemies as Jesus' foundational ethical teaching in *The Sermon on the Mount: A Commentary on the Sermon on the Mount, Including the Sermon on the Plain (Matthew 5:3–7:27 and Luke 6:20-49).* Edited by Adela Yarbro Collins. Hermeneia (Minneapolis: Fortress, 1995) 296–300. Of the material in the exhaustive bibliographies in Fitzmyer and Betz, *ad loc.,* most important for me were Krister Stendahl, "Hate, Non-Retaliation, and Love," *HTR* 55 (1962) 343–55; Oscar Seitz, "Love Your Enemies," *NTS* 16 (1969–70), 39–54; Dieter Lührmann, "Liebet eure Feinde (Lk 6,27-36/Mt 5:39-48)," *ZThK* 69 (1972) 412–38; Luise Schottroff, "Non-Violence and the Love of Enemies," in Reginald H. Fuller, ed., *Essays on the Love Commandment* (Philadelphia: Fortress, 1978) 9–39; John Piper, *"Love Your Enemies": Jesus' Love Command in the Synoptic Gospels and in the early Christian Paraenesis: A History of the Tradition and Interpretation of its Uses."* MSSNTS 38 (Cambridge and New York: Cambridge University Press, 1979); Jürgen Becker, "Feindesliebe—Nächstenliebe—Bruderliebe," *ZEE* 25 (1981) 5–17; Anton Vögtle, "Das Zwiegespräch der Liebe zwischen Gott und dem Menschen," *WuW* 44 (1981) 143–53; Jürgen Sauer, "Traditionsgeschichtliche Erwägungen zu den synoptischen und paulinischen Aussagen über Feindesliebe und Wiedervergeltungsverzicht," *ZNW* 76 (1985) 1–28.

[24] Exodus 23:22; Ps 6:10; Werner Foerster, "ἐχθρός," *TDNT* 2:11–14.

[25] Roland de Vaux, *Ancient Israel* (New York: McGraw-Hill, 1957) 10–11; S. David Sperling, "Blood, Avenger of," *ABD* 1:763–64.

[26] This *lex talionis* appeared not only early in the Ancient Near East, but can be seen as enunciating the basic notion of justice behind Western law codes; Betz, *Sermon* 275–76.

lying hatred in our comment on 6:22) provides religious sanction to one's own hatred of enemies.

Further, while a host of commands in Israel's legal materials prescribe practical assistance to others, especially the weak and marginalized, there are only a few biblical commands to love other humans.[27] Leviticus 19:18 commands every person in Israel to love as oneself one's neighbor, understood as one's covenant partner.[28] Deuteronomy 10:19 expressly commands love of the alien in Israel's land, and so, with Lev 19:34; Exod 22:21; 23:9, brings the alien into the circle of Israel's love of the neighbor.[29] Although the motive for such love is not articulated, compassion for the other as a fellow human being throbs in such laws as "If ever you take your neighbor's garment in pledge, you shall restore it to him before the sun goes down, for that is his only covering; it is his mantle for his body, in what else shall he sleep?" (Exod 22:26-27) or "and you shall love [the stranger] as yourself, for you were strangers in the land of Egypt" (Lev 19:34).

It is not surprising, then, that Judaism has no command to love one's enemy.[30] Still, a few texts speak of benevolent actions toward one's enemies. The three laws that demand the return of the enemy's ass (Exod 23:4-5; Deut 22:1-4) and prohibit hatred or vengeance against the neighbor (Lev 19:17-18) extend love of neighbor to love of one's personal

---

[27] In the Decalogue sixty or seventy per cent of the commands refer to service of neighbor; in the Book of the Covenant (Exod 20:22–23:33) eighty-two per cent of the verses deal with the Israelites' obligations to their neighbor; see L. John Topel, *The Way to Peace: Liberation Through the Bible* (Maryknoll, N.Y.: Orbis, 1979) 23–31. Emphasis on practical action rather than on interior motive may account for the rarity of formal commands to love the neighbor; H. von Rücker, "Warum wird ʾahab (lieben) im Alten Testament selten zur Bezeichnung für Nächstenliebe gebraucht?" in Joseph Reindl and Georg Hentschel, eds., *Dein Wort Beachten: Alttestamentliche Aufsätze* (Leipzig: St. Benno Verlag, 1981) 9–15.

[28] Πλησίον normally translates *rēaʿ*, which, both in its etymology (from *rʿh* "to have dealings with someone, to associate") and in its usage (where relationship within YHWH's covenant is implied) identifies the neighbor with a covenant partner, even if the generalized language of the commands can extend beyond the Jews to all humankind; Johannes Fichtner, "πλησίον," *TDNT* 5:312–15. See also Rudolf Bultmann, "Aimer son prochain, commandement de Dieu," *RHPR* 10 (1930) 222–41; Victor P. Furnish, *The Love Command in the New Testament* (Nashville: Abingdon, 1972); Andreas Nissen, *Gott und der Nächste im antiken Judentum: Untersuchungen zum Doppelgebot der Liebe. WUNT* 15 (Tübingen: Mohr, 1974); W. Wolpert, "Die Liebe zum Nächsten, zum Feind und zum Sünder," *ThGl* 74 (1984) 262–82; Katherine Doob Sakenfeld, "Love (OT)," *ABD* 4 (1992) 375–81. These authors rarely deal with reciprocal loving, which emerges in later Wisdom works (e.g., Prov 8:17, 21; Sir 4:14; 12:1-6; 13:15).

[29] Piper, *"Love Your Enemies"* 35–49 shows that this love of the neighbor is a constant in the intertestamental Jewish literature from Palestinian and Hellenistic provenance.

[30] See the short survey in ibid. 28–35. Nor is there, as some infer from Matt 5:43c, an OT command to hate one's enemy. The only explicit command to hate one's enemy occurs

enemy, whether Israelite or alien. In effect, these laws make the enemy into one's neighbor, and so provide some foundation for Jesus' teaching.[31]

Although later Judaism occasionally enjoined doing righteousness to all the peoples among whom the Jews lived, it mostly continued the emphasis on the brother in the covenant as the object of one's love.[32] Nevertheless, a significant passage from Hellenistic Judaism has remarkable resonances with Jesus' teaching:

> a good man . . . shows mercy to all, even though they are sinners. And, though they devise evil against him, he overcomes evil by doing good, since he is protected by God and loves righteousness as his own self. . . . He praises the virtuous; on the poor he has mercy, on the weak, compassion, and to God he sings praises. . . . . If, then, you have a good mind, wicked men will be at peace with you, and the profligate will reverence you and turn to good, and the covetous will not only abandon their desire, they will give the objects of their covetousness to the afflicted. . . If anyone does violence to a holy person, he repents because the holy person is merciful to his reviler and holds his peace. If anyone betrays a righteous person, the righteous person prays. (*T. Benj.* iv,1–v,4)[33]

This passage, enjoining not only mercy to enemies but a strategy of non-retaliation to convert the sinner to good, shows some similarity with Hellenistic ethics.[34] Could Greek thought, then, provide closer background for Jesus' teaching?

---

in the sectarian 1QS 1:2-10 "that [the saints] may love all the sons of light . . . and hate all the sons of darkness." Piper shows that even the sectary does not carry this "hatred" into action: *"Love Your Enemies"* 40–41.

[31] Gianni Barbiero, *L'Asino del Nemico: Rinuncia alla vendetta e amore del nemico nella legislazione dell'Antico Testamento (Es 23,4-5; Dt 22,1-4; Lv 19,17-18.* AnBib 128 (Rome: Biblical Institute Press, 1991) demonstrates the relatedness of these texts from the three great moral codices of the Old Testament and shows how each in its own time and social condition extends love of neighbor to love of enemy. For a similar attitude in the Wisdom literature cf. Prov 25:21-22 (= Rom 12:20).

[32] The succinct survey of Pheme Perkins, *Love Commands in the New Testament* (New York: Paulist, 1982) 12–21 indicates that *Jub.* 7:20 continues to interpret the neighbor as the covenant partner, but *Jub.* 20:2-10 extends the command to Gentiles. Later tradition mostly confines the love of neighbor to one's fellow Jew, as at Qumran (CD 6:14–7:2; 9:2-5) and among the rabbis; Klaus Berger, *Die Gesetzauslegung Jesu. Teil I. Markus und Parallelen.* WMANT 40 (Neukirchen-Vluyn: Neukirchener Verlag, 1972) 130–33.

[33] From the Testaments of the Twelve Patriarchs *T. Jos.* 18:2; *T. Gad* 6:7; *T. Iss.* 7:6; *T. Zeb.* 7:2-4 enjoin love of neighbor. Some of these identify the neighbor with an Israelite, others with all humans; some speak of love of enemy, others of love of the neighbor. Although the author was a Hellenistic Jew, Stoic influence on motivation is not manifest (Piper, *"Love Your Enemies"* 43–45).

[34] *The Letter of Aristeas*, 225, 227; 4 Macc 2:10-14; Philo, *Virt.* 116–118 are passages from Hellenistic Judaism enjoining love of enemies whose motivation is strongly influenced

b. *Hellenistic ethics* also takes the *lex talionis* as fundamental to its sense of justice, as is witnessed by the ancient playwrights (Aeschylus, *Choephori* 304; Sophocles, *Oed. Tyr.* 100), so that Lysias, *Pro Milite* 20, can state, "I consider it established that one should do harm to one's enemies and be of service to one's friends."

But Hellenstic ethicists tend to identify virtue in a self-centered way. From the Homeric notion of ἀρετή to the Hellenistic moral perspectives at the time of the formation of the gospel (Middle Platonism, Stoicism, Cynicism, Epicureanism) the ethical question is always, "What must *I* do to be happy? How am *I* to be good?"[35] Aristotle's ethics are baldly teleological: right action is what conduces to a person's end (her good). Even his treatise on friendship in the *Nicomachaean Ethics* considers friendship as a perfection of the person: "in loving a friend men love what is good for themselves" (1157b33)—it is doing the good "for his own sake (for the sake of the intellectual element in him, which is thought to be the man himself)" (1166a14-16). Giving to a friend in need ennobles the giver: "while a man's friend gains wealth, he himself achieves nobility; he is therefore assigning the greater honor to himself" (1169a27-30).[36] The happy man needs friends because he is by nature social and needs to be benevolent (1169b2-22).

Nevertheless, this remarkable treatise begins by locating friendship in the category of beneficence (1155a7-9), defines friendship as wishing what is good for the friend's sake (1155b31; 1156b6-9; 1157b31-32; 1159a8; 1166a1-5; 1168b2-3).[37] Friends so come together in love that they

---

by Stoic notions of virtue. On the other hand, *Joseph and Asenath,* which stereotypically affirms that it is not right for the godly to repay evil for evil, shows no Stoic influence on this ethical stance and so may simply be an extension of the OT doctrine of nonretaliation; Piper, *"Love Your Enemies"* 35–39.

[35] Werner W. Jaeger, *Paideia: the Ideals of Greek Culture.* Translated by Gilbert Highet. 3 vols. (New York: Oxford University Press, 1939–44); Arthur W. H. Adkins, *Moral Values and Political Behaviour in Ancient Greece; From Homer to the End of the Fifth Century* (New York: Norton, 1972); Kenneth J. Dover, *Greek Popular Morality in the time of Plato and Aristotle* (Berkeley: Univ. of California Press, 1974; Phillip Mitsis, *Epicurus' Ethical Theory: the Pleasures of Invulnerability* (Ithaca: Cornell Univ. Press, 1988); William F. R. Hardie, *Aristotle's Ethical Theory* (Oxford: Clarendon Press, 1980) 325.

[36] Hendrick Bolkestein, *Wohltätigkeit und Armenpflege im vorchristlichen Altertum* (Utrecht: A. Oosthoek, 1939) 170 summarizes the Greek motivation for beneficence: "The mainsprings of the εὐ ποιεῖν have been shown to be the following: the *joy* which the giver gets from his act, the *honor* which he expects, and the *reward* or advantage which he counts on," and he cites Isocrates' examplary "I assert that all men do everything for the sake of pleasure, or gain or honor" (Piper, *"Love Your Enemies"* 180 n. 2).

[37] Cf. *Rhet.* 1371a21. Aristotle distinguishes friendship of utility and friendship of pleasure from perfect friendship because only in the latter do people love their friends for their own sakes (1156ab).

become "a single soul" and "have all things in common" (1168b7). Thus the friend is "a second self [αὐτὸς, ἄλλος]" (1166a29-32). Indeed, the much controverted statement that "Friendly relations with one's neighbors . . . seem to have proceeded from a man's relations to himself" (1166a1-2) appears to be the model according to which Aristotle united the altruism of friendship with one's self-perfection.[38]

Of course this kind of loving friendship is between equals, between comparably accomplished free citizens of the polis. The best friendship for Aristotle is based on the proximity of the friend (e.g., kinship), or his goodness; there is no friendship of the citizen with the slave, or with the gods. *But* this best friendship is *not for the evil person* (1157a16-19); indeed, "it is impossible to love the bad" (1165b13-14). One can have good will toward those with whom one is not close (1155b32-1156a5; 1166b30-1167a2), yet this good will consists only in wishing well to another, not in doing anything effective for him or her (1167a8-9). Thus Aristotle agrees with Plato's rejection of doing evil to one's enemies (*Rep.* 335a7-e), not out of avoidance of harm to the enemy or even the state (though there is some consideration of the latter), but to avoid the harm done to one's own virtue.

Mostly Hellenistic philosophy backed away from this Aristotelean thread of altruism in favor of a Cynic αὐτάρκεια (self-sufficiency) or a Stoic ἀπάθεια (impassivity) that would make human happiness invulnerable to external and uncontrollable influences. But strands of Hellenistic philosophy expanded Aristotle's restriction of care to the *polis*. The proto-Cynic Diogenes proclaimed, "I am a citizen of the world [κοσμοπολίτης]" (6.63).[39] The Stoics developed a pantheistic doctrine of the λόγος everywhere in the cosmos, so that there was everywhere one law of nature, and

---

[38] John Benson, "Making Friends: Aristotle's Doctrine of the Friend as Another Self," in Andros Loizou and Harry Lesser, eds., *Polis and Politics: Essays in Greek Moral and Political Philosophy* (Aldershot, England, and Brookfield, Vt.: Avebury, 1990) 50–68, takes Aristotle's argument that a man's relations with himself are the source of friendly relations with others as the key to his understanding of the friend as another self. As a craftsman puts himself into the thing made (*Nicomachean Ethics* IX, 7), so the lover's self is found in the friend as the product of mutual sharing of ideas and goals and mutual effective willing of the good for one another. Thus altruism is a form of enlightened self-love, and self-love must issue in altruism.

[39] In the case of Diogenes this appears more a revolt against the customs and laws of any society than an appeal to benevolence of all humans. Since Cynics left few writings, one must capture their words from others. The Stoic Epictetus records the Cynic's concern for the welfare of his enemy: ". . . the Cynic has made all mankind his children . . . in that spirit he approaches them all and cares for them all . . . as a father . . . as a brother and as a servant of Zeus, who is Father of us all" (*Disc.* III.22.81-2). But this altruism is incidental to the Cynic's desires to be sovereignly serene in adversity; Adolf F. Bonhoeffer, *Epiktet und das Neue Testament* (Giessen, 1911); Piper, *"Love Your Enemies"* 24.

all humans, even slaves and foreigners, have a spark of the divine λόγος, with a claim to good will. In this cosmopolitan Stoicism even enemies have Zeus as father, and so have a kinsmen's right to mercy and forgiveness. This inclusiveness would seem to lead to loving others as we love ourselves because humanity at large is connected with self. In Seneca's late Stoic ethical perspective, "We shall engage in affairs to the very end of life, we shall never cease to work for the common good, to help each and all, to give aid even to our enemies when our hand is feeble with age" (*De Otio* 1.4).[40] But when Stoics explain the motives for their concern for others the reasons are quite different. When Seneca prohibits returning evil for evil the underlying motivation is concern for one's own virtue: "for it is not honorable as in acts of kindness to requite benefits so to requite injuries with injuries . . . the man who returns a smart commits merely the more pardonable sin" (*De Ira* II.32.2-5). At its worst, the motive is that a disdainful ignoring of the slight is the best revenge.[41] But even at its best it is not the cosmopolitan kinship status of the other that is the Stoic motive for forgiveness of the enemy, but the maintenance of a distance from others in which one's tranquility is preserved: "the attempt [to injure the wise man] will be made but the injury will not reach him. For the distance which separates him from contact with his inferiors is so great that no baneful force can extend its power all the way to him" (*De Constantia* 4.1).

Consequently, love of neighbor among the Greeks seems to be rooted in either a desire for advantage or a concern for one's own happiness or practice of virtue. There is hardly anything of the compassion for the other underlying Exod 22:26-27 or Lev 19:34.[42] In sum, although one can find traces of the motive for loving the enemy in both Judaism and Greco-Roman thought, there is nothing nearly so explicit and clear as Jesus' bald command in the Sermon.

Ἀγαπᾶτε: ἀγαπᾶν in Greek literature lacks the passion of ἐρᾶν and the warmth of φιλεῖν and occurs much less frequently than either. It has the connotation of detachment, "to satisfy, to prefer;" it is a love that makes distinctions, choosing its object freely, and so serves to describe the love of a higher for a lower. Perhaps for these reasons it is almost always the LXX translation for *ʾahēb*, the Hebrew word that describes a range of feelings and commitments from sexual passion (2 Samuel 13) to the

---

[40] Other texts of Seneca in which love of neighbor extends even to love of those who have injured us are *Ep.* 48.2 and *De vita beata* 24.3.

[41] Marcus Porcius Cato refused even to remember being struck accidentally in the baths; Piper, *"Love Your Enemies"* 22.

[42] This higher ethic will be reduced to a more utilitarian level in the ethic of reciprocity, which will be discussed in the exegesis of Luke 6:32-34.

personal love that leads to self giving in marriage (Song 8:5; 1 Sam 1:5; 18:20), in the family (Gen 22:2; Ruth 4:15), among intimate friends (1 Sam 18:1, 3; 20:17), and beneficent action for neighbor (Lev 19:18).[43] Often *ʾhb,* under the influence of usage found in second- and first-millennia political treaties, can mean political loyalty (1 Sam 18:16, 22, 28), and this use can color other expressions of love.[44] Indeed, God's love for Israel and Israel's for God, though sometimes expressed in emotional terms (Hos 3:1; Isa 49:15; Jer 31:3), is strongly influenced by notions of deliberate choice, expressed in covenant, with overtones of political loyalty (Exod 20:6; Deut 6:4-5; 7:7-14; 10:12-22; 11:1, 22; Hos 9:15).

In the NT ἀγαπᾶν, ἀγάπη, ἀγαπητός occur 318 times; the root occurs in every book. In the gospels and Acts the frequency is: Matthew 12, Mark 9, Luke 15, John 43, Acts 1.[45] The synoptics never explicitly describe God's love, and, except for the Great Commandment of the Law (Matt 22:37-40//Mark 12:29-31//Luke10:26-28), do not enjoin disciples to love God.[46] Luke uses the verb thirteen times, six of them in 6:27-35. His other uses may give us a clue about the kind of affection or beneficent action that is meant in the Sermon's uses.

7:5: The centurion "loves" the Jewish people, and has built their synagogue in Capernahum.[47] Here ἀγαπᾷ does not mean special intimacy or friendship with individual Jews, but an esteem for the people. If, as Bruce J. Malina conjectures, the centurion is brokering imperial resources for the local population, the "love" could be merely instrumental.[48] However, the verb ἀγαπᾷ,[49] the friendly nature of the negotiations described in 7:2-6, and

[43] Gottfried Quell, "ἀγαπάω," *TDNT* 1:21-35; Katherine Doob Sakenfeld, "Love (OT)," *ABD* 4:376–77.

[44] William L. Moran, "The Ancient Near Eastern Background of the Love of God in Deuteronomy," *CBQ* 25 (1963) 77–87; Michael A. Fishbane, "The Treaty Background of Amos 1:11 and Related Matters," *JBL* 89 (1970) 313–18, shows that even Jonathan's love for David (1 Sam 18:1, 3; 20:17) can mean commitment to David's political cause.

[45] The Johannine gospel and letters use the group 105x, and Paul 135x, so the terms cannot be said to be a strong emphasis of the synoptic gospels or Acts.

[46] Indeed, this holds true of John as well; Thomas Barrosse, "The Relationship of Love and Faith in St. John," *TS* 18 (1957) 538–59.

[47] The verb could indicate that he was the or a primary contributor to its construction. J. M. Creed, *The Gospel According to St. Luke* (London: Macmillan, 1930) 101 cites a second-century Egyptian manuscript attesting to a Gentile's contributions to a Jewish place of prayer, and there is later evidence cited in Billerbeck 4/1:142–43.

[48] Bruce J. Malina and Richard L. Rohrbaugh, *Social-Science Commentary on the Synoptic Gospels* (Minneapolis: Fortress, 1992) 326–29. The centurion then would be making the Jewish elders into clients of Rome, or of himself as its representative, as a way of pacifiying the region.

[49] Josephus describes as honoring the people (ἐτίμα ἡμῶν τὸ ἔθνος in *Contr. Ap.* 2, 4, 43) Alexander's rewarding the Jews' fidelity to him by letting them hold Samaria tax-free.

the openness to faith described in 7:6-10 most probably point to a deep personal esteem for Jewish customs and mores that carries into beneficent action, securing the building at the center of those customs and mores.[50] Thus ἀγαπᾶν denotes, at the least, esteem that leads into supportive action.

7:42: Jesus asks which of two debtors more "loves" the creditor who has forgiven their unequal debts. The parable gives ἀγαπήσει a color of gratitude springing from the unexpected and generous absolution (ἐχαρίσατο) of the debt. Hence ἀγαπᾶν means the kind of personal gratitude and loyalty that would reciprocate with some kind of service to one's benefactor. The action could be the establishment of a patron-client relationship.

7:47: The application of this parable to the sinful woman (v. 47e, "one who has been forgiven a small debt 'loves' little") indicates that the acts of braving a hostile audience, bewailing her sins, bathing his feet with her tears and wiping them with her hair, and anointing his feet with expensive myrrh are acts of loving gratitude.[51] If one takes the ὅτι clause as causal,[52] then the loving acts expressing sorrow are part of the actual process of forgiveness and manifest a love that exceeds even more the description of the love as "merely" gratitude. But in either case the love issues in very personal acts of benevolence toward the other.

10:27: The citation of Deut 6:5 and Lev 19:18 employs ἀγαπήσεις but once, because the two form only one commandment in Luke's theology (contrast δευτέρα in Matt 22:39 and Mark 12:33). Whatever *ʾhb* meant in these original passages,[53] Luke has transformed these meanings by the following parable of the Good Samaritan. Love of neighbor now means feelings of compassion (10:33b, ἐσπλαγχνίσθη) and actions of healing (10:34a) and hospitality (10:34b-35) for one's enemy.[54] Again, Lukan ἀγαπᾶν has taken on connotations of personal engagement with the other, here an enemy.

[50] Possibly the centurion, like Cornelius in Acts 10:2, was a "God-fearer," at least in the loose sense attested in Kirsopp Lake, *The Beginings of Christianity* (London: Macmillan, 1933) 5:84–88.

[51] This, the almost unanimous interpretation of contemporary exegetes, makes the "love" of the forgiven debtor in 7:42, 47e a gratitude expressed by acts of loving care.

[52] While ὅτι *can* express "this is true because I see the signs of it" (*GB* §421–22, which gives no other examples from the Bible or Greek literature), only 1 John 3:14c, of the 1285 uses of ὅτι in the NT, manifests this usage. The following pronouncement of the forgiveness of sins in 7:48 indicates a more complex description of the process of forgiveness than contemporary exegetes allow.

[53] Both of them occur in covenantal contexts, stressing the loyalty the subject owes his Lord and the obligation to carry that loyalty into action. This kind of love is closer to duty or *pietas*.

[54] The lawyer's active animosity toward a Samaritan is revealed in his inability to pronounce the word "Samaritan" in answer to Jesus' question in 10:37b; Joachim Jeremias, *The Parables of Jesus* (London: S.C.M., 1963) 205.

11:43: This woe pronounced on the Pharisees uses ἀγαπᾶν in the opposite way, signifying a greedy and self-centered seeking after positions of honor, more like lust than love.[55]

16:13: The proverb that ends the parable of the dishonest steward parallels ἀγαπᾶν to serving (δουλεύειν) a master and opposes it to hating (μισεῖν) a master. Thus it is like the covenant usage of *ʾhb*, formally committing oneself to a dutiful life of loyalty and service.

Thus Lukan ἀγαπᾶν encompasses a wide range of meanings, from gross desire for base things (11:43) to compassionate acts arising from deep personal affection (7:37-47; 10:33-37 as exemplification of 10:27). In all uses it goes beyond feeling, to a commitment to action for another. Most often ἀγάπη arises in response to the prior benevolence of another. Sometimes the response derives from a formal commitment one has made, more comparable to the English phrase "dutiful service" (10:27; 16:13), sometimes from gratitude for a prior act of benevolence by another in which the obligation of gratitude is not formally spelled out (7:42, 47). Sometimes, however, the act springs from the initiative of the one loving, as in 7:5 and the acts of the Samaritan (10:30-37) used to describe love of neighbor.

Love of enemy (6:27b), then, describes a commitment to help the enemy.[56] Luke 6:27b tells us nothing about the compassion or duty that underlie the acts, but if, as has so far been common in Lukan usage (4:18; 6:20b), the first colon is a topic sentence to be spelled out by the subsequent cola of the strophe, we may get in 6:27-36 a description of the kind of love required by 6:27b.

Τοὺς ἐχθροὺς: ἐχθρός in secular Greek usage described one's personal enemy. Israel, which had from its beginning a more focused sense of national identity, used *ʾôyeb* (almost always translated by ἐχθρός) to describe national enemies, enemies of God, as well as personal enemies.[57] But whether the enemy is national or religious or personal, the personal dimension of enmity dominates Hebrew usage.[58] Among the rabbis hatred itself is bad, but hatred of heretics or other enemies of God is good. In the NT also, ἐχθρός means primarily personal enemies (Gal 4:16), but it can also mean the foes of Israel or those hostile to God and God's people (Phil 3:18 and the many passages that quote Ps 110:1).

---

[55] Cf. 16:14 for the Pharisees' love of money, now expressed by the φιλ- stem (φιλάργυροι).

[56] The present tense of the imperative makes the command general, to be followed regularly through the disciple's life. The same is true for all the commands and prohibitions of 6:27-31, except v. 29b.

[57] J. Moulder, "Who Are My Enemies?" *JTSA* 25 (1978) 41–49 shows that the LXX principally uses ἐχθρός to describe civic or national enemies.

[58] Werner Foerster, "ἐχθρός," *TDNT* 2:811–12.

In view of this wide usage a brief survey of Lukan usage is necessary to determine the meaning here. The subsequent injunctions in 6:27-36 seem to speak of personal enemies of the disciples, who afflict them directly with all kinds of evils. But all other Lukan uses of ἐχθρός refer not to a Christian's personal enemy but to the enemy of the People of God (1:71, 74; 20:43; Acts 2:35), the (Roman) enemies of Jerusalem (19:43), those who refuse to accept Jesus as messianic king (19:27), whether in Jesus' ministry or in that of the Church. Paul calls Elymas the magician an enemy of all righteousness for trying to turn Sergius Paulus from faith in Jesus (Acts 13:10). Ultimately, Satan is the enemy (Luke 10:19, reflecting on 10:18).

Thus one expects that Jesus' command in 6:27b addresses enemies of larger scope than the disciple's personal enemies.[59] This would throw us back to the persecution that forms the proximate context of the command— the persecution of Christians for the sake of the Son of Man (6:24).[60] Such persecutors would be the enemies of the People of God, of Jesus himself, of all righteousness identified with faith in Jesus. If so, then the command asks for a staggering reversal of human values. Jesus commands the disciple not only to counteract the natural desire for a "justified" retaliation against one's personal or tribal enemies, but also to reverse the larger "religious" impulse to retaliate against the enemies of God! This contradiction of the pattern of the world and even OT hatred of the enemies of God recalls the paradoxical nature of the beatitudes with which the Sermon began.[61] Perhaps expanded description of these enemies in 6:27-36 will reveal further how Luke's Jesus functionally defines them in the Sermon.

6:27c: καλῶς ποιεῖτε τοῖς μισοῦσιν ὑμᾶς, "do good to those who hate you" continues the series of four cola in synonymous parallelism specifying the actions of love of the enemy. These acts progress from attitude (hatred) to word (a curse) to deed (mistreatment);[62] to counteract these, however, Jesus proposes deeds (doing good, blessings, and prayer), which become more spiritualized as the actions of the persecutors become more externalized.

---

[59] This seems to be the meaning in Matt 5:43-44, where attitude to enemies is contrasted to love of the neighbor as member of God's people; Foerster, *TDNT* 2:814.

[60] Although I. Howard Marshall, *The Gospel of Luke* (Exeter: Paternoster, 1978) 259 takes the enemies to be the persecutors of 6:24, by making the enemy "a person who has hostile feelings towards me" who becomes the object of my hostility, he extends the Lukan reference beyond persecutors to enemies in general and personal ones in particular.

[61] How Jesus can make this demand (how it becomes possible and coherent for his disciples) will be discussed in Chapter 8. Here we only note that it is consistent with Jesus' own actions in 9:55; 23:34.

[62] Walter Grundmann, *Das Evangelium nach Lukas* (Berlin: Evangelische Verlagsanstalt, 1961) 147; Josef Ernst, *Das Evangelium nach Lukas übersetzt und erklärt* (Regensburg: Pustet, 1977) 224.

Τοῖς μισοῦσιν: We already saw in Chapter 4 the hatred that God's enemies show to those who follow God's ways. People can be hated because they are of God's people (1:71), because they are of Christ (19:14), or especially because they are destined for persecution by their allegiance to Christ (21:17). In the context of the Sermon, Jesus has pronounced a beatitude on his disciples who, for his sake, experience hatred issuing in exclusion, disgrace, and slander (6:22-23). So again the hatred to which Jesus refers in 6:27c is primarily the kind of hatred the disciples experience as followers of Jesus.

Καλῶς ποιεῖn: εὖ ποιεῖν is normal Greek for benevolent action, but it occurs rarely in the LXX.[63] Καλῶς ποιεῖν is even rarer, used only eight times in the LXX, to mean "to do good" (Lev 5:4; Zech 8:15), "to do well" (1 Kings 8:18 = 2 Chr 6:8), or simply "please" (1 Macc 12:18, 22; 2 Maccabees 16). It occurs more frequently in the NT, where eight uses refer to doing the morally right thing (Acts 10:33; 1 Cor 7:37, 38; Phil 4:14; Jas 2:8, 19; 3 John 6).[64] But all three synoptic uses refer to doing benevolent acts to another:

> Matthew 12:12 "is it lawful on the Sabbath to act benevolently [healing the sick]?"
>
> Mark 7:37 "He has done all things well," where the immediate reference is to healing;
>
> Luke 6:27 "Do good to those who hate you."

In all three of these uses the concern of the action is not its moral character but its healing effect for the other. Further, in its Lukan context καλῶς ποιεῖτε, as part of a series of verbs explicating love of enemies in 6:27-28, is parallel to ἀγαθοποιεῖν, to do good (to someone), the middle of the triad of verbs in 6:32-34 and the same triad in 6:35. Thus the meaning here is not to do well morally, but to do benevolent acts to those who hate oneself. Finally, this benevolent action (6:27c) as explicitation of love of enemies (6:27b) stresses the active character of that love.[65]

6:28a: εὐλογεῖτε τοὺς καταρωμένους ὑμᾶς, "bless those who curse you."

Καταρᾶσθαι since Homer was the normal word for "to curse, call a curse upon, imprecate." It is used 70x in the LXX, normally to translate the

---

[63] Of some 3300 uses of ποιεῖν in the LXX, εὐποιεῖν occurs only some twenty-four times. In both classical Greek and in the LXX a number of expressions convey the same idea: ἔλεος ποιεῖν, δικαιοσύνην ποιεῖν, ἀγαθὸν ποιεῖν, etc.

[64] The meaning indicated by the etymology of καλῶς, beautifully, *nobly*.

[65] Jesus' command goes far beyond Aristotle's refusal to do evil to the other (see above) by requesting a benevolence for the enemy that carries into action.

pi'el or *pu'al* of *qll*. In the OT a curse is an utterance designed to bring harm by a supernatural agency.[66] Although the ultimate harm is to separate humans from God, most OT curses seek to deprive the one cursed of prosperity or physical health. Although God can curse directly (Gen 12:3; Mal 2:2), as can prophets and other divine agents (Numbers 22–24; 2 Kings 2:24),[67] the OT more normally implies, often by the divine passive, that lack of prosperity for Israel or its enemies arises from a divine curse. Rarely are good persons or divine agents cursed by enemies (1 Sam 17:23; 2 Kings 2:23; Pss 62:4; 109:17, 28); in most of these instances the just man prays that the curse fall upon those who curse him. The Qumran sectaries were to bless their own members, who have cast their lot with God, and curse outsiders and defectors, who have cast their with Belial (1 QS 2:2-17). The most notable exceptions in which the cursed does not retaliate are 2 Sam 16:5-14 and especially Jer 15:10-11, where he entreats the Lord for his enemies' good.

The verb is used only five times in the NT.[68] James 3:9-10 has an implicit injunction to Christians not to curse other humans. Romans 12:14 contains such strong resonances of Luke 6:28 that many exegetes think it derives from the Jesus tradition.[69] Even if this is not so, the verbal resonances are so strong that Rom 12:14 offers the best NT commentary on Luke 6:28: "Bless those who persecute you; bless and do not curse them" may indicate that the persecution itself involves a curse on the Christians, who do not retaliate in kind (Rom 12:17).[70]

[66] In the OT both blessings and curses were not simply declarative, but factitive, having the power to effect objectively and permanently what they declared (Gen 27:33-37; Num 22:6). As such, the curse is somewhat more than the *Wort* Grundmann found intermediate between attitude and deed.

[67] Jeremiah frequently asks God for vengeance on his enemies (11:20; 12:3, etc.), but the LXX never translates these prayers as curses.

[68] Matthew 25:41 and Mark 11:21 do not relate to the blessing or cursing of enemies.

[69] Dale C. Allison, "The Pauline Epistles and the Synoptic Gospels. The Pattern of the Parallels," *NTS* 28 (1982) 1–32; Peter Stuhlmacher, "Jesustradition im Römerbrief? Eine Skizze," *ThB* 14 (1983) 140–50; David Wenham, "Paul's Use of the Jesus Tradition: Three Samples," in idem, ed., *The Jesus Tradition Outside the Gospels* (Sheffield: JSOT, 1985) 7–37; J. D. G. Dunn, "Paul's Knowledge of the Jesus Tradition: the Evidence of Romans," in Karl Kertelge et al., eds., *Christus Bezeugen: Für Wolfgang Trilling.* ETS 59 (Leipzig: St. Benno Verlag, 1990) 193–207. Others think that the imperatival participles betray an early Christian Semitic source; C. K. Barrett, *A Commentary on the Epistle to the Romans.* NTC (New York: Harper, 1957) 240; Charles H. Talbert, "Tradition and Redaction in Romans xii, 9-21," *NTS* 16 (1969–70) 83–94. That in a Christian exhortation that reverses the ordinary ethics of society both passages have (1) rejection of retaliation (Rom 12:17, 19; Luke 6:27-29) and (2) blessing (εὐλογεῖτε) of persecutors and those who curse (Rom 12:14; Luke 6:28) persuades me that the source is the Jesus tradition.

[70] Betz, *Sermon* 594 gives Polycarp's list of countermeasures for the curse (including the countercurse), but none of these magical means were acceptable to Christians.

Consequently, those who curse in Luke 6:28 may be any of those who object to Christian beliefs or conduct, but in the context of the enemies of 6:27b and the haters of 6:27c it seems to point to those who consistently oppose the disciples as bearers of the Gospel.

Εὐλογεῖν can mean to praise, give thanks, or bless; in the context of reversal of attack, persecution, or curses (Gen 12:3; Luke 6:28; Rom 12:14ab; 1 Cor 4:12; 1 Pet 3:9) "to bless" is preferred (BAGD 322). It is the usual LXX translation for *brk,* which admits of a wide range of use, from the commonplace greeting to the highest gifts of God's favor. Ultimately the source of all blessings is God. Ordinarily a superior—God, who gives life, prosperity, and personal relationship to himself (Gen 12:1-3; 24:35; Ps 65:10), the father of the family (Gen 27:27-29), the king (2 Sam 6:18); the priest (1 Sam 2:20; Num 6:23-26)—invokes a blessing on an inferior. But often the inferior blesses the superior. Acknowledging the gifts they have received, humans bless God as an act of praise and thanksgiving (Gen 24:48; Deut 8:10; Ps 31:21; 103:2). Humans also bless other humans, usually ones who have already conferred a favor on them (1 Sam 23:21; 2 Sam 2:5; Ruth 2:20).[71] This blessing conveys a wish or prayer. In all uses *brk* seeks to strengthen solidarity in social, racial, and religious relationships.[72]

New Testament use of εὐλογεῖν echoes Old Testament usage. That it is God who blesses (Matt 25:34; Gal 3:9; Heb 6:14) is implied in all the *barûk* formulae translated by εὐλογημένος (Mark 11:9, 10; Matt 23:39; Luke 1:28, 42; John 12:13).[73] In Luke, humans bless God (1:64; 2:28; 24:53) and other humans (2:34).[74] Jesus himself says the Jewish blessing at meals (Mark 6:41; 8:7; Luke 24:30) in ways that recall his institution of the Eucharist (Mark 14:22; 1 Cor 10:16). Jesus blesses his disciples with a high-priestly blessing (Luke 24:50-51; Acts 3:26). Something distinct begins to emerge when Jesus blesses little children (Mark 10:16).[75] But the real break with Jewish practice emerges when Jesus' command to bless those who curse one becomes part of

---

[71] The blessing formula *barûk ʾattāh* is the obverse of the curse formula *ʾarûr ʾattāh* (1 Sam 25:33; Ruth 3:10; Ps 115:15).

[72] Jacques Guillet, "Blessing," in Xavier Léon-Dufour, ed., *Dictionary of Biblical Theology* (New York: Seabury, 1973) 47–51; Josef Scharbert, "Blessing," in Johannes B. Bauer, ed., *Encyclopedia of Biblical Theology* (London: Sheed and Ward, 1976) 69–75, and in his longer article on *brk, TDOT* 1:279–308.

[73] In Luke five of his thirteen uses of εὐλογεῖν occur in a participial blessing of humans (εὐλογημένος). In the NT εὐλογητός (8x) refers only to God as the subject of human praise.

[74] Heb 7:1, 6-7; 11:20-21 recall Melchizedek's blessing of Abraham and Isaac's blessing of Jacob and Esau.

[75] This is the only use of κατευλογεῖν in the NT; it is not clear what calling down such a blessing actually means (is it a prayer?). That it was unusual may be deduced from the silence of the OT about such a blessing of children and more expressly from the disciples' chasing the children away.

Christian life[76] and paraenesis. Romans 12:14 not only asks for blessing of persecutors but implies that such persecutors have cursed the disciples (12:14b). First Peter 3:9 enjoins a blessing on those who have reviled the disciples. Thus the Christian community seems to have understood the importance of this reversal of sinful or inadequate religious practice.

But what is the content of such a blessing? Luke's contrast with a curse is our best clue to what εὐλογεῖν means in 6:28a—to reverse the action of calling down divine harm on one's enemy by instead calling down God's favor and gifts on the enemies. In the absence of explicit naming of such favor or gifts, it must mean the gift of God's drawing the opponents to himself. If the blessing is even more factitive than the curse, it should reveal ultimately that their opposition to these Christian disciples is opposition to God's salvific work in Jesus. Such a content is most congruent with the context of the injunction in the blessings and woes and in the injunctions of the love commandment itself.

6:28b: προσεύχεσθε περὶ τῶν ἐπηρεαζόντων ὑμᾶς, "pray for those who abuse you." Ἐπερεάζειν from the time of Herodotus means "to threaten, mistreat, abuse." The LXX does not use the word; it occurs only twice in the NT,[77] and so its content must be deduced from the Sermon itself. It may refer to any sort of attack, but in the context of increasingly externalized actions in 6:27-28 it probably denotes the kinds of abusive social actions described in Luke 6:22 as due to the Christian's association with the Son of Man. As Hans Dieter Betz points out, a citizen would ordinarily bring such abuse to the courts, but 6:22-23 has made it clear that this recourse is not effective or even available for Christians.

Προσεύχεσθαι: In the Hebrew Bible the specific words for prayer, 'tr and the hithpael of pll, are rarely used. In the LXX εὔχεσθαι and εὐχή normally translate ndr or 'tr; slightly more common are προσεύχεσθαι and προσευχή as the normal translations of the hithpael of pll and tephillah. In the OT all prayer is directed to God, who is all-wise and all-powerful, and committed to Israel's well-being through his covenant. In confidence and trust, then, Hebrews pray for bodily goods, the overthrow of enemies, and spiritual goods. They also, in cult and in individual prayer, praise and thank God for all favors received.[78]

---

[76] Paul's own practice was to bless those who reviled him (1 Cor 4:12).

[77] In view of its infrequency of use in the Bible and its strong Greek character, I take it as Lukan redaction; the Q original was probably closer to the προσεύχεσθε ὑπὲρ τῶν διωκόντων ὑμᾶς of Matt 5:44. Still, 1 Pet 3:16 uses ἐπερεάζειν for those who are abusing Christians, which reinforces the idea that 1 Pet 3:8-18 has been influenced by the Jesus tradition, perhaps that of the Lukan Sermon.

[78] Johannes Herrmann, "εὔχομαι," *TDNT* 2:785–800; Johannes B. Bauer, "Prayer," *EBT* 679–81.

In the NT προσεύχεσθαι and προσευχή predominate. (Luke-Acts has forty-one per cent of the eighty-six NT uses of προσεύχεσθαι, and thirty-three per cent of the thirty-six uses of προσευχή.)[79] As a pious Israelite, Jesus says the customary prayers of his people. His recorded prayers are all addressed to his "Father:" he prays for food (Luke 11:3), for deliverance from death (Mark 14:35 and *parr.*), in thanksgiving for his Father's plan (Matt 11:25//Luke 10:21), in petition that God's will be realized (Luke 11:2), for spiritual gifts for his disciples (John 17:9-19), and for forgiveness for his enemies (Luke 23:34). In Luke-Acts the classic topics for the disciples' prayer are given in the Our Father (11:2-4): that God's name be held holy, that the Reign of God come, that the disciples receive their daily bread, forgiveness of sins,[80] and deliverance from temptation. In Luke-Acts the content of the disciples' prayer is rarely specified, but they are to pray for mercy (18:11-14)[81] and for deliverance from temptation.[82] In Acts the disciples are presented as obeying Jesus' injunction to pray always (Luke 18:1), both cultically and personally (Acts 1:14; 2:42; 3:1; 6:4; 9:11; 10:4, 9, 30; 11:5; 16:13, 16; 22:17). The content of the disciples' prayer is barely discernible, but it includes requesting God's direction and choice (1:24), asking for the gift of the Spirit in conjunction with laying on of hands (6:6; 8:15; 13:3; 14:23), asking for the power to work miracles (9:40; 28:8), praying for Peter's safety (12:5, 12; 13:14, 23), and, in the context of Paul's departure, prayer for mutual safety (20:36; 21:5). Thus in Acts προσεύχεσθαι does not express the disciples' prayer for their enemies, but Stephen in 7:60 does pray for those stoning him in words quite similar to those of his master.

This varied usage hardly specifies the exact object of the disciples' prayer for those who abuse them. But in the context of increasingly external action against them, and increasingly spiritual response on their part (6:27-28), one assumes persistent prayer for the forgiveness, well-being, and even conversion of the enemy to amity with God and the Christian community.

---

[79] Ευχεσθαι is used only six times, and εὐχή only three times; δέησις for prayer of petition is used only eighteen times (only in Luke in the gospels and Acts), εὐλογεῖν forty-two times for "to bless, thank," εὐχαριστεῖν thirty-eight times for "to thank," αἰτεῖν twenty-nine times for "to ask God for."

[80] For our exegesis of 6:28 note that in all accounts, the disciples' forgiveness is related to their own forgiveness of those who have offended them (Luke 11:4//Matt 6:12; 18:32-33; Mark 11:25).

[81] By implication the Pharisee is rejected for his subtle self-praise, while the publican is commended for a petition for mercy for his sins.

[82] Luke 22:40, 46 specifies the deliverance from temptation in his version of the Lord's Prayer as the ability to persevere through human persecution. In Luke-Acts temptation refers to the constant danger of apostasy under persecution, as in 8:14-15; Acts 20:19; Fitzmyer, *Luke* 907.

6:29-30: After illustrating love of enemies (6:27b) by three generic sorts of actions against hatred and verbal abuse (6:27c-28b), Jesus now descends to four concrete physical actions against individual disciples and the recommended non-retaliatory response to each. The four-beat rhythm continues, now with participles preceding the imperatives. The change to second-person singular verbs marks not another source, but Jesus' articulation of those specific physical actions against individual Christians that evoke deeply visceral feelings in the listeners/readers.

6:29a: τῷ τύπτοντί σε ἐπὶ τὴν σιαγόνα πάρεχε καὶ τὴν ἄλλην, "to the one striking you on the cheek, turn the other cheek." The blow on the cheek[83] is the first act of physical violence to be directed against the person of Jesus' hearers. In the Mediterranean honor- and shame-based culture in which one retains ascribed honor or acquires honor by responding agonistically to the challenge of the other, a blow on the cheek was an egregious insult that demanded retaliation to re-establish one's position in society.[84] As such it was a far greater injury than it is for moderns, who find it difficult enough. Although this injury, like the others of the Sermon, could be enacted against the disciple *qua* disciple,[85] the intense personal nature of the injury may argue to injuries on other bases as well.[86]

How literally does one take πάρεχε καὶ τὴν ἄλλην?[87] Πάρεχειν in the NT means "to give up, offer, present, grant, show" (BAGD 626). Although

[83] Matthew 5:39 specifies a blow on the right cheek (ῥαπίζει εἰς τὴν δεξιὰν σιαγόνα), implying the greater insult of a left-handed or backhanded blow. First Esdras 4:30 (LXX) details the special insult involved in a left-handed slap, and *b. Qam.* 8.6 (Billerbeck 1:342) the double penance required for a backhanded slap; Ulrich Luz, *Matthew 1–7* (Minneapolis: Augsburg,1992) 325. In view of Luke's fondness for the "right" (6:6; 22:50), it is not likely he omitted it here, and so the right cheek is ascribed to Matthaean redaction; Fitzmyer, *Luke* 638.

[84] In Plato's *Gorgias* (486C) Callicles hyperbolically describes an unrequited blow to the head (κόρρη = temple) as the greatest of all dishonors, forcing its victim to live in his own city like an outcast. Although Socrates asserts in 508CD that to return the blow is more shameful than to suffer the injury, he agrees on the magnitude of the insult and its effects; see Betz, *Sermon* 596 for a jumbled account of the texts. For other citations from ancient literature see Gustav Stählin, "τύπτειν," *TDNT* 8:263; for various possible motivations for nonretaliation in Hellenistic Jewish and Greek literature see Luise Schottroff, "Non-violence," 18–22; for a social-science view of the insult's magnitude see Bruce J. Malina, *The New Testament World: Insights from Cultural Anthropology* (Atlanta: John Knox, 1981, rev. 1993) 25–48; Bruce J. Malina and Richard Rohrbaugh, *Social Science Commentary* 55.

[85] Joachim Jeremias, *The Sermon on the Mount* (Philadelphia: Fortress, 1963) 28. E. Earle Ellis, *The Gospel of Luke* (London: Nelson, 1966) 115 makes this a slap on the cheek of the heretic Christian in the synagogue, and 6:29b the robbing of a Christian missionary on the road. Perhaps; there is no evidence for either assertion.

[86] Some commentators (T. W. Manson, Heinz Schürmann, Josef Ernst) think 6:29ab describes robbers' acts.

[87] Many exegetes reduce Jesus' command to Semitic hyperbole or figurative language to inspire Christians to less recourse to violence; e.g., Robert C. Tannehill, *The Sword of*

it is a Lukan word (fifty-six per cent of sixteen NT uses), his usage is too broad to give us a clear interpretation of the action. It means "to grant as a favor" in 7:4; Acts 28:2 and perhaps Acts 17:31; 22:2; this would ground a presentation of the cheek as a gift, inviting not more abuse but a counteroffer of personal gift from the abuser.[88] Other usage merely means "provide" (11:7; 18:5; Acts 16:16; 19:24) and leaves open what meaning such "presentation" has. In any case the present imperative, as opposed to Matthew's aorist, lays down a general rule in such cases, not an isolated action.

We make four points about the meaning of the injunction. (1) Jesus clearly reverses the OT *lex talionis* (Exod 21:24; Lev 24:20; Deut 19:21) so that automatic or planned retaliation is not an ethical option for Christians.[89] (2) Some suggest an allusion to the nonviolent response of the Servant of YHWH; such an allusion, however, is far from clear.[90] (3) But if Jesus' words may best be interpreted by his own actions in the same gospel, then Luke's silence about Jesus' response to his beating in 22:63-65 illustrates the principle of nonretaliation, but it gives no indication of how or why.[91] (4) Inter-

---

His Mouth (Philadelphia: Fortress, 1975); Georg Strecker, *Die Bergpredigt* (Göttingen: Vandenhoeck & Ruprecht, 1985) 67–77; 88; Jan Lambrecht, "The Sayings of Jesus on Non-Violence," *Louvain Studies* 12 (1987) 291–305. Others think Jesus' demands apply only to the Christian's private sphere of morality; e.g., Ingo Broer, "Plädierte Jesus für Gewaltlosigkeit?" *BiKi* 37 (1982) 61–69. Others think the demands apply to both private Christian morality and the social sphere of the Church; e.g., Gerhard Lohfink, "Der ekklesiale Sitz im Leben der Aufforderung Jesu zum Gewaltverzicht (Mt 5,39b-42/Lk 6,29f)," *ThQ* 162 (1982) 237–53. Walter Wink thinks Jesus' command of an active nonviolent resistance forcing oppressors to make choices they would rather not make provides a middle ground between violent response and passive pacifism even for nations in "Beyond Just War and Pacifism: Jesus' Nonviolent Way," *RevExp* 89 (1992) 197–214, and in his response to Lambrecht in *Louvain Studies* 18 (1993) 3–20.

[88] Betz, *Sermon* 596 supports this interpretation by reference to Jesus' Golden Rule in 6:31.

[89] The context of the injunction in Matt 5:38-39 makes this unavoidably clear; still, even the Lukan wording contradicts the OT "stripe for stripe."

[90] Ernst, *Lukas* 225 cites Isa 53:7, but neither the MT nor the LXX speaks of a blow, still less a blow on the cheek; Schürmann, *Lukasevangelium* 347 suggests a reference to Isa 50:6, where the LXX has τὰς δὲ σιαγόνας μου εἰς ῥαπίσματα. But in that case Luke surely would have retained from Q or formulated something like Matt 5:39, ῥαπίζει εἰς τὴν . . . σιαγόνα; on the contrary τύπτειν is probably a Lukan redactional touch. (Luke has seventy per cent of thirteen NT uses.) And so Luke seems not to have either of these allusions consciously in mind.

[91] More illustrative of Jesus' manner is his healing of the ear of the high priest's slave in Luke 22:50-51, but even that falls short of Jesus' purpose in not returning the Temple guard's slap in John 18:22-23. There Jesus' response goes beyond passively turning the other cheek to a confrontation with the temple guard: asking him to justify his actions shows Jesus' concern for the ethical conversion of his attacker. Betz, *Sermon* 596 thinks

preting 6:29a in the context of the Sermon's rhetorical structure gives us the best purchase on the text. In 6:27-28 Jesus enjoins the disciples to a love of the enemy, expressed by benevolent action, blessing, and prayer. This *love of enemy* reverses hostile actions not out of self-seeking, but out of concern for the enemies themselves.[92] Soon in 6:31 the Golden Rule will summarize all the actions in 6:27-30 as concern for the other. In this context the offer of the other cheek either literally or figuratively indicates the kind of action that challenges the other to reflect on his action and be converted to a more authentic relation to his neighbor.[93] The best answer to the question of the literalness of Jesus' commands will arise in the exegesis of 6:31.

6:29b: καὶ ἀπὸ τοῦ αἴροντός σου τὸ ἱμάτιον καὶ τὸν χιτῶνα μὴ κωλύσῃς, "and to the one taking your coat, do not refuse your shirt." The first and third examples (6:29a, 30a) are stated positively; the second and fourth (6:29b, 30b), negatively. Whereas Matt 5:40 depicts a court scene in which a creditor has sued the disciple for his shirt,[94] Luke's version is more ambiguous. It could refer to someone seizing the coat out of court but on legal grounds,[95] or to a case of robbery.[96]

Ἄιρειν means generically "to lift up, take up, take away," more rarely "to remove by force, sweep away" (BAGD 24). Luke's twenty uses manifest the full range of its meanings; only six (8:12, 18; 11:22, 52; 19:24, 26) speak of losing something to superior force. It is clear from the parallel usage in 6:30b that the opponent in 6:29b has taken the disciple's coat against his will. In a case of robbery the sense of outrage and the impulse

---

Acts 23:2-5 witnesses Paul as conforming to Jesus' example: Paul, however, does not respond by turning the other cheek, but with a threat and an epithet.

[92] This was the interpretation of the Fathers (John Chrysostom, *Homil.* 18 on Matt, PG 57, 265) and older commentaries (G. L. Hahn, *Das Evangelium nach Lukas erklärt.* 2 vols. [Breslau: Morgenstern, 1892, 1894] 431; Marie-Joseph Lagrange, *L'Evangile selon Saint Luc* [Paris: Gabalda, 1921] 193).

[93] Again, this conversion is not for the sake of the Christian, to make his or her life easier, but out of concern for the personal integrity of the neighbor.

[94] Κριθῆναι is "to be haled into court, be sued" (BAGD 451); the creditor has sued for the shirt because the coat is exempt from debt service (Exod 22:25-27; Deut 24:12-13). The sequence "shirt, then coat" means that a poor Christian gives away not only all he has on his back, but also in the end his shelter against the cold.

[95] Fitzmyer, *Luke* 639; this would presume a more Greek environment that could envisage the taking of the outer garment as a pledge. Frederick W. Danker, *Jesus and the New Age* (rev. ed. Philadelphia: Fortress, 1988) 145 seems alone in assuming that Luke's case is also a juridical court procedure.

[96] And so the upper and most valuable article would be taken first; Alfred Plummer, *A Critical and Exegetical Commentary on the Gospel According to St. Luke* (Edinburgh: T & T Clark, 1896) 185; Alfred Loisy, *L'Evangile selon Luc* (Paris: E. Noury, 1924) 205; Schürmann, *Lukasevangelium* 347; Fitzmyer, *Luke,* also entertains this possibility.

to defend oneself by violent means is much greater than in a case of non-forensic forfeiture. But Luke's language does not permit us to say precisely what kind of a taking is envisioned.

The ἱμάτιον is the outer garment, a "coat" or heavy "cloak'; the χιτών is the undergarment, worn next to the skin, a "tunic" or "shirt." The former served the poor Jewish man as a blanket, even a shelter, in which to sleep, and so if taken as a pledge it could not be kept from him as night drew on (Exod 22:25-27; Deut 24:12-13; Amos 2:8). If the cloak was so protected in legal process, how much more wrong was it to steal one!

Μὴ κολύσῃς, "do not hinder, prevent, forbid" is, as a Lukan word (fifty-two per cent of twenty-three NT uses), probably a Lukan redactional choice.[97] The αφες in Matt 5:40 is a more positive action; in Luke 6:30 the disciple is not offering the shirt but simply not keeping the other from taking it. The aorist subjunctive speaks of a more situation-bound, single-instance response. These two factors may point to a case of robbery, but Luke's lack of specificity about this "exchange"[98] forces us to approach the problem more phenomenologically.

If it is a creditor, acting on some "right," who claims the coat, then he will be satisfied with the coat, to which he has the right. He will not be looking for the shirt, and so offering him the shirt, not denying him the shirt, would be the action that would appeal to his better nature. But if a robber has seized the coat, then he would take a shirt, too, if he had the time or the shirt had value. (In Luke 10:30 the robbers strip the man.) In this case the refusal to hang onto one's shirt is an appeal in the face of the robber's next step. Thus the action in 6:29b seems most probably a robbery. The willingness to relinquish the shirt is an appeal to the robber to consider his victim as a person rather than an object to be exploited.

[97] Κολύειν ἀπὸ was considered a Semitic construction, but it is also found in classical Greek: κολύειν ordinarily takes the accusative, as in Justin's citation of this passage: καὶ τὸν αἴροντά σου τὸν χίωνα ἢ τὸ ἱμάτιον μὴ κολύσῃς (*Apol.* 1.16,1); ἀπὸ with the genitive occurs in the LXX of Gen 23:6. However, κολύειν with ἀπὸ and the genitive occurs in Xenophon, *Cyrop.* I.3.11.

[98] The series of injunctions from 6:27-30 speak of a disciple whose innocence is part of the surprise and paradoxical nature of Jesus' injunctions. In 6:27-28 it appears that the disciple is being attacked because he is a Christian; in 6:29-30 he is attacked not so much for his adherence to the new sect but because of the generalized violence of the world. First Peter 2:20-25 points out that it is no special credit to the Christian to suffer when guilty. If the disciple has forfeited his coat there is no merit in letting it go. The creditor sees himself as "just" in taking the garment; on the level of "rights" he is untouchable, and so argument is of no avail. But the dramatic act of giving the shirt, as an appeal like turning the other cheek, would indicate that something is wrong with the system. Perhaps this is a protest against the regularity of debt in first-century Palestine, even for those working hard to eke out a living. But in the case of robbery the whole situation is clearer: not denying the shirt is an appeal against a criminal action by the other, and an appeal for personal conversion.

6:30a: παντὶ αἰτοῦντί σε δίδου, "give to everyone who begs." Luke continues his discussion of despoliation of possessions, repeating the positive + negative pattern. In comparison with Matt 5:42a,[99] Luke's 6:30a is striking for its double generalization, making this the most outrageous and difficult command of the whole Sermon.[100]

Πᾶς is a Lukan word, usually ascribed to his redaction.[101] It refers to *every* request for money or possessions, day in and day out, from that of the beggar to that of the rich friend. Ἀιτεῖν means "ask, ask for, demand," (BAGD 25–26); normal Lukan usage is "ask, request."[102] Perhaps the asker is a beggar,[103] but Luke's Jesus leaves the case open to anyone in need. Δίδου: the present imperative expresses a general rule rather than an ad hoc experience. Besides this double (with παντί) generalizing tendency, Jesus here allows of no qualifications that restrict this limitless giving.[104] Nor does Luke give any way in which this astonishing demand is to be lived.[105]

---

[99] Matthew 5:42 has the simple τῷ αἰτοῦντι and the aorist imperative δός.

[100] Many take the prohibition of retaliatory physical violence (Luke 6:29a//Matt 5:39b) as the most difficult of the Sermon's injunctions. But the command habitually to refuse no request for money is, in its daily demands, much more stringent; in a short time one following this counsel will have no money left to take care of his or her own needs or those of others. Betz, *Sermon* 598 cites the example of Lucian's *Timon the Misanthrope,* whose unlimited philanthropy led him to a beggar's state, and shows that Christian experience of abuse of such unlimited generosity led to warning to such opportunists, and advice to the givers to be prudent, in *Did.* 1:5-6.

[101] Henry J. Cadbury, *The Style and Literary Method of Luke* (Cambridge, Mass.: Harvard University Press, 1920) 115–16; Joachim Jeremias, *Die Sprache des Lukasevangeliums* (Göttingen: Vandenhoeck & Ruprecht, 1980) 30–31.

[102] John Nolland, *Luke 1–9:20,* 297, seems to be the only commentator to identify the one "asking" in 6:30a: "the 'asking' is no longer the request of a beggar, but rather the request made by one who has the upper hand, which if not acceded to leads easily to 'taking.'" But of Luke's twenty-two uses of αἰτεῖν only one (the variant reading of Luke 12:20 in 𝔓75, B) can be interpreted as the "demand" that one with an upper hand makes of an inferior, and that one uses ἀπὸ with the genitive instead of the accusative for the one asked. The Lukan word for "demand" is ἀπαιτεῖν (6:30b; 12:20); "beg" is ἐπαιτεῖν (16:3; 18:35).

[103] Beggary is not the object of OT legislation, and ἐπαιτεῖν and ἐπαίτης occur only four times in the LXX, in later Wisdom literature (Sir 40:28-30; Ps 109:10). The NT word for beggar (προσαίτης, Mark 10:46) does not occur in the LXX. But begging must have been an activity of the blind and poor in Israel before NT times.

[104] "The absolute form of the command excludes any consideration of the person's background or condition, or the purpose of the begging," Fitzmyer, *Luke* 639; "Disciples must give freely, even to those who have no legitimate claim on them," Marshall, *Luke* 261.

[105] Augustine, *In Sermone Domini* 20, (67), *"non omnia petenti; ut id des, quod dare honeste et juste potes"* excludes giving something that will be wrongfully used, but leaves open an unlimited demand for just need. Marshall, *Luke* 261, like most commentators, says this demand (like the others) is not to be taken literally, but "seriously." For him this means,

6:30b: καὶ ἀπὸ τοῦ αἴροντος τὰ σὰ μὴ ἀπαίτει, "and do not demand back your possessions taken by force." Again (cf. 6:20b) we have the case of something taken by force;[106] Jesus' command is that one not demand its return. Ἀπαιτεῖν, "to ask for something back, demand," is used only twice in the NT, here and in Luke 12:20. It is not clear how one would "demand" something from a robber, or even from one who took something on a legal pretext. But Jesus' position assumes that the victim is, by his refusal to demand the article back, taking the moral high ground, and there is some kind of love of the plunderer in the refusal, even though it is less generous than the relinquishing of the shirt in 6:29b.

Summary: On top of the bewildering paradoxes of the beatitudes and woes, Jesus has now given a command to love enemies that flies in the face of human experience and custom. Further, he has fleshed this command out rhetorically with seven increasingly concrete examples whose very concreteness make even more astonishing the original command. Each of these examples strikes especially hard at the values and ways of doing things of a Mediteranean honor-and-shame-based culture in which one retains ascribed honor or acquires honor by responding agonistically to the challenge of the other.

By now the reader at least subliminally wonders what might be the motive or motivating power behind such bizarre behavior. Many of Jesus' non-retaliatory responses intimate some kind of concern for the perpetrator of violent actions; the blessing and praying of 6:28 are the most explicit about this concern. Now in the next verse Jesus clearly enunciates the reason for the requested actions in concern for the other.

"There is no place for the claims of self over against generosity to others." Plummer, *Luke* 186, says, "The wish to keep what we have got is not the right motive for refusing."Fitzmyer, *Luke* 639, "Need must not encounter selfish reserve among the disciples." Ernst, *Lukas* 226, goes a step farther in ascribing this astonishing demand to the new power of the Reign of God, "The motive for such an attitude is . . . the will to replace power with the new principle of service and 'being for the other.'" We will further consider this possibility in Chapter 8; here we only note that Luke witnesses to comparable acts of total generosity in 9:3-6; 10:4-7; 14:33; 18:22; 21:2-4; Acts 2:43-47; 4:32-37.

[106] Danker, *New Age* 146, arguing from a context of borrowing and from a commercial use of ἀπαιτεῖν, "to press for payment" takes αἴρειν [sic] to mean "to borrow." I like this creative idea, for it would prepare for the use of borrowing in 6:34. However, "borrowing" is not within the interpretative range of αἴρειν, especially in view of the parallel usage in 6:29.

2. *The Golden Rule* (6:31)[107]

Καὶ καθὼς θέλετε ἵνα ποιῶσιν ὑμῖν οἱ ἄνθρωποι, ποιεῖτε αὐτοῖς ὁμοίως, "and as you want people to do to you, so do to them."[108] Jesus now breaks from the four-beat rhythm of the parallel imperatives (6:27-30) to state a general moral maxim that underlies their interpretation and practice; this maxim will itself be interpreted by the three-beat rhythm of the three rhetorical questions in 6:32-34.

Καὶ joins this moral maxim to the immediately preceding commands (6:27-30) as the underlying general rule that explains them.[109] Καθώς is a Hellenistic adverb, used mostly to indicate comparison, often with ὁμοίως or a correlative pronoun in the main clause. Among the synoptics it is a Lukan expression. In comparison with πάντα ὅσα ἐὰν in Matt 7:12, Luke's καθώς is concise, more suited to the gnomic character of the maxim. Θέλετε is present plural, as is common in general maxims. Θέλειν, a Hellenistic verb meaning to wish or desire, is much more common (207x in the NT) than its classical synonym βούλεσθαι (37 NT uses). Luke uses θέλειν 28x in the gospel and 14x in Acts, but βούλεσθαι only twice in the gospel and fourteen times in Acts. Although βούλεσθαι may more often connote intending and planning than does θέλειν (Acts 12:4; 18:15), they are mostly synonymous (BDF §101, θέλειν). Luke's usage is broad, covering the whole range of human desire and intent, and so offers no clue to the meaning here. Still, it is significant that Jesus has Christians consult their own desires, left unspecified, in beginning the process of deciding what they should do to others.

Ἵνα ποιῶσιν ὑμῖν: The NT often uses ἵνα in place of the complementary infinitive after verbs of asking, exhorting, commanding, and

---

[107] For a critical overview of the background to the exegesis of the Golden Rule and an analysis of its literary form see my article, "The Tarnished Golden Rule (Luke 6:31): The Inescapable Radicalness of Christian Ethics," *TS* 59 (1998) 475–85.

[108] The Golden Rule seems closer to its original context in Luke's love commandment than it is in Matthew, where it has been postponed to form an inclusion with 5:17-20 on the Law and the prophets; Schürmann, *Lukasevangelium* 351; Hans-Theo Wrege, *Die Überlieferungsgeschichte der Bergpredigt.* WUNT 9 (Tübingen: Mohr, 1968) 132 n. 1; Marshall, *Luke* 261; Luz, *Matthew 1–7*, 425. Matthew features a generalizing expression (πάντα . . . ὅσα ἐὰν), an emphatic use of ὑμεῖς, and a summarizing assertion that the Golden Rule contains all of "the Law and the prophets." Although it is possible that Luke omitted the latter clause as of no interest to his Gentile readers, it is hard to think of his omitting a generalizing tendency expressed by πάντα. (Betz, *Sermon* 599, is wrong to infer that the Sermon on the Plain avoids πάντα; Matthew's more abundant use can be explained by his Sermon's being almost four times longer than the Sermon on the Plain!) It is impossible to determine the priority of either version; both authors are using favorite redactional expressions.

[109] The older commentaries (H. A. W. Meyer, Paul Schanz, Bernhard Weiss, F. L. Godet, Theodor Zahn) have seen this better than the more contemporary ones, but see also Schürmann, *Lukasevangelium* 349.

wishing,[110] and then it ordinarily, as here, takes the subjunctive. Again, ποιεῖν is the most general verb for human action, and so continues the open-ended character of the Golden Rule. Οἱ ἄνθρωποι generically covers all humans, and so it reinforces the basis of the Golden Rule in human nature and the universal outreach of Jesus' ethic beyond the covenant community.

Ποιεῖτε αὐτοῖς ὁμοίως: The present imperative indicates the regular applicability of general precepts. Ὁμοίως, as a Lukan touch (thirty-five per cent of NT uses), conveys more applicability than Matt 7:12 οὕτως. Οὕτως indicates that one should do exactly the same thing as one wishes would be done to self, but ὁμοίως, "similarly," allows for some variation according to what best suits the occasion.

Literary analysis reveals Jesus' Golden Rule as a maxim, a short and pithy general rule of conduct, expressed by a present imperative in the second person plural. The literary form of the Golden Rule includes a triple symmetry: the same verb (ποιεῖν) used in both clauses, καθώς in the subordinate and ὁμοίως in the independent clause, and a grammatically expressed mutuality between moral agents, so that the indirect object of the antecedent becomes the subject of the consequent, and the subject of the antecedent becomes the indirect object of the consequent.

Ordinarily one would speak of this mutuality as reciprocity, but that term has been assigned, in the history of exegesis of the Golden Rule, to a species of retribution. There is no strict retribution in Jesus' Golden Rule, since the Christian is not responding to the prior act of another but is discerning what should be his or her own prior act toward another. Nor is there Paul Ricoeur's mitigated reciprocity in which one acts in such a way as to evoke a corresponding benevolent action from another, for in that case the Golden Rule should read "what you intend, or expect," which θέλειν never conveys, in classical, Hellenistic, or biblical Greek.[111] Further, the context (Luke 6:27-36) explicitly rejects any notion of self-interest. The maxim is a rule of general altruism.

This generalized maxim refers not to specific acts but to the whole range of human conduct, since ποιεῖν is the most generalized verb for human acts. Further, the mutuality is not between discrete individuals, but is generalized to all humans (οἱ ἄνθρωποι). Consequently, the Golden Rule is a maxim of general altruism in which the actions commanded are

---

[110] Mark 6:25; 10:35; Max Zerwick, *GB* §408.

[111] "The Golden Rule: Exegetical and Theological Perplexities," *NTS* 36 (1990) 392–97. Ricoeur finds a logic of equivalence that implies a *do ut des,* an intent to bring the other to respond in kind to my prior initiative. Christoph Theobald, "La regle d'or chez Paul Ricoeur. Une Interrogation théologique," *RechScRel* 83 (1995) 43–59 is a convincing theological refutation of Ricoeur; Topel, "Tarnished," 477–78 provides a literary and theological refutation.

left open and so is the whole range of persons to whom such benevolence must be directed. The mutuality is between all humans inasmuch as all humans are implicated in the rights and duties that apply to any one.

We come then to the theological meaning of the Golden Rule. Since the maxim, like all expressions, takes its meaning from its literary context,[112] we must look first at what 6:27-30 has prepared us to understand, then at the theological meaning of the formulation itself, and finally (in the next section of this chapter) at Jesus' own interpretation of the Golden Rule in the following verses (6:32-36).

a. *The Context:* 6:27-30 is a unit on love of enemies. Verses 27-28 give the general principle of loving enemies, described generally as those who hate, curse, and mistreat the Christian reader. Verse 29 describes specific actions that illustrate this enmity—physical attack, stealing one's clothes— while v. 30 describes the Christian's generous attitude toward those who beg and those who have already taken from the Christian. In all of these there is a sharp reversal of the *lex talionis,* and indeed of any principle of retaliation. There is no motive adduced for such actions, leading the reader to ask what might be the cause of such surprising behavior. The Golden Rule in 6:31 begins to answer such questions by asserting that one is to treat other humans as one wishes to be treated. By using θέλειν instead of ἐλπίζειν, προσδέχεσθαι, προσδοκᾶν, the Golden Rule excludes the motive of *do ut des* ("I give that you give").[113] Then 6:32-34, a series of three contrasts with the way of sinners (responding in kind to others' generous treatment), implicitly rejects a morality of exchange underlying a *do ut des.* Finally, 6:35 returns to the principle of loving enemies with which the section began, and then explicitly rejects any seeking of temporal reward as inconsistent with the Christian's true measure of conduct, which is God's boundless love without expectation of reward in 6:35-36. Consequently, the whole context of 6:31 forces us to interpret the Golden Rule in a revolutionary way, beyond the motives underlying the Greco-Roman and Jewish maxims adduced as the predecessors of Jesus' Golden Rule.[114]

b. *Theologically* the Golden Rule's genius lies in making one's wishes for oneself the standard of Christian conduct toward others. What I want others to do for me is as *unlimited* as my desires, ranging from

---

[112] Werner Wolbert, "Die Goldene Regel und das *ius talionis,*" *TThZ* 95 (1986) 170–72.

[113] The *ut* in *do ut des* may be taken as introducing a purpose clause, in which my own gain is central to the action, or a result clause, in which altruism plays a stronger part; see "Tarnished," 478 n. 16, for explanation of the syntax. Outside of θέλειν, however, it is the context, not the vocabulary or syntax, that excludes the *do ut des.*

[114] Topel, "Tarnished," 479–85.

simple physical needs (food, money), to needs for security and status, for friendship and community,[115] for spiritual relationship to God in divine community. Jesus' positive form of the Golden Rule, as opposed to the negative formulation of the "Silver Rule" ("what you do not want"), underlines this unlimited character of human desires.[116] Such unrestricted expression of human hungers transcends all talk of concrete rights and limited duties, and intimates the unlimited hunger for God that the Creator and Redeemer has placed in each human.[117]

c. *Second, the unexpressed motivation* of the Golden Rule is altruistic: there is no trace of the Greek preoccupation with my actions being authentic so that I am free from hostile emotions or so that I am good; my concern is that the Other receive the good that my best self would want[118] Underlying this step is the presupposition of a commonality of human desires, perhaps rooted in a common human nature.[119] The Other, then, is a subject with her own desires to find fulfillment in God. This explains why the Golden Rule takes the love command of Lev 19:18 one huge step farther,[120] beyond the covenant community, to those farthest outside, the "enemies," understood not only as personal enemies, but as the enemies of God's People,[121] and yet those summoned to union with their God.

---

[115] My desire for friendship and community makes me want to be held accountable, corrected, even punished, as part of the process by which I enter and build community. This corrects the fear that naïve living of the Golden Rule will produce self-indulgent chaos in society.

[116] Topel, "Tarnished," 479–81 demonstrates that the positive and negative formulations are not logically equivalent because of the greater extension and the deeper quality of the positive one. Of all the commentators only Grundmann, *Lukas* 149 seems to have caught these depths of human desiring, in two short sentences underlining the vast difference between the Golden Rule and Silver Rule.

[117] Vindication of this interpretation must await theological exposition of the Sermon in Chapter 8, but a first justification of it is found in 6:35-36, where Jesus promises that we will be sons and daughters of the Most High, and ought so to act.

[118] Although my wish may be mistaken because I have not probed deeply enough into what I want, nevertheless what I want is an "objective" first step I can make in discerning what I should do.

[119] Peder Borgen, "The Golden Rule with Emphasis on its Usage in the Gospels," in his *Paul Preaches Circumcision and Pleases Men: and Other Essays on Christian Origins* (Trondheim: Tapir, 1983) 104. G. B. Shaw's cynical "Don't do to others what you want others to do to you—their tastes may be different," ignores the fact that what I want others to do is to consult my wants, and so implies that I will consult with others before I act.

[120] As the Golden Rule finds its deepest interpretation in the *imitatio Dei* of 6:35-36, so had the commands of Leviticus 19 begun from imitation of Yʜᴡʜ: Lev 19:2 "You shall be holy, for I the Lord your God am holy," followed by the reminder "I am the Lord your God" after Yʜᴡʜ's commands in 19:4, 10, 11, 18, 25, 28, 30, 31, 34, 37.

[121] J. Moulder, "Who Are My Enemies?" 41–49.

3. *The Contrast with the Ethic of the World* (6:32-34)

The literary structure of three-beat rhythms, embodying the same invariant sequence of conditional clause, identical rhetorical question, and rejection of the proposed conduct as that of sinners: all manifest 6:32-34 as a unit.[122] The unit serves as a commentary on 6:31, protecting it from a false interpretation of the Golden Rule as *do ut des*.[123] However, Jesus is not just defending his articulation of the Golden Rule but announcing that his ethic revolutionizes the prevailing ethic of the Greco-Roman world. The series of rhetorical questions is meant to engage the reader's personal judgment.

6:32a: καὶ εἰ ἀγαπᾶτε τοὺς ἀγαπῶντας ὑμᾶς, "for if you love those who love you": Jesus continues the second-person plural address (6:27-28, 31), which indicates that he is speaking to all the disciples listening to him, elaborating the general command of the Golden Rule. Although εἰ + present indicative says nothing about the fulfillment of the condition, it so often applies to actions that actually do occur that grammarians call it a "real" condition.[124] Jesus points to ordinary conduct in the Greco-Roman culture of Luke's community.

6:32b: ποία ὑμῖν χάρις ἐστίν; "What kind of credit is that to you?" Ποία is an interrogative pronoun, "what kind of?" Χάρις is used from Homer on to denote what delights, charms. Although Aeschylus uses it for the "favor" of the gods, it is not a religious term. In Hellenistic Greek it becomes a regular term for "favor, gracious disposition," of rulers and other dignitaries. In recipients χάρις means "thanks."[125] In the LXX it usually translates *ḥēn,* denoting benevolence, a gracious disposition expressed in a gracious action. Although in its earliest uses it relates to humans, soon it especially describes God's own loving and merciful actions toward his people. Later, but much more rarely, χάρις translates *ḥesed,* love, merciful help springing from committed relationship, as in God's covenant with the Jews.[126]

---

[122] The literary structure, with its fondness for a triple pattern, interest in economic exchange, and specifically Lukan vocabulary like χάρις, υἱοί, ὑψίστου, ἀγαθοποιεῖν, derives from Luke; Robert Morgenthaler, *Die lukanische Geschichtsschreibung als Zeugnis. Gestalt und Gehalt derKunst des Lukas.* 2 vols. ATANT 14, 15 (Zürich: Zwingli Verlag, 1949) 1:73–79; W. C. van Unnik, "Die Motivierung der Feindesliebe in Lukas VI 32-35," *NovT* 8 (1966) 287–88; Halvor Moxnes, *The Economy of the Kingdom: Social Conflict and Economic Relations in Luke's Gospel* (Philadelphia: Fortress, 1988) 155.

[123] Danker, *New Age* 147.

[124] Max Zerwick, *GB* §303–305; contrast the more hypothetical ἐάν + subjunctive in Matt 5:46.

[125] Hans Conzelmann, "χάρις," *TDNT* 9:359–76.

[126] Walter Zimmerli, "χάρις," *TDNT* 9:376–87.

In the NT χάρις occurs regularly only in Luke-Acts, Paul, 1 Peter, and Hebrews.[127] Ordinarily it means grace, attractiveness, favor, good will, or the practical outcome of benevolence—a gracious deed, a gift. From God such a benefaction means standing in God's favor or grace, or it can refer to the extraordinary effect of that favor. In response to a gift it can mean thanks, gratitude (BAGD 877–78). Thus in Luke-Acts it can mean the charm of beauty (Luke 2:52), benevolence leading to action (Acts 2:47), God's favor on his chosen ones (Luke 1:30; 2:40), a concrete benefit, a "bonus" conferred by humans (Luke 6:32; Acts 24:27; 25:3, 9).

Most modern commentators take χάρις in 6:32a as God's favor, grace; thus these actions of sinners may have limited value, but they fall short of God's grace.[128] But W. C. van Unnik holds that it forms part of the normal vocabulary of reciprocity in Greek social relations,[129] and Luke probably intends that here, for he has used ἀγαθοποεῖν, a word that does not belong to Christian paraenetic vocabulary, but rather points to the Greek ethic of reciprocity.[130]

Hendrick Bolkestein had already proved, with many examples, that "the principle of reciprocity formed one of the foundations of Greek social relations."[131] Van Unnik focused on texts using expressions functionally identical to Luke 6:32-33, ἀγαθὸν ποιεῖν, εὐποεῖν, εὐεργετεῖν, ἀποδιδόναι, in ways that clearly express doing something in the hope of a return gift (a *do ut des*), or to return a favor to someone. The *Rhetoric to*

---

[127] Χαρίζεσθαι, "to show pleasure" or "to be agreeable" occurs only in Luke-Acts (seven times) and Paul (seventeen times); χαριτοῦν occurs only once in Luke and once in Paul. For what follows, Ceslas Spicq's analysis of χάρις in *TLNT* 3:500–506 is more penetrating than Conzelmann's.

[128] H. J. Holtzmann, Josef Schmid, and Erich Klostermann call actions done to repay favors worthless, but most speak of such acts as simply falling short of God's favor. To ground this interpretation most argue from a parallel with Matt 5:46, μισθός; some argue from parallel passages in Acts 7:46; Luke 2:40, 52; 14:12-14), others from the whole context in 6:27-36, especially from μισθός in 6:35. Only J. Norval Geldenhuys, *Commentary on the Gospel of Luke*. NICNT (Grand Rapids: Eerdmans, 1952) 212, Danker, *New Age* 148, and perhaps the many-sided analysis in Fitzmyer, *Luke* 640 take χάρις as referring to human credit or thanks.

[129] "Motivierung,"284–300, especially 290, 293, 295–97.

[130] Outside of Luke, ἀγαθοποιεῖν occurs only in 1 Pet 2:20, a passage that also contains χάρις and attacks the basic Greek notion of equal reciprocity. It does not occur in classical Greek; in Hellenistic Greek it occurs only in an astrological context. In the LXX it translates *hetîb* four times, none of these in a meaning similar to Luke 6:33. But 1 Macc 11:33, describing the intentions of the Hellenistic king Demetrius, uses ἀγαθὸν ποιεῖν to speak of doing a reciprocal benefit for the Jews. The synonyms regularly used in classical Greek are εὐποιεῖν or καλῶς ἐργάζεσθαι. See van Unnik, "Motivierung," 289–91 and our own comment on καλῶς ποιεῖν at 6:27.

[131] Hendrick Bolkestein, *Wohltätigkeit* 158. The witnesses to this principle, ranging from Hesiod to Dio Chrysostom (d. 120 C.E.?), are found mostly on pp. 156–70.

Alexander offers a parade example: "Everyone gives presents in the hope of receiving some repayment [ὀφειλεθήσεσθαι] or as a recompense for prior benefits [χάριν ἀποδίδοντες]."[132]

Contemporary exegetical studies utilizing cultural anthropology and economics of preindustrial societies confirm this literary evidence. Halvor Moxnes asserts that in peasant societies the most important form of exchange is reciprocal, aiming at symmetry between the two parties.[133] Reciprocities would be of three kinds:

(1) *Generalized reciprocity* describes altruistic transactions; the ideal form is the "pure gift." Generalized reciprocity obtains in links of close kinship where the exchange for the gift is honor, loyalty, solidarity.

(2) *Balanced reciprocity* attempts to reach near-equivalence in goods and services. This form of reciprocity occurs between those who have regular relationships. In towns, but also in the countryside, money often would be the medium of exchange.

(3) *Negative reciprocity* is the asocial attempt to "get something for nothing." It occurs more often between strangers. Strictly speaking it is not reciprocity.

The truly reciprocal relationships (generalized and balanced) are all-pervasive in Greco-Roman society. In Luke 6:32-34 Jesus refers to a balanced reciprocity in which anyone who gives a good or service to another expects a comparable return, and anyone who receives a good is expected to make a return. Not to do so in a timely manner threatens the relationship.

Χάρις is frequently used in a technical sense in those texts. Of van Unnik's many texts,[134] perhaps Thucydides' Periclean funeral oration is most illustrative:

> Now he who confers the favor [ὁ δράσας τὴν χάριν] is a firmer friend in that he is disposed, by continued good will toward the recipient, to keep the feeling of obligation alive in him, but he who owes it is more listless in his friendship, knowing that when he repays the kindness [ἀποδώσων τὴν

---

[132] *Rhetoric to Alexander* 1446b 36-38. Other texts close to 6:32 include Xenophon, *Cyropaedia* XIII, 2, 22; *Memorabilia* II, 2, 1-2; II, 9, 8; IV, 4, 24; Thucydides, *War* II, 40,4; Dio Chrysostom, *Or.* VII, 88-89, showing the range from classical to Hellenistic Greek.

[133] Moxnes, *Economy* 34–35. Although Moxnes draws from the previous social-scientific studies of ancient civilizations of Karl Polanyi and Moses I. Finley, here he especially relies on Marshall D. Sahlins, *Stone Age Economics* (Chicago: Aldine-Atherton, 1972) 185–276.

[134] Χάρις occurs with words of reciprocity (ἀγαθοποιεῖν, εὐποιεῖν, ἀποδιδόναι, εὐεργετεῖν, etc.), most clearly in Thucydides, *War* II, 40,4; Xenophon, *Memorabilia* II, 2, 1-2; Aristotle, *Rhetoric to Alexander* 1446b 36-38; 1 Macc 11:33; Sir 12:1; Dio Chrysostom, *Or.* VII, 88-89; 1 Pet 2:20, but also in other texts imbued with the Greek notion of reciprocity: van Unnik, "Motivierung," 290–97.

ἀρετὴν] it will count not as a favor bestowed [οὐκ εἰς χάριν], but as a debt repaid [ἀλλ' ὡς ὀφείλημα].[135]

Consequently van Unnik summarizes the use of χάρις in the ethic of reciprocity:

> When one has received a benefit and makes some return for it, this may be called a χάρις, but it is really only a debt. And he also ought not to receive thanks for the act, because the one who in this way has received something from him, has not received anything special, but has only been repaid.[136]

Therefore Luke 6:32b really says, "If you love those who love you, what kind of gift is that? You are merely absolving a debt and so returning the relationship to equilibrium. You have no credit with the other." Jesus shows that by the common ethic of Luke's society the return in balanced reciprocity is not gracious or praiseworthy; it can be no more than honor among thieves, and at its best is simply the redemption of a debt. Only the one who takes the initiative has done a true χάρις. In exposition of the Golden Rule Jesus says that one must first love one who has not already done one a favor to have any credit even in the secular ethic of reciprocity.[137]

6:32c: καὶ γὰρ οἱ ἁμαρτωλοὶ τὸ αὐτὸ ποιοῦσιν, "for even sinners do the same."

Καὶ γάρ, "for even," gives a surprising reason (BAGD 151) drawn from experience. After the argument drawn from secular codes Jesus now argues from example, using a religious term that prepares for the religious argumentation of 6:35e-36. Ἁμαρτωλοί:[138] ἁμαρτία in Greek literature can refer to morally missing the mark, but it has no clear religious meaning. The Jew takes sin as an offence against God that disrupts the divine plan of salvation for humans and brings alienation on sinners themselves.[139] In the synoptics and Acts ἁμαρτία occurs less often than in the rest of the NT; evidently Jesus did not speak much of the nature and consequences of sin but was simply conscious of its reality and acted accordingly.[140]

---

[135] Thucydides, *War* II, 40,4; translation by C. F. Smith in *Thucydides* I. LCL (Cambridge, Mass.: Harvard Univ. Press, 1951) 329–30.

[136] Van Unnik, "Motivierung," 296–97, my translation.

[137] As Betz, *Sermon* 600 documents, both Plato and Aristotle had distinguished love as a free gift from the exchange of favors. Jesus points out that even in the exchange of favors reciprocity accrues no credit nor praise.

[138] It is impossible to say whether Matt 5:46, τελῶναι, was originally in Q, since Luke uses τελώνης oftener than Matthew (ten times, versus eight for Matthew; Luke has forty-eight per cent of NT uses). But Luke has so rewritten the whole passage for Greek listeners that the use of "sinners" may be a move away from a Judaic notion of τελῶναι as sinners. Still, neither is ἁμαρτωλός a familiar word for Greeks.

[139] Johannes Bauer, "Sin," *EBT* 849–62.

[140] Walter Grundmann, "ἁμαρτάνω," *TDNT* 1:302–303; Jesus knew he was the victor over sin.

Ἁμαρτωλός occurs only five times in Greek literature, never clearly connected with a significant notion of ἁμαρτία. In the LXX, 74 of 94 uses translate raš'îm,"the evil ones;" 68 of the 74 are in the Psalter, where raš'îm are a definite religious type: those who break the Law, trust in their own power, and oppress others. For the rabbis Torah was not only a code of ethics for persons, but the manifestation of God to the whole people. When the Gentiles rejected Torah they rejected God and forfeited the possibility of a life according to God's will, and so for the Jews Gentiles were, *ipso facto,* ἁμαρτωλοί.[141] Again, Jesus is not specific about the nature of sinners' sin. He uses the vocabulary of his time: τελῶναι καὶ ἁμαρτωλοί describes those who live a flagrantly immoral life, or those whose profession leads to dishonesty and injustice.[142]

Luke's own usage (thirty-eight per cent of NT occurrences) may prove our best guide to the meaning here. Prescinding from 6:32-34, Luke uses ἁμαρτωλός (1) as the Pharisees' stereotypical phrase τελῶναι καὶ ἁμαρτωλοί, in their mouths (5:30; 15:2; 19:7) and in the narrator's words when Jesus' opponents are in view (5:32; 7:34; 15:1). But Luke does not confine the phrase to those who simply do not follow the Pharisees' prescriptions: these tax collectors and sinners confess their personal guilt in 15:7, 10;[143] 18:13; 19:7. (2) Ἁμαρτωλός describes a person guilty of publicly scandalous acts (5:30; 7:37, 39). (3) It is used in a general moral sense (13:2; 24:7); (4) to describe a person guilty of personal sin (15:7, 10; 18:13; 19:7); and (5) to describe a human's sense of unworthiness in the presence of the Holy (5:8). The most difficult verse to interpret may be the key to our passage: in 24:7 Jesus is said to have prophesied in Galilee that he had to be handed over into the hands of sinful people (ἀνθρώπων ἁμαρτωλῶν). The phrase "sinful people" does not occur in any of Jesus' three Galilean Passion predictions.[144] Thus the sinful people could be the Jewish authorities, any humans, or this generation. Nothing seems to link these three groups except sinful complicity in putting the Son of Man to death.

---

[141] Karl H. Rengstorf, "ἁμαρτωλός," *TDNT* 1:317–25.

[142] Rengstorf, "ἁμαρτωλός," 327; the synoptics sometimes let the Pharisees use the term in their own sense for those who do not subject themselves to Pharisaic ordinances, the *'am hā'āreṣ*. So Jesus and his disciples are also called ἁμαρτωλοί. But Jesus seems to have transcended the view that certain groups are sinners; for him human autonomy from God makes humans sinners who need that divine forgiveness and grace he offers as the One sent to the lost.

[143] Even if the wandering of the sheep or loss of the coin is not depicted as human responsibility for sin, the μετανοοῦντι in 15:6, 7 expresses repentance from real guilt.

[144] In 9:22 he must be rejected by the elders and chief priests; in 9:44 he is going to be handed over into human hands; in 17:25 the Son of Man must be rejected by this generation. In 18:32 he will be handed over to the Gentiles (ἔθνεσιν). The sinful men of 24:7 then could be the Gentiles. But this prediction is not in Galilee, so it is not the passage referred to by 24:7.

In short, Luke has no consistent meaning for ἁμαρτωλοί except the Christian meaning in which Luke's readers have been catechized: humans alienated from God. It means all five characteristics listed above. Jesus in 6:32 points to the lack of merit in returning a favor because even evil persons, those part of the problem of what is wrong with the world, engage for their own purposes in such acts of simple reciprocity. The world gets no better through what sinners do. Just as sanctioned retaliation cannot heal wounds or create community, neither can civil relations built on exchange. Simple reciprocity is the way of the world, not that of a disciple.

In strict logic 6:32 does not argue against *do ut des*.[145] But asserting, according to the common ethic of the time, that reciprocation of another's gift is not a χάρις, a praiseworthy credit, undermines any attempt to find a *logic of equivalence* (Paul Ricoeur) in the Golden Rule. As we have seen, χάρις is a polyvalent term, and it has religious resonances for a Christian reader who knows of God's grace. Jesus' argument in 6:32 forms the first step in an implied argument *a minore ad maius:* if return of a good deed is not meritorious in the eyes of the world (even sinners do it), how much less meritorious is it in the eyes of God?

6:33: καὶ ἐὰν ἀγαθοποιῆτε τοὺς ἀγαθοποιοῦντας ὑμᾶς, ποία ὑμῖν χάρις ἐστίν; καὶ οἱ ἁμαρτωλοὶ τὸ αὐτὸ ποιοῦσιν, "and if you should do good to those who have done good to you, what credit is that? For sinners do the same."[146] The repetition of the same structure, now centered on the action of ἀγαθοποιεῖν, rhetorically emphasizes the point. Our discussion of καλῶς ποιεῖν above found the concept embedded in the Greek thought-field of balanced reciprocity. Luke here has changed the protasis to ἐὰν + subjunctive, implying a general condition. The shift suggests that such conduct (of sinners) will never bring favor.

6:34: καὶ ἐὰν δανίσητε παρ᾽ ὧν ἐλπίζετε λαβεῖν, ποία ὑμῖν χάρις ἐστίν; καὶ ἁμαρτωλοὶ ἁμαρτωλοῖς δανίζουσιν ἵνα ἀπολάβωσιν τὰ ἴσα, "and if you lend to those from whom you expect a return, what kind of credit is that? Even sinners lend to sinners to get an equal return."[147] This rhetorical unit denying virtue to balanced Greek reciprocity comes to a climax with a third instance of hypothetical conduct of sinners challenged by

---

[145] In a *do ut des* the agent initiates the exchange, does not respond to a prior gift as in 6:32-33. The argument that excludes a *do ut des* as praiseworthy appears in 6:35e-36.

[146] I have omitted the γὰρ after καὶ because for once I think that the probability of dittography outweighs the attestation by better MSS (B, ℵ, 892, W) and the criterion of *lectio difficilior.*

[147] This sentence has no equivalent in Matthew, but the notion of borrowing presumably was in Q (Matt 5:42//Luke 6:30). However, the sentence structure, grammar (the suppressed antecedent), and vocabulary (δανίζειν, ἀπολαμβάνειν) show strong traces of Lukan redaction.

a rhetorical question. However, Jesus now shifts from disparagement of *re*action to denial of merit to the *initiator* of a transaction that legally binds the receiver to a return.

Ἐὰν + aorist subjunctive once again presumes a general practice, although the aorist points to each single act of lending, not a regular practice. Παρ' ὧν is a classical expression in which the antecedent τούτοις is suppressed. The reciprocity is now changed: one does not loan to those from whom one has already received a loan, but to those from whom one expects to get a return. This would mean that the lender would accrue a credit, as the one who must be repaid.

Δαν(ε)ίζειν means to lend or borrow money.[148] More than ἀγαπᾶν or ἀγαθοποιεῖν, δανίζειν legally requires return: there is a contract on the part of the debtor to return the loan (plus interest?) to the creditor. Such a formal obligation removes the transaction from the category of *do ut des*. Ἐλπίζετε λαβεῖν then expresses the anticipation that underlies the loan: the lender expects to get a return.[149]

Once again Jesus gives as reason for the denial of merit that sinners are willing to loan to sinners, with the assurance that even sinners will follow the mandatory code of balanced reciprocity. The denial of χάρις has a different motive; the lender is only "doing a deal." Ἵνα ἀπολάβωσιν gives the anticipation as the very purpose for which the loan was made: this is a business deal,[150] or, at best, helping another without any risk of loss. The creditor hopes to get back the same amount as was loaned.

Τὰ ἴσα: ἴσος means "equal in number, size, quality;" τὰ ἴσα would mean "the same amounts" or "an equal amount" (BAGD 381). The word is used only eight times in the NT. Commentators have found three possible meanings of "in order to receive equal amounts" in 6:34c: repayment of principal with interest, recovery of the principal, or reception of loans in exchange.[151] I rule out the third because τὰ ἴσα does not describe return services or services in kind, but talks about equal *amounts*. Even a return loan for an equal amount does not correspond to ἴσα.[152] Further, such a re-

---

[148] LSJ 369 gives no examples of anything but money used as the object of the verb. Any other object would have to be clearly named and the verb then would have a figurative meaning. Luke has three of its four uses in the NT.

[149] If Luke means an expectation of a return, as in a *do ut des*, he uses ἐλπίζετε, not θέλειν.

[150] Ἀπολαμβάνειν is a regular business term; BAGD 94; see also Gustav Stählin, "δανίζω," *TDNT* 3:344–45, and the excellent discussion in Betz, *Sermon* 604.

[151] Stählin, "δανίζω," *TDNT* 3:344–45.

[152] Both Marshall and Nolland in affirming the expectation of a comparable loan seem dependent on Stählin's analysis. But Stählin's argument against the parallel from P. Ryl. 65,7, which clearly takes τὰ ἴσα to mean an exact amount, is very weak.

turn loan would be more in accord with a modern economy. In the highly stratified first-century economy one did not move from debtor to creditor with such rapidity.

Consequently, we can decide between the first and second interpretations above. It is possible that Luke is here describing Christian practice taken over from the Jews, and in that case τὰ ἴσα would probably mean return of the principal without interest.[153] But the whole context has been the economic world of Greek reciprocity, and so we should analyze the possibilities in that context: (1) One expecting both principal and interest is doing a business deal, indicated by ἀπολαμβάνειν. This abandons the specious virtue of the *do ut des;* there is no expectation that a business deal would constitute a χάρις for the lender; rather the debtor has an ὀφείλημα pure and simple. (2) Expecting only the principal would be going beyond expected business practice to the behavior of a patron or a friend, in realms where the lender could receive a χάρις, and so this interpretation is more congruent with 6:32-33.[154]

Although it may make no difference which interpretation is taken, since all three describe actions at variance with Jesus' own sense of χάρις,[155] it appears preferable, in either the Jewish or Greek thought-world, to understand the loan as interest-free, expecting only the return of the exact amount of the principal. This interpretation best fits the vocabulary and rhetorical structure of 6:32-34. Jesus is here attacking the best-case argument for Greek reciprocity as a χάρις, the lender who does not

---

[153] If money lent to foreigners could be exacted in the sabbath year (Deut 15:1-3), Jews could charge interest on a loan to foreigners (Deut 23:21). The Law prohibited Jews from taking interest on loans to their compatriots (Exod 22:25; Lev 25:35-37; Deut 23:19-20; Ps 15:5; Prov 28:8). Of course there were violations of these laws, and the prophets condemned usury (Ezek 18:8, 13, 17) because their contemporaries were practicing it (Ezek 22:12; Neh 5:6-13). But in all these texts there is no challenge to the conception of usury as sin. Thus in the Jewish Christian world (1) one expecting both principal and interest would be breaking the Jewish law against usury. In that case the lender would not expect God's favor, but punishment. (2) One expecting only return of the principal would act meritoriously according to the Law (Deut 15:7-8; Pss 37:26 and 112:5 equate lending with giving generously), and so could expect a χάρις. See also Betz, *Sermon* 602–603.

[154] Plummer, *Luke* 187 mounted the most serious attack on this interpretation, because in classical Greek to make a friendly, interest-free loan is κιχρῆναι, not δανίζειν. However, this distinction must have disappeared in Hellenistic Greek, since in Ptolemaic Egypt a δάνειον can be ἔντοκος (interest-bearing) or ἄτοκος (interest-free). Δανίζειν describes an interest-free loan in 4 Macc 2:8 and Luke's own use of δανίζειν in 6:35 seems to describe interest-free loans, such as were made to kin or friends. The discussion in Betz, *Sermon* 605–607 concludes with Philo's opinion (*Spec. Leg.* 2, 78) that interest-free loans constitute a benevolence (χάρις).

[155] This is the position taken by Josef Ernst, *Lukas* 227.

return a favor but initiates a loan to one hard-pressed. Although Aristotle would deny a χάρις to the one demanding any sort of return on a loan, Philo of Alexandria considered interest-free loans to be benevolences (χάριτες).[156] Jesus says that sinners sometimes make interest-free loans (for whatever motive sinners might have) as long as they are assured of getting the principal returned. But even this economic transaction that most approximates the ἀγαπᾶν and ἀγαθοποιεῖν of Greek reciprocity contains no χάρις, presumably because there is less risk for the lender, and no freedom for the borrower.[157]

Thus ends Jesus' rejection of any interpretation of his Golden Rule as Greek reciprocity: it is the morality of sinners. This reference to sinners leads his argument into an exalted notion of χάρις in 6:35-36, which thereupon is seen as what has been at play in all of 6:27-36.

4. *Positive Repetition with a Reward* (6:35)

6:35a: Πλὴν ἀγαπᾶτε τοὺς ἐχθροὺς ὑμῶν καὶ ἀγαθοποιεῖτε καὶ δανίζετε μηδὲν ἀπελπίζοντες, "but love your enemies, and do good, and lend without hope of return." With the strong adversative πλήν (6:24) Luke returns to Jesus' positive teaching, which overthrows the Greek ethic of reciprocity. Ἀγαπᾶτε τοὺς ἐχθροὺς ὑμῶν (6:35a) resumes the exact formulation of 6:27a and reverses 6:32a; καὶ ἀγαθοποιεῖτε (6:35a) resumes 6:27b and reverses 6:33a; καὶ δανίζετε μηδὲν ἀπελπίζοντες (6:35a) resumes 6:30a and reverses 6:34a. All this vocabulary has already been discussed, with the exception of the troublesome μηδὲν ἀπελπίζοντες. Both words are Lukan.[158] In Koinē Greek the participle ordinarily uses μή for the negative, which still conveys something of the subjective sense it had in classical Greek (BDF §426). Ἀπελπίζειν means "to give up hope, despair" in all Greek texts before and contemporaneous with the writing of the gospels.[159] This is the meaning found in the LXX of Isa 29:19; Jdt 9:11; Sir 22:21; 27:21; 2 Macc 9:18, and in *1 Clement* 59:33.

---

[156] Again the references and argument are from Betz, *Sermon* 605–607.

[157] Betz argues, taking ἐλπίζειν as "hope," that the creditor takes a risk. But ἐλπίζειν here rather means "expect," an expectation grounded in a fairly risk-free and enforceable contract. Indeed, Betz himself refers to careful investigation of the credit risk involved: *Sermon* 602–603.

[158] To the special Lukan words of 6:32-34, note that Luke-Acts has sixty-one per cent of NT usage of πλήν, thirty-five per cent of NT usage of μηδείς, and the single NT usage of ἀπελπίζειν.

[159] BAGD 82–83; Rudolf Bultmann, "ἀπελπίζω," *TDNT* 2:534. The scribal substitution of μηδένα for μηδὲν (‭א‬, W, X, Ξ, Π, syr^{s, p, h, pal} and some minuscules) witnesses to the fact that the scribes of the first four centuries wanted to understand ἀπελπίζειν as giving up hope on the debtor.

Hence older commentators have translated it "never doubting, never despairing."[160] The translation "to hope for some return" is attested from the time of John Chrysostom (early fifth century).[161] Because "never despairing of" fits so badly with the context,[162] the principal dictionaries of the NT (BAGD, *TDNT, EWNT*) and all contemporary commentators have preferred "not expecting any return."[163] Thus Jesus' own ethic is a generalized reciprocity that converts every loan into a gift, a position articulated by Aristotle for true benevolence to friends and by Philo of Alexandria for observing the Law.[164]

Thus πλήν in 6:35a marks an adversative transition from Jesus' rejection of the sinners' code of conduct in 6:32-34 to the articulation of his own radical interpretation of the Golden Rule in 6:31. By using the very verbs of 6:32-34, now in the present imperatives expressing the repeated action of an ethical code, Jesus reverses the balanced reciprocity of Greek social life by an unlimited giving of generalized reciprocity. Luke's practical ethic has him concentrate on the practical conduct that lies closest to every Christian's everyday life—the readiness to lend assistance to anyone

[160] This translation was favored by the Latin commentators, the earliest vernacular translations, and German commentators from the nineteenth century. Those who read μηδέν understand it as "never despairing, never doubting (that God will repay you)": Plummer, *Luke* 188.

[161] The Vulgate had *nihil inde sperantes,* confirmed by similar Coptic and Armenian translations (Adalbert Merx, *Die vier kanonischen Evangelien nach ihrem ältesten bekannten Texte. Übersetzung und Erläuterung der Syrischen im Sinaikloster gefundenen Palimpsesthandschrift.* 2 vols. in 4 [Berlin: G. Reimer, 1897–1911] 2/2:223–26), and so great scholars like Beda, Erasmus, Jansenius, and Grotius preferred this alternative translation.

[162] If μηδένα ἀπελπίζοντες means not giving up on a debtor's repayment, this contradicts the πλήν that begins a line of argumentation opposed to that of sinners and is incoherent with the emerging emphasis on God's reward in 6:35bc. If μηδέν ἀπελπίζοντες means not despairing of God's reward, then one would expect γὰρ instead of καὶ in 6:53c (Hahn, *Lukas* 437). Indeed, this interpretation cannot be reconciled with the opposition to 6:34 or with the love of enemies in 6:35, or with the radical new nature of Jesus' ethic throughout 6:27-36, or with the whole Sermon.

[163] Note that μηδέν includes all transactions, whether of a loan with interest or a friendly interest-free loan. I have not found a single commentary of this century that does not prefer this translation. The consensus is formidable because it includes men (e.g., Fitzmyer and Danker) usually exigent of historical attestation. Chrysostom's translation could have been influenced by coherence with 6:35, but it is also possible that this meaning was used for the word for three centuries before his writing. Frederick Field, *(Notes on the Translation of the New Testament being the Otium norvicense (pars tertia).* Reprinted with additions by the author [Cambridge: Cambridge University Press, 1899] 40), M.-J. Lagrange (*Luc* 196), and Christopher F. Evans (*Saint Luke* [Philadelphia: Trinity Press International, 1990] 336) suggest that Luke creates the meaning by catachresis from ἀπολαμβάνειν = "receive in return" and "hope to receive" (ἐλπίζειν) in v. 34.

[164] Aristotle, *Rhet.* 2.6,6-7 (1383b 25-34); 2.7,2 (1385a 18-190; Philo, *Spec. Leg.* 271–72.

who asks for it (6:30a), without expecting any return for it.[165] Jesus' injunctions are such a radical interpretation of the Golden Rule that they force the question of the warrants for such action, to which Jesus now proceeds in 6:35bc.

6:35b: καὶ ἔσται ὁ μισθὸς ὑμῶν πολύς, "and your reward will be great." In 6:32-34 Jesus' rejection of the Greco-Roman code of balanced reciprocity implies a different standard of behavior for a different kind of reward, which he now describes.

Ὁ μισθὸς ὑμῶν πολύς in itself has the same meaning as it had in 6:23, but there the eschatological dimension of the reward was secured by ἐν τῷ οὐρανῷ; here the reward is merely designated as future. Whether it applies to the disciples' earthly future constituted by their actions here or to their eschatological reward is left open.[166] Some object that the introduction of reward here subtly insinuates egoism into what has been portrayed as altruism. As we will see, however, the reward is participating in the divine altruism!

6:35c: καὶ ἔσεσθε υἱοὶ ὑψίστου, "and you will be sons of the Most High" repeats the vague future (καὶ ἔσεσθαι), but the reward now is specified as their being children of God. As a synonym for God ὕψιστος is Lukan (Luke-Acts has sixty-nine per cent of NT uses). "Most high" is used frequently for God in the LXX, some forty times as a translation of *'elyôn,* and another sixty times when there is no Hebrew Vorlage.[167] It stresses the transcendence of God in contexts of contact with Gentiles (Gen 14:18).[168] Luke uses it as a divine name uttered by angels (1:32, 35), by demons (8:28; Acts 16:17), and by those speaking under the influence of the prophetic spirit (1:76). In Acts 7:48 the usage stresses the transcendence of God. Luke probably uses it here in his argument about Greek ethical practice to stress the identity of the transcendent God as his Greek Christian listeners would understand it.

[165] Though μηδὲν ἀπελπίζοντες immediately modifies δανίζειν, it can also modify the immediately preceding ἀγαπᾶτε and ἀγαθοποιεῖτε of 6:35a.

[166] The synoptic tradition thinks of a future reward that is both eschatological and already here on this earth (Luke 18:28-30//Mark 10:28-30//Matt 19:27-29). The commentaries, e.g., Schürmann, *Lukasevangelium* 355, take the reward to refer to that following on the eschatological judgment.

[167] The usage ranges from the earliest writings to its more abundant use in the Hellenistic age (Genesis to Wisdom and 3 Maccabees); it is represented only three times in the classical prophets (Mic 6:6; Isa 14:14; 57:15), but abundantly in the Psalms (24x) and Wisdom literature (some 45x in Sirach). It occurs in later Jewish literature (*Jub.* 16:8; 1 Enoch 9:3; 10:1; 46:7; 60:1, 22), and eight times in QL (Fitzmyer, *Luke* 348).

[168] *'Ēl 'elyôn* was a Canaanite name for God, whose cult and name the Hebrews gradually appropriated for YHWH; ὕψιστος was a Greek name for Zeus, and so in dialogue with Gentiles became a name for YHWH; Georg Bertram, "ὕψιστος," *TDNT* 9:614–20.

Ὑιοὶ ὑψίστου occurs but twice in the OT. Thus it will help to consider the more common related concept of υἱός θεοῦ to understand the title here.

a. *The Jewish Usage: bᵉnēi*, in common Semitic use, designates membership in a class or group. In the OT and later Jewish literature *bᵉnēi 'elohîm* refers to two groups:

1. *Polytheistically conceived gods,* who by the time of the writing of the Bible had been subordinated to YHWH and formed his heavenly court or council (Job 1:6; 2:1; Pss 29:1; 82:6; 89:6-7; Deut 32:43).[169] In later Judaism this title gets fused with the notion of angels, who share God's home, holiness, and immortal life (Dan 3:25; Wis 5:5; the LXX of Gen 6:2; Job 1:6; 2:1; 1 Enoch 6:2; 69:4-5; 1 QH 2:3);[170]

2. *Israelites,* conceived metaphorically as sons of God because of their intimate and unique relationship to YHWH, who chose and created them (Deut 14:1-2; 32:6, 18-19; Isa 43:6-7; 45:11; Hos 1:10; Mal 2:10).[171] This unique relationship, expressed by a covenant, requires a faithful moral life (Exod 4:22-23; Deut 14:1-2; 32:5-6; Isa 1:2-4; Hos 11:1-2). In later Judaism eschatological purification creates an ideal Israel, whose fidelity to the covenant leads to its acknowledgment as God's son by the Gentiles (Isa 61:9; Esth 16:15-16; Ps Sol 17:26-32; *Jub.* 1:23-28),[172] and ultimately to the fullness of life.[173] Even in these later texts (Esth 16:15-16) the Jews are already sons of God, whose purified conduct in eschatological times will *reveal them* to the nations as such. Thus "sons of God" is not simply a final eschatological state or title. Usually the singular "Son of God" refers to the king (Pss 2:7; 110:3; 2 Sam 7:14), not as generated

---

[169] This usage probably lies behind the consultative plural of Gen 1:26; 3:22; 11:7. Much of this survey I have drawn from Brendan Byrne, *"Sons of God" —"Seed of Abraham": The Sonship of God of all Christians In Paul Against the Jewish Background.* AnBib 83 (Rome: Biblical Institute Press, 1979) and Jarl E. Fossum, "Son of God," *ABD* 6:128–37. Both contain exhaustive bibliographies.

[170] The distinction between the sons of God and the sons of men is that the former share God's deathless "spirit" of life, while the latter remain mortal unless given a share in the "spirit" common to YHWH and his host; Byrne, *"Sons of God"* 13. Perhaps "life" is as close as the Hebrew mind can come to a description of God's "nature."

[171] Underlying this usage is an Ancient Near Eastern metaphor for the bond between a tribe and its god. All of these texts speak of sonship as a present historical reality.

[172] Byrne's thorough survey of sonship of God in the intertestamental literature (*"Sons of God"* 18–78) reveals that in eschatological times the nations will *recognize* purified Israel as sons of God because of their righteousness. In honor/shame societies, this recognition is very akin to *being.*

[173] This eschatological life is the immunity from death that humans had before the fall (1 Enoch 69:11; 2 Enoch 30:11; Wis 1:13-16; 2:23-24).

by God but because he is called as God's vicegerent to effect God's justice in the people.[174] When there was no longer a Davidic king, the idea was loosely tied to the notion of a Messiah.[175] The title was also used of an individual *righteous Jew,* whose immunity to death and destiny to eternal life is acknowledged by his persecutors (Wis 2:13–3:9; 5:5).

In sum, by the time of Jesus "sons of God" refers to (angelic) beings who possess God's immortal life, to historical Israel, whose righteous life manifests them as God's sons, and to eschatological Israel, whose purified conduct enables them to receive eternal life. Although God's choosing and creating his people remains foundational to "sons of God," right conduct is a marker of God's children in this historical life.

b. *Greco-Roman Usage:* Heroes (Dionysos, Heracles) and rulers (Alexander, Caesar, Augustus) were called θεοῦ υἵος or *divi filius,* but this usage smacked too much of a living polytheism to have influenced Christian usage.[176] *Thaumatourgoi* were often called θεῖος ἀνήρ,[177] and famous historical persons (Plato, Pythagoras, Apollonius of Tyana) were seen in a filial relationship to a god. If this did influence Christian usage, it was because designation of a filial relationship to a god was consequent upon some god-like ethical conduct of the person.

c. *NT Usage:* υἱοὶ θεοῦ is used nine times (five of them in Paul) and τέκνα θεοῦ nine times (including four in 1 John). These bald statistics reveal that "sons of God" is principally the concern of Paul and John. In both writers Jesus as the transcendent Son of God enables those who believe in

---

[174] The notion of the king as adopted son of the god and executor of the god's justice is widespread in the Ancient Near East. In Israel this filial relationship "is set firmly within the frame-work of the covenantal theology typical of the religion of Israel," Byrne, *"Sons of God"* 18. "Son of God" is nowhere conceived as meaning lineal or genetic descent from YHWH.

[175] Joseph A. Fitzmyer, "The Contribution of Qumran Aramaic to the Study of the New Testament," *NTS* 20 (1973–74) 382–407, has demonstrated that there is no *explicit* identification of the titles Messiah and Son of God in the OT or intertestamental literature. Still, texts like 4QFlor 1-2.i.10 and 4QpsDan probably intimate some ideal of royal sonship in the ill-defined notion of the Messiah in intertestamental times.

[176] So Peter Wülfing-von Martitz, "υἱός," *TDNT* 8 (1972) 338–40; for a survey of the texts see Jarl E. Fossum, "Son of God," *ABD* 6:132–33, and his bibliography. At the other, more naturalistic end of the spectrum, the Stoic conception of a common humanity with one God as father also had no influence on gospel usage, either because it ignored the privileged place of the Jews or it was too theoretical.

[177] The investigation of θεῖος ἀνήρ enjoyed a vogue in twentieth-century scholarship, but has proved methodologically deficient as a comparative term for understanding Jesus as miracle-worker; John P. Meier, *A Marginal Jew: Rethinking the Historical Jesus.* 2 vols. to date (Garden City, N.Y.: Doubleday, 1991, 1994) 2:595–601, and his bibliography.

him to become children of God now and in the final time.[178] For Paul, "Son
of God" referred

> primarily and properly to the exalted status of Christ. It pertained to him in
> his pre-existent state, was concealed during his earthly lowliness, became
> manifest in his risen glory. This view of Christ as Son of God corresponds
> perfectly to the way in which Paul speaks of Christians as "sons." . . . As
> sons of God "in Christ" Christians are alive with his resurrection life . . .
> despite the fact that the sonship status is as yet something awaiting public
> revelation. . . . But the Spirit, crying "*Abba,* Father" is the first instalment
> and guarantee of the fullness to come.[179]

For John, the pre-existent Word's power to make believers τέκνα θεοῦ is
the central affirmation of the prologue (1:12-13)[180] and remains the criterion of the true children of God in Jesus' dispute with the Pharisees (3:1-
5; 8:31-47) and also within the fractious Johannine community itself (1 Jn
3:1-2; 5:1-5). Thus both authors say, in effect, that Christians have inherited through Jesus, the eternal Son of God, the Israelite title "sons of God,"
which they are now, in the present eschatological age, and which will be
fully manifested in the *parousia.*

"Sons of God" is not a significant idea in the synoptics.[181] Appendix
G shows that Luke also has unmistakable tendencies to elevate beyond the
functional the transcendent status of Jesus as Son of God. This development might well have influenced his rare notion of the "sons of God/Most
High," but it is not clear how, and so we must construe the precise meaning of the title from our text in its context.

Ὑιοὶ ὑψίστου: Of the two OT uses, only Sir 4:10 applies the title to
humans.[182] Set in an instruction (4:1-10) on ethical conduct toward the
poor, the hungry, the suppliant, and those unjustly oppressed—precisely
the people of Luke's beatitudes and love command—Sir 4:10 almost perfectly parallels Luke's use in 6:35b: "Be like a father to the orphan, and a
husband to their mother; you will then be like a son of the Most High, and

---

[178] In the same way, the Jewish "sons of God" had two tenses. Appendix G shows
Jesus' own sonship in Paul moving from a purely functional meaning to a much more existential one evoked by his pre-existence and his role in creation.

[179] Byrne, *"Sons of God"* 213.

[180] R. Alan Culpepper, "The Pivot of John's Prologue," *NTS* 27 (1980) 1–31.

[181] This is a commonplace in NT research since Wolfgang Schweitzer, *Gotteskindschaft, Wiedergeburt und Erneuerung im Neuen Testament und in seiner Umwelt* (unpublished doctoral dissertation at Tübingen, 1943). In the synoptic tradition only Matt 5:9 (a
Sermon beatitude) and 5:45 (// Luke 6:35c) refer to disciples as υἱοὶ θεοῦ.

[182] Psalm 82:6 sets υἱοὶ ὑψίστου in synonymous parallelism with the subordinate gods
whom Yhwh condemns for their failure to uphold justice for the powerless in the areas assigned them by the supreme God.

he will love you more than does your mother."[183] Conduct like YHWH's love for orphans makes Sirach's disciples sons of the Most High *in this life.*[184]

d. Lukan Usage: Outside of 6:35c only once does Luke refer to humans as sons of God. In an eschatological context, Jesus says in 20:36 that the just become in the resurrection like the angels (= sons of God with eternal life), neither marrying nor dying, and so are sons of God. It is this clear final eschatological use, coupled with the eschatological use of Matt 5:9, that has persuaded some exegetes to take Luke 6:35c as referring to a hope of becoming sons of the most High in a risen life.[185]

This is possible, after the promise of reward in 6:35b, but is very unlikely.[186] As we have seen, "sons of God" usually refers to Israelites' historical status. There is no apocalyptic context here in 6:35c to demand an other-worldly meaning of υἱοὶ ὑψίστου. Rather the whole context of the love commandment makes the model for 6:35c Sir 4:10, where unconditional loving makes one now, in the doing, υἱός ὑψίστου.[187] Ἔσεσθε υἱοὶ ὑψίστου in 6:35c means that the disciples' radically new actions (6:27-31, 35ab), reversing the "normal" human ethics of the Greeks (6:32-34), manifest them as Sons of God, imitating in their lives God's unconditional love, as υἱός ὑψίστου in Sir 4:10 had led us to expect. Self-transcending participation now in God's altruistic unconditional love is the reward, as the following clauses confirm.

6:35d: ὅτι αὐτὸς χρηστός ἐστιν ἐπὶ τοὺς ἀχαρίστους καὶ πονηρούς, "because he is helpful to the ungrateful and wicked." Ὅτι confirms our interpretation of ἔσεσθε υἱοὶ υἱίστου. The disciples will be

---

[183] Marshall, *Luke* 264 points out that in both Sir 4:10 and Luke 6:35c "Sons of the Most High" occurs without the article, which he takes as a Hebraism, but Evans, *Luke* 336, takes as Greek usage. In either case the relation between the two texts is thus more secure.

[184] Among post-exilic works, Esth 16:15-16 also equates the Jews' righteous conduct in this world with being sons of the Most High.

[185] Hans-Werner Bartsch, "Feldrede und Bergpredigt: Redaktionsarbeit in Luk. 6," *TZ* 16 (1960) 12; Ernst, *Lukas* 227–28; Schürmann, *Lukasevangelium* 355; Betz, *Sermon* 609, 612. Most commentaries take the moral conduct of 6:27-36 as making Christians Sons of the Most High now, on this earth, as does even Schürmann, 356.

[186] There are three principal possibilities for interpretation; in the first two being Sons of the Most High describes the reward of 6:35b, in the third it does not: (1) your (eschatological) reward will be great, i.e., you will be (eschatological) sons of the Most High; (2) your (undefined) reward will be great, i.e, you will be in your actions sons of the Most High; (3) your (undefined) reward will be great, and you will (also) be sons of the Most High. Each of these interpretations has its defenders among the commentaries, but the context convincingly favors either (2) or (3).

[187] Καὶ + future tense here has the sense of a consequent clause, like the ὅπως of the parallel, Matt 5:45 (BAGD on καὶ, I. f., p. 392). This usage is common in informal speech ("Do this and you will be . . ."), and it is the usage in Sir 4:10!

children of the most high *because* the actions of loving enemies, doing good (to those who hate them, v. 27c) and lending without hope of return are the actions of God, their Father, who is helpful to the useless and the wicked. God's love is unconditional, not predicated by what humans do first, or even in response to God's love.

The notion of God as the one who gives to all is found in the OT and Greek literature. In the OT, Yʜwʜ is most often the just God who rewards the good and punishes the wicked (Exod 34:6-7; Num 14:18; Isa 5:18-19; Jer 32:18), but since his compassion outweighs his justice (Neh 9:17, 31; Jonah 4:2) he comes in rabbinic literature to be seen as the One who gives good gifts to both the good and the bad.[188] In Greco-Roman literature the even-handed benevolence of nature to both the wicked and the good served as indicator of the divine benevolence to all humans,[189] a benevolence to be imitated by humans.[190]

Χρηστός in secular Greek usage means "excellent, useful, serviceable" when applied to things; it is a weak term for morally good humans, meaning "decent, kind, good hearted," doing what they ought to do. It is used only some thirty times in the LXX, mostly as a translation of *tôb* in the Hebrew *Vorlage*. When used of God it generally refers to divine benevolence to those of inferior status who need God's help: Ps 105:1; Jer 33:1; Ps 34:8, all referring to God's merciful goodness in delivering his people.[191] Thus it may be conscious Lukan redaction to refer to God's benevolence to the ἀχαρίστους.[192]

Ἀχάριστος is used only four times in the LXX, all in the late Greek writings, to mean ungrateful (Sir 29:17; Wis 16:29; 4 Macc 9:10). Therefore, in contrast to Matt 5:45, where the provision of sun and rain to the evil and unjust stresses God's love of enemies, Luke 6:35 emphasizes constant giving to those whose past ingratitude promises that they will not return the good things that Jesus is enjoining his disciples to give them. Ἀχάριστος emphasizes lending without hope of reward, and so 6:35d refers to the notion of χάρις in 6:32-34.

---

[188] Billerbeck 1:374–76 for a wealth of examples.

[189] Cicero, *De Natura Deorum* II, 131; Seneca, *De Beneficiis* IV, 26, 1; see Betz, *Sermon* 316–17.

[190] "If you are imitating the gods . . . then bestow benefits also upon the ungrateful" (Seneca, *De Beneficiis* IV, 26, 1).

[191] Karl Weiss, "χρηστός," *TDNT* 9:483–87. In Dan 3:89 and often in the Psalms (135:1; 99:4) it is connected with God's ἔλεος. This idea of patient mercy underlies NT usage in Rom 2:4; 1 Pet 2:3.

[192] Luke's only other use of χρηστός in 5:39 is the secular Greek usage referring to the old wine as still good, and so does not illumine our text.

Πονηρός means morally bad, evil, and in biblical Greek refers to those who reject and oppose God and God's ways (see 6:45b).[193] That Luke does not specify (as does Matt 5:45) the way in which God is generous to the ungrateful implies that, like his injunctions, God loves and does good to those alienated from him, and lends without asking for return. Note that Jesus does not refer to God's enemies; evidently God refuses to take even the wicked as enemies. Their Father's generosity to the ungrateful, and even to the evil ones who consciously reject him, is then the model of the disciples' generosity as scions of the Most High. This strongly implied notion of patterning one's actions on God comes to explicit expression in the next verse.[194]

5. *The Deeper Christian Principle* (6:36)

6:36: γίνεσθε οἰκτίρμονες καθὼς [καὶ] ὁ πατὴρ ὑμῶν οἰκτίρμων ἐστίν, "be compassionate, as your Father is compassionate." As in 6:31, Jesus summarizes his preceding teaching in a general imperative.[195] Ὀικτίρμων, in classical Greek, denotes a compassion close to lamentation; humans may seek such active sympathy from the gods.[196] In the LXX the stem is used some 87 times, mostly to translate the Hebrew stem *rḥm*, "to be sympathetic, have compassion."[197] In the LXX it is used mainly of God's compassion, especially in the Psalms. The classic text is Exod 34:6,

---

[193] Ἀχάριστος καὶ πονηρὸς is a commonplace in Stoic writings; Betz, *Sermon* 611. For the understanding of πονηρός as moral evil see the comments on 6:45.

[194] Since the gospels do not use the terminology of *imitatio Dei*, we need not delve into the probable derivation of this notion from a Hellenistic-Jewish syncretistic milieu (as does Hans-Dieter Betz in *Nachfolge und Nachahmung Jesu Christi in Neuen Testament*. BHTh 37 (Tübingen: Mohr, 1967). Nor need we investigate the fact that *hālāk 'aharē 'elohîm* in the OT refers to obeying God's commandments rather than patterning one's actions upon God's. However, the notion of the divine pattern for human conduct is found in the Holiness Code, where the Israelites are exhorted to a range of just actions *because* YHWH is holy (Lev 19:2, *passim*). Closer to home, God's pattern of unwonted justice to alien nations underlines for the people of Israel the injunction to treat them justly in Exod 22:20-22//Deut 10:17-19; 24:17-18; Lev 19:33-34. Jesus especially patterns his contact on that of his Father; the classic example is John 5:17, but the motif occurs also in Luke 15:1-32, where Jesus refers to God's actions to justify his own conduct. Luke makes God's conduct the standard for humans, especially in the parables in which God reaches out to outcasts and sinners (14:15-24; 15:1-32; 18:1-14).

[195] While Matt 5:48 has a future indicative with imperative force (ἔσεσθε), Luke has a present imperative (γίνεσθε), underscoring the continuing general obligation.

[196] Rudolf Bultmann, "οἰκτίρω," *TDNT* 5:159.

[197] At its root, *rḥm* derives from *reḥem*, the womb, and so denotes the most moving sort of heartfelt compassion. In the LXX οἰκτίρειν is used some thirty-three times, mostly to translate Hebrew *ḥānan*, "to have mercy on" or *rāḥam*, "to have compassion on;" the noun some thirty-six times, almost always translating *rāḥam*, the adjective some eighteen times, almost always translating *raḥûm*.

κύριος ὁ θεὸς οἰκτίρμων καὶ ἐλεήμων, "the LORD, a God compassionate and merciful;" this same pair of adjectives refers to YHWH in Pss 85:15; 102:8; 108:12; 110:4; 111:4. But οἰκτίρμων can refer to human persons as well (Lam 4:10). A perfect parallel to Luke 6:36 is in Jerusalem Targum Pseudo-Jonathan on Lev 22:28 "My people, children of Israel, as your Father is merciful in heaven, so should you be merciful on earth."

In the NT the stem is rarely used.[198] Ὀικτίρμων is used only in Luke 6:36 and in Jas 5:11, where it describes God's compassion as parallel with God's gut-felt sympathy (πολύσπλαγχνος). Since this is the only occurrence of the stem in the gospel tradition, it is likely to be Lukan redaction,[199] and indeed it displays a basic theme of the Lukan gospel. Jesus is moved with compassion (ἐσπλαγχνίσθη) for the suffering in 7:13 and 10:33, and the forgiving father has that same compassion on the prodigal son in 15:20. This compassion is made part of the larger theme of God's mercy by the phrase in 1:78, διὰ σπλάγχνα ἐλέους θεοῦ ἡμῶν.[200] Mercy is given as the essence of the Good Samaritan's actions in 10:37, and the following imperative (v. 38) enjoins this kind of merciful action on those who hear Jesus' teaching. Without ἔλεος or οἰκτίρμων being used, the theme still underlies the great scenes of forgiveness and seeking the lost (the ἀχαρίστους) in 7:36-50; 15:1-32; 19:1-10, 41-42; 23:34, 39-43.

Πατήρ is used of God extensively in Greek religion, literature, and philosophy, where the notions of the divine progenitor, patriarchy, and monarchy intersect.[201] Its literal use for YHWH is infrequent in the OT, although the notion is affirmed in theophorous proper names and is implied in other relationships.[202] Nevertheless, in the NT the more Jewish gospels use Father for God more frequently (Matthew 45, John 117). Luke uses the word most often (thirty-nine times) for a human progenitor or ancestor. While Matthew's Jesus divides his usage fairly evenly between his Father, the disciples' Father, and the Jews' Father, Luke has Jesus refer to God as his Father twelve times and as the disciples' Father only four times (6:36; 11:2; 12:30, 32).[203] As we saw in Chapter 1 and below in Appendix

---

[198] The verb and noun occur only in the Pauline literature, their six uses equally divided between divine and human compassion.

[199] This does not mean that τέλειος in Matt 5:48 was original; contemporary commentators take it as Matthaean redaction to stress the Jewish notion of perfection through keeping the new commands expressed in the antitheses; Betz, *Sermon,* and Luz, *Matthew 1–7,* 345–47.

[200] The theme of God's mercy had already been announced in the two canticles of the prologue, where God's ἔλεος is mentioned in 1:50, 54, 72, 78 as the source of his actions in Israel's history.

[201] Gottlob Schrenk, "πατήρ," *TDNT* 5:945–59.

[202] Gottfried Quell, "πατήρ," *TDNT* 5:959–74.

[203] Although ὁ πατὴρ ὁ ἐξ οὐρανοῦ is in itself ambiguous, the context seems to point to the disciples' Father in 11:13.

G, God was Jesus' Father in a unique way, expressed in an exclusive reciprocal intimacy. Yet Jesus has the disciples address his Father as their Father (11:2). In fact, Jesus' four uses of Father for the disciples' God are all in a context of prayer. In 11:2 they are to ask their Father not only for their daily bread, but for the sanctification of God's name in the coming of God's Reign. Jesus' following clarification on prayer (11:5-13) assures them that their Father not only cares for their physical needs but will give the Holy Spirit to those who ask for it (11:11, 13). The same message recurs in 12:22-32, where Jesus assures them that their Father will grant them God's Reign. Therefore in the intimacy of prayer to their provident Father the disciples will receive gifts far beyond their ability to conceive or achieve. Thus with this one word πατήρ, used only once in the Sermon, in the climactic place of the love commandment section, Jesus makes clear that his ethic is not about obedience, but about personal love.

Thus the climactic motive for the whole of the love commandment is *imitatio Dei*. Although μίμησις τοῦ θεοῦ and similar notions are attested in Greek literature,[204] the emphasis here on compassion makes it more likely to have derived from the Bible and Jewish literature.[205]

Like the Golden Rule, Jesus' second principle makes not the other's conduct but one's own benevolent feeling the rule of conduct. Like the Golden Rule, this principle begins with the affective realm, with the spontaneous human intersubjectivity that is our primordial engagement with the Other. Whereas the Golden Rule began with my own desires, οἰκτίρμων implies already primordially the face of the Other that summons my aid, out of my *Mitmenschsein*.

---

[204] Becoming like the divine is an ideal for human conduct in Plato, *Theaetetus* 176ab; *Laws* IV, 716; it was asserted as the teaching of Pythagoras in Areios Didymos *Var. hist.* XII, 59; the later Stoics inculcate virtue as an imitation of god in Cicero, *De nat. deorum* II, 153, in Seneca, *De ira* II 16, in Epictetus, *Diss.* II 14, 11-13. Cicero says that "virtue is nothing else than nature perfected and brought to its peak; it is therefore human likeness to god," *De leg.* I, 25. These Stoics conceived of this likeness to god as doing good (εὐεργετεῖν) to others; see Gerhard Schneider, "*Imitatio Dei* als Motiv der 'Ethik Jesu,'" in Helmut Merklein, ed., *Neues Testament und Ethik: für Rudolf Schnackenburg* (Freiburg: Herder, 1989) 71–83; Jacques Dupont, "L' Appel à imiter Dieu en Matthieu 5,48 et Luc 6,36," *RivBib* 14 (1966) 137–58 and the bibliographies cited there and in Betz, *Sermon* 325 n. 1021.

[205] Although the LXX does not use μιμεῖσθαι or its noun forms, Lev 19:2, 4 and Deut 10:18-19 imply that Israel's justice is an imitation of YHWH's holiness. The terms for imitating God occur first in *T. Abr.* 4:3-5; *Ep. Arist.* 187-88, 280. Rabbinic literature has similar expressions: "We ought to resemble Him; just as he is compassionate and merciful, you also ought to be compassionate and merciful." *Mekh. Ex.* 15:2; *Ex. R.* 26 (87b); see other citations in Dupont, "L'appel," 280, and Schneider, "*Imitatio*," 75–76.

But the *imitatio Dei* transcends human measures of conduct to measure us by what we are, daughters and sons of a compassionate God who unconditionally loves (6:35-36). He loves those who are ungrateful and wicked. Again, Luke's Jesus does not identify them as God's enemies (because the divine compassion cannot see them as enemies). But humans do see them as enemies, and it is precisely this identification that must be transformed if God's reign and its peace are to come on earth. Here the Golden Rule helps—beginning with our desires and assuming those in the Other transforms the enemy into my fellow traveler, my companion. The *imitatio Dei* tells us that love is not a *quid pro quo* or even a *do ut des;* the Other must be loved even in his inimical alterity.

In short, Luke's Jesus sums up all of his ethical teaching about love of enemies, doing good to those who hate and abuse you, giving to those who steal or simply keep asking from you, doing to others as you would have them do to you as having that deep and heartfelt compassion for another that characterizes their divine Father's relations to his creatures. Although Jesus here speaks of God's compassion on the useless and wicked, the fact that God is their Father implies that he also has compassion on the disciples' slowness to grasp the magnitude of the empowerment he is giving them.

Finally, note how artistically Luke has constructed 6:36 to be an echo and expansion of his other general rule in this section, the Golden Rule. The Golden Rule had asked the disciple to search her own deepest desires, to presume that these were also the desires of the other, and to act accordingly. Luke 6:36 likewise makes not the other's conduct but the rule of benevolence the norm of Christian action. Yet that norm has been infinitely enlarged to the measure of God's own compassion.

Summary and Conclusions

1. *The Love Command (6:27-36)* is an artistic rhetorical structure, consisting of

a. the command to love one's enemies as a topic sentence and six examples of nonretaliatory love in four-beat rhythm (6:27-30);

b. the Golden Rule as a general interpretative principle (6:31);

c. repetition of these injunctions in negative form as critique of Greco-Roman balanced reciprocity in three-beat rhythms (6:32-34);

d. positive repetition of the injunctions with motive of reward (6:35);

e. the Christian principle of morality: *imitatio Dei* (6:36).

2. *Luke highlights the love of enemies* as the topic sentence of Jesus' morality by placing it first, as the prime example of his morality. This

highlights the uniqueness of Jesus' ethic.[206] The six following examples speak of an attack on one's person or possessions by a personal enemy. The verbs "hating" and "cursing" may recall the attack on Christians mentioned in 6:22, 25, but all the verbs are general enough to speak of any personal attack. The responses of the Christian victim, read by contrast off the actions of the attackers, seem to speak—especially in "blessing" and "praying for" (6:28)—of a consideration for the moral state of the neighbor, and so the nonretaliation intimates the conversion to the neighbor of which the next verse speaks.

3. *The Golden Rule (6:31)* gives as motivation for such Christian nonretaliation a sense of fellow-feeling for another human being (6:31). As a moral maxim of general altruism, expressed by mutuality between subject and object, the principle is unique to Jesus. In the literary context of 6:20-30 Jesus moves beyond the love of neighbor in Lev 19:18 to love of enemies. By beginning with one's own desires, Jesus' Golden Rule forces one to consider the other as a person with her own correlative desires. Further, beginning with desires opens the disciple herself to the range of desires of the human heart, not only for money and food, but also for friendship and community, even to being in communion with God. Ultimately these desires are rooted in the fact of, and desire of, being children of God (6:35). Jesus' formulation of the Golden Rule ultimately is rooted in radical altruism, found in God.

4. *Repetition in Negative Form (6:32-34):* Lest the Golden Rule be understood in terms of customary Greco-Roman balanced reciprocity expressed by χάρις, Jesus explicitly excludes three examples of such exchange: loving those who have previously loved oneself, doing good to benefactors, and lending in hope of return (6:32-34). These are actions of self-interested sinners, receiving their reward in reciprocal exchange, comparable to those who have already received theirs in 6:24-25.

5. *Positive Repetition with Motive (6:35):* Jesus now repeats the general commands to love, changing the third imperative to lending without hope of return. Yet these nonretaliatory acts of love of the enemy as a neighbor, as a fellow human being, even as another self, do receive a great

---

[206] Judaism had stressed love of one's neighbor, one's fellow Jew as covenant partner. Although the OT has abundant examples of retaliation against one's personal enemies and the national enemies (who are therefore God's enemies), the OT never enjoins hatred of one's enemies, nor does it command love of the enemy. But there is a series of three texts (Exod 23:4-5; Deut 22:1-4; Lev 19:17-18) that enjoin benevolent action toward the enemy. Hellenistic philosophy speaks of nonretaliation against a personal attacker, but the motive for nonretaliation is rooted in self-centered concern for one's own happiness and practice of virtue rather than in love of enemies.

reward. The future tense ἔσται (6:35b) recalls the reader to the promises of the beatitudes: disciples will receive their reward in the immediate and ultimate futures of the Reign of God.[207] As the actions Jesus requires go beyond human "reason," so their proportionate reward exceeds human agency. The great reward they hope for can come only from God, and so is an object of faith, not secured by human conduct but by reliance on the sovereign goodness of God.

In doing such generous actions the disciples will be "children of the most High," for God acts generously toward the useless and the wicked without regard to what they have done in the past or what they might do in the future (6:35d). Ἔσεσθε υἱοὶ ὑψίστου in 6:35c describes not just an eschatological state, but an empowerment that allows Jesus' disciples to act with his power as Son of God on this earth. The disciples' radically new actions (6:27-31, 35ab), reversing the human ethics of the Greeks (6:32-34), manifest them as Children of God.

6. *The Deeper Christian Principle (6:36):* The OT often describes God as compassionate (οἰκτίρμων). Here Luke's Jesus focuses all of the disciples' imitation of God not on the eschatological power of healing or raising from the dead, but on having the compassion that could drive them to nonretaliatory love of the neighbor. Thus Luke 6:36 concludes this section on love of enemies by echoing and expanding the other general rule in this section, the Golden Rule. But the norm has been infinitely enlarged to the measure of God's own compassion. Luke does not specify how this is to be done, except perhaps by way of the tantalizing hint in 6:35c, that we are to be "sons of the Most High." Further explanation of the "how" of this Love Command will be taken up in Chapter 8.

---

[207] Indeed, the contrast between the true reward from God and a humanly attained reward in this life manifests the relationship of 6:32-34 with 6:35, just as it had revealed the relationship between 6:20-23 and 6:24-26.

Chapter 6

The Critique of Judgment
(6:37-42)

Thematic Division of This Section

Now Jesus takes a step even beyond the command to love enemies, proscribing the judgment that the other is my enemy!

We have judged that its rhetorical parallel with 6:31 makes 6:36 into the conclusion of the Love Command (6:27-36). But we cannot know what structure Luke intended for 6:37-42. Many commentators, noting the literary aside in 6:39 and the switch from imperatives to parabolic discourse in 6:39-49, take 6:37-38 with 6:36 as part of the Love Commandment (6:27-38), and begin a new, parabolic, section in 6:39.[1] The return to the four-beat rhythm of the imperatives in 6:37-38b, parallel to the rhythm of 6:27b-30, reinforces that division.

But determinative for me is that the parabolic language of 6:41-42 echoes and develops the theme of judgment introduced in 6:37-38, and so makes 6:37-42 into a unit.[2] Probably an equation of compassion with mercy enabled Luke to see 6:36 not only as the climax of the Love Commandment, but also as a hinge linking that commandment to the non-judgmental attitude of Jesus, now enjoined on the disciples in 6:37-42.[3] In short, the desires of the human heart in 6:31 also exclude harsh judgment

---

[1] Paul Hahn, in his unpublished Ph.D. dissertation, *Structure in Rhetorical Criticism and the Structure of the Sermon on the Plain (Luke 6:20-49)* (Milwaukee: Marquette University, 1990) 274–92, indicates the substantial difficulty with beginning a new unit at 6:39, especially when this break means joining 6:37-38 with 6:36.

[2] So divided, for roughly these reasons, by C. G. Montefiore, T. W. Manson, Josef Schmid, Wilfrid J. Harrington, Joseph A. Fitzmyer, and Johannes Schneider.

[3] This notion of a bridge does rough justice to the insight of Erich Klostermann, J. M. Creed, and Josef Ernst that 6:36 introduces the theme of judgment articulated in 6:37-38, and grounds the resumption of the four-beat rhythm of the imperatives in 6:37-38a.

in 6:37-42.[4] As a rhetorical unit, it has two parts: 6:37-38 resumes the four beat-rhythm of the imperatives in 6:27b-30, but 6:39-42 switches from the imperative mood to the figurative language of three images relating to the theme of not judging. Only exegesis can demonstrate that the theme forms a unit.

Exegesis of Luke 6:37-42

1. *Parallel Prohibitions of Judgment and Commands to Give* (6:37-38)

6:37ab: Καὶ μὴ κρίνετε, καὶ οὐ μὴ κριθῆτε, "and do not judge, and you will not be judged." Καὶ leaves the connection with 6:27-36 unclear.[5] All four imperatives in 6:37-38a are in the present tense, expressing general rules, as has been the pattern throughout the Sermon.[6] Μὴ is the regular negative particle for general prohibitions; κρίνειν is the ordinary LXX translation for *špt,* which means either to rule or to judge.[7] In Semitic culture the god is ruler and judge of the people; the king receives the right to judge from the god. God's judgment in the OT and in Judaism is a matter of establishing a right relationship between God and the Jews, between the Jews themselves, and between the Jews and the nations that oppress them (or seek God's will).[8] Although throughout all strata of OT and Judaism God's judgment is primary and ultimate, human agents do exercise the function of judging: first the judges and the elders in the gate, then the king and his royal courts, and finally the religious leaders, like the Pharisees and scribes, who render judgment on what the *mishpatim* and oral traditions mean.

Although divine judgment plays its part in Greek culture, the word also refers to human acts of distinguishing, estimating, discerning, choosing, deciding, and to judgments in law courts (LSJ 996). In the NT κρίνειν is used 114x, most often of God's ultimate judgment on human actions.[9]

---

[4] It is true that this seems to make 6:39a a maladroit insertion. But, against those who divide the Sermon on the basis of imperatives vs. parabolic language, parabolic language had already begun in 6:38b!

[5] Some manuscripts (D, and its related traditions) left καὶ out, probably feeling that 6:37-38 does not continue 6:27-36. As will appear, I think that 6:37-38 does continue the thought of the Love Command.

[6] All ten positive commands in 6:27-36 are present imperatives, and of the two prohibitions only 6:29 contains an aorist subjunctive, prohibiting a future action.

[7] The ruler's principal duty is to execute justice for the people. Since in the NT only Matt 19:28//Luke 22:30 means "to rule," the Jewish meaning of judging forms the background of the usage here.

[8] Volkmar Herntrich, "κρίνω," *TDNT* 3:923–26.

[9] Friedrich Büchsel, "κρίνω," *TDNT* 3:935–40.

Sometimes Jesus is the ultimate judge (Matt 7:22-23), most often as Son of Man (Mark 8:38 *parr.*; Mark 14:62 *parr.*; Matt 24:30-31; 25:31-46). In Luke-Acts, however, κρίνειν rarely refers to ultimate divine judgment.[10] Rather it refers to human judgment and condemnation, in many ways:

> (1) humans making a (right) decision (7:43; 12:57; 19:22; Acts 4:19; 16:15; 26:8; 27:1);
>
> (2) an authoritative Christian decision in the Spirit (Acts 15:19; 16:4; 21:25);
>
> (3) a forensic procedure, religious or civil: to stand trial (Acts 23:3, 6; 25:9, 10, 20; 26:6), be judged guilty, condemned (Acts 3:13; 13:27; 24:21), be judged innocent (Acts 25:25);
>
> (4) humans condemning themselves as unworthy of eternal life (Acts 13:46);
>
> (5) the apostles' governance of the tribes of Israel (Luke 22:30).

Thus Luke's usage is too wide of itself to define what is being prohibited here. Prohibition of all human decision-making is not what Jesus had in mind, as subsequent exegesis will make clear.[11] Here we can only say that the upcoming synonymous parallel with καταδικάζειν in 6:37c and the actions of the parable of 6:41-42 make it probable that Jesus is prohibiting condemnatory judgment.

Καὶ οὐ μὴ κριθῆτε: καὶ here seems to express a result of the preceding clause (BAGD 392). Οὐ μὴ + the aorist subjunctive expresses an emphatic denial of a future action (BDF §365.3). The lack of an agent leaves the future consequence ambiguous: it could refer to an imminent future in which the neighbor who is not judged will not judge the one who has not judged.[12] But in this literary context the eschatological future is probably meant: the theological passive expresses a divine judgment. Luke 6:32-35 is filled with the notion of ultimate eschatological reward, which coheres with the promise and threat of divine judgment that is the

---

[10] Acts 7:7; 17:31. Cf. similar usage of its cognates: κριτής refers to a judge in a civil suit in Luke 12:58; 18:2, 6; Acts 18:15, and to a ruler in Acts 13:20; 24:10; only Acts 10:42 speaks of Jesus as divine judge. But κρίσις refers to the last judgment in Luke 10:14; 11:31, 32, while Luke 10:42 and Acts 8:33 speak of human judgment of justice and right.

[11] In 6:41-42 Jesus himself made such judgments and expected his followers to do the same. Hans-Dieter Betz, *The Sermon on the Mount: A Commentary on the Sermon on the Mount, Including the Sermon on the Plain (Matthew 5:3–7:27 and Luke 6:20-49)*. Edited by Adela Yarbro Collins. Hermeneia (Minneapolis: Fortress, 1995) 490 demonstrates convincingly that Jesus here uses κρίνειν to refer to "negative and destructive conduct," and so the prohibition attacks the common human practice of condemning others through gossip, rash judgments, and even court actions.

[12] Betz, *Sermon* 616 is the only commentator to make this his preferred interpretation; he cites Alfred Plummer and Marie-Joseph Lagrange as predecessors, but this does not seem to be the case. This position is favored by those who treat the Golden Rule as a *do ut des*.

sanction for the Sermon as a whole (6:20-26, 35, 46-49). Jesus promises his disciples who refuse to judge others that God will not judge them.[13]

6:37cd: καὶ μὴ καταδικάζετε, καὶ οὐ μὴ καταδικασθῆτε, "and do not condemn, and you will not be condemned." Jesus now continues with a perfect synonymous parallel. Καταδικάζειν is used only nine times in the LXX, mostly translating *ršᶜ* (evenly divided between human and divine condemnation), sometimes with legal force, sometimes not. It is used only five times in the NT: in Matt 12:7 and Jas 5:6 it refers to humans condemning the innocent; in Matt 12:37 it refers to God's ultimate judgment. Here it probably intensifies its parallel κρίνειν (6:37ab) and so refers to a kind of formal condemnation. Again the reward is divine acquittal, and possibly a non-condemnatory world in the disciple's own lived future.

6:37ef: ἀπολύετε, καὶ απολυθήσεται, "forgive and you will be forgiven," continues the four-beat rhythm of general imperatives, but now shifts to a positive command with positive reward, as in its parallel 6:38ab. Ἀπολύειν occurs only 36 times in the LXX, and no one meaning predominates.[14] In the NT, with the exception of Heb 13:23, it occurs only in the gospels and Acts, where it has the same range of meanings as it had in Greek literature from Homer on: to set free (as a slave), pardon, release from a bond (debt, contract), dismiss (BAGD 96). In Luke-Acts it means to release from custody (23:16, 18, 20, 22, 25; Acts 3:13; 4:21, 23; 5:40; 16:35, 36; 17:9; 26:32; 28:18), to send away, dismiss (8:38; 9:12; 14:4; Acts 19:40; 23:22), to send on a mission (Acts 13:3; 15:30, 33), to divorce (Luke 16:18), to release from a burden (Luke 2:29; 13:12), to leave (Acts 28:25). None of these meanings fits Luke 6:38, and so we must construe from context. There seems to be a progression from not judging someone (κρίνειν) on the basis of some evidence, to not condemning (καταδικάζειν) where the evidence is more certain and public, to pardoning (ἀπολύειν) where the debt or personal offense is established. Jesus asks his disciples not to avoid false judgment, but to pardon when they have correctly judged that an offense has been done them. He asks them to pardon unrestrictedly, a message carried elsewhere in Luke-Acts by forgiveness of debts (6:35; 16:1-13) and by unrestricted forgiveness (Luke 7:47; 11:4). With the prohibitions of judging and condemning, the command to pardon specifies the command to love one's enemies.

Καὶ describes the result: the disciple herself will be pardoned definitively by God, and so again the eschatological reward for actions ex-

---

[13] Nevertheless, Betz's warning to include both interpretations for all four of these maxims is well taken (*Sermon* 616).

[14] Of these, only four or five have a Hebrew *Vorlage*. Twenty of the thirty-six uses occur in 1–4 Maccabees.

presses the compassion of God (6:36) toward those who are evil (6:35-36). The disciple will also live in a world where pardon is freely given.

6:38ab: δίδοτε, καὶ δοθήσεται ὑμῖν, "give and it will be given to you" is the last of the four commands set in parallel. Here the personal indirect object of the verb is not someone who has done something wrong (to be judged or condemned in 6:37a-d, to be forgiven in 6:37ef), but someone who is simply in need. Διδόναι is one of the most commonly used verbs in the NT (416x), since love and grace are understood as God's *gifts.* This fourth imperative, in the climactic position, is another summary of Jesus' teaching of the Golden Rule and the imitation of God.[15] The series of divine passives in 6:37 has set the pattern of God's saving mercy; now the disciple who is to be a daughter or son of God (6:35c) is summoned to the same generosity.[16] The disciple had already been summoned to generosity to any beggar in 6:30a. Although the object is ordinarily understood to be some material means of support, corresponding to δίδου in 6:30 and to the very material image in 6:38c, lack of any expressed direct object leaves the action open to the giving of spiritual gifts as well.

6:38c: μέτρον καλὸν πεπιεσμένον σεσαλευμένον ὑπερεκχυννόμενον δώσουσιν εἰς τὸν κόλπον ὑμῶν, "a generous measure, pressed down, shaken together, and running over will they pour into your bosom." Μέτρον καλὸν: μέτρον ordinarily means an instrument of measuring, and in an agricultural economy usually a measure of volume, a cup and larger measures. If the cup is meant, then καλὸν would mean "beautiful," or at least "in good repair." However, μέτρον can also be used figuratively to mean the quantity measured (e.g., a cup of flour as a quantity). In that case καλὸν would mean "fair" or a "good measure" in the sense of generous (BAGD 400 and 515).[17] Luke here uses metonymy to express the generous quantity, while at the same time keeping the graphic image of the merchant's container before the eyes of his reader in the following phrases.

The three verbs are Lukan: πιέζειν, "to squeeze, press down" and ὑπερεκχύνεσθαι, "to pour out over, overflow" are hapax in the NT, while Luke-Acts has eight of the fifteen NT uses of σαλεύειν, "to shake"). The rare perfect passive participle form embodies Greek conciseness in creating one

---

[15] "The fourth maxim presents the act of giving as the culmination of Jesus' teaching as explained through the Golden Rule (6:31). In that context all of Christian ethics is a form of giving" (Betz, *Sermon,* 617).

[16] The idea occurs not only in the gospels (//Matt 7:1-2; Mark 4:24), but also in 2 Cor 9:6-8, where, in the context of the collection, Paul reminds the Corinthians that God, who scatters abroad and gives to the poor, loves a bountiful and cheerful giver.

[17] Bernard Couroyer, "De la mesure dont vous mesurez, il vous sera mesuré," *RB* 77 (1970) 366–70.

of the most graphic images in the whole NT.[18] The image is a reversal of a merchant's normal business practice in which grain was sold by volume. Biblical literature is so replete with warnings against using different measures for selling and buying to defraud the buyer[19] that getting a level measure for one's money was virtue enough. But Jesus' image strikingly elevates expectations: the merchant will first press the grain down to pack it into the container, then shake it so that air spaces will be filled with grain, and then will pour in more grain until it heaps up, spills over the container and overflows into the fold of the disciple's garment (εἰς τὸν κόλπον ὑμῶν).[20] The image conveys unprecedented, almost unimaginable generosity.

Who will give this reward? Δώσουσιν continues Luke's instructive ambiguity. For those who have been interpreting the passive verbs of 6:38 as done by those to whom the disciples have extended tolerance and forgiveness, the third-person plural means that Luke has finally made those agents explicit. But δώσουσιν is to be read as a parallel explaining the δο-θήσεται of 6:38b and so in continuity with the (divine) passives of 6:37. Further, since this verse is so clearly Lukan redaction it is even more legitimate to see the third-person plural as referring to divine agency, as in Luke 12:20, 48; 16:9; 23:21.[21] In this astonishing generosity, so unlike human practice, surely the image symbolizes divine reward. The ambiguity is instructive: tolerance, forgiveness, and generosity come from God in abundance, whether in this life from those whom the disciples forgive and to whom they give, or from God in the decisive judgment.

6:38d: ᾧ γὰρ μέτρῳ μετρεῖτε ἀντιμετρθήσεται ὑμῖν, "for the measure you use will be measured out to you," now sums up the relationship of 6:38a to 6:38b (and the whole argument of 6:37-38c) with a gnomic expression whose passive reiterates the divine passives. The proverb appears in almost the same form in Mark 4:24//Matt 7:2,[22] and is approximated in

---

[18] Heaping up adjectives is non-Semitic, a feature of Hellenistic Greek style. Note also the artistic use of different moods and tenses of the same verb (δίδοτε, δοθήσεται, δώ-σουσιν).

[19] From the Law, Deut 25:13-15; Lev 19:35-36; from the prophets, Amos 8:5; Hos 12:8; Ezek 45:10; from Wisdom literature, Prov 11:1; 16:11; 20:10.

[20] The κόλπος is ordinarily the chest, bosom, and then comes to mean in both Greco-Roman and biblical literature the fold of the garment that hangs over one's belt, used by the ancients as a shopping bag; BAGD 442. John Nolland's suggestion (*Luke 1–9:20*. 3 vols. [Dallas, Tex.: Word Books, 1989] 301) that it may mean the lap is not borne out by the texts he cites and is not attested elsewhere.

[21] Friedrich Rehkopf, *Die lukanische Sonderquelle: ihr Umfang und Sprachgebrauch.* WUNT 5 (Tübingen: Mohr, 1959) 99. The construction is also a rabbinic and Qumran periphrasis for God; I. Howard Marshall, *The Gospel of Luke* (Exeter: Paternoster, 1978) 267.

[22] Mark 4:24-25 has a quite different context and application. Lukan redaction added ἀντί το μετρηθήσεται, probably to reinforce the notion of perfect reciprocity.

the OT,[23] Greco-Roman,[24] and rabbinic literature.[25] At first the proverb seems to contradict the theological argument of 6:35-38 and return to the principle of retribution in the *lex talionis*. But the *lex talionis* calculated a reasonable limit for *re*tribution ("an eye for an eye"), while Jesus asks his disciples to imitate in faith the unlimited initiative of their Father, acting altruistically without reference to human return (6:35-38). If you, as a daughter of God, act with the unlimited generosity of God (6:35d), believing that your loving Father will give you the unlimited recompense that a perfect father gives, you will receive an unlimited reward.[26]

2. *The Parables on the Blindness of Those who Judge* (6:39-42)

6:39a: εἶπεν δὲ καὶ παραβολὴν αὐτοῖς, "and he told them a parable" constitutes a strange narrative aside in the midst of discourse material. Αὐτοῖς refers to the same audience addressed in 6:27-38.[27] No one has explained what this narrative aside is doing in the midst of connected speech by Jesus. What can literary criticism tell us about Luke's usage here?[28] Luke uses such narrative asides, which do not change subject matter, speaker, or addressee, mostly in introducing parables (5:36; 6:39; 12:16; 13:6; 18:1; 21:9; [18:9; 20:9]) and infrequently in other cases (11:5; 13:20; 15:11; 21:10). Such asides reveal nothing about the sources of the composition, nor do they begin a new rhetorical section of the speech, but rather connect what follows with what went before. Such a narrative aside is merely a stylistic variation, providing a breather in a long speech and calling attention to the intricate and mysterious meaning of the following figurative language.

---

[23] Hans-Peter Rüger, "Mit welchem Mass ihr meßt, wird euch gemessen werden," *ZNW* 69 (1960) 174–82.

[24] Johann Jakob Wettstein, *He kaine diatheke* [Romanized form] = *Novum Testamentum graecum: editionis receptae cum lectionibus variantibus codicum mss., editionum aliarum, versionum et patrum nec non commentario pleniore ex scriptoribus veteribus hebraeis, graecis et latinis historiam et vim verborum illustrante*. 2 vols. (Amsterdam: Dommer, 1751–1752) 1:697 gives examples from as far back as Hesiod, *Erga* 349–51; for fuller documentation see Betz, *Sermon* 619.

[25] The principal example is *m. Sota* 1.7, "With what measure a man metes it shall be measured to him again;" other citations in Billerbeck 1:444–46.

[26] The heavenly reward for faith that does charitable works finds classic expression in Luke 14:14, whose ἀνταποδοθήσεται echoes the ἀντιμετρθήσεται of 6:38d, and whose μακάριος recalls the Sermon beatitudes. Of course, only the infinite Creator can act without any need of reward.

[27] I.e., primarily the Twelve (6:17a) and the larger crowd of disciples (6:17b), but in a lesser way also the crowd who has come to hear (6:17c); see my comment on 6:27.

[28] Appendix F surveys previous approaches and supports the position taken here.

Παραβολὴ: Jesus now shifts to figurative language to demonstrate the truth of his prohibitions of judgment.[29] Παραβολη is singular, yet Jesus actually adds three figures: (1) 6:39b is a proverb expressed as a rhetorical question with the obvious answer adjoined (6:39c); (2) 6:40a is another proverb, with an explanation added in 6:40b; (3) 6:41-42c is a similitude, with an application supplied in 6:42de. To what does παραβολὴ refer? Most naturally it refers to the immediately following parable, but, as Frederick W. Danker points out, this parable is itself an introduction to the tropes that follow, and so, implicitly, it refers to the series of figures in 6:39b-42.[30]

6:39b: Μήτι δύναται τυφλὸς τυφλὸν ὁδηγεῖν; "can a blind man lead a blind man?"[31] Μήτι: μὴ is the ordinary interrogative particle expecting the answer, "no;" μήτι may be an emphatic form, "surely not," but is often used as an alternative form of μή.[32] The παραβολὴ is a proverb expressed as a rhetorical question expecting the answer "no;" it is "answered" by a rhetorical question expecting "yes." Δύναται, "can," emphasizes the physical impossibility of the action. Τυφλός denotes one who is blind from birth or so injured that he can no longer see well enough to avoid a pitfall. The commonness, irreversibility, and drastic effect of the physical condition are the grounds for its frequent use in proverbs, not only in Greco-Roman literature,[33] but also in many cultures. It is not a Lukan

---

[29] For selective bibliographies of the immense literature on the NT parable see John R. Donahue, *The Gospel in Parable* (Philadelphia: Fortress, 1988) and Bernard Brandon Scott, *Hear Then the Parable* (Minneapolis: Fortress, 1989). Common to all expositions of the biblical parable are these notions: (1) Hebrew *māšāl* and Greek παραβολή refer to various forms of figurative speech from proverbs to extended narratives; (2) parables range from didactic to metaphoric literary functions; (3) by engaging the hearers' experience and imagination they move them to judgment on a preconscious level and reveal depths of meaning that cannot be exhausted by rational analysis. Consequently, they are the perfect tool for Jesus' invitation to the Reign of God and imitation of God's unconditional love, which both exceed the grasp and assent of unaided human reason and will.

[30] Frederick W. Danker, *Jesus and the New Age* (rev. ed. Philadelphia: Fortress, 1988) 153; commentators take for granted that παραβολή refers to 6:39bc.

[31] The proverb occurs in Matt 15:14 as a reference to the Pharisees as blind guides, especially in the subject of stringent rules of ritual cleanliness (15:1-20//Mark 7:1-23). The priority of Matthew's or Luke's form and context is irrelevant to our interpretation, but it is clear that Luke's form is more literary and rhetorical (cf. the balanced rhetorical questions and the postponement of the verb ἐμπεσοῦνται to the end of the sentence).

[32] BDF 427 (2); BAGD 520.

[33] The proverb is used in Plato, *Rep.* VIII, 554b; Philo, *Virt.* 7, and occurs in exactly the same form as in Q (perhaps influenced by it) in Sextus Empiricus, *Pyrr. Hyp.* III, 259; Wolfgang Schrage, "ὁδός," *TDNT* 8:270–94 and Betz, *Sermon* 620 nn. 271and 272. The proverb does not occur in the LXX, but τυφλός is used in a figurative sense in the Isaian school, beginning with 6:9-10.

word; he usually uses it in the physical sense (7:21-22; 14:13, 21; 18:35; Acts 13:11), but it can have a transferred meaning (4:18).

Ὁδηγεῖν is a combination of ὁδός, "way, path, road," and ἡγεῖσθαι, "to lead, guide," and so means "to lead, guide on the way."[34] When the subject is concrete the verb is concrete, but it can have a figurative meaning, as in Acts 8:31, where the eunuch asks Philip to guide him through an interpretation of a biblical passage. In Luke-Acts, where ὁδός often means a way of life (Luke 20:21; Acts 13:10; 14:16) or life in the Christian community (Acts 9:2; 18:25-26; 19:9, 23; 22:4; 24:14, 22), this transferred meaning may underlie ὁδηγεῖν for Luke's readers.

6:39c: οὐχὶ ἀμφότεροι εἰς βόθυνον ἐμπεσοῦνται; οὐχί is a strengthened form, expecting the answer "of course!" The other words are to be taken simply in their literal meaning, "will not both fall into a pit?"[35] The meaning is clear: the blind are dangerous guides. But who are the blind in the Lukan figure? Commentators are divided:

> (1) the vast majority consider them to be the disciples addressed in 6:37-38;[36]
>> (a) the wider group of disciples who are led, now warned of false teachers,[37]
>> or
>> (b) those who exercise leadership in the community,[38]
> (2) the Jewish rabbis outside the community (Friedrich Hauck).

In fact, there is no evidence in Luke 6:39 of any definite group. We know only that the proverb is addressed to the larger group of disciples who were disjoined from judging and enjoined to unlimited generosity in 6:37-38; perhaps the following verses give more insight into the identity of the blind.

6:40a: οὐκ ἐστὶν μαθητὴς ὑπὲρ τὸν διδάσκαλον, "a disciple is not superior to the teacher." Jesus adds another proverb asyndetically and

---

[34] The verb occurs in the NT only in Matt 15:14; Luke 6:39; John 16:13; Acts 8:31; Rev 7:17.

[35] Βόθυνος, used only in Matt 12:11; 15:14; Luke 6:39, in the LXX refers to a ditch, sometimes dug as a trap. It does not denote or connote "the pit" as the grave or Sheol as places for the dead; those meanings are taken by *sāḥat,* translated by διαφθοράν in Ps 30:10, or untranslated in Ezek 28:8.

[36] Theophylact, Fridolin Stier, Hans Achelis, M.-J. Lagrange, Karl H. Rengstorf, Eduard Schweizer.

[37] G. L. Hahn, I. Howard Marshall, Joseph A. Fitzmyer, John Nolland; Jacob Kremer. Heinz Schürmann thinks of a group of false teachers in the community, probably of a Christian pharisaical persuasion.

[38] J. J. van Oosterzee, F. L. Godet, August Bisping, J. C. K. Hofmann, C. F. Keil, Paul Schanz; Walter Grundmann think of them as apostles, or those with the office of teaching; Rudolf Bultmann, *The History of the Synoptic Tradition* (New York: Harper & Row, 1963) 99; Theodor Zahn, Josef Ernst, and François Bovon take them as those who assume spiritual leadership without office.

epexegetically: the guiding takes place through teaching.[39] In the Greek world μαθητής denotes a learner or pupil. In the philosophical schools, as well as in the mystery religions, the disciple had a moral commitment to, and an almost religious veneration of, his master. The word is entirely lacking in the LXX, probably because God is the revealer and teacher of all Jews (and so has no special disciples); nor do prophets and other leaders have disciples. Only under the influence of Hellenism does the rabbinic tradition develop its *talmîdîm*. In the NT μαθητής describes an even more personal relationship to Jesus than it does to the Greek master. This relationship originates in a call by Jesus (rather than in a request by would-be learners), and demands complete obedience to his aims and commands, including the obligation to suffer.[40] Μαθητής is used only in the gospels and Acts and relatively rarely by Luke.[41] It refers almost always to disciples of Jesus, except for seven mentions of the Baptist's disciples[42] and this one proverb that speaks of the role of any disciple and teacher.[43] Thus Luke's reader would ordinarily hear the connotation of discipleship of Jesus when she heard μαθητής, all the more so when the proverb is set in a speech explicitly addressed to disciples.

Ὑπὲρ τὸν διδάσκαλον: ὑπέρ with the accusative is axiological, "superior to." In the realm of teaching and learning such superiority would mean that the disciple knows more and better than his teacher. In the Academy such a proverb would not be true: Socrates or Plato could expect that a pupil would exceed his own knowledge.[44] But in a rabbinic tradition, where the object is mastery of a tradition, the subject could not exceed the mastery of the tradent. In the gospel tradition, however, the impossibility of surpassing the teacher lies in the authority of Jesus as *the* teacher.[45] Διδάσκαλος, the correlative of μαθητής in Greek culture and in the NT, is

---

[39] Walter Grundmann, *Das Evangelium nach Lukas* (Berlin: Evangelische Verlagsanstalt, 1961) 153.

[40] Karl H. Rengstorf, "μαθητής," *TDNT* 4:400–61.

[41] Even when one considers that Luke uses οἱ δώδεκα and οἱ ἀπόστολοι (forty-three per cent of seventy-nine NT uses) relatively frequently, the number of references to disciples is considerably fewer than in Matthew, Mark, and John.

[42] Mark 2:18//Matt 19:14//Luke 5:33; Mark 6:29//Matt 14:12; Matt:11:2//Luke 7:18; Luke 11:1; John 1:35, 37; 3:25; 4:1.

[43] The two proverbs from John that illustrate the disciple's call to humble service of one another (13:16) and even to die for Jesus' cause (15:20) use not the relationship of teacher and disciple, but that of master and slave.

[44] See the instances in Wettstein, *Novum Testamentum graecum* 1:373 and in Betz, *Sermon* 623 n. 293.

[45] Betz, *Sermon* 622 sees this as a general rule for the early community's instructional schools. By the time of Q, Jesus was firmly established as the teacher of the community. In the context of Luke's Sermon, the teacher can be no one but Jesus.

the one whose doctrine, life-style, and character the disciple takes on.[46] It is used fifty-eight times in the NT, forty-eight times in the gospels, where in forty-one uses it refers to Jesus. Although it usually carries only the respect due a rabbi, sometimes the person and the special call of Jesus give the title added weight, so that he becomes the subject of much greater devotion than the Hellenistic philosophical teachers or adepts of the mysteries. Since Luke avoids Aramaic *rabbi* he uses διδάσκαλος more than the other evangelists. Of his seventeen uses only two refer to persons other than Jesus, and twelve of the fourteen times the word refers to Jesus it is used in the vocative, as a translation for *rabbi*. Such preponderant usage for Jesus must have connoted Jesus as the reader's teacher, but the identity of the proverb's διδάσκαλος is clarified only by the second half of Jesus' sentence.

6:40b: κατηρτισμένος δὲ πᾶς ἔσται ὡς ὁ διδάσκαλος αὐτοῦ, "but each (disciple) having been corrected will be like his teacher." Δὲ introduces mild opposition to the supposition of superiority already denied in the preceding clause. Πᾶς (see comment on 6:30) "each one, everyone" could indicate a range of people who could be prepared to be like the master, and yet it must, in the context of the proverb, be taken to mean "every disciple."[47]

Καταρτίζειν is emphasized by being placed first in the clause. In Greek culture it means "to adjust, put in order again, mend, restore; to make complete, furnish completely." It is literary language, but can also be technical, referring to the surgical resetting of bones.[48] It occurs seven times in the LXX of Ezra in its normal Greek usage, referring to rebuilding the city walls and restoring the Temple. Otherwise it occurs eleven times in the LXX of the Psalms, where it translates eight different Hebrew roots, rarely in the sense of its normal Greek usage. In the NT it has that normal usage of "repairing, restoring" in half of its twelve uses, as in Mark 1:19//Matt 4:21, the Zebedees mending the holes in their nets. In four of Paul's five uses it denotes a correction or restoration of something that has lost its good condition (1 Cor 1:10; 2 Cor 13:11; Gal 6:1; 1 Thess 3:10.[49] Especially congruent with Luke 6:40 is Gal 6:1, where καταρτίζετε not only means to amend and restore to an originally good state, but lies in a context where the corrector must attend to himself (6:1de), similar to what

---

[46] Karl H. Rengstorf, "διδάσκαλος," *TDNT* 2:140–60. So correlative is the concept that the LXX likewise avoids διδάσκαλος, except in two late Hellenistic texts.

[47] Julius Wellhausen, Theodor Zahn, Erich Klostermann, Walter Grundmann, and Josef Ernst take πᾶς as an adverb, "wholly," like Aramaic *kulleh,* neither a necessary nor even a likely translation.

[48] LSJ 910; see the examples cited in Wettstein, *Novum Testamentum graecum,* on Matt 4:21.

[49] The exception is Rom 9:22, where κατηρτισμένα means not "amended, restored to prior good condition," but rather "outfitted for destruction" from the outset.

will follow in Luke 6:41-42. Thus one would expect from normal Greek usage and from NT usage that it would mean the restoration or refurbishing of something that has lost its original good condition.[50] In the perfect passive participle it emphasizes something done to one in the past, and affecting one's present condition: "Every disciple (having been) restored to right order will be like his teacher."[51]

Again, this proverb is without introduction or application that would guide interpretation. We have only its proximate and immediate context (following on 6:39, and leading into 6:41-42) to guide our interpretation, but that is enough to provide a secure beginning. As we have repeatedly seen, the Sermon is addressed to disciples (6:12-16, 17, 20). Even the designation τοῖς ἀκούουσιν (6:27) is still addressed to disciples, who are contrasted with the sinful world (6:32-34) and are called υἱοὶ ὑψίστου (6:35-36). Indeed, the extraordinary demands of the Sermon can be understood only by and for those who are disciples of Jesus.[52]

I. Howard Marshall lists four possible interpretations of these verses:

(1) Josef Schmid takes the blind man as the teacher: a pupil learning from an ignorant teacher cannot surpass the teacher's ignorance.[53] But this identification of the blind man is unlikely, since it has no connection with the preceding context.

(2) Heinz Schürmann takes the blind to be false teachers in the Christian community, who go beyond Jesus' words in the Sermon. This is possible, but it falls to Occam's razor: there is no reason to postulate another group

---

[50] It is amazing that all the commentators overlooked this obvious denotation of the verb in Greek, LXX, and NT usage, translating it as "well-instructed, fully trained, perfected;" Betz, *Sermon* 624–25 notes the correctional meaning, but still chooses to translate as "fully-trained" in the sense of "graduated."

[51] Already in 1892 G. L Hahn had discussed the four different ways in which interpreters had taken κατηρτισμένος as subject and predicate, and demonstrated that only "every pupil, when he has been perfectly instructed, will be like his teacher," was *philologically* possible. When κατερτισμένος is translated as "restored to right order," interpretations that construe the participle with Jesus as the διδάσκαλος are seen as *theologically* impossible for Luke's community.

[52] Even if the crowds who have come to hear and be healed (6:17-18) are also addressed, they can receive the designation "sons of God" only by becoming disciples. As we will see, the doing of the extraordinary commands of the Sermon demands a disciple's union with God in faith and love.

[53] Josef Schmid's problem is that he cannot understand Jesus as the teacher because he has not judged. But that is precisely the point: Jesus *is* the teacher because, although he has the authority to judge (12:8-12, 35-48, 57-59; 17:20-37; 21:25-28; 22:24-30), he has not judged (5:20-24; 7:36-50; 12:13-14; 19:1-10; 22:61; 23:34, 43), and so is the living model of what he teaches in 6:37, 41-42!

when the Sermon is addressed directly to disciples who themselves are going to find the teaching too difficult (6:47-49).[54]

(3) Johannes Weiss thinks the disciples are not to behave in a way judged superior to that of Jesus, who refused to judge. But this shifts the focus from teaching to behavior, which is incongruous with the text's dominant images of seeing, blindness, the eye, teaching, all of which intimate knowing.[55]

(4) Consequently, I prefer Julius Wellhausen's position: only complete agreement with the one authoritative teacher makes the disciples authentic, seeing, teachers of the church and the world.[56] This interpretation not only conforms best to the preceding context (6:37-40), but also to what now follows.

By form and content, then, 6:37-38 continues the commands addressed to disciples. Suddenly the Lukan narrative aside (6:39a) warns us that figurative language difficult to interpret is coming, presumably to explain what preceded: the blind cannot lead the blind (6:39bc), but we have no clue about who the blind are. A second proverb is adjoined, presumably to illustrate its predecessor: a disciple is not greater than his teacher (6:40a). Now the blind person is seen to be a disciple who considers himself above his teacher, more enlightened or more practical than his teacher. In the context of these imperatives (6:27-38), he is one who does not accept Jesus' radical denial of judgment. Such a disciple will lead those whom he teaches into a pit. Thus the disciple must be refurbished, brought into the correct order of the teacher's instruction, so that he may be like the teacher, the true seeing guide.

6:41a: τί δὲ βλέπεις τὸ κάρφος τὸ ἐν τῷ ὀφθαλμῷ τοῦ ἀδελφοῦ σου; "why do you see the particle in your brother's eye?" Jesus secures the preceding teaching with a final similitude expressed in paired rhetorical questions, each with two clauses containing opposing actions, which move from seeing to judging, to self-criticism, to renunciation of judging.[57] The

---

[54] Heinz Schürmann may be interpreting Luke 6:39-42 by Matt 7:15-20; Betz, *Sermon* 620 n. 274.

[55] *Die Schriften des Neuen Testaments* (Göttingen: Vandenhoeck & Ruprecht, 1917) 1:447. The emphasis on behavior is not unimportant, but is secondary here; it comes to the fore in 6:47-49.

[56] Julius Wellhausen, *Das Evangelium Lucae übersetzt und erklärt* (Berlin: G. Reimer, 1904) 25. There is no evidence in this text, or in Luke-Acts generally, of disciples who have an institutional status as teachers. It is of the nature of discipleship itself to be first a follower and then a guide.

[57] The passage comes to Luke from Q (//Matt 7:3-5), which explains some uncharacteristic Lukan vocabulary. The parallels adduced from classical literature (Plutarch, *De curios.* 515d; Horace, *Sat.* I, 3.25) speak of one's judging one's own (worse) case more leniently than the (milder) case of another, but do not use the image of wood in the eye. The only true parallel is the *baraita* of R. Tarphon (ca. 100 c.e.) in *Arakh.* 16b, which may derive from the gospels.

argument is expressed in the second-person singular characteristic of polemical, diatribal, style.

Τί δὲ βλέπεις: The neuter interrogative pronoun τί, used adverbially, asks "why?" (BAGD 819 §3); δὲ is simply transitional, with a tone of explanation, "why, then . . . ?" (BAGD 171 §2). I. Howard Marshall (*Luke* 270) suggests "how is it possible for you to see . . . ?" but "why?" probing for motivation and cause is better, because it leads more directly to the lack of explanation in which the rhetorical question is grounded. βλέπειν: Greek is rich in words for seeing: ὁρᾶν, ἰδεῖν, βλέπειν, ὀπτάνεσθαι, θεᾶσθαι, θεορεῖν, σκοπεῖν.[58] They all have the root meaning of ocular sense perception, but they can also refer to intellectual perception and spiritual vision. The combination of ὁρᾶν in the present and perfect tenses and ἰδεῖν in the aorist tenses is by far the most used and means predominantly both sense and cognitive perception. Βλέπειν places stronger emphasis on the function of the eye in sense perception and is used when seeing is contrasted with blindness. These tendencies remain in the LXX and into the NT, although in Koinē βλέπειν and σκοπεῖν tend to replace ὁρᾶν without any change of meaning.[59]

Βλέπειν occurs 132x in the NT and not often in Luke-Acts, where it usually means the physical act of seeing, the opposite of physical τυφλός.[60] Jesus is not referring to a process of discernment, but to a simple physical seeing.

Κάρφος is proverbial in Greek literature to denote something insignificant.[61] In the NT it is used only three times here and three times in the parallel Matt 7:3-5. Its original meaning is a dry stalk, chaff, a chip of wood, a speck.[62] From the figure itself we understand something very small, in contrast to δοκός, and yet something large enough to be seen by another.

---

[58] In contrast, there is really only one root for hearing: ἀκούειν. There are other words that come to mean "to see," such as ἀτενίζειν and κατανοεῖν in Luke. For this and most of the discussion of vocabulary, see Wilhelm Michaelis, "ὁράω," *TDNT* 5:315–82.

[59] Θεᾶσθαι, "astonished or attentive seeing," and θεορεῖν, "being aware of, attending (religious festivals)" tend towards a spiritual seeing, as in visions. In the LXX ὁρᾶν is used some 520x and ἰδεῖν some 930x (= 1450x); βλέπειν occurs 130x, and θεορεῖν occurs almost 50x.

[60] There are only three exceptions: in Luke 8:10 it means to comprehend the inner meaning, but it may be used there as *paranomasia,* repetition of the same term for rhetorical effect. In 8:18; 21:8 it means "to take care."

[61] BAGD 405 cites Aristophanes, Lysias, Herodas, and Ion of Chios.

[62] Alfred Plummer, *A Critical and Exegetical Commentary on the Gospel according to St. Luke* (Edinburgh: T & T Clark, 1896) 191, derives it from κάρφειν, to dry up and wither. The image is of something that gets in the eye during the harvest or threshing of grain. German exegesis has taken it as a splinter, perhaps, with Ernst Curtius, deriving it from σκάρφιον, a less likely etymology.

Ἐν τῷ ὀφθαλμῷ τοῦ ἀδελφοῦ σου: The eye is the physical organ of sight, in which chaff might lodge. Ἀδελφός ordinarily means a blood brother, but it can mean a countryman or simply a neighbor (BAGD 16). Jesus calls "brother" everyone devoted to God's will (Mark 3:35//Matt 12:50//Luke 8:21). Under this influence and perhaps that of the mystery religions, which called initiates brothers, the early Christian community referred to its members as brothers and sisters. It is not a Lukan word. (Luke-Acts has only twenty-four per cent of NT uses.) Eighteen of Luke's uses in the gospel refer to blood relatives. In 8:21; 17:3; 22:32 and in these three uses in 6:41-42 ἀδελφός names a spiritual relationship. In Acts it overwhelmingly refers to members of the Christian community. What is problematic in the interpretation of 6:41 as correction in the community[63] is that 6:27-36 had directed the disciples' actions not to fellow Christians, but to enemies and outsiders. Nothing in the text urges a Christian meaning of ἀδελφός. Perhaps it is better to understand it as "neighbor," but translating it as "brother" preserves the ambiguity of the original Greek text.

6:41b: τὴν δὲ δοκὸν τὴν ἐν τῷ ἰδίῳ ὀφθαλμῷ σου οὐ κατανοεῖς; "but do not notice the beam in your own eye?" Δοκός means a large beam, usually the load-carrying beam in the room or floor of a house. The impossibility of such a beam being in the eye forms the hyperbole that points to the incongruity of a disciple's judging the speck in another's eye.[64] Κατανοεῖν, from its stem (νοῦς) and intensifying compound (κατὰ) denotes an intellectual act, "to consider, understand," but in both classical and Koinē Greek it also means "to perceive, notice, observe well." Although Luke may have received κατανοεῖν from Q (cf. the parallel Matt 7:3), it is a Lukan word (Luke-Acts has fifty-seven per cent of NT uses), and his usage could give us a clue to the meaning here. In the majority of cases (12:24, 27; 20:23; Acts 7:31-32) it means not only to see but to ponder the meaning; in Acts 11:6; 27:39 it rather seems to mean "to notice or perceive." Rhetorically, κατανοεῖς in 6:41b is contrasted to βλέπεις in 6:41a, but is parallel to βλέπων in 6:42c, and so "perceive, notice" seems more likely. Overall, "notice" probably best reproduces the hyperbole, for it accentuates the blindness and stupidity of not even adverting to the log in one's own eye.

What is the *tertium comparationis* for the δοκός? Although the similitude is polysemic, the context suggests at least two possibilities:

[63] Most exegetes understand this passage as enjoining fraternal correction within the community; see Jean Duplacy, "Le Veritable Disciple; un essai d'analyse sémantique de Lc 6,43-49," *RSR* 69 (1981) 71–86 for discussion and bibliography.

[64] Beyond the bald fact that one cannot get a δοκός into a human eye is the fact that one could not see the beam if it were there. Out of the good eye one cannot see into the blocked eye; the blocked eye can only see that its vision is obstructed, and cannot see the beam itself as a beam.

(1) If the similitude followed immediately upon the prohibitions of judging (6:37-38), the obvious meaning for δοκός would be the sin or fault of the one judging, since the combination κρίνειν, καταδικάζειν, ἀπολύειν implies that a transgression or sin is being judged.[65] The proverb about the blind as a false guide does follow on 6:37-38 and so bridges to the blindness of the one with the beam in his eye. The beam need not suggest that the judge's own sin is that much greater than that of the one being judged, only that it is sufficient to obscure his view of the one being judged.

(2) Since the similitude in fact follows upon the proverb about the disciple not being greater than the master (6:41), the δοκός might be the disciple's failure to follow the master's own example and teaching about not judging others (6:37-38), or even the whole preceding teaching about love of the other (6:27-36). In that case the disciple would be especially guilty of not attending to Jesus' Golden Rule in which attention to her own state and desires would keep her from condemning others. Perhaps the following verses or interpretation of the Sermon as a whole can further specify the meaning of δοκός, which will, ultimately, remain polysemic.

6:42abc: πῶς δύνασαι λέγειν τῷ ἀδελφῷ σου, Ἀδελφέ, ἄφες ἐκβάλω τὸ κάρφος τὸ ἐν τῷ ὀφθαλμῷ σου, αὐτὸς τὴν ἐν τῷ ὀφθαλμῷ σου δόκον οὐ βλέπων; "how can you say to your brother, 'Brother, let me cast out the speck in your eye,' while you ignore the beam in your own?" This longest verse in Luke (sixty-nine words) uses the same similitude in a further rhetorical question, moving from seeing to acting. The disciple wishes to help his neighbor, but cannot because inattention to his own failure as a disciple distorts his judgment of the other. Luke's rhetorical question, πῶς δύνασαι, denies the possibility of correcting another's fault when one has not even seen one's own. Jesus envisions a three-stage strategy for correction: first recognize one's own defective vision (6:42c), then mend it (6:42d), and finally heal the neighbor's vision (6:42e).

6:42d: ὑποκριτά, ἔκβαλε πρῶτον τὴν δοκὸν ἐκ τοῦ ὀφθαλμοῦ σου, "hypocrite, first cast the beam out of your eye." Ὑποκριτά: In classical Greek ὑποκρίνεσθαι meant "to discern, interpret, explain;" the original meaning of ὑποκριτής was an actor, an interpreter of a role. From the time of Plato the actor is seen as taking an identity that is not his, and so comes to mean "to pretend," but not with an ethically negative tone. The LXX uses the noun only twice (Job 34:30; 36:13) to mean the ungodly, and Philo and Josephus use it to connote the ungodly as pretenders and shams.[66] In the NT it occurs only in the synoptics, and only on the lips of Jesus attacking those who profess piety and righteousness (especially in

---

[65] Ὑποκριτά (6:42), with its connotation of sinfulness, will reinforce this meaning.
[66] Ulrich Wilckens, "ὑποκρίνομαι," *TDNT* 8:559–65.

censuring others), while they are themselves inconsistent in conduct. Thus it denotes pretense, an inconsistency between one's public role and one's actual practice. Ordinarily Jesus uses the term to attack the Pharisees and this was undoubtedly the root of its usage in the synoptic tradition. Indeed, Joachim Jeremias thinks that ὑποκριτά in Matt 7:5//Luke 6:42 must have originally been addressed to the Pharisees, since the word is never otherwise applied to disciples.[67] But Jesus does address harsh words to the disciples, especially accusing them of inconsistency.[68] In Luke, where harsh judgment of the disciples is often omitted (cf. the parallels to Mark 7:18; 8:17; 8:33), the disciples are called hypocrites only here in 6:42. Crowds, synagogue leaders, and chief priests and scribes are called hypocrites for their failure to discern what is right when they certainly should know it.[69]

When applied to the disciples in 6:42d ὑποκριτά seems to have its full double meaning: (1) they fail to judge a situation that ought to be obvious to them—because of their own sinfulness they are in no position to judge anyone else; (2) they are a sham—they say they are disciples (6:40) of one who prohibits judgment (6:37) and refused to judge in his own life (12:14), and yet they judge others.[70] The following clauses reveal that (2) is the meaning emphasized. If (1) is stressed, then cleaning up one's sin enables the disciple to judge the other, which is contrary to the teaching of 6:37. But if (2) is stressed, then the disciple is able to help the other, not by judging him from a position of superiority but precisely because of the nonjudgmental attitude present in the help offered.

6:42e: καὶ τότε διαβλέψεις τὸ κάρφος τὸ ἐν τῷ ὀφθαλμῷ του ἀδελφοῦ σου ἐκβάλειν, "and then you will see clearly enough to cast the speck out of your brother's eye." This clause continues the idea that it *is* possible to clear the beam from one's own eye and then see clearly to cast the particle out of the neighbor's eye. The way to do so is to relinquish the condemnatory attitude that underlies judging the neighbor. Jesus did not judge in the gospel, but he certainly discerned the difference between right and wrong, and where people stood in that discernment. He was clearsighted and forthright about the presence of evil to be exorcised (3:35-36; 8:26-36; 9:37-42) and conquered (10:18), about the situation of sin in others (3:25-27; 5:8-10, 27-32; 6:22, 24-26, 32-34, 43-49; 7:31-34; 8:11-14;

[67] *The Parables of Jesus* (New York: Scribner's, 1972) 167.

[68] Cf. ἀσύνετοι, Mark 7:18//Matt 15:16; hardness of heart, Mark 8:17; Σατανᾶ, Mark 8:33//Matt 16:23; ὀλιγόπιστοι, Matt 6:30//Luke 12:28; ἀνόητοι, Luke 24:25.

[69] The crowds (12:56) fail to discern the signs of the time; the synagogue leaders (13:15) are inconsistent in judging permissible work on the Sabbath; the scribes and chief priests (20:20) pretend, ὑποκρινομένους, to be righteous.

[70] This judgmental attitude is later manifested in Luke 9:54-55 and perhaps in Acts 15:37-39.

9:23-26, 41; 10:10-15; 11:17-26, 29-32, 39-54; 12:1-15; 13:1-5, 15-17, 22-30, 32, 34-35; 16:14-15; 17:1-4, 17-18, 25-30; 18:9-14, 24-25; 19:10, 41-44; 20:9-19, 46-47; 22:21-22, 34, 48, 53) and about the virtuous state of others (7:24-28; 8:21; 9:23-26, 47-48, 50; 10:21, 41-42; 11:28, 33-36; 18:22; 21:3-4). Jesus' response to such situations, however, was not judgment, but forgiveness (5:20-24; 7:47-50; 19:1-10; 23:34, 39-43) arising from mercy (6:36; 7:13; 9:55; 10:29-37; 13:8; 15:1-32). Even so his followers are to be aware of sins and even correct each other for them, but the underlying virtues that make such correction fruitful are not innocence, but forgiveness and mercy (17:3-4).[71]

Summary and Conclusion

Now that we have seen how the imperatives and the three diverse images have unfolded their meaning into one another, we can attempt to see the unity of the section and interpret its meaning as a unit growing out of, and applying, the preceding sections of the Sermon.

1. The unit has a kind of thematic inclusion built on the theme of not judging:[72] Luke 6:37 begins with the notions of not judging (κρίνειν, καταδικάζειν) and 6:41-42 concludes with a similitude that expresses the impossibility of the disciple's judging another. To 6:39b's τυφλός respond the themes of the disciple's not seeing (οὐ βλέπων) his own fault in 6:42c, which leads to the ultimate blindness of hypocrisy (6:42d), which in turn makes it impossible to see the true situation of both oneself and the other.

2. The prohibition of judging and condemnation (6:37ab), echoing the four-beat rhythm of 6:27-30, further specifies the Golden Rule (6:31), which is at the heart of the love commandment. But this prohibition challenges not only the disciple's spontaneous human tendency to criticize, but also their upbringing in a Law that clearly articulated the offenses the community was to avoid, correct, and punish. Further, the attitude of unrestricted forgiveness and boundless generosity (6:37c-38) strikes them as irrational. In their hearts they reject this teaching as they did the teaching on riches and ease (6:24-26), on balanced reciprocity (6:32-34), and on the radical nature of the Sermon as a whole (6:46-49).

---

[71] Peter's correction of Simon Magus in Acts 8:20-25 includes a recommendation of prayer for forgiveness; other examples of nonretaliation and forgiveness occur in Acts 5:41; 7:60.

[72] Many commentators speak of a catchword association between blindness, not seeing, inability to judge, and the prohibition of judging. Catchword is not the right expression, since a *Stichwort* or *mot-crochet* uses the same stem to secure its bond. Rather one should speak of these as a thematic echo of ideas or images.

Consequently, Jesus attacks their blocked minds with parabolic language expressed in almost polemical rhetorical questions (6:39-42). Just as the blind cannot lead the blind, so disciples who reject Jesus' teaching are blind and cannot lead other blind ones (disciples or the world) who also do not grasp Jesus' teaching (6:39). Jesus uniquely teaches unconditional love as God's way (6:35de-36), which the beatitudes (6:20-23) and the love commandment (6:27-36) specify. Because of the uniqueness of the Teacher and his message, no disciple can be superior to Jesus, and so (s)he must be set straight (κατηρτισμένος), to be like that Teacher (6:40).

Once again: the disciple is unseeing because he does not see the log (resistance to Jesus' prohibition of judgment) in his own eye, and so cannot see the true fault (or way to healing) of the neighbor (6:41). This blind judgmental attitude to the brother's blindness links 6:39b-42 with the prohibition of the judgmental and unforgiving attitude of 6:37 and the inculcation of the generosity of 6:38ab. Only when she is reformed (6:40b) and accepts Jesus' nonjudgmental love of the neighbor can she really see in order to help the other to see.

Interestingly, this section does not begin from the compassion for the other described in 6:36. Instead the figures force disciples to look at themselves, their complicity in the evils of revenge, stinginess, cagey reciprocity, and alienating judgment of others that blocks their true help of the other. Thus the figures lead back to the Golden Rule's emphasis on looking at oneself, at one's own best desires. What one wants is not judgment, but fraternal help.

3. Ultimately, however, the focus is not on the disciple, or on his sins, but on the Teacher. The passage on the teacher, which seemed a foreign body in the section on blindness and judgment, is now seen as integrated into its structure. When the μαθητής is restored (κατηρτισμένος) by accepting Jesus' teaching she will not judge, but will see clearly, like her δι-δάσκαλος. Further, the passage is central to the thought of the whole Sermon. Our culture has taught us the way of blindness and we need teachers of greater vision. Those who reject the teaching cannot escape the cycles of violence a vindictive judgmental attitude spawns.

The critique of judgment attacks a judgmental attitude, which opposes the Golden Rule's focus on the good one desires and extends to the other. The hypocrite of 6:41-42 represents the attitude of self-protecting vindictiveness proscribed by 6:27-36. More central to Jesus' message, a judgmental attitude is the opposite of God's own generosity to the unworthy and wicked (6:35d): God has compassion on them (6:36) and grants them freely what they need. This is the true sight Jesus as Teacher would engender in his disciples, called to be sons and daughters of God (6:35c).

Chapter 7

True Discipleship
(6:43-49)

Luke 6:43-45 could appear to be part of the critique of judgment (6:37-42). The γάρ of 6:43 vindicates the implication in 6:42 that when the disciple purifies her own eye she will be able to see clearly enough to purify her brother's eye. The criterion is the fruit produced by the one being judged (6:43), since such fruit reveals one's true being (6:45). Thus knowing (γινώσκεται, 6:44) the fruits of a person's actions justifies the διαβλέψεις in 6:42.

Yet the assertion that one *can* judge clashes with the rejection of judgment in 6:37-42. Rather, judging by its proper fruit (6:44a) is rooted in the congruence between the interior nature of the producer and its products (6:43), and so climaxes in an affirmation that the goodness of the human heart is at stake (6:45). This emphasis on fruits leads into the necessity not only of hearing the Lord's words, but also of doing them (6:46-49).[1] In this sense, although they contain linking and bridging elements to 6:37-42, vv. 43-45 should be interpreted in connection with vv. 46-49, a final concluding paraenesis for the Sermon.[2]

While ancient law codes frequently ended with sanctions for the performance or nonobservance of the laws,[3] Jesus casts his final exhortation in figurative language that highlights the parabolic character of the Sermon as a whole.

---

[1] Jacques Dupont, *Les Béatitudes*. 3 vols. (Paris: Gabalda, 1969) 1:200 lists exegetes who have read the repetition of ποιεῖν in 6:43 (2x), 46, 47, 49 as demonstrating a unit on the disciples' conduct.

[2] French-speaking exegetes have already demonstrated that 6:43-49 is a unit; Dupont, *Béatitudes,* 1:200; Augustin George, "Le disciple fraternel et efficace. Lc 6, 39-45," *Assemblées du Seigneur* 39 (1972) 68–77; Jean Duplacy, "Le véritable disciple Duplacy, "Le Veritable Disciple; un essai d'analyse sémantique de Lc 6,43-49," *RSR* 69 (1981) 71–86.

[3] Cf. the epilogue to the Code of Hammurabi (*ANET* 177–80). Likewise OT law codes end with exhortations to do the words and laws of the law codes, often by means of sanctions or of blessings and curses (Leviticus 17–26 with the sanctions of 26:3-45 and Deuteronomy 12–26 with the curses of Deuteronomy 27, and blessings and curses in ch. 28).

The Literary and Rhetorical Structure of 6:43-49

We have here two different series of images: an agricultural series with application to the human heart and the actions that proceed from it (6:43-46), and a pair drawn from house construction (6:47-49). They are loosely connected by means of the verb ποιεῖν (6:43, 46, 47, 49) and by a rhetorical question (6:46).

The *first series* consists of

> 6:43: a proverb about good trees producing good fruit, with its converse in antithetical parallelism, linked with weak causality (γὰρ) to the preceding sentence;
>
> 6:44a: an explanation for the proverb, linked to it by illustrative causality (γὰρ)—you can judge a tree by its fruit;
>
> 6:44bc: two further examples in synonymous parallelism confirming (γὰρ) the proverb;
>
> 6:45ab: a concluding application to (judging) good humans, with its converse in antithetical parallelism;
>
> 6:45c: an epichiretic reason (γὰρ) grounded in the human heart's determination of human speech (as an action, fruit).

Emphasis on the quality of the heart leads to a *second similitude* on house construction, which reveals the true grounding of the good disciple:

> 6:46: a question challenging the hypocritical conduct of disciples;
>
> 6:47: a description of the true disciple (who both hears and does the words of his master) and the promise of a comparison;
>
> 6:48: a similitude likening the true disciple to one building a house on a foundation of rock;
>
> 6:49: the description of the false disciple, and a similitude likening him to one building a house on bare ground.

Exegesis of 6:43-45, on the Fruits of the Human Heart

6:43: Οὐ γάρ ἐστιν δένδρον καλὸν ποιοῦν καρπὸν σαπρόν, οὐδὲ πάλιν δένδρον σαπρὸν ποιοῦν καρπὸν καλόν, "for no good tree produces bad fruit, nor does a bad tree produce good fruit." Γάρ connects the quite disparate material in 6:43-44[4] to 6:41-42, as an illustration of how the disciple can see clearly (διαβλέψεις, 6:42) to cast out the speck in the brother's

---

[4] Source-critically, 6:43-44 may have belonged to a criticism of false teachers, as in Matt 7:16-18. There is no evidence, *pace* Heinz Schürmann, *Das Lukasevangelium* (Freiburg: Herder, 1969) 373, that this is the reference in Luke.

eye.[5] Καρπός means what a tree produces, but can also mean a product or gain. In the OT (Isa 5:1-7), and increasingly in later Judaism it refers to human works and deeds.[6] Ποιοῦν καρπὸν is a Septuagintalism (Gen 1:11, 12; Ps 106:37), which Luke uses of seeds and trees (8:8; 13:9), but also metaphorically of human deeds (3:8).

Δένδρον in classical Greek is the generic word for tree, but it also means a fruit tree (as it does here), as opposed to lumber (ὕλη) (LSJ 378). Καλόν in the esthetic sense means "beautiful, fair, elegant," in the moral sense "noble, virtuous;" generically it means simply "good, of fine quality" (LSJ 870). The precise sense here is read off its contrast with σαπρός, "rotten, stale, worn out" (LSJ 1583) In that case the proverb would run, "a healthy tree does not produce rotten fruit, nor a rotten tree healthy fruit." But this more specific translation proves incorrect.[7] The more generic language of the small farmer is more likely to be apposite: "A good tree does not produce bad fruit, nor a bad tree good fruit."[8] Jesus means to emphasize, especially in the context of 6:44-45, that what is intrinsic to the tree determines the quality of the fruit produced,[9] the message, indeed, of the following verse.

6:44a: ἕκαστον γὰρ δένδρον ἐκ τοῦ ἰδίου καρποῦ γινώσκεται, "for (the quality of) each tree is recognized by its proper fruit." Ἴδιος means "one's own, private, personal, peculiar, distinct, proper" (LSJ 818); here it means to recognize each tree by its own kind of fruit. Γινώσκειν refers to a knowledge of the essence or character of a person or thing, a judgment of its quality or value.[10] Γὰρ connects a reason for the proverb: people normally recognize and call a tree bad when it produces bad fruit and good

[5] Ibid. 373 and I. Howard Marshall, *The Gospel of Luke* (Exeter: Paternoster, 1978) 272 cite BAGD, *s.v.* §4 to argue that γάρ is equivalent to δὲ and has not even weak causal (illustrative) meaning here. But the examples in BAGD are from Paul, who uses γάρ loosely and abundantly (forty to forty-four per cent of the 1036 NT uses!). Luke-Acts, on the other hand, uses it sparingly (only seventeen per cent of NT uses), always with some causal effect.

[6] Friedrich Hauck, "καρπός," *TDNT* 3:614–15.

[7] Alfred Plummer, *A Critical and Exegetical Commentary on the Gospel according to St. Luke* (Edinburgh: T & T Clark, 1896) 192 says that "a rotten tree would produce no fruit," which is wrong: rotten and decaying trees can produce fruit, even healthy fruit. In fact, a dying tree most often produces its most abundant harvest the year it dies. On the other hand, healthy trees can produce fruit spoiled by blight, worms, drought, or freezing. Further, a good tree unpruned can produce inferior fruit.

[8] Σαπρός does have this generic meaning in classical Greek (LSJ 1583 II, §5).

[9] Technically a tree that is neglected, has inferior genes, or is decayed and so cannot process water and photosynthesize properly will produce inferior ("bad") fruit, and so will be called a "bad" tree.

[10] It appears that BAGD 160–61 has located the passage in the wrong category; it should be under §7, not §1.

when it produces good fruit,[11] and so they form a maxim that no good tree produces bad fruit and vice versa.[12]

6:44bc: οὐ γὰρ ἐξ ἀκανθῶν συλλέγουσιν σῦκα οὐδὲ ἐκ βάτου σταφυλὴν τρύγωσιν,[13] "for people do not gather figs from thorn bushes, nor harvest grapes from a bramble." Since the figure of good fruit from bad trees might be ambiguous, Jesus adds an example so clear that it borders on absurdity. Yet another illustrative γάρ connects these additional examples of the proverb: the kind of fruit is determined by the kinds of flora that produce it. Συλλέγειν means to gather or simply pick from a plant or tree. An ἄκανθα can be the cammock *(ononis spinosa),* but in biblical usage it refers to any thorny plant or bush (BAGD 29), often with thistles (Gen 3:18; Hos 10:18). Used in opposition to βάτος, it probably refers more to a plant than a bush. Thorns generally produce only seeds, nothing resembling a fruit. The σῦκον is the fig, the most common fruit in the Levant, which grows on a moderately tall tree (the Mediterranean *ficus carica*). Absurd, then, is one trying to get the common fruit grown on a large tree from a small shrub or plant that not only does not resemble it but, in fact, produces no fruit—a mistake no one is likely to make.[14]

In the paired example, τρυγᾶν refers to a reaping process, in the case of grape harvest using a knife or sickle to cut the cluster of grapes from the vine.[15] Βάτος is a thorny bush or shrub, a bramble (BAGD 137).[16] Again, such a shrub produces nothing resembling a fruit. Σταφυλή is not the individual grape, but the cluster of grapes on a vine. The disparity in size between a bramble bush and a vine is not as great as that between a

---

[11] Any other reason (e.g., the beauty of its blooms or its shape) would be judged frivolous by Jesus' hearers or Luke's readers.

[12] Johann Jakob Wettstein, *He kaine diatheke* [Romanized form] = *Novum Testamentum graecum: editionis receptae cum lectionibus variantibus codicum mss., editionum aliarum, versionum et patrum nec non commentario pleniore ex scriptoribus veteribus hebraeis, graecis et latinis historiam et vim verborum illustrante.* 2 vols. (Amsterdam: Dommer, 1751–1752) 1:697, locates rough parallels to Luke 6:44 in Plutarch, Hesiod, and Dioscurides; the adage is a bit of folk wisdom in many cultures.

[13] The parallels in Matt 7:16 and Jas 3:12 have similar expressions with different ordering and different flora, but the comparison does not aid the exegesis of Luke 6:44.

[14] Thus Schürmann, *Lukasevangelium* 374 misses the point entirely when he comments on the deceptive nature of weeds that grow as tall as bushes and produce what looks like fruit. François Bovon, *Das Evangelium nach Lukas.* 2 vols. to date. EKK 31/1, 2 (Zürich: Benziger; Neukirchen-Vluyn: Neukirchener Verlag, 1989, 1996) 377 points out that Luke's rhetorical strategy in these figures is to stress their dissimilarity.

[15] Συλλέγειν is not used of harvesting in classical Greek (LSJ 1672), but is so used in the LXX, Josephus, and the NT (BAGD 777); τρυγᾶν specifically means to reap or harvest in classical and Koinē Greek (LSJ 1829).

[16] Luke's other use refers to the thorn bush from which God spoke to Moses (20:37).

fig tree and a thistle, but again for a Mediterranean person to be unable to distinguish between a vine and a bramble bush would be ludicrous.

In summary, Jesus in 6:43-44 enunciates the principle that good trees produce good fruit and bad trees bad fruit, adduces as proof the adage that you can tell a tree by its fruit, and adds two obvious examples that secure the same point. The argument depends on understanding that there is an intrinsic connection between what a plant or tree produces and what it itself is, so that we do not expect a kind of fruit from a plant that, by its very nature, cannot produce it.

Having made his point by examples from the world of flora, Jesus now applies it to the human world, the human actions of disciples and others: **6:45a:** ὁ ἀγαθὸς ἄνθρωπος ἐκ τοῦ ἀγαθοῦ θησαυροῦ τῆς καρδίας προφέρει τὸ ἀγαθόν, "the good person produces good from the good treasure of the heart." In a sermon devoted to morality, this is the only use of ἀγαθός! In classical Greek moral good was only one of its meanings, but it was increasingly used in a moral and religious sense in Hellenistic thought.[17] In the OT God is good (1 Chr 15:34) and does good (Exod 18:9), and those who do good are of God, are good.[18] Jesus in Matt 19:17//Luke 18:19 continues in this vein, so that "Only God is good." All of Luke's uses in Acts have moral and religious denotation (9:36; 11:24; 23:1), and nine of his sixteen gospel uses have moral or religious meaning (6:45; 10:42; 18:18, 19 (2x); 19:17; 23:50). Thus the triple repetition of ἀγαθός here emphasizes the moral character of the good human and the acts she performs. As good fruit reveals the καλόν tree, so good moral acts manifest the ἀγαθόν moral character of their doer.

More difficult is ἐκ . . . θησαυροῦ τῆς καρδίας, where τῆς καρδίας is Lukan redaction.[19] Luke may have supplied the specifying genitive to link with the proverb to come in 6:45c. If one takes it as an epexegetical or appositional genitive (BDF §167) it makes explicit the metaphor latent in the proverb: the heart is a person's treasure house.[20] θησαυρός literally means the place where something is kept—a treasure chest, a storeroom— and what is stored within it, ordinarily material treasures. Classical Greek also uses treasure in a spiritual sense, as in treasures of wisdom.[21] The LXX, too, uses it mostly to describe material treasures, but wisdom and

---

[17] The good is salvific, "pleasing to God," and "god-like" in Hellenistic thought; in Hermetic writings only God is truly good; Walter Grundmann, "ἀγαθός," *TDNT* 1:11.

[18] See the numerous examples in ibid. 14-15.

[19] It is absent in the parallel Matt 12:35. Luke has probably also substituted the more appropriate verb προφέρειν, "produce," for the clumsier ἐκβάλλειν in Matt 12:35.

[20] Matthew 12:34c-35 has reversed the order of clauses in Luke 6:45, but has still equated the heart and the treasure, if more implicitly than has Luke.

[21] Friedrich Hauck, "θησαυρός," *TDNT* 3:136, cites Plato, Xenophon, and Epictetus.

fear of God are treasures in Isa 33:6, and good works provide heavenly treasure in Tob 4:9—a concept frequent in Judaism.[22] The NT contains most of these uses, and Luke's Jesus specifically uses the notion of heavenly treasure in 12:33-34 and 18:22. The treasure is, then, either as container or contained, as material or spiritual, what is most precious to a person. Nowhere in Greek or biblical literature outside of Luke 6:45 is the heart called a treasure. Thus Luke means to speak of the most precious recess of the heart, at the core of a person's being.

Καρδία for the Greeks was the seat of feeling and passion (especially of fear or courage) and the source of inclination and desire. It also meant mind, especially for engaged thinking.[23] Finally, it could mean the substance or core of a thing, and so came to be used metaphorically, as in the heart of the sea. In the LXX it is coextensive with Hebrew *lēb* and this OT usage dominates the NT as well.[24] *Lēb* denotes the main organ that moves the body. Lying deep in the chest, it connotes the inward and real character of a human. It affects feelings and moods, wishes and desires, but it most often describes functions we ascribe to the head or brain. In Deut 29:3; Prov 15:14; 19:8; Dan 2:30; Job 12:3 *lēb ab)* clearly means the mind, knowing, understanding, insight, even reason. "Keeping words in one's heart" refers to memory (Dan 7:28). Largely in the OT, however, this thinking leads to decisions: *lēb* describes planning (Prov 16:9), intention (Isa 10:7; Jer 23:20), and especially conscience (1 Sam 24:6), the place of decision (Prov 4:23) leading to moral conduct (1 Sam 12:20). So it means the inmost being of a human (1 Sam 16:7; Jer 31:33), or the whole person with her inner being and willing (Josh 22:5; Deut 6:5). The NT even more strongly than the LXX identifies καρδία as the main organ of psychic and spiritual life, the source of feelings and emotions, desires and passions, thinking and understanding, willing and deciding, and the moral conduct that flows from all of these.[25]

Καρδία is not a favorite Lukan word (only twenty-nine per cent of NT usage), but he uses it oftener than other evangelists. Eight times he makes it a center of intentionality and thinking that leads to decision and action (1:51; 2:35; 3:15; 5:22; 9:47; 12:45; 21:14; 24:38), once the source of belief (24:25), and twice the place of remembering (1:66; 2:51). Twice it is the source of emotional commitment (10:27; 24:32). Five passages,

---

[22] Again see the citations in ibid. 137.

[23] LSJ 877. Over time νοῦς comes to describe contemplative mind or calculating reason.

[24] With 814 Hebrew and Aramaic uses dealing exclusively with the human heart, it is the commonest of OT anthropological terms; Hans-Walter Wolff, *Anthropology of the Old Testament* (Philadelphia: Fortress, 1974) 40. My analysis of *lēb* is drawn mostly from Wolff, 41–55.

[25] Johannes Behm, "καρδία," *TDNT* 3:612; BAGD 403–404.

three from his *Sondergut* and two from his editorial changes of his synoptic sources, show that for Luke καρδία is the root of true character that authors one's proper moral conduct (as in 6:45): In *1:17* (SG) καρδία represents the moral concern of fathers in effecting reconciliation with their children, as in Mal 4:5 (LXX). In *16:15* (SG) God knows the Pharisees' καρδίας as the thinking that informs their true moral character. In *21:34* (SG) καρδίαι represents the disciples' clear thinking, free from distractions, that enables them to make the correct moral choice in the last days. In *8:12* (Mark) the devil takes the word of God from people's hearts, from the source of their knowing, deciding, and acting *that produces fruit,* as Luke points out by his insertion of καρδία καλῇ καὶ ἀγαθῇ as the source of καρποφοροῦσιν in 8:15. Note here Luke's intentional combination of καρδία, ἀγαθὴ, καλὴ, and καρπὸς just as in 6:45. Again, in *12:34* (Q), "Where your treasure is, there also your heart will be," καρδία is the place of one's personal commitment and conduct, based on one's treasured desires. Note the combination in this Q pericope of θησαυρός and καρδία, as in (Q-based) 6:45.

This predilection for the moral dimension of καρδία is confirmed by Luke's usage in Acts, where of twenty uses none refers to the heart as a source of ideational thought.[26]

A paraphrase, then, will illustrate this meaning of heart as the place of deliberation leading to moral action in the interpretation of 6:45: "The (morally) good person produces virtuous action from the treasure of her conscience." But the specificity of "conscience" disguises the fact that the vital and concrete word "heart" connotes many additional meanings in the metaphor of the treasure of the heart: Jesus means that a person spontaneously, naturally, and inevitably produces, from what is most precious to her, from the place of her emotional roots and passion as these issue in commitment and decision, from her conscience, which derives its criteria from a lifetime of this commitment, from the very core of her being (from her substance, quality), the good action that reveals the character that inevitably produced them. This inevitability underlies Jesus' continued argument that it is possible to judge what kind of a character a person is, just as one can judge a tree from the kind of fruit it produces.[27]

---

[26] Only four uses (2:26; 7:54; 14:17; 21:13) refer to the heart as the seat of emotions, and all the rest refer to the heart as (1) the place or source of moral intent and decision (5:4; 7:23, 39, especially of conversion to the good news or a moral life 2:37; 15:9; 18:27), (2) the place of moral character, whether of sin (5:3; 7:51; 8:21, 22; 28:27) or of virtue (2:46; 11:23), (3) the source of good deeds (13:22), and of moral union in the community (4:32).

[27] Someone might object that, because of the limitations of human experience and knowing, and because of the multiplicity of human desires, a good person sometimes produces a bad act. Jesus would calmly reply that the act reveals precisely that character, and

Jesus again argues by a converse illustration:

6:45b: καὶ ὁ πονηρὸς ἐκ τοῦ πονηροῦ προφέρει τὸ πονηρόν, "and the bad man out of his evil (treasure), evil." Πονηρός, from its root (πένο-μαι, "to be poor") originally meant "painful, sorrowful," then what causes sorrow. In the social sense it was opposed to οἱ καλοὶ κἀγαθοί, the social elite, and so came to mean "the wretched" or "the worthless," who contributed nothing to society. From the fifth century on it took on the moral sense, "bad, depraved, base, cowardly," and so Aristotle used it of those who do harm with evil intent.[28] In the LXX it translates Hebrew *ra*ʿ, the bad by nature or condition, the useless, the harmful. But its overwhelming use is of the culpably bad, who reject God and God's ways. This biblical sense dominates usage in Hellenistic Judaism, the rabbis, and the NT. If God alone is good, then humans are generally called πονηροί (Matt 7:11//Luke 11:13). But the word applies more generally to those who willfully reject God, and so do evil (Luke 11:29); in this they evince the classical NT use of πονηροί to describe the evil spirits.[29]

Πονηρός is a Matthaean word (twenty-six occurrences, twice as many as in Luke).[30] Luke uses it exclusively in its moral sense. Three times it refers to the evil spirits opposing God's reign and oppressing people (7:21; 8:2; 11:26). We have already seen in 6:35 that Luke distinguishes evildoers (πονηροί) from those who are merely useless or ungrateful. Πονηρός refers to the murderous deeds of the quintessentially evil Herod (3:19), to the name of an apostate (6:22), to the evil generation who turn a blind eye to signs and do not respond to Jesus' preaching (11:29), and to the covetous eye that darkens one's whole being (11:34). Thus this biblical sense informs even the one passage that seems to refer to one less morally culpable (19:22).[31] Clearly, then, in the present passage where πονηρός is contrasted with the ἀγαθός producing good deeds we are dealing with an evil man recognized by his evil deeds because they proceed from the evil storehouse of his heart.[32]

---

so would assert, "No one is (unrestrictedly) good but God" (Luke 18:19), an insight that underlines Aquinas' *bonum ex integra causa, malum ex quocumque defectu*. See the discussion immediately below of all humans as πονηροί in Luke 11:13//Matt 7:11.

[28] Günther Harder, "πονηρός," *TDNT* 6:546–48.

[29] Ibid. 554–58.

[30] Bernard Brandon Scott, *Hear Then the Parable: A Commentary on the Parables of Jesus* (Minneapolis: Fortress, 1989) 285–86 develops John Dominic Crossan's thesis that Matthew prefers an ἀγαθός/πονηρός contrast.

[31] The servant of 19:22 could be simply worthless, but his unwillingness to do the bidding of his master and (in the application of the parable) his view of the Lord are morally reprehensible.

[32] Τοῦ πονηροῦ as a masculine adjective must refer to θησαυρός (m.) and not καρδία (f.), but the short form recalls the whole phrase ἐκ τοῦ . . . θησαυροῦ τῆς καρδίας from the preceding clause.

6:45c: ἐκ γὰρ περισσεύματος καρδίας λαλεῖ τὸ στόμα αὐτοῦ, "for out of abundance of heart his mouth speaks." Jesus adds another witness of one's character: what a person says witnesses to what dominates her heart. Περίσσευμα: although the stem, meaning "to abound, be rich in, overflow, exceed," occurs in six different forms in the NT, the noun occurs only in this Q passage (//Matt 12:34), in Mark 8:8 (where it refers to the leftovers of the feeding miracle), and twice in 2 Cor 8:14, "surplus."[33] The literal meaning of anarthrous ἐκ περισσεύματος καρδίας is "from an abundance of a heart." This keeps close to the image, "what the heart is filled with, is rich in; from the overflow of one's heart."

Λαλεῖ τὸ στόμα αὐτοῦ: στόμα, "mouth," in conjunction with a verb of speaking, rather than of tasting or eating, means the physical mouth as the organ of speech, the tongue. Λαλεῖν originally derived from childish babbling, and connoted the making of sounds or the ability to speak. In the LXX it almost exclusively translates Hebrew *dābār,* while λέγειν translates *'āmar.* Since the noun *dābār* often carries the prophetic word of God and ὁ κύριος ἐλάλει often refers to prophetic speech (Isa 1:2, 20 and *passim*), λαλεῖν can mean the act of revealing.[34] Luke uses λαλεῖν in the sense of revealing (1:19, 45, and most of the fourteen uses in chs. 1–2), and to mean the simple ability or act of speaking (1:20, 22); sometimes both meanings are possible (2:38). Here the meaning of the mouth connotes both speaking and revealing the heart.

Some have thought that the mouth revealing what is in the heart indicates that all of 6:42-45 (or even 6:37-45) is not about deeds, but about speech, either judgments (6:37-42) or false prophets (6:39-45).[35] But this does not do justice to the meaning of καρπός in the Bible or in Luke. Rather it appears that speech is the fifth example in a series of illustrations of the principle that the interior quality of a thing determines the kind of thing it produces.

But isn't this a commonplace, to judge people by their works? Was this not what his opponents were doing to Jesus and the disciples to one another? No; in fact they offer the counter-example of those who judge in spite of the good works issuing from their opponent. In Luke 11:14-23, in the face of Jesus casting out a demon from a deaf-mute his opponents ascribe

---

[33] It occurs only once in the LXX, in Eccl 2:15, and may be an interpolation there; see the literature cited in BAGD 650.

[34] In the NT also λαλεῖν means both the act of speaking and that of revealing. The verb occurs twenty-four times in 1 Corinthians 12–14, referring to speaking in tongues, or in other charismatic ways.

[35] Schürmann, *Lukasevangelium* 365–79 makes 6:39-45 refer to false prophets in Luke's community; Marshall, *Luke* 273 thinks that all of 6:37-42 refers to speech and not deeds.

his work to an alliance with Beelzebul. In 13:10-17, in the face of Jesus' healing a woman crippled by a spirit the Pharisees attack him for breaking the law of the Sabbath rest.[36] John seems to judge an outsider exorcising in Jesus' name, and Jesus looks rather to the work than the profession of discipleship (9:49-50), precisely the point of the following 6:46! But being aware of one's own sinfulness (6:41-42) opens one's eyes to the goodness (or evil) in the other's actions, and so enables the correct judgment of her character.

Even though the application of the proverb is given in 6:45, commentators differ widely on the meaning of 6:42-45 as a whole.[37]

(1) centering on the word spoken by leaders of the community (6:42, 45c):

(a) one can expect no good teaching from false teachers (Heinz Schürmann);

(b) a leader must preach a word that comes out of a good heart (Theodor Zahn, Marie-Joseph Lagrange, Walter Grundmann);

(c) to be a teacher or minister one must be free of error or fault (Theodor Zahn);

(2) centering on the deeds produced by the disciple (6:43-44):

(a) those with a beam in their eye are unhealthy trees that can produce no good work; only the good man can do good to his neighbor (Paul Schanz, Alfred Plummer, Erich Klostermann, Friedrich Hauck, Christopher F. Evans);

(b) "Jesus' location of goodness in love of enemy and non-judgment is a call to a true inner goodness of the heart, of which one's concrete acts of goodness will be the natural fruit" (John Nolland).

(3) integrating deeds and words: If you want to correct others (6:41-42) you must first show your own goodness by good deeds (6:43-44), for then your speech will flow out of the goodness of your heart (6:45) (Joseph A. Fitzmyer).

The difficult relationship of the various proverbs and examples to each other can be resolved only if one attempts to interpret the three verses in their immediate context and in the overall argument of the Sermon.[38] Jesus has given his disciples his radical new command to love and do good

---

[36] The same false judgment can be found in his opponents in 5:17-6:11; 7:36-50.

[37] John Nolland, *Luke 1–9:20* (Dallas, Tex.: Word books, 1989) 308–309 briefly indicates the diversity of exegetical opinions about the rhetorical function and actual point of 6:43-45.

[38] Joseph A. Fitzmyer and François Bovon began this process; Christopher F. Evans' "the effectiveness of the disciple will depend upon his having his eye and mind purified and rendered sound by obedience to the Lord's teaching" (*Saint Luke* [Philadelphia: Trinity Press International, 1990] 339) carries it further.

to one's enemy (6:27-36), summarized in a unique formulation of the Golden Rule (6:31-34), made possible by the new life of divine adoption (6:35cd-36). Such love of enemies rules out harsh judgment of them (6:37ab), and demands unlimited forgiveness (6:37c) and generosity (6:38a) that evokes an unlimited reward from God (6:38bc). The one who accepts this teaching is not blind (6:39), but is restored to her proper being, is like Jesus, her teacher (6:40). The one who does not live as Jesus teaches has a log in her eye and so not only cannot see others' faults but will make false judgments about them (6:41-42, rounding off the theme of judgment introduced in 6:37).

The hint that one *could* see clearly to correct the neighbor (6:42de) leads to an explanation (γάρ) of how this is possible: one's heart must be transformed by Jesus' teaching (6:43-45). Once one begins to love enemies, do good unrestrictedly and give freely (good deeds as fruit of the treasury of one's heart, 6:43-45), one no longer judges hostilely and hypocritically (6:42d), but sees clearly to help the neighbor (6:42e).[39] This restored heart produces, out of a divine abundance, not only the good works that manifest the Christian character of the disciple's heart, but also a *spoken* good judgment that helps the brother (6:45c).

Exegesis of 6:46-49, on the Security of the True Disciple

Doing (6:43-44) and speaking (6:45) form the bridge to the next passage,[40] where Jesus' emphasis on both profession of faith and doing the Sermon's works forms the paraenetic conclusion of the Sermon.

6:46: Τί δέ με καλεῖτε· κύριε κύριε, καὶ οὐ ποιεῖτε ἃ λέγω; "why do you call me 'Lord, Lord' and do not do what I say?" The eighth rhetorical question in the twenty-nine verses of the Sermon intimates how essential is *doing* these radical directives of Jesus' Sermon. Καλεῖν in classical Greek, the LXX, and the NT means "call, summon," and, with a double accusative, "to name, call someone by name." It is a favorite verb of Luke (forty-one per cent of NT usage), who has a predilection for the ancient biblical notion that a person is what he is named (1:31, 35, 36, 76; 15:19, 21; BAGD 399). The meaning here is, "Why do you by mouth make me your Lord, when . . . ?" The reinforcing repetition κύριε, κύριε not merely names, but *pretends to make* Jesus one's Lord.[41]

---

[39] Further, one known to be good from her good actions will have a good woman's credibility with those whom she wishes to help (6:44a).

[40] As noted by Alfred Plummer, Theodor Zahn, and Béda Rigaux.

[41] Cf. Rom 10:13. The doubled vocative occurs in Gen 22:11; 46:2; Exod 3:4; 1 Sam 3:10, and often in Judaism; Billerbeck 1:943; 2:258. Luke used it frequently (8:24; 10:41;

Κύριος is a much-discussed title, both for God and for Jesus.[42] It means "lord, master," and was used only of men in classical Greek. The first use of κύριος for God is in the LXX, translating the *qere 'adōnai* for the *ketib YHWH* 6156x.[43] Thus in the LXX it is the personal and generic name for Israel's God.

Since it is Christian copies of the LXX that witness this practice, scholars have debated whether reading *'adōnai* for *YHWH* was Hebrew practice (whether "Lord" was the name for God in the Hebrew Bible) or a Christian interpretation.[44] Now Joseph A. Fitzmyer has demonstrated that pre-Christian Palestinian Jews referred to YHWH absolutely as "the Lord" by the Hebrew title *'adōn,* the Aramaic *mārê'* and *māryā',* and Greek κύριος. Therefore the primitive Christian confession "Jesus is Lord" (1 Cor 12:3) probably derived from the early Palestinian kerygma, and so naming Jesus κύριος put him on the same level of power and due reverence as YHWH.

Κύριος is a favorite Lukan word (even with Paul's overwhelming use, Luke has twenty-nine per cent of NT usage). It is his favorite title for Jesus (thirty-nine times, although in a couple of these the title probably means little more than "master" (6:5) or "sir" (9:59). Luke has retrojected this Christian post-resurrection confessional title into Jesus' earthly ministry, as

---

13:34; 22:31; Acts 9:4; 22:7; 26:14) to express Jesus' reproach of others, except for 8:24, which, like our 6:46, expresses the disciples' cry to their Lord for saving.

[42] The principal works are Wilhelm Bousset, *Kyrios Christos; A History of the Belief in Christ From the Beginnings of Christianity to Irenaeus.* Translated by John E. Steely (Nashville: Abingdon, 1970 [1913]); Oscar Cullmann, *The Christology of the New Testament.* Translated by Shirley C. Guthrie and Charles A. M. Hall (Philadelphia: Westminster, 1959); Ferdinand Hahn, *The Titles of Jesus in Christology; Their History in Early Christianity.* English translation by Harold Knight and George Ogg (London: Lutterworth, 1969); Reginald H. Fuller, *The Foundations of New Testament Christology* (New York: Scribner, 1965); Werner R. Kramer, *Christ, Lord, Son of God.* Translated by Brian Hardy. SBT 50 (Naperville, Ill.: A. R. Allenson, 1966); Ignace de la Potterie, "Le titre κύριος appliqué à Jésus dans l'évangile de Luc," in Albert Descamps and André de Halleux, eds., *Mélanges bibliques en hommage au R. P. Béda Rigaux* (Gembloux: Duculot, 1970) 117–46; D. L. Jones, "The Title Κύριος in Luke-Acts," in George W. MacRae, ed., *SBL 1974 Seminar Papers.* 2 vols. (Cambridge, Mass.: Society of Biblical Literature, 1974) 2:85–101. A thorough investigation of the NT background of κυριος is found in Joseph A. Fitzmyer, "The Semitic Background of the New Testament *Kyrios*-Title," in his *A Wandering Aramaean: Collected Aramaic Essays.* SBLMS 25 (Missoula: Scholars, 1979) 115–42, and "New Testament *Kyrios* and *Maranatha* and their Aramaic Background," in his *To Advance the Gospel: New Testament Studies* (New York: Crossroad, 1981) 218–35.

[43] Gottfried Quell, "κύριος," *TDNT* 3:1058–59. It translates other divine names (*'el, 'elôah, and 'elohîm*) only 286x.

[44] For the evidence adduced, see Werner Foerster, "κύριος," *TDNT* 3:1081–89 and Joseph A. Fitzmyer, *The Gospel According to Luke.* 2 vols. AB 28, 28A (Garden City, N.Y.: Doubleday, 1981, 1985) 201 and the bibliography cited there.

witnessed by his absolute use of the title ὁ κύριος nineteen times, in contrast to Mark's single use.[45] Further, the Prologue has already indicated the divine meaning of the title as Luke intends to use it in his gospel (1:43; 2:11). There is no doubt that "Luke is simply using the title that had become current in his own day, as the narrative in Acts also witnesses."[46] Consequently, με καλεῖτε κύριε, κύριε now must be the cry of disciples who confess that Jesus is their Lord with divine powers. But in spite of their verbal and notional commitment to Jesus they do not do what he has been asking of his disciples throughout the Sermon; they are not true disciples.

Καὶ might be a simple connective "where more discriminating usage would call for other particles."[47] But if it indicates a surprising turn, ". . . you call me Lord, Lord, *and yet* (in spite of that), you do not do what I say," the simple καὶ is more powerful, since it merely connects the two behaviors in such a way as to let the contradiction explode in the reader's imagination.

Οὐ ποιεῖτε ἃ λέγω: ἃ λέγω refers to everything that Jesus asks the disciples to do throughout the gospel, but here, in the concluding paraenesis of the Sermon, it denotes what Jesus has commanded in the Sermon itself. Ποιεῖν, the generic word for action, good or evil (3:12, 14) occurs nine times in the twenty-nine verses of the Sermon. The OT had emphasized the importance of not only hearing God's will, but doing it.[48] Luke uses ποιεῖν in many ways to describe doing what God has commanded (2:27; 12:43) or doing good deeds as producing fruits (3:8; 6:43). Luke's Jesus uses ποιεῖν with λέγειν/λόγος to speak of doing God's will in 8:21; otherwise he varies expression: in 11:28 φυλάσσοντες, in 12:47 τὸ θέλημα, in 17:9-10 διαταχθέντα. Thus four times explicitly and many times implicitly the mark of a disciple is doing what the master commands. Calling one "master" and not doing his bidding is a contradiction; calling one (divine)

---

[45] Many maintain that κύριε originally addressed to Jesus at the time of the Sermon could have meant only "sir, master" (i.e., teacher), either from the mouths of the crowds who come to hear him (6:18) or from those of his disciples. But Luke uses διδάσκαλε when he wishes to make this historical distinction. These scholars ignore the fact that it is Christian confession that delivers the tradition to Luke and Luke's confessing Christians who now read the text.

[46] For the data and argument that support Fitzmyer's quotation see *Luke* 203.

[47] BAGD 392 §2. This usage could fall under paragraph e, "connecting negative and affirmative clauses," or under g, "emphasizing a fact as surprising or unexpected or noteworthy," although the editors do not cite 6:46 under either of these. Adversative adverbs— καίτοι, καὶ ἔπειτα, ὅμως, μέντοι—are common enough in classical Greek but extremely rare in the NT: perhaps ὅμως in 1 Cor 14:7 or Gal 3:15, certainly ὅμως μέντοι in John 12:42 and καίτοι in Acts 14:17 are adversative.

[48] John R. Donahue, *The Gospel in Parable* (Philadelphia: Fortress, 1988) 137 cites Deut 4:5-6; 28:13-14; Ezek 33:31-32 and suggests its dominance in the NT while citing only Rom 1:13; Jas 1:22; cf. also 1 Cor 3:11-15; John 13:17.

Lord and not doing what he says is not only a contradiction, but a disaster, as Jesus now illustrates in the following paired similitudes.

6:47: Πᾶς ὁ ἐρχόμενος πρός με καὶ ἀκούων μου τῶν λόγων καὶ ποιῶν αὐτούς, ὑποδείξω ὑμῖν τίνι ἐστὶν ὅμοιος, "everyone coming to me and hearing my words and doing them, I will show you what she is like." Πᾶς ὁ ἐρχόμενος πρός με: the participial construction at the beginning of the sentence, similar to the *casus pendens* of Hebrew syntax, emphasizes the doer of the action. Πᾶς, marking Lukan universality, emphasizes Jesus' plan as the sure way to salvation for all who do it.[49] Surprisingly, since the form of Luke-Acts is a travel narrative, ἔρχεσθαι and even προσέρχεσθαι are Johannine and Matthaean, not Lukan words.[50] Ἐρχόμενος πρός, designating an approach to Jesus as the first step of discipleship (the others are hearing, confessing, doing), occurs in 4:42 and 5:17; in each case it implies that people have come to hear Jesus. Such coming *to hear* is made explicit in 6:18 and here in 6:47; see the parallel usage in 11:31). These phrases and clauses connote the more explicit phrase for discipleship, ἐρχόμενος ὀπίσω μου as the translation of hālāk ʾaharê (9:23; 14:26, 27).[51] Thus the Lukan addition of ἐρχόμενος (see the parallel Matt 7:24) is not simply to recall the crowds coming to hear in 6:18, but to emphasize the first steps of discipleship, which lead up to the actual confession of 6:46.[52] Luke adds καὶ ἀκούων[53] and καὶ ποιοῦν to clarify the three steps of discipleship. All three are essential to reap the reward of discipleship, the burden of this concluding parable.[54] Ὑποδείξω ὑμῖν τίνι ἐστὶν ὅμοιος is probably Lukan redaction, for ὑποδεικνῦναι is

[49] Πᾶς ὁ with participle is a favorite Lukan construction; Joachim Jeremias, *Die Sprache des Lukasevangeliums* (Göttingen: Vandenhoeck & Ruprecht, 1980) 72.

[50] Although subtracting Matthaean usage from the totals reveals that Luke-Acts has fifty-four per cent of the remaining NT usage of προσέρχεσθαι, it is still true that Luke avoids ἔρχεσθαι and its compound forms, sometimes in favor of his favorite, πορεύεσθαι (Luke-Acts has fifty-nine per cent of NT usage), which carries theological freight; Henry J. Cadbury, *The Style and Literary Method of Luke.* HTS 6 (Cambridge, Mass.: Harvard University Press, 1920) 177–78.

[51] This usage is equivalent to ἀκολουθεῖν as the fundamental action of the disciple; 5:11, 27-28; 9:57-62, expressed differently in 22:28. See Fitzmyer on following Jesus in *Luke* 241–43.

[52] Ἐρχόμενος πρός με is missing in the otherwise parallel 6:49, probably because discipleship language cannot characterize one who does not do as Jesus says.

[53] We have already seen that ἀκούειν often means not only hearing but obeying the one heard (Acts 3:22; 28:28). But Luke 8:15, adding κατέχουσιν and καρποφοροῦσιν to specify the effective nature of hearing the word by the true disciple, is more typical Lukan usage.

[54] For similar NT paraenesis on not only hearing but also doing see Jas 1:22-25 and also 1 Cor 3:11-15, which includes the notion of building on Christ as the θεμέλιος.

Lukan, as is the doubled ὅμοιος (in 6:48a).[55] This more elaborate introduction (in comparison with the parallel Matt 7:24) makes the use of the similitude more didactic.

6:48a: ὅμοιός ἐστιν ἀνθρώπῳ οἰκοδομοῦντι οἰκίαν ὃς ἔσκαψεν καὶ ἐβάθυνεν καὶ ἔθηκεν θεμέλιον ἐπὶ τὴν πέτραν, "he is like a person building a house who dug, and went deep, and laid a foundation on the rock." Ἀνθρώπῳ οἰκοδομοῦντι οἰκίαν: Where Matt 7:24 has ἀνδρὶ φρονίμῳ Luke's more generic ἀνθρώπῳ (his favorite use in parables)[56] emphasizes the work of building rather than Matthew's contrast between the prudence and stupidity of the builders.

Ὃς ἔσκαψεν καὶ ἐβάθυνεν καὶ ἔθηκεν θεμέλιον ἐπὶ τὴν πέτραν: σκάπτειν (Luke has the only three NT uses), βαθύνειν (*hapax* in the NT), and θεμέλιον (Luke has the only three gospel uses) reveal conscious Lukan redaction. In contrast to the pallid language of Matt 7:24, "who built his house on rock," Luke's three vigorous action verbs produce a striking artistic effect: the three parallel finite verbs echo the three parallel participles that described discipleship in 6:47, and call attention to the toil involved in making the house solid. In pre-technological society digging itself is laborious; going down deeper, to the rock itself, and laying the foundation on that rock, speaks of many long days of back-breaking work.[57] This image evokes the enormous task involved: not simply to come to Jesus and listen to his words, but to put into practice the radical ethic of the Sermon.

---

[55] Nolland, *Luke 1–9:20,* 309 points out that Luke-Acts has 5/6 of NT uses of ὑποδεικνῦναι. For doubled ὅμοιος see Luke 6:47-48; 7:31-32; 13:18-19, all uniquely Lukan.

[56] Luke 10:30; 11:24, 26; 12:16, 36; 13:19; 14:16, 30; 15:4, 11; 16:1, 19; 18:10; 19:12; 20:9. Thus Marshall, *Luke* 275 is wrong in denying that ἄνθρωπος is Lukan redaction. Probably οἰκοδομοῦντι οἰκίαν was originally in Q, since Luke generally avoids the Greek accusative (Jeremias, *Sprache* 75). Although the parable seems to come from Q it is a futile exercise to decide what the original text might have been.

[57] Joachim Jeremias, *The Parables of Jesus* (London: S.C.M., 1963) 27 n. 9 asserts that Palestinian houses lack cellars, a point confirmed indirectly by J. S. Holladay, "House, Israelite," in ABD 3, 308-310. The last synthesis of what little we know of Greco-Roman domestic architecture, Bertha Carr Rider, *The Greek House; Its History and Development from the Neolithic Period to the Hellenistic Age* (Cambridge: Cambridge University Press, 1965 [1916]), did not mention cellars or basements. The only treatment of cellars in these houses is by Marie-Christine Hellmann, "Caves et sous-sols dans l'habitat grec antique," *Bulletin de correspondence hellénique* 116 (1992) 259–66, where she discusses the scant evidence for cellars as storerooms for wines and other perishables in the homes of rich merchants, who could afford the extravagance of such excavation. But, although Luke 11:33 *may* speak of a cellar (κρύπτη), there is no mention of a cellar in 6:48. Luke here refers to excavating deep enough to lay the foundation of the house on bedrock. By 70 C.E. the Roman practice of the well-to-do cementing foundations to bedrock would have come into any place where Luke would have been writing his gospel.

6:48b: πλημμύρης δὲ γενομένης προσέρηξεν ὁ ποταμὸς τῇ οἰκίᾳ ἐκείνῃ, "and when a flood rose, the river crashed against that house." Luke's description of the construction was more detailed than Matthew's, but Matthew's description of the storm attacking the construction is more detailed than Luke's. Matthew describes a Palestinian autumn storm, whose torrential rains fill the wadis, whose waters break upon the house with a force redoubled by winds. Luke thinks of a flooded river overflowing its banks and breaking upon the house with tremendous force.[58] Still, Luke's own classical vocabulary describes his scene vividly.

Πλήμ(μ)υρα (*hapax* in the NT) originally refers to a flood tide of the sea, then to a flood of a river, and then to figurative meanings, such as a flood of words or tears (LSJ 1419). In the LXX it occurs only in Job 40:23, referring to a violently flooding river, as here. Perhaps Luke's readers would think such a flood more likely to sweep a house away than the storm in Q. Προσρήσσειν/προσρηγνύναι, "dash against, beat upon," occur only in the Christian era and then very rarely (LSJ 1525). Thus Luke has chosen rare words to speak of a powerful flood, so strong that in an immense rush it will break the house apart (the root meaning of ῥηγνύναι).

6:48c: καὶ οὐκ ἴσχυσεν σαλεῦσαι αὐτὴν διὰ τὸ καλῶς οἰκοδομῆσθαι αὐτήν, "and it was not powerful enough even to shake it, because it was so well built." The image concludes with Lukan language, manifesting his own literary formulation.[59] Καὶ represents rapid oral discourse where more literary usage would be δὲ or ἀλλὰ to express a result contrary to expectation. Ἰσχύειν, from ἰσχύς, "strength, power, might," in Greek literature meant "to be strong in body, prevail" (LSJ 844). In comparison with δύνασθαι (which Luke uses three times more often), it connotes forceful physical power to do something (16:3; 13:24). Σαλεύειν in classical Greek meant "to rock, shake to and fro," as in an earthquake, or "to toss" as a ship on the sea (LSJ 1581). Luke uses it as a synonym of σείειν, to cover the range of meanings from the gentle shaking of grains in a cup (6:38) or the shaking of a reed in the wind (7:24) to the cosmic forces of heaven being shaken at the end of time (21:26). This denotative range serves Luke well: not only cannot the flood destroy the house; it cannot shake it, violently or gently! I render the gap between the reader's expectation of destruction and the impotence of the storm as "was not strong enough *even* to shake it."

---

[58] So Jeremias, *Parables* 194, basing his interpetation on Gustaf Dalman, and followed by all the commentators.

[59] Luke-Acts contains fifty per cent of the NT usage of ἰσχύειν and fifty-three per cent of NT usage ofσαλεύειν; the construction of διὰ with the accusative of the articular infinitive to denote cause is Lukan; BDF §402 (1) and §406 (3) and also Jeremias, *Sprache* 29, 79.

Διὰ τὸ καλῶς οἰκοδομῆσθαι αὐτήν: Here, in reference to the laborious and careful building of 6:48b, καλῶς means "because it was *so securely* built." The explanation seems redundant after the vivid description of the construction in 6:48b, but Luke's Jesus does not want his hearers to miss the point of how potent his words are. He next drives home the point by the antithetical similitude that follows.

6:49a: ὁ δὲ ἀκούσας καὶ μὴ ποιήσας ὅμοιός ἐστιν ἀνθρώπῳ οἰκοδομήσαντι οἰκίαν ἐπὶ τὴν γῆν χωρὶς θεμελίου, "but the one who has heard and not done (them) is like one who built a house on the ground without a foundation." Since this shorter similitude takes its language from the preceding one we need only comment here on χωρὶς θεμελίου. Building one's house flat on the ground, which seems improvident to us with poured concrete, was common throughout the Greco-Roman world, normal for the poorer classes, and universal in Palestine. By taking as dangerous what everyone did, Jesus teaches that those who reject his radical ethic because it is not what everyone does ("reasonable") are making a dreadful mistake.

6:49bc: ᾗ προσέρηξεν ὁ ποταμός, καὶ εὐθὺς συνέπεσεν, "against which the river crashed, and it immediately collapsed." Luke's only use of εὐθύς as an adverb (he prefers εὐθέως) means "straightaway, immediately." Συμπίπτειν, "to fall in, collapse," the ordinary word for the (inward) collapse of a building, is used only here in the NT.[60] Again, by means of rare and exact language Luke graphically depicts the sudden and total destruction of the house. While the house founded on rock was not even shaken, the house laid on the ground collapsed.

6:49d: καὶ ἐγένετο τὸ ῥῆγμα τῆς οἰκίας ἐκείνης μέγα, "and complete was the ruin of that house." Following upon 6:48c, this conclusion is rhetorical redundance. Ῥῆγμα, from ῥήγνυμι, literally means "breaking," but is the usual word for the ruin or collapse of buildings (BAGD 735). Luke (like Q) has postponed the adjective μέγα, "complete, utter" (BAGD 497 §2,a, α and g) to the end of the sentence so that the totality of the ruin of those who do not observe Jesus' words rings in the hearers' ears as the Sermon comes to an end.

In summary, the short similitudes in 6:47-49 are didactic; they produce no imaginative shock as do Jesus' more metaphorical parables. Jesus himself, the tradents of the original form in Q, as well as Matthew and Luke as final authors have simply drawn on real life experiences of construction, storm, and flood as the best description of the effect of Christian

---

[60] Marshall and others ascribe the form to Luke's fondness for συν– compounds, ignoring the fact that this is the exact word for the collapse of a building, as in German *zusammenbrechen;* BAGD 779.

discipleship.[61] It is possible that these images or some elements of them might have allegorical identifications in the Christian community. Patristic authors have seen in the storm a reference to the last judgment,[62] and so an allusion to the events described in Luke 17:26-37. But the imagery in Luke 17, as well as in the last judgment as a whole, is not of a flood breaking on a house, but of fire or cosmic signs. It is more likely that Jesus and the tradents of the story simply took the flood crashing on the house as a picture of the most powerful force known to them,[63] one that had become mythical in its power, whose impotence against the one doing God's word is a vindication of the disciple's placing his trust in these words of Jesus.[64] The similitudes make clear that it is of no value to hear the words of Jesus and profess allegiance to him if one does not obey the words of this Sermon. One who goes through the immense toil and risk in building his foundation on doing the demanding words of Jesus has a firm foundation that can withstand any onslaught, and so secures his life.

These parables are part of a whole NT theology in which having faith in Jesus, following him, and doing his behest produces life and salvation.[65] Luke expresses this theology by highlighting the authority of Jesus as Messiah, Son of God, the Holy One of God, and showing that one's position with regard to the Son of Man determines one's eternal destiny (12:8-9; 17:22-37; 21:25-28). In the parables, too, adherence to Jesus as master of the house (13:22-30), the nobleman with kingship (19:11-27), the beloved Son (20:9-19) is the criterion of life and salvation. Because of this authority Jesus necessarily provokes a decision for or against himself (12:49-53), and decision for him supersedes the most sacred human commitments (9:59-62; 14:25-33). Because as Son of God he has a unique knowledge and revelation of the Father (10:21-22), his proclamation of the Reign of God is greater than what prophets and kings have seen and heard (9:23-24), greater than the preaching in Sodom, Tyre, Sidon (10:12-16), or

---

[61] Paul (1 Cor 3:10-17) has also used the image of construction to describe the apostles' work in founding Christian communities that withstand fire. Many commentators refer to Ezek 13:11-14 as a parallel, but there the figure does not illustrate the kind of construction being tested.

[62] Matthew 7:22, ἐν ἐκείνῃ τῇ ἡμέρᾳ, can evoke expectation of the final judgment.

[63] Rooting the similitudes in the immediate experience of Luke and his predecessors makes most sense out of Luke's deliberate choice of technical terms to describe the construction and storm phenomena known to his readers.

[64] Nevertheless, the figure of the flood partakes in the eschatology that has permeated the Sermon from the future tenses of the beatitudes and woes through the great reward of 6:35 to the divine measure of 6:38.

[65] NT authors' expressions of the necessity of doing what Jesus commands are many; the ones most commonly seen as germane to Luke 6:47-49 are Jas 1:19-24; 1 John 2:17; 3:18.

the message of Jonah or even the wisdom of Solomon (11:29-32). He proclaims God's Reign as the central event of human history (16:16). Consequently disciples and all humans are divinely summoned to listen to him (9:28-36), especially when he is articulating the role of the cross in human authenticity (9:21-27). Acts, too, makes Jesus' way central to the whole human way of salvation (4:12; 16:16-17). Consequently, the concluding paraenesis, so centered on the necessity of doing the commands of the Sermon, no mattter how radical, is its fitting conclusion.

Conclusion

When one reaches the end of this section the Christian reader has undergone a subtle shift in her interpretation of the whole. One now sees that in 6:39-49 each image underscores somehow the decisive importance of learning and doing Jesus' teaching on love of enemies and of not judging others.

1. *6:39-42* indicates that to judge others is not to be a disciple of Jesus. The τυφλός of 6:39 is the hearer (quasi-disciple) who is blind to Jesus' own teaching on not judging; he cannot lead. The μαθητής of 6:40 cannot be beyond his master's teaching, but must be renewed like him in not judging. The one who judges in 6:41-42 is not a disciple of Jesus because he does not recognize as evil his tendency to judge others harshly. Only by accepting Jesus' teaching on love of enemies and not judging can he see clearly to be of help to his brother.

2. *6:42-45* begins as an explanation (γάρ) of how one can come to see so clearly. As tropes accumulate and develop it becomes clear that it is one's actions that reveal whether one is truly a disciple of Jesus. In 6:43-44 agricultural figures demonstrate that the kind of fruit produced determines whether a tree is good or bad, nourishing or not. Luke 6:45 draws the application: a man is known to be interiorly good or bad by his actions, e.g., not judging.

3. *6:46-49:* The final two similitudes drawn from house construction now serve as the application of this series of images and form the conclusion of the Sermon. The rhetorical question in 6:46 reveals that discipleship is what this series of images, and the Sermon as a whole, have been about. The one who comes to Jesus, hears his words about love of enemies and not judging, and puts them into practice is a true disciple whose house is secure against any storm. The one who professes to be a disciple but does not do what Jesus has been commanding is not a disciple and he will fall in the struggles of life, just as he will lead the blind into a pit (6:39),

will be a false disciple for not being like his master (6:40), and will not be able to correct his brother (6:41-42) because (γάρ) he inevitably produces bad fruit since his heart is not set on Jesus as is that of a true disciple.

Jesus then has concluded his Sermon with an ultimatum: "Do this or die." How can he be so adamant about so radical an ethic, which the natural human mind misunderstands, and from which the human heart of his would-be disciples recoils? That is the burden of our final chapter.

Part III

The Interpretation of the Sermon

Chapter 8

The Theology of the Lukan Sermon

The inquiry that generated this book began in Christian hearers' blank incomprehension of the paradoxical and challenging commands of Jesus' Sermon. Commentaries on Luke have inadequate space to describe how these radical demands can be good news for the bewildered hearer, and most attempts to interpret the ethic of the Sermon relate it to Matthew's Sermon on the Mount.[1] Attempts at such a description of the Lukan ethic have been few and brief.[2]

The task is daunting, and these few pages can only begin it. First we will synthesize the findings of our minute analysis of the individual pericopes, so we can understand the overall message of Jesus' Sermon on the Plain. Then we must investigate the nature of the difficulty in interpreting Jesus' countercultural message. Third, the radical nature of Jesus' ethic will force us to investigate how Jesus empowers his disciples to respond to the radical claims he makes on them. This will imply a Christian anthropology, not in the explanatory terms of systematic theology but in the descriptive terms of Luke's first-century Hellenistic rhetoric.[3] Only when

[1] Two of the major surveys of work on the Sermon, Harvey K. McArthur, *Understanding the Sermon on the Mount* (New York: Harper, 1960) and Warren S. Kissinger, *The Sermon on the Mount: A History of Interpretation and Bibliography* (Metuchen, N.J.: Scarecrow Press, 1975) concern themselves only with Matthew's Sermon. The rather exhaustive bibliography in Hans-Dieter Betz, *The Sermon on the Mount: A Commentary on the Sermon on the Mount, Including the Sermon on the Plain (Matthew 5:3–7:27 and Luke 6:20-49)*. Edited by Adela Yarbro Collins. Hermeneia (Minneapolis: Fortress, 1995) 652–63 lists no studies on the ethic of Luke's Sermon.

[2] The one monograph on the Lukan Sermon, Heinrich Kahlefeld, *Der Jünger; eine Auslegung der Rede Lk 6, 20-49* (Frankfurt: J. Knecht, 1962) does devote sixteen pages, a comparatively generous eighth of its bulk, to the topic.

[3] For the distinction between explanatory and descriptive categories see Bernard Lonergan, *Insight; A Study of Human Understanding* (New York: Philosophical Library, 1957) 291–92, 295–96 and its elaboration into primal and secondary intentional fields by John F. Haught in *Religion and Self-Acceptance* (New York: Paulist, 1976) 34–50. Jesus' discourse

such an anthropology describes the Christian indicative can we explore, in the fourth place, the coherence and power of the Christian imperative that Luke's Jesus gives his Christian community as good news.

Summary of Jesus' Sermon on the Plain

1. Luke's Sermon really begins with his establishment of Jesus' authority to teach.[4] Luke's *Prologue (chs. 1–2)* establishes Jesus as not just another prophet, but the Messiah, who as Lord and Son of God is more than human. The salvation this divine messenger brings is continuous with God's covenant with Israel, but is addressed to all nations. It will comprise a reversal of oppression through mercy and the forgiveness of sins, resulting in joy and peace. Disciples' participation in this salvation requires obedience to God's word and to the Holy Spirit. Already at twelve Jesus' vision of God's will makes him an original interpreter of the Law.

2. *The beginning of Jesus' ministry in Luke 3:1–6:16* sees the eschatological age already begun in the Elijah-like prophecy of John the Baptist, by Jesus' programmatic overthrow of Satan's reign in his temptation and exorcisms, and by his reconstitution of Israel's twelve tribes on the twelve apostles. God proclaims Jesus as the Son of God and Jesus proclaims himself as the eschatological prophet like the Isaian Servant, announcing a Jubilee year that liberates captives and the oppressed. This redemption is the good news of the Reign of God, comprising a reversal of the lot of the poor, forgiveness of sins, and healings. Jesus' unique authority issues a radical call: his disciples are to leave all and follow him. He acts against the Pharisaic construal of the Law and is often shown teaching, but we do not know the content of his teaching.

3. *The Sermon reveals his ethical teaching,* primarily to disciples but also to outsiders eager to hear him. Its first word, μακάριοι, sets a theme of rejoicing for the Sermon as a whole. The reward offered in *the first beatitude (6:20),* ἡ βασιλεία τοῦ θεοῦ, supplies not only the final, but also the efficient cause for all of the beatitudes. Thus Jesus transforms the platitudinous OT wisdom form into paradoxical proclamations of the reversed conditions of the eschatological Reign of God he is ushering in. He proclaims blessed those considered the most wretched in his society, the des-

---

is not couched in the theoretic terms of a Hellenistic philosophical system, but rather in the figurative terms of first century Hellenistic rhetoric. We are attempting to ground a NT ethic stemming from Jesus himself and formulated by a pastoral theologian in narrative, rhetorical, and literary forms.

[4] Evidence for each number of this summary is found in the corresponding chapter of this monograph.

perately poor. Jesus' disciples, by distributing to the poor, abolish poverty. The present inbreaking of the eschatological Reign of God makes possible this distribution.

Thus the poor are proclaimed happy because the rich are summoned by eschatological judgment to distribute their wealth to the poor now. The poor who receive such distribution are no longer needy, and so blessed. Disciples who make such distribution are happy because they become eschatologically rich toward God. When such distribution is not complete, the poor at least know that by seeking the Reign of God they are now in the process of receiving their reward in the perfect Reign of the apocalyptic Son of Man. This Reign transforms the earthly existence of those who live it and vibrantly hope for it.

4. *The rest of the beatitudes (6:21-23)* likewise proclaim happy those who are neglected or despised in Luke's society.

a. Hunger is a correlative of poverty, and here, as elsewhere in Luke-Acts, it refers to hunger for adequate food. Jesus addresses this hunger throughout the gospel, and satisfies it with food in 9:10-17. Further, he commands his disciples to feed the hungry in 14:13. Consequently, the blessed state of the hungry arises both from their being fed in the present Reign of God and also from knowing they will be satisfied in the final consummation of God's reign.

b. Those who are destitute and starving are going to die; wailing for the dead is the chief meaning of κλαίοντες. Consequently, Jesus proclaims blessed those who weep for the poor, the hungry, and the oppressed. They will laugh joyfully in the full eschatological possession of justice. (Any disciple who carries the cross through to the resurrection will both weep and rejoice.)

c. The different form of the concluding beatitude reveals its formulation in the church's experience of persecution for discipleship of its crucified Lord. Jesus proclaims blessed those hated by Gentiles and Jews for their commitment to the Son of Man's way. The generic "hated" refers to the hostile rejection of the good by the evil and godless. The specifying verbs "exclude, reproach, revile" are not technical terms of official persecution, but rather describe the kind of labeling and shunning everywhere used to discredit and discourage those who upset the declining mores of the status quo. Jesus spoke of his own rejection as a prophet, and promised his disciples that as members of his prophetic movement they would suffer. He foresees no historical end of such persecutions. The disciples will leap for joy only in the perfect peace of the eschatological Reign of God. Thus the beatitudes end with otherworldly reward as the source of disciples' joy.

d. The woes (6:24-26), on the other hand, are a prophetic form. Here the woes present the obverse of the beatitudes, to reinforce and clarify them. Jesus names the states that humans call good and pronounces a condemnation on them. While the adjectives in the beatitudes describe states from which God will liberate his people, the adjectives in the woes imply a summons to conversion, demand an ethical response. As poverty implies hunger and bewailing one's state, so wealth implies being well-fed and blissfully ignorant of the state of the wretched who surround one. In a first-century economy the rich are exploiters who can enjoy their feasts only at the expense of the vast majority. Those who live for this world have already had their reward: in the world to come they will starve and lament. The woes hang eschatological judgment over the heads of the rich, the fat, and the mirthful, and this judgment can work conversion of human conduct now.

e. The final woe also springs from the experience of the early church: teachers of a way of salvation not founded on Christ's cross have arisen in the community. They are praised for teaching a way of life that condones the injustice endemic in their world. To ease their way in this world they have abandoned the prophetic way of Jesus. Alas! they will suffer the same fate as did the Jewish false prophets. Thus the final woe of the Sermon's exordium performs two rhetorical functions: (1) It summarizes the message of the exordium: Jesus' way, in which the cross reverses the condition of the oppressed, radically challenges worldly powers, and so provokes persecution of the true disciples who share his prophetic message. Nevertheless, these true disciples will triumph in the eschatological Reign of God. (2) It foreshadows the coming passages that summon disciples to listen to (6:27) and live out (6:46) the Sermon's message.

Each beatitude and woe embodies a paradox needing to be pondered, yet Jesus' rapid-fire delivery allows no time for such pondering, and so creates an increased befuddlement about this good news that cries out for clarification.

5. *The Love Command (6:27-36)* now details what Christians must do to realize the astonishing promises of his exordium, in commands just as astonishing as the beatitudes! He addresses those who have made the first step toward discipleship, coming to listen, but his commands will make sense only to those who have moved to the further steps of discipleship, professing faith in Jesus and obeying his commands (6:46-49). Still, these commands are also addressed to the world at large (6:17-19; 7:1), which hungers for this message as much as do the disciples.

a. Jesus begins with the command to love one's enemies as the prime example to be specified in the following series of commands (6:27-36, 37-

42). Love of the enemy so far exceeds both Judaic and Hellenistic moral demands that it shatters the boundaries of human rationality itself. Jesus exemplifies this general command with a series of seven imperatives. Their concreteness (turning the other cheek, giving to the one robbing you) manifests how counter-cultural they are. To various attacks on their person, the disciples' responses—especially in "blessing" and "praying for" the one causing injury—bespeak a consideration for the moral state of the neighbor that intimates the conversion to the neighbor of which the next verse speaks.

b. The Golden Rule (6:31) makes human fellow-feeling a motivation for such Christian nonretaliation. As a moral maxim of unlimited altruism, expressed by mutuality between subject and object, the principle is unique to Jesus. Beginning with one's own desires forces one to consider others as persons with their own correlative desires. This principle seems consonant with human experience and reason (until one reflects on the inhuman way in which he has been attacked!). However, the Golden Rule stretches human reason in its own way: beginning with desires opens the disciple herself to the whole range of desires of the human heart, not only for money and food but also for friendship and community, even to being in communion with God. Ultimately these desires are rooted in the fact of, and desire for, being children of God (6:35).

c. Human reason can interpret the Golden Rule as a system of just exchange. Lest it be understood in terms of customary Greco-Roman balanced reciprocity, Jesus explicitly excludes three examples of such exchange (6:32-34) as actions of self-interested sinners, who have already received their reward.

d. But Jesus does not exclude all hope of reward. Those who love enemies, do good to them, lend without hope of return will receive a great reward (6:35). The future tense ἔσται reminds the reader of the beatitudes' promises: disciples will receive their reward in the immediate and ultimate futures of the Reign of God. As the actions Jesus requires go beyond human "reason," so their reward exceeds human agency. Such reward comes only from God, and so is an object of faith, not secured by human conduct but by reliance on the sovereign goodness of God.

By such generous acts the disciples will be "sons of the most High," who is generous to the useless and the wicked without regard to what they have done in the past or might do in the future (6:35d). Υἱοὶ ὑψίστου describes not just an eschatological state, but also Jesus' empowering his disciples to act on this earth with his love as Son of God. The disciples' radical actions, reversing the "normal" human ethics of the Greeks, manifest them as children of God.

e. The OT describes this God as compassionate (οἰκτίρμων). Jesus focuses the disciples' imitation of God not on the power of healing or raising from the dead, but on living the divine compassion which impels them to nonretaliatory love of the neighbor. This is the Christian principle. Thus 6:36 concludes this section on love of enemies by expanding the other general rule in this section, the Golden Rule. It had asked the disciple not to use the conduct of the other as criterion for her action but to search her own deepest desires, to presume that these were also the desires of the other, and so act. Luke 6:36 likewise makes compassion, not the other's conduct, the norm of Christian action, but the norm has been infinitely enlarged to the measure of God's own compassion. Outside of the tantalizing hint that we are to be children of God, Luke does not specify for the bewildered disciple how this is to be done.

6. *The Critique of Judgment (6:37-42)* embodies not just a special case of love of enemies but also an attitude that underlies it, the Golden Rule, and the Christian principle.

a. The prohibition of judging and condemnation (6:37ab), resuming the four-beat rhythm of 6:27-30, attacks not only the disciples' spontaneous human tendency to criticize but also their upbringing in a Law that articulated the offenses the community was to avoid, correct, and punish. Many disciples reject unrestricted forgiveness and boundless generosity (6:37c-38) as irrational, as they do the rest of the Sermon (6:24-26, 32-34, 46-49).

b. Consequently, Jesus attacks their blocked minds with parabolic language expressed in almost polemical rhetorical questions (6:39-42). Just as the blind cannot lead the blind, so disciples who reject Jesus' teaching are blind and cannot lead other blind ones who also do not grasp Jesus' teaching (6:39). Again: the disciple is blind because she does not see the log (rejection of Jesus' prohibition of judgment) in her own eye, and so cannot see the way to healing the neighbor (6:41). This blind judgmental attitude (6:39b-42) opposes the prohibition of the judgmental and unforgiving attitude of 6:37 and the corresponding inculcation of generosity of 6:38ab. Only when reformed (6:40b) by Jesus' nonjudgmental love of the neighbor can the disciple help the neighbor to see with nonjudging eyes.

c. The puzzling verse on the teacher (6:40) is now seen as integral to the argument. Jesus uniquely teaches God's way of unconditional love, of which the beatitudes and the love commandment are explications. Since the Teacher and his message are unique, no disciple can be superior to Jesus, and so must be set straight (κατηρτισμένος) so as to be like that Teacher. When the μαθητής is restored by accepting Jesus' teaching she will not judge, but will see clearly, like her διδάσκαλος.

d. The hypocrite of 6:41-42 enacts the attitude of self-protecting vindictiveness proscribed by 6:27-38a. The one who judges does not recognize as evil his tendency to judge others harshly. Even more: a judgmental attitude is the opposite of God's own generosity to the unworthy and wicked; God has compassion on them and freely grants them what they need. This Christian principle is the true sight Jesus as Teacher would engender in his disciples as sons and daughters of God, to enable them to heal their brothers and sisters.

7. *The Concluding Paraenesis (6:43-49)* reveals that not only 6:39-42, but each image of 6:39-49 develops the decisive importance of learning and doing Jesus' teaching on love of enemies and of not judging others.

a. 6:43-45 begins as an explanation (γάρ) of how one can come to see clearly, but at once shifts from not judging to doing. In 6:43-44 agricultural figures demonstrate that the kind of fruit produced shows whether a tree is good or bad. Then 6:45 draws the application: a person is known to be interiorly good or bad by the kind of acts one does. The nature of the acts (not judging, loving enemies?) is unspecified, and so can be understood as the context (6:39-49) urges: doing as a disciple all that the Teacher commands.

b. 6:46-49: Two similitudes drawn from house construction conclude the Sermon. The rhetorical question in 6:46 reveals that discipleship is what this series of images, and the whole Sermon, have been about. The one who comes to Jesus, hears his words about love of enemies, and practices them is a true disciple whose house is secure against any storm. The one who professes to be a disciple but does not do what Jesus commands is not a disciple and will be utterly destroyed. Against all interpretations of Jesus' commands as rhetoric or hyperbole these similitudes proclaim that these commands can and must be done, for the life of the world.

In sum, the ethic of Jesus' Sermon can be summarized by four imperatives: **Love all** (6:27-28, 29a, 31, 32-34, 35ab); **Give all** (6:29b-30, 34, 35c, 38); **Forgive all** (6:37c, implied in 6:27-28?); **Do not judge** (6:37ab, 39-42).[5]

---

[5] I owe this succinct formulation to Quentin Quesnell.

The Sermon as Counter-Cultural and "Irrational"

1. *Two Essential Qualities of the Sermon* drive these four imperatives of the Sermon:

a. *Maximalization:* In contrast to many ethical systems, Jesus' Sermon does not ask for a golden mean or for something within the reach of the average good person. Rather Jesus asks for the peak of human authenticity: not for limited retaliation, but for no retaliation at all, not for moderate sharing, but for wholehearted and repeated giving. Indeed, the standard of conduct is not human virtue, but the unrestricted compassion of God as Father.

b. *Conversion to the Neighbor:* Just as the large majority of the OT Law Codes' injunctions were regulations of interhuman justice, so Jesus' Sermon does not speak of one's duties to God, but is concerned with the disciples' relations with their neighbors. The welfare of the neighbor, the Other,[6] takes precedence over the disciple's own concerns, and results in loving the enemy, not retaliating against evil, in unlimited giving, unrestricted forgiving. One so converted to the neighbor will, in the short run, enter the poverty, hunger, and weeping of the beatitudes.[7] But in the long run God will deliver and reward this disciple, in this and in the final Reign of God.

Thus the Sermon is bewildering because the qualities Jesus commends and the actions he commands are strikingly counter-cultural for Jewish, Greco-Roman, and modern cultures and are, indeed, beyond human reason.

2. *Countercultural:*

a. *For Jews:* The OT covenant theology of retribution, from Adam to Abraham and to the various forms of Mosaic covenants, as well as in the prophets, promised physical prosperity, happiness, and peace in this life to those who observed God's commands.[8] Consequently those who prospered—the rich and well-fed, the fecund, the happy—were considered the

---

[6] For a philosophy of the supremacy of the Other, see Emmanuel Lévinas, *Totality and Infinity; an Essay on Exteriority* (Pittsburgh: Duquesne University Press, 1969); idem, *Ethics and Infinity* (Pittsburgh: Duquesne University Press, 1985); for a psychological appropriation of this work see George Kunz, *The Paradox of Power and Weakness: Lévinas and an Alternative Paradigm for Psychology* (Albany: S.U.N.Y. Press, 1998).

[7] If the disciple gives to all who ask (6:30) she will soon be poor and hungry; if she offers her tunic to the one who has taken her coat (6:29) she will be naked; and if she persists in calling this the authentic human ethic she will be ostracized and persecuted (6:22).

[8] Even those books that work the reversal of this theology—Job, Qoheleth, Wisdom—witness to its prevalence and power in their culture. In rabbinic Judaism this view is normative.

good.[9] That the poor were the good was always a marginal view. But Jesus pronounces prophetic woes against the rich, the well-fed, the mirthful, and counts blessed the poor, hungry, and sorrowing.

Even if there is no command to hate the enemy, the Law and Jewish culture strongly sanctioned retaliation against an offender.[10] But Jesus forbids retaliation in kind, and recommends benevolent action toward the offender.

The Law articulated the offenses the community was to avoid, correct, and punish. Indeed, there was a high priority given to paternal and fraternal correction of the faults of others.[11] But Jesus eschews judgment and asks his disciples to do the same. All of this is the more counter-cultural since first-century Mediterranean culture was an agonistic honor/shame society in which one lost not only honor but position in society by not responding to the challenge of another's offense. To lose one's reputation (6:22) and worse, to be ostracized from family, tribe, or town, were much more intolerable in a culture with dyadic personality than they are to us.

b. *Greece* and late republican *Rome* had no restrictions on the accumulation of wealth, and so throughout the empire there was a huge gap between the rich and the poor.[12] Although in Greco-Roman thought wealth and a happy life were a gift of the gods,[13] wealth was not a divinely-sanctioned proof of virtue. Greek and Roman thought are ambivalent about wealth and poverty.[14] Poverty was a badge of virtue only if it was the result of supporting one's kin or of generosity to the community. In sum, the

---

[9] The synoptic tradition witnesses to its prevalence in the disciples' astonishment at Jesus' statement that the rich cannot get into the Reign of God (Mark 10:23-26//Matt 19:23-25//Luke 18:24-26).

[10] "The very ancient custom of blood-vengeance, carried out by the *gô'ēl,* never disappeared and was recognized by law," Roland de Vaux, *Ancient Israel: Its Life and Institutions* (New York: McGraw-Hill, 1961) 160. The case-laws of the various Hebrew law codes realize the principle of vindicative justice.

[11] Deuteronomy 19:15; Lev 19:17; among the Covenanters 1 QS 5:24–6:2; among the rabbis Billerbeck 1:787–93.

[12] Earlier Greek public policies that limited accumulation by requiring or expecting the rich to use some of their wealth for public benefit, especially in the Athenian "liturgies," and the later notion of "benefaction," had either disappeared or lost their effeciveness; John Kenyon Davies, "Wealth, attitudes to," in Simon Hornblower and Antony Spawforth, eds., *The Oxford Classical Dictionary* (3rd ed. Oxford: Oxford University Press, 1996) 1620.

[13] This is true from Homer, *Odyssey* 24.527 on; for the Hellenistic view see Kenneth J. Dover, *Greek Popular Morality in the Time of Plato and Aristotle* (Berkeley: University of California Press, 1974) 174.

[14] Although Aristotle saw a comfortable independence as essential to the virtuous life and enabling a generous magnanimity (*Nicomachean Ethics* IV, 1120-1121), in the popular mind wealth led to *hybris,* greed, and softness (Dover, *Popular Morality* 110–11; Davies, "Wealth," 1620). Those who acquired wealth were not admired for their entrepreneurship,

poor in Greece and Rome do not, as they do in Judaism, have an identity ("good," "bad") or a face that evokes compassion or almsgiving. No one but the Cynics considered poverty or hunger a blessing, and wailing or mourning was certainly not associated with tranquillity, still less happiness. Hence Jesus' beatitudes and woes would have evoked in Luke's Gentile reader as much incredulity as they did in his Jewish reader.

In social and economic exchange, balanced reciprocity was the rule of the day.[15] Even when exchange was unequal, as in client-patron relations, there was a *quid pro quo* observed in all transactions. Jesus' command to give without asking or even hoping for return (6:30, 35a), independent of any history of benefactions (6:32-34), would have struck Gentiles as absurd.

Balanced reciprocity led the Greeks and Romans to return good for good and evil for evil; returning good for evil may have been a Platonic ideal, but it does not occur in popular literature.[16] Nonretaliation was as unacceptable in their honor/shame Mediterranean culture as it was to the Jews.[17] Hence the Sermon countered the "givens" of Greco-Roman culture.

c. *Contemporary American Culture.*[18] In the land of unlimited possibilities, where meritocracy has replaced ascribed honor and is measured

---

and new wealth was usually considered dishonestly acquired (in comedy the dishonest become rich, the poor remain poor; Dover, *Popular Morality* 172–73). Poverty could be the result of sloth or of divine displeasure, or it could be an inducement to crime; in such cases the poor man would not be treated compassionately (ibid. 109–110, 239). Still, poverty and wealth were often a matter of luck, and the possibility of reversal of fate made people less judgmental of the poor; reproaching the (honest) poor was wrong; ibid. 174, 240, 269–70.

[15] This is true from the time of Homer; Gilbert Highet, "Reciprocity," *OCD* 1295.

[16] Dover, *Popular Morality* 180–89, 192. Indeed, in hostile encounters over-retaliation (Dover's "head for an eye" principle) was the norm.

[17] In addition to the witness of Cratylus in Plato's *Gorgias* (see p. 149), cf. Dover, *Popular Morality* 184.

[18] I take the culture of the United States as exemplary of modern cultures because it seems to be, through the interlocked mechanism of the market, communicative diffusion, and technological development, one toward which the world's developing economies are moving. The following over-generalized argument is partially indebted to Alexis de Tocqueville, *Democracy in America* (New York: Doubleday, 1969); David Riesman, *The Lonely Crowd* (New Haven: Yale University Press, 1950); Robert Bellah et al., *Habits of the Heart* (Berkeley: University of California Press, 1985); Robin M. Williams, *American Society: A Sociological Interpretation* (3rd ed. New York: Knopf, 1970), especially 438–504; Richard L. Means, *The Ethical Imperative: The Crisis in American Values* (New York: Doubleday, 1969); Rodger van Allen, ed., *American Religious Values and the Future of America* (Philadelphia: Fortress, 1978), especially 5–23; Gerald F. Cavanagh, *American Business Values* (2nd ed. Englewood Cliffs, N.J.: Prentice-Hall, 1984); Robert Wuthnow, *God and Mammon in America* (New York: Free Press, 1994); Henry J. Aaron et al., eds., *Values and Public Policy* (Washington, D.C.: Brookings Institution, 1994).

by wealth, the poor and hungry mostly are deemed lazy and responsible for their state. Further, as a lingering result of Puritan emphasis on prosperity as a sign of God's election, they are likely to be thought of as bad. To name them happy or blessed by God contradicts the American cult of prosperity. Further, American culture seeks to eliminate suffering, illness, and death, and so weeping is a sign of failure. Nor is it polite to show one's grief, lest others be saddened by it, for after all, in a truly individualist society there is no reason why others should grieve with one. However, in an individualist society where social bonds are frayed by social and physical mobility being persecuted or reviled is not as great an injury as it would be in a society of dyadic persons and familial and civic bonds. Still, the fact that so few politicians are willing to contravene the self-seeking of their constituencies indicates that Americans, too, find unacceptable Jesus' calling blessed the persecuted and unpopular.

No less than the Mediterranean, American justice is based on balanced reciprocity, and so Jesus' advocacy of general reciprocity jars us. Further, some of the rhetoric surrounding capital punishment and other sanctions for crime, and policies like "Mutually Assured Destruction" indicate that retaliation for injury is as much a part of American culture as it was of a first-century one. Jesus' turning the other cheek seems to invite more violence and so is baffling to people who from childhood have been warned to look out for "Number One."

3. *Beyond Human Reason:* This persistent opposition between Jesus' commands and human cultures invites us to inquire whether it is "unnatural" to human culture. There are at least four lines of confirmation of this hypothesis:

a. *The Christian Tradition:* In elaborating Paul's analysis of Genesis 2–3 and the history of human sinfulness (Genesis 3–11; Rom 1:18–5:14) as Original Sin, Augustine found a universal human rebellion against God's plan of harmonious community between God, humans, animals, and cosmos. Humans define the good as what is pleasing to them or exalting to their egos, without reference to God or others, and this they define as "rational." This rebellion against God's plan is both inherited from previous generations and ratified in the lifetime of each human, and so is pandemic in human culture. Recent theologians[19] have located this rebellion in the customs and institutions of society, so that humans reject Jesus'

---

[19] Recent theological understandings of this inherited sin as both individual and (anti-) social are Piet Schoonenburg, *Man and Sin* (Notre Dame: University of Notre Dame Press, 1965); Henri Rondet, *Original Sin: The Patristic and Theological Background.* Translated by

articulation of God's will as contrary to the received wisdom of the culture and so "unreasonable."

b. *Social Science* investigates the intrinsic human mechanisms that produce in Western cultures this egocentrism leading to anxiety and violence:[20]

(1) Sigmund Freud's mechanistic theory of psychoanalysis locates anxiety in the compromises that the child's dominant pleasure principle has to make with reality as it is presented by parental and societal powers (whose values are in turn sedimentations of their own pleasure principles). Still, this narcissistic drive for one's own pleasure remains the dominant human motive throughout life.[21] This egocentrism in adult human relations leads to preemption of others' desires and neutralization of their opposing narcissistic drives through calculation and trade at best, manipulation and domination at worst; in national governments it leads only to laws that protect the citizens' individual rights; in international relations it prohibits the development of a world community, which would require surrender or mitigation of national sovereignty, and so the best it achieves is protection through nonaggression pacts and armed peace.[22]

In spite of various attempts to broaden perspective, western psychology after Freud has mostly remained an egology,[23] and so defines any al-

---

Gajeten Finegan (Staten Island, New York: Alba House, 1972); George Vandervelde, *Original Sin: Two Major Trends in Contemporary Roman Catholic Reinterpretation* (Amsterdam: Rodopi, 1975); Karl Rahner, *Foundations of Christian Faith* (New York: Seabury, 1978) 106–116; Marjorie Hewitt Suchocki, *The Fall to Violence* (New York: Continuum, 1994).

[20] Tribal societies have an altogether different relationship of society and the (submerged) individual, but our concern is with Western Christians' inability to hear Jesus' message.

[21] For the most extended discussion in Freud himself see James Strachey, et al., eds., *The Standard Edition of the Complete Psychological Works of Sigmund Freud* (London: Hogarth, 1963). Vol. 16, *Introductory Lectures on Psychoanalysis, Part III;* Vol. 18, *Beyond the Pleasure Principle;* also Paul Ricoeur, *Freud and Philosophy: An Essay on Interpretation* (New Haven: Yale University Press, 1970).

[22] Sigmund Freud, *Civilization and its Discontents.* Translated by Joan Riviere (London: Hogarth, 1939); Jean-Claude Sagne, *Conflit, changement, conversion. Vers une éthique de la réciprocité.* Cogitatio Fidei 78 (Paris: Cerf-Desclée,1974). This narcissism is obvious in Western liberal democracies influenced by Hobbes's natural state of war and Locke's individualism. See Roger Burggraeve, *From Self-Development to Solidarity: An Ethical Reading of Human Desire in its Socio-Political Relevance According to Emmanuel Lévinas* (Leuven: Peeters, 1985) 19–61 for Lévinas's description and critique of such an "ethical system."

[23] This is Lévinas's term. Even Carl G. Jung's valiant use of Eastern symbols to broaden the notion of the Self remained at root egocentric. For an attempt to move beyond egology to an altruistic psychology see Kunz, *The Paradox of Power and Weakness.*

truism as masochistic self-seeking. Reciprocity in this fragile system of egocentric rights and duties is merely self-maintenance and self-promotion. Such narcissism must immediately object to *everything* in Jesus' Sermon.

(2) Ernest Becker's *The Denial of Death* is a cultural anthropologist's broader description of the human problem. Human nature is paradoxical, made up of a symbolizing mind that speculates about atoms and infinity and a corrupting body that is food for worms. We are haunted by a repressed fear of death that drives activity designed to disprove that death is our final destiny. We seek by success, money, and power to overcome our animal nature and make ourselves more than other animals. We create a symbol system of beliefs, values, and goals that give us independent existence and self-worth. Chief among these is heroism.

Human heroics based on the delusion that we have absolute control, the conviction that we shape our own lives, consumes people. All humanly-caused evil is based on attempts to deny creatureliness, overcome insignificance, sustain our self-esteem in egoistic cultural dramas. The problem of yielding our individualistic self-assertion, of rooting ourselves in a secure self-transcending framework has become difficult for moderns because the beliefs and values of western technological society are increasingly based on the *causa sui* project.

The answer to the anxiety of (non-)existence lies in giving up the Oedipal project of heroic self-assertion. The self must be destroyed before any true self-transcendence can begin. Kierkegaard pointed out that nakedly faced and lived anxiety leads to the possibility of freedom because it demolishes all finite aims and leads to yielding to the love and service of the transcendent God.

Becker's humans must reject Jesus' Sermon. Lack of food is a threat to life, and, where money buys food, poverty is always to be avoided. In a culture where increasingly expensive surgical intervention can forestall death from previously lethal sickness like neoplastic anemia, any resources shared with the poor and hungry may well deprive one of the means necessary to save one's life. Lament for the dying is banished since it witnesses to the reality of death that psyche and culture have repressed. And so Jesus' command to unfailing generosity to those in need is taken as a threat. Conversely, Christian disciples who proclaim these beatitudes threaten the whole modern belief structure, and so must be isolated and shunned. The *causa sui* project caps human desires, and so perverts Jesus' Golden Rule into the measured reciprocity he counts as the conduct of the sinner. Ironically, Jesus' eschatological promise of the Reign of God and of being a scion of the everlasting God by accepting death in this life,[24] precisely that to which Becker points, is what moderns reject.

c. Although Becker found psychologists and psychiatrists pointing to this need for self-transcendence,[25] he believed that in an adequate and comprehensive science of the human, *psychology* must dialogue with *theology.*[26]

One theologian who enters this dialogue is Bernard Lonergan, who begins with humans concretely described by the empirical human sciences, and so with human egoism.[27] As creatures we are naturally egoistic, needing to acquire the food, protective security, and (ultimately) the leisure in which our spirits can flourish. But equally natural, from our earliest days, no matter how furiously we assert our omnipotence and control, is our experience of receiving what we need from others, and so of needing them, as well as our experience of a spontaneous intersubjective affectivity that binds us to others and drives us to help them.[28] We are social animals, and become most truly ourselves in communion with others.

These two primary drives are in tension, and egoism enjoys an immediate priority. But the interference of this egoism with the development of intelligence, particularly in its concern for intersubjectivity, leads to bias. When the pleasure principle remains dominant, but is hidden by the work of the censor or other mechanisms of repression, we suffer unconsciously from *neurotic bias.* When egoism drives a more conscious choice of my own immediate satisfaction over what is more ultimately good for me and for my fellow human beings, I suffer *individual(istic) bias* ("Look out for number One"). When this self-seeking is shared by family, social class, nation, we get *group biases* such as racism, classism, sexism, and "natiosis." These prove the more resistant to recognition and change as

---

[24] Jesus had already solved the anxious clinging to life that Becker's modern human exhibits: "whoever wishes to save his life will lose it, and whoever loses his life for my sake will save it" (Luke 9:24; 12:13-34).

[25] Otto Rank, *Beyond Psychology* (New York: Dover, 1958); Robert Jay Lifton, *Revolutionary Immortality* (London: Heidenfeld & Nicholson, 1969); idem, *The Protean Self* (New York: Basic Books, 1993).

[26] Ernest Becker, *The Denial of Death* (New York: Free Press, 1973) 281–85.

[27] His philosophical book *Insight; A Study of Human Understanding* begins by dialogue with mathematics, physics, and psychology. The start of his inquiry was the longer cycles of social decline as the manifestation of the problem of evil, and he concluded his career with an economic analysis of them. His disciples have further developed his insights and method, especially, for our purposes, Patrick Kerans, *Sinful Social Structures* (New York: Paulist, 1974 and, at a more technical level, Robert M. Doran, *Theology and the Dialectics of History* (Toronto: University of Toronto Press, 1992).

[28] One and the same child both collects as much as he can under the rubric, "It's mine!" and cries with compassion when his playmate is hurt.

they become the commonly shared wisdom of the dominant group. Ultimately, these biases are secured by *general bias,* the conviction that the common sense of our ancestors or of the dominant group is all the wisdom needed to cope with complex situations. But since common sense focuses on particular short-term solutions, exclusive recourse to it as the solution to societal problems necessarily excludes the drive of intelligence for deeper questions about the decline that only explanatory frameworks at the service of the common good can answer.[29] Thus arises in individuals, groups, and humanity as a whole a universally shared sin, the seeking of short-term individual gains instead of long-term social goals. This way of defining sin does not deny legitimate goals of the ego, but rather makes clear that seeking individualistic pleasure to the exclusion of the larger values of our shared common good is destructive for the individual.[30]

Thus arise and perdure concrete sinful social structures, in which humans feel compelled not only to compete for scarce resources but to accumulate them to protect themselves against the fragility of life, even if such hoarding means that the earth is exploited and others must hunger and even starve.[31] This aggressive world provokes in us a defensive reaction in which we must provide for ourselves, and so our egoism overrides our spontaneous intersubjectivity and reinforces in these social structures individualism and the rationalization of it that generally reinforce the longer cycle of social decline.

If this, then, is the human situation, Jesus' Sermon will always be spontaneously rejected, for his message of conversion to the neighbor challenges the primacy we spontaneously give to our most immediate individual needs. His blessing of the poor and hungry challenges our fear

[29] For two explanations of the dynamics of bias see the chapters by Vernon Gregson and Matthew Lamb in Vernon Gregson, ed., *The Desires of the Human Heart; An Introduction to the Theology of Bernard Lonergan* (New York: Paulist, 1988) 29–34, 270–79.

[30] Under my analysis lies Aristotle's and Aquinas's notion of the common good as the full perfection of the person. For two different analyses of that tradition see Jacques Maritain, *The Person and the Common Good* (New York: Scribner, 1947) and Charles De Koninck, *De la Primauté du Bien Commun* (Quebec: Université Laval, 1943). In modern thought the concept is so shriveled through disuse that for many authors it is a cipher unable to be defined or grounded. Only the Thomist concept of the common good seems capable of responding to a postmodern critique; contemporary restatements of that concept appear in M. Shawn Copeland, "Reconsidering the Idea of the Common Good," in Oliver F. Williams and John W. Houck, eds., *Catholic Social Thought and the New World Order* (Notre Dame, Ind.: University of Notre Dame Press, 1993), 309–27; Stephen J. Pope, "Knowability of the Natural Law: A Foundation for Ethics of the Common Good," in James Donahue and Mary Theresa Moser, eds., *Religion, Ethics, and the Common Good.* CTS 41 (Mystic, Conn.: Twenty-Third Publications, 1996) 53–63.

[31] Unequal distribution of goods occurs not only in societies where the accumulation of capital is unrestrained, but even in the purest communist societies.

that in an acquisitive society we will not have enough in the future. His demand that we give all to the beggar asks us to reach beyond our class to intersubjective concern for those whom society has designated as lazy or unworthy, and shakes the foundations of our group bias. His demand that we not retaliate for evil asks us to go beyond our common sense bias that balanced reciprocity is the only way a society can be maintained. His rule of attending to others' desires through the medium of our own asks us to elevate our spontaneous human intersubjectivity to a more comprehensive position than our pleasure-seeking egoism, and raises speculative questions about how a truly human sociopolitical and economic order might operate more adequately.

d. Now Luke himself seems to have recognized this "beyondedness" in the way in which he contrasts the Baptist's more "reasonable" ethic with that of Jesus:

John (Luke 3:10-13)	*Jesus (Luke 6:20-49)*
He who has two coats, let him share with him who has none (3:11)	Give to the one stealing your coat your shirt as well (6:29-30)
Collect no more than is your due (3:13)	Do not ask a return of your loan; [make it into pure gift] (6:34-35)
Rob no one by violence (3:14)	Offer the other cheek to the person striking you (6:29)

While John's demands are reasonable applications of the OT ethics of sharing and justice, Jesus, in each comparable content, makes demands on his disciples that go beyond the bounds of reason, that even violate our sense of justice.[32]

The Sermon itself bears witness, in the woes (6:24-26), the misinterpretation of the Golden Rule (6:32-34), the references to the blindness of disciples (6:39-42) and to false disciples who produce bad fruit (6:43-45) and so are utterly destroyed (6:49), that Jesus' disciples did not understand or practice his teaching in the Sermon.

Nevertheless, Jesus concluded his Sermon with an ultimatum: "Do this or die." How can he be so adamant about so radical an ethic, which the natural human mind misunderstands, and from which the merely human heart of even his would-be disciples recoils?

---

[32] While it is true that John's ethic will, over time, impoverish the one who shares with each successive coatless person, the initial command seems reasonable and possible. Jesus' ethic attacks the "reasonableness" of human egoism from the outset, in the first encounter.

Interpretations of the Sermon

Interpretations range from those that assert the literal validity of its every phrase through those that reduce it to a more "reasonable" application to those who find it unreasonable, and so unsuitable as the basis of a realistic Christian ethic.[33] Harvey K. McArthur synthesized twelve different types of interpretation of the Sermon, but here it will be enough to deal with three generic understandings of it[34] as

1. *Law,*[35] expressing literally the unconditional will of God, which the Christian is bound to fulfill.[36] This interpretation takes seriously the imperative form of Jesus' commands and reflects the absoluteness of Jesus' final exhortation that his disciples must do these commands. But the radical content of Jesus' demands undermines this interpretation. For law is an ordinance of reason setting out the *minimal* observances necessary to promote the common good of a society, but Jesus' demands call for the *maximum* in human conduct. Luke's Sermon does not merely forbid the most egregious acts of revenge, but prohibits *all* retaliation. Further, Jesus prohibits judgments about others that are not actionable at law. In short, it does not make sense to call *law* "Give your coat to the one suing you for your shirt."

2. *Unrealizable Ideal,* whose high standards awaken disciples to their sinfulness and so to their need for repentance and God's mercy. This position accepts the maximal nature of the commands, the standards of conduct that faith-filled Christians should measure themselves against. But our fallen human nature always falls short of these demands, and so comes to a profound awareness of its own sinfulness. Hence Pharisaism is overcome because we *cannot* observe the law and so must cry out to God, who justifies us because of our faith in Christ.[37] But this interpretation is un-

---

[33] See n. 1 above.

[34] Like the ones selected by Joachim Jeremias, *The Sermon on the Mount* (Philadelphia: Fortress, 1963).

[35] McArthur calls this the Absolutist interpretation. Matthew's version, with its location on the mountain and Jesus' sitting to teach, the legal form of the antitheses, and taking the Golden Rule as a statement of the Law and prophets are features that emphasize the Sermon's legal character more than Luke's.

[36] Very few (e.g., Leo Tolstoy) interpret Jesus' every phrase absolutely; most adapt their applications of Jesus' commands by masking some of them as hyperbole or merely illustrations. The best scholarly exposition of this interpretation is by Hans Windisch, *The Meaning of the Sermon on the Mount* (Philadelphia: Westminster, 1951 [1929]).

[37] This is the classical Lutheran (not Luther's!) position, deriving from Paul's justification by faith, most recently expressed by Carl Stange, "Zur Ethik der Bergpredigt," *ZST* 2 (1924–25) 37–74, and Gerhard Kittel, "Die Bergpredigt und die Ethik des Judentums," *ZST* 2 (1924–25) 555–94. McArthur calls this the Repentance interpretation.

dermined by the Lord's demands that we do this law, and the warning that if we do not we will be destroyed (6:46-49).

3. *Gospel of the Realizable Ideal.* Jesus' sayings portray the lived faith of the Christian disciples, who are forgiven children of God, members of the Reign of God. Out of the thankfulness of a redeemed child of God a new life grows, which issues in the exigent ethics of the Sermon.[38] The Gospel as "ideal" accepts the radical nature of Jesus' commands, and as "realizable" expects them to be done by more than human agency. An expanded view of this third kind of interpretation seems likeliest to reveal the ethic underlining the precepts and figures of the Sermon.

But how do biblical theologians explain how these divine ideals become realizable for very human Christian disciples? Most exegetes speak of Jesus' (or Paul's) imperatives as flowing from the Christian indicative: that the redemption God has accomplished in Jesus and given to the faith of the believer enables her to do the works of Jesus "and greater works than these" (John 14:12). But these exegetes hardly develop how that indicative works in the Christian.

Hermeneutics for New Testament Ethics

There are grounds for thinking that Luke had some awareness of how salvation worked in his readers. Every author has some world-view, a kind of preconscious ontology that makes the various elements of his work hang together and provides the framework for interpreting any part of that work.[39] Especially when passages are difficult to understand, the interpreter is forced to look for the author's underlying world-view, in which otherwise unintelligible statements might make sense.[40] This world-view, even if expressed in narrative and symbolic language, always implies an

---

[38] This is the formulation of Jeremias, *Sermon* 34–35. It is closest to, but something more than, McArthur's Unconditioned Divine Will interpretation. But Jeremias' theological fear of "works" keeps him from taking these commands as a "Christian ethic;" rather, he speaks of "lived faith." Nowhere does he say that Jesus' commands can be observed in their entirety, though his argument should lead to saying so.

[39] For the existence of such a world-view in literary authors see Richard E. Palmer, *Hermeneutics: Interpretation Theory in Schleiermacher, Dilthey, Heidegger, and Gadamer* (Evanston, Ill.: Northwestern University Press, 1969) 30–31.

[40] A clear synthesis of the theories of historiographers and philosophers on interpretation theory can be found in Peter Chirico, *Infallibility: The Crossroads of Doctrine* (Kansas City, Kan.: Sheed, Andrews, and McMeel, 1977) 3–29. For the necessity of the interpreter's seeking the author's world-view underlying his surface expression see my articulation of Chirico's hermeneutical theory in Robert J. Daly, ed., *Christian Biblical Ethics: From Biblical Revelation to Contemporary Christian Praxis: Method and Content* (New York: Paulist, 1984) 49–52.

existential structure of reality. Thus if we are grounding Luke's ethics we must identify his anthropology (the indicative) that enables his ethics (the imperative).

But this implicit anthropology is rarely theoretically or systematically expressed, and never in literature. New Testament writers use images, similes, metaphors, and symbols to point to these deeper views of God and humans. Thus three different NT authors use images to convey their sense of how the Christian has been transformed in Christ so as to be able to live a new ethic:[41]

1. In *John 15:1-11* abiding (μένειν) in Jesus, as the branch vitally exists in and from the vine, causes the disciple to bear much fruit (and sets the context and possibility for the love commandment in 15:12).

2. In *2 Cor 5:17* anyone in Christ is a new creature (καινὴ κτίσις), reconciled to God. This union ἐν Χριστῷ has ethical consequences in 5:21, "so that in him we might become the righteousness of God."[42]

3. In *Eph 4:22-24* Christians are to put off the old man with its deceitful lusts and put on the new person (τὸν καινὸν ἄνθρωπον) with its true righteousness.

These authors used literary figures (vine and branches, Body of Christ, new creature, new person) to describe a personal bond with Christ (remain, in Christ) so real as to constitute a new being (new creature, new humanity) who is to effect a radically new Christian action. Thus these authors root their description of appropriate Christian action in their artistic preconscious sense of the Christian's transformed personal identity, and express this preconscious sense through symbols and figures of speech. When such a personal bond seems to be followed by ethical conduct quite unattainable by normal human striving we are obliged to probe deeper into the nature of that bond, asking what existential changes might ground such new action.

4. Luke also argues in this vein. As we will see, Luke's Sermon contains five tropes that point to the radicalness of the Sermon's ethics. Of these, the good tree bringing forth good fruit, together with its surrounding

---

[41] For an earlier and fuller formulation of what follows see my discussion in *Christian Biblical Ethics* 51–54.

[42] In 5:19 God is ἐν Χριστῷ, just as ἐν Χριστῷ was used in 5:17. Paul actually has two other striking images of transformed Christian existence in 1 Cor 12:12-27 (cf. Rom 12:4-8), where Christians are members of the Body of Christ, and in Rom 8:12-17, where the Spirit makes Christians adopted children of God, able to address God as Jesus, Son of God, did, "*Abba.*" For the ethical implications of these images of transformation see *Christian Biblical Ethics* 52–53.

images (6:43-45), is a clear literary way of saying one's way of being determines one's kind of action. If one's conduct manifests the otherworldly goodness of not judging and love of enemies there must be some special kind of goodness intrinsic to the Christian that produces such fruit.

Indeed, exegetes and theologians have already presumed precisely this move by their formula, "the Christian imperative flows from the Christian indicative:" what Christ has done for us affects the way Christians now live and act. This expression leaves vague the kind of causality Christ's life has on the Christian's.[43] Early Christian theologians sometimes specified that causality by reference to a divine elevation of the Christian's being: in faith and baptism the Christian is incorporated into Christ in such a way as to be "divinized,"[44] and so interiorly empowered to live a new, divine mode of life.[45] But this new mode of existence, responding to the radical new demands of Christ in the beatitudes, imperatives, and paraenesis of the Sermon on the Plain, is not explained in the New Testament in the theoretical terms of philosophy (nature, essence, substance, act).

What we must seek, then, to make sense out of the radical demands of the Sermon, is the pre-theoretical anthropology that underlies Luke's description of the Christian's new mode of acting. Luke could have expressed this world-view in a biblical anthropology that would speak of the organs or interior activities from which Christian action flows, or of external agents that move Christians (spirits, demons), or of a dynamic new personal relationship that drives new modes of acting. We will now take up in order each of these possibilities.

[43] I have surveyed the range of positions in "The Lukan Version of the Lord's Sermon," *BTB* 11 (1981) 50–51. Briefly, they range from the more extrinsic and generic to the more instrinsic and structural. Those who fear to admit a transformation that Christians might then claim as their own speak of "the spirit of love," "faith," "openness to the Kingdom communication." Others who wish to intimate some God-given power that enables radical ethical action speak of "the reception of salvation." Walter Grundmann finds in the transformation of the whole human personality ("in their emotions, love replaces hate; in their words, blessing replaces curses; in their deeds, prayer replaces mistreatment") a demonstration that Christian love is a *Dasein für den anderen vor Gott.* Finally, those who are more willing to speak of an interior change in the Christian develop the Christian's presently being a Child of God. Béda Rigaux speaks of this filiation being effected by the Father's gift of grace.

[44] The words of the Greek Fathers Clement of Alexandria (*Paed.* 1.6; 3.1), Origen (*C. Cels.* 5.23), Cyril of Alexandria (*In Hos.* 4), and the Latin Augustine (*Ennarr. in Ps.,* Ps 49:2). Often their analysis begins from or implies the "participators of the divine nature" (θείας κοινωνοὶ φύσεως) of 2 Pet 1:4.

[45] This expression implies an underlying ontological world-view that later Catholic theologians correctly understood by the philosophical principle *agere sequitur esse,* "action flows from one's mode of being." This principle explains Christ's influence on Christian life by a (quasi-)formal causality.

Luke's Description of Christian Empowerment

1. *Human Structures of Knowing and Acting:* Our search for the intrinsic components of human behavior could begin from the text of Luke's Sermon itself: "The good person out of the good treasure of the heart produces good . . . for the mouth speaks out of the abundance of the heart" (6:45ac). In the context of agricultural figures that illustrate the principle that the quality and kind of fruit produced depends on the nature of the tree Jesus says that the quality of one's conduct depends on the quality of one's heart. Thus Luke's text itself asks us to look for the aspects of human personality that determine the quality of one's conduct.

a. But the quest for the faculties that initiate human action turns out to be fruitless, for Luke shares the synoptic lack of interest in developing such an anthropology. Luke uses sparingly the general NT vocabulary for the faculties of human life and action—flesh, guts, body, heart, mind, will, soul, spirit—and, in contrast to Paul's distinct uses of σάρξ, ψυχή, and πνεῦμα, he does not distinguish these faculties from one another, nor does he articulate how they ground or issue in human thought and action (see Appendix G).

Further, there is no indication in Luke-Acts that any of these faculties or human powers are changed by faith, baptism, or the arrival of the Reign of God, so as to be the vehicles of new Christian conduct. We do not read in Luke-Acts of a new creation, new life, a changed soul, or even a converted heart. In fact, characters like Elizabeth and Zechariah are righteous and observe the Law without further ado (1:5-6); the Baptist's preaching intends to evoke a willing response in good works without any reference to the baptism he preaches (3:3-14), and even Jesus' radical calls to discipleship (9:57-62; 14:25-33; 16:16-18) do not presuppose special empowerment.[46]

b. Nevertheless, the whole gospel is suffused by an atmosphere of *faith:* Elizabeth and Zechariah live in God's world—the Temple, sacrifices, visions, and prophecies—and so under divine influence.[47] The Baptist's work grows out of the prophetic word received according to divine predestination from the womb (3:2-6, corresponding to 1:17). Faith in God's faithful love and compassionate action everywhere drives the actions of the gospel's heroes.

---

[46] This "natural" tone is set by the preface, which describes Luke's process of writing according to the canons and language of historiography of his day, without any reference to visions or any mediated influence of the Holy Spirit.

[47] Zechariah says that God gives the ability to worship in holiness and righteousness (1:73).

Luke uses the noun πίστις more than other evangelists. In Luke-Acts it almost always means faith in, and commitment to, God's saving plan and power in Jesus.[48] Seven of Luke's eleven uses describe faith in Jesus' eschatological power to heal physically (5:20; 7:9; 8:25, 48; 17:19; 18:42) and spiritually (7:50). As with the disciples' reception of the Holy Spirit, the disciples' faith enables them to act with Jesus' power. In Acts 3:16 and 14:9 faith in Jesus enables Peter and Paul to heal cripples. In Acts 6:5; 11:24; 15:9 faith enables the Spirit, working through the individual disciple's faith, to move the community in new directions (in all three cases, toward the Gentiles).[49] Finally, faith in Jesus implies both a consecration that leads to an eternal inheritance (Acts 26:18) and an ethical life to be lived (which frightens Felix off in 24:24). These ecclesial and ethical dimensions of faith connect with what Luke says of the disciple's faith in the gospel. The disciples ask for the increase of faith that will empower them for Jesus' kind of radical and total forgiveness, symbolized by forgiving a brother seven times in one day (7:5). Such faith could enable a disciple to plant trees in the sea (17:6), a power over nature found in Jesus in 8:24-25. It is faith that enables the disciples to persevere in prayer (18:8) and Peter to persist through his sinful cowardice to strengthen his brothers (22:32).

Thus faith in Jesus implies an empowering of disciples to act like Jesus, not only in healing but in radical (and irrational) forgiveness and a radical life of goodness that frightens the world—in short, to the ethical life of the Sermon. Underlying all of these uses of πίστις (and the verb πιστεύειν) is the element of personal trust in Jesus (or in God working in and raising Jesus), which leads to personal conversion, commitment, fidelity.[50] In short, one is talking of transformed personal relationships by which the believer identifies with Jesus' aims and destiny, and indeed his very person, and so lives as he lived. Can we further specify the nature of this personal relationship of the Christian believer to Christ?

---

[48] In Acts' fifteen uses of πίστις only 17:31 does not refer to Christian faith but to the confirmation of that faith through the resurrection. Curiously, only at the beginning (3:16) and end (20:21; 24:24; 26:18) is faith explicitly described as faith in Jesus. But it is clear throughout that the object of faith is God's saving plan in Jesus.

[49] The most common use of "*the* faith" in Acts makes it an identifier of the Christian community, which faith constitutes (6:7; 13:8; 14:22, 27; 16:5).

[50] Rudolf Bultmann, "πιστεύω," *TDNT* 6:199–215; Dieter Lührmann, "Faith," *ABD* 2:752–55, and the bibliography cited there.

2. External Spiritual Agents Affecting Human Actions

a. *Oracular Spirits and Demons:*[51] In Acts 16:16 an oracular spirit, not described as good or bad, prophesies in a young slave girl. Thirteen times in Luke-Acts unclean spirits or demons inhabit persons so as to act in their bodies. They use the person's voice (Luke 4:31-37, 41; 8:28; 9:39) or make him mute (11:14), or even cripple a woman (13:11). Such demons can bring a man to all kinds of feral behavior (8:27, 29). They cause a man to leap on the sons of Scaeva and subdue them (Acts 19:16). Such diabolical possessions do not cause humans to sin, but they are not outside of moral categories either, as the strange repossession of Luke 11:24-26 intimates. Satan himself, however, can tempt humans from outside (4:1-13; 22:31), take God's word from their hearts (8:12), and enter human hearts to lead them to sin (22:3; Acts 5:3). So, in Luke's world-view, human actions can be influenced by the spirit world.

b. *God's Word and the Holy Spirit:* Positively, God inspires and moves humans to act in salutary ways that are moral acts of the human person. The word of God comes to the Baptist (Luke 3:2) as an agent in his prophetic ministry that is not only salvific for those addressed and baptized (3:7, 18; 7:29-30; Acts 19:1-4) but also for John himself (Luke 7:26-28). But in Luke-Acts God chiefly moves humans to good through the Holy Spirit,[52] and that in

3. A New Relationship to God Constituted by the Reign of God

a. *The Reign of God:* In Chapter 3 we saw that Jesus' proclamation and enactment of the Reign of God was the synoptic gospels' summary of his ministry and the meaning of his life. Our question here is how this Reign becomes effective in human life and history.

In Luke-Acts the Reign of God refers primarily to the healing presence of Jesus as the eschatological *Heilsprophet* anointed in the Spirit to proclaim and effect the Jubilee year of release for the poor and oppressed (4:16-22). This proclamation and its real and symbolic enactment by overcoming Satan's temptations (4:1-13) and human bondage to Satan's reign (4:6, 31-41) is clearly what Jesus means by proclaiming God's reign also to the other towns (4:43). Jesus' ministry of healing and exorcising is the

---

[51] Here we exclude angels, who work as messengers and so are agents external to the human person addressed.

[52] The Baptist was filled with the Holy Spirit from his mother's womb (1:15) as a constant principle of growth (1:80) to fulfill Elijah's spiritual role (1:17) and to point to Jesus while still in the womb (1:41). Others whom the Spirit leads to prophesy in Luke 1–2 are Elizabeth (1:41-43), Zechariah (1:67), and Simeon (2:25-26).

Reign of God already present (11:20; 16:16; 17:21) and a sign that he is the Messiah (7:19-23 in light of 3:15-16; Acts 10:36-38).

Proclamations of the imminence of the Reign of God (9:27; 10:9, 11) are then transformed into predictions that the Reign of God will enter a new stage with Jesus' gift of the promised Spirit (24:49; Acts 1:3-5), which will enable his disciples to do the same works of the Kingdom that he had done. In this second stage (Luke's own time) preaching or teaching about the Reign of God is explaining from the Scriptures that this Jesus as Spirit-bringer is the Messiah, whose dying and rising inaugurates a second stage of the Reign into which hearers are persuaded to enter (Luke 16:16; Acts 1:3; 8:12; 19:8; 28:23, 31), and on account of which they leave all to follow Jesus (Luke 18:29). And yet, even though life in this Kingdom feeds the poor so that there are no needy among the disciples (Luke 14:33; 18:22; Acts 2:43-47; 4:32-37), the perfect and final Reign of God will occur only when the Son of Man reappears for the apocalyptic judgment (17:20-22; 21:25-31; Acts 1:11). But this third stage occurs in an undetermined future, after the time of the Gentiles (Luke 21:24); in the meantime, disciples live the Way of Jesus (Acts 9:2; 19:9, 23; 22:4; 24:22), doing his works in the Reign of God, and at death they enter into some other condition of it (Luke 23:42-43; cf. 12:20). Now it is the Spirit of God that overthrows Satan's reign and establishes the Reign of God, both in Jesus' career and in that of his disciples.

b. *The Spirit in Jesus' Person and Mission:* The principal work of the Holy Spirit is to make Jesus Son of God. The Spirit's overshadowing of Mary is his conception as Son of God (διό in 1:32-35). This conceptional Son of God programmatically affects all uses of the title. The Spirit's descent at his baptism, anointing him for his prophetic career (4:18), makes him Son of God in his ministry (3:21-22). Through the agency of the Spirit (4:1) he overcomes the devil in the desert as the obedient Son of God (4:3, 9). Finally, when Jesus reveals his exclusive and intimate relationship as Son to his Father (10:22), he does so while rejoicing in the Holy Spirit (10:21). Thus, throughout the gospel, Luke ascribes Jesus' Sonship to the Spirit.

More relevant to Christian conduct, the Holy Spirit drives Jesus' work.[53] In the Spirit's power he takes up his preaching ministry (4:14). His inaugural sermon at Nazareth announces that his anointing by the Spirit in his baptism has made him the prophetic Servant of YHWH sent to announce good news to the poor, free captives, give sight to the blind, and proclaim the Lord's Jubilee year (4:16-18), which he subsequently enacts

---

[53] The Spirit still inspires Jesus' final instructions to the disciples before his ascension (Acts 1:3).

in Capernaum by miraculous healings, which the demons immediately recognize as the work of "the Son of God (4:41).[54] This same Spirit gives him power over demons. The Spirit leads him into personal combat with and triumph over Satan (4:1,14). Jesus' mission from the anointing Spirit (4:18) was this overthrow of Satan's rule (4:34, 41), which comes to perfect expression in 11:20 where Jesus' ability to drive out demons manifests that the Reign of God has arrived in his work.[55]

Thus the Spirit confers a unique divine sonship on Jesus, who overthrows the reign of Satan by his preaching, healing, and even raising from the dead (7:11-17; 8:49-56), and these actions inaugurate the eschatological Reign of God.[56]

c. *The Spirit in the Disciples' Activity:* During his career Jesus gives disciples the Holy Spirit so they can do his works;[57] indeed, they participate in the final overthrow of Satan (10:17-18).[58] Jesus promises a further gift of the Holy Spirit to those who ask (11:13) and as a defender of the persecuted (12:12). This "Promise of the Father" (24:49; Acts 1:4), which will clothe the disciples with power from on high and actually descends on them at Pentecost, is the gift of the Spirit (Acts 1:5; 2:4, 33) which animates them to speak in tongues and do the other works of Jesus.

As Jesus began his career through baptism by the Holy Spirit, so do Jesus' disciples begin theirs with the baptism of the Spirit at Pentecost (Acts 1:5).[59] This Spirit comes "in the last days" (2:17), Luke's conscious

[54] Though 4:41 clearly associates the demons' title "Son of God" with messiahship ("they knew he was the Christ," 4:41), the string of sonship relationships constituted by the Spirit going back to his conception does not lose its force.

[55] Probably Luke understood the finger of God as the Spirit, since the Spirit is the source of his power over demons; for the OT equation of "hand of God" and Spirit see Robert Hamerton-Kelly, "A Note on Matthew xii.28 par. Luke xi.20," *NTS* 11 (1964–65) 165–67. Luke also equates the wisdom Jesus will give to the persecuted (21:15) with the gift of the Spirit (12:12). For further equation of the Holy Spirit with the Reign of God in Luke see 12:32, where the Father's gift of the Kingdom sounds like the gift of the Spirit in 11:13 (both redactional changes in Luke).

[56] The raising of the dead is an eschatological phenomenon since Isaiah 24–27; Ezek 37:1-14; Dan 12:2; 1 Enoch 22–27; 102–104; 2 Maccabees 7; see the survey by George W. E. Nickelsburg, "Resurrection (Early Judaism and Christianity)," *ABD* 5:684–88.

[57] Without any mention of the Spirit they are given power and authority over demons and diseases (9:1-2; 10:17), works Jesus did through the Spirit. While others can have this power apart from explicitly being in the circle of disciples (9:49), the disciples cannot excercise it apart from Jesus (9:40). In Acts 8:7 Philip also exorcises demons.

[58] Susan R. Garrett, *The Demise of the Devil: Magic and the Demonic in Luke's Writings* (Minneapolis: Fortress, 1989) 46–54 argues that the vision in Luke 10:18 is both apocalyptic and anticipatory of the disciples' power over demons in the early church.

[59] Since the Lukan Spirit makes Jesus God's Son, it might well make the disciples eschatological sons of God. That position is explicit in Rom 8:14-15; Gal 4:6.

insertion identifying the work of the Spirit with the final Reign of God.[60] Thus the disciples' works in the name of Jesus will be a continuation of the Reign of God, which was manifested in his exorcisms (11:20; 17:21).[61] As Jesus had identified himself as the eschatological "one to come"[62] by curing the lame and raising the dead (Luke 7:22; cf. 5:25; 7:14-15; 8:49-56), so Peter and Paul exercise this eschatological power through the Spirit given them in their own baptism in Acts 2:4 and 9:17.[63] Peter cures cripples in Acts 3:1-10; 9:32-34; Philip cures the paralyzed and crippled in Acts 8:7; Paul cures a cripple in Acts 14:8-11. Peter raises the dead Tabitha in Acts 9:36-41; Paul raises a dead boy in 20:7-12.

Further, as Jesus was empowered by the Spirit to cure the sick (4:38-40), so the Spirit-filled disciples cure the sick. Peter's shadow cures the sick in Acts 5:15-16. Sometimes this is done by the touch of their clothes, as had been the case with Jesus (Luke 8:44-48): Paul cures through face cloths and aprons in Acts 19:12. Thus the actions that manifest the arrival of the eschatological one, done by those baptized in the Spirit, manifest

---

[60] The outpouring of the Spirit is Jesus' answer to Peter's question about the restoration of the Reign in Acts 1:6-8. Jesus is the eschatological Messiah, raised and exalted at the right hand of God, who pours out this Spirit (Acts 2:33) so his disciples can continue his eschatological saving work. This Spirit enables Stephen to see the apocalyptic Son of Man at God's right hand in Acts 7:56-57.

[61] In Chapter 3 we saw that in Luke-Acts God's Reign is both a present and future reality. That argument extended and made more concrete the interpretation of Lukan theology found in Robert H. Smith, "History and Eschatology in Luke-Acts," *CurTM* 29 (1958) 881–901; Ulrich Luck, "Kerygma, Tradition und Geschichte bei Lukas," *ZTK* 57 (1960) 51–66; Helmut Flender, *St. Luke, Theologian of Redemptive History.* Translated by Reginald and Ilse Fuller (Philadelphia: Fortress, 1967) 135–62; E. Earle Ellis, "Present and Future Eschatology in Luke," *NTS* 12 (1965–66) 27–41, and idem, *Eschatology in Luke* (Philadelphia: Fortress, 1972); Fred O. Francis, "Eschatology and History in Luke-Acts," *JAAR* 37 (1969) 49–63; Josef Zmijewski, *Die Eschatologiereden des Lukas-Evangeliums; eine Traditions-und Redaktionsgeschichtliche Untersuchung zu Lk 21, 5-36 und Lk 17, 20-37.* BBB 40 (Bonn: P. Hanstein, 1972); Werner G. Kümmel, "Lukas in der Anklage der heutigen Theologie," *ZNW* 63 (1972) 149–65; Otto Merk, "Das Reich Gottes in den lukanischen Schriften," in E. Earle Ellis and Erich Grässer, eds., *Jesus und Paulus. Festschrift für Werner Georg Kümmel zum 70. Geburtstag* (Göttingen: Vandenhoeck & Ruprecht, 1975) 201–20; Emilio Rasco, *La Teología de Lucas: Origen, Desarrollo, Orientaciones.* AnGreg 201 (Rome: Gregorian University Press, 1975); Robert Maddox, *The Purpose of Luke-Acts.* Edited by John Riches (Edinburgh: T & T Clark, 1982) 100–157; Robert O'Toole, *The Unity of Luke's Theology* (Wilmington, Del.: Michael Glazier, 1984) 149–59.

[62] Although it is impossible to identify the precise referent of ὁ ἐρχόμενος (suggested are the Messiah of Zech 9:9, the prophet like Moses of Deut 18:18, YHWH's messenger of Mal 3:1, an apocalyptic Son of Man, Luke 9:26), each possibility is an eschatological figure.

[63] Ananias restores Paul's sight in Acts 9:17, another of the eschatological signs of Luke 7:22.

the presence of the Reign of God in the disciples' actions no less than they had in Jesus' own actions (Luke 11:20).[64]

Finally, as the Spirit had inaugurated and guided Jesus' ministry, so it guides the progress of the Church, especially in its turn to the Gentiles; Acts 8:29; 10:19; 13:2-4; 15:28; 16:6-7 (and perhaps 20:22). Indeed, Acts seems to identify its ecclesial community with the Spirit: in 5:9 lying to the Church is testing the Spirit.

These parallels make it clear that the disciples are transformed by baptism in the Spirit and fire (Luke 3:16; Acts 2:3) to carry on Jesus' own eschatological mission of the overthrow of Satan (Luke 4:1-44) through the curing of diseases, healing of the lame, and raising from the dead (7:22), which manifest the presence of the Reign of God in their work as they did in Jesus' (11:20). Although the last text connects the work of the spirit with the Reign of God, in Acts that nexus can only be inferred through texts indicating that the last days have arrived (2:17).

Now if the Spirit enables Jesus' disciples to do the works he did, it could also enable them to live the life he led—the poverty (Luke 9:58), the hunger (4:2), the mourning (7:13), the slander (7:34) and persecution (20:20; 21:1-6; 23:2)[65]—the life of the beatitudes. It could also enable them to live the radical ethics by which he lived: prayer for those mistreating him (22:14-22; 23:34), turning the cheek (22:47-53, 63-65), not judging (7:39; 12:14), forgiving (5:17-26; 7:39-48; 12:10; 22:61; 23:34). But although Luke-Acts everywhere witnesses to the disciples' en-Spirited power to be as Jesus was and do as he did, it never makes explicit this ethical empowerment. We know only that the disciples who elaborated, heard, and read the Sermon on the Plain acted under the guidance and in the power of the Spirit in the presently established eschatological Reign of God. If that Reign is a present reality, then the Reign of God promised to the poor in 6:20 can be taken as empowerment for the unique and radical ethics of the Sermon. But the link of the Reign of God to the ethics of the Sermon is weak and the link of the Spirit to those ethics is at most implicit. We need again to look more closely to the Sermon itself to see if it offers a clue to what would make possible the radical ethics of the Sermon.

---

[64] The Spirit is associated with the Messiah or an eschatological prophet in Isa 11:2; 28:5; 42:1; 61:1; 1 Enoch 49:3; 62:2. That the Spirit is an end-time gift is increasingly witnessed from early post-exilic thought (Ezekiel 36–39, especially 36:26-27; 37:14; Joel 3:1-5) into intertestamental literature (1 QS 4:18-23). It is the eschatological identity of the Spirit as in conflict with the evil spirits that links Jesus' exorcisms to the Reign of God; Victor H. Matthews, "Holy Spirit," *ABD* 3:260–80.

[65] We have already seen that the Spirit enables them to endure persecution (Luke 12:12).

d. *Sons and Daughters of God:* Can we discover, especially in the Sermon itself, images of the Christian that would further describe this personal commitment and empowerment, and even offer a clue about Luke's deeper world-view underlying such images?

(1) The Sermon's Image of the Christian: As I have shown elsewhere,[66] the Sermon contains five figures of speech (the beatitudes as oxymorons, "sons of the Most High," the shopkeeper, the good tree, the prudent housebuilder) that point to the singular radicalness of the Sermon's ethics. Two of these directly describe the Christian as ethical agent. The good tree bringing forth good fruit, together with its surrounding images (6:43-45), is a crystal-clear and indisputable literary way of saying *agere sequitur esse*. If someone's conduct manifests the otherworldly goodness of not judging and the rest of the Sermon's ethics, there must be some special kind of goodness in the Christian heart.

(2) But "Sons of God," with its adjoined charge to be imitators of God, is the image central to the Sermon's ethics, as can be shown in two ways:

(a) In Luke's rhetorical structure, "Children of the Most High" forms the climax of the love commandment's three movements:

• a four-beat pattern of imperatives (6:27-28, 29-30) with an arhythmic summary rule;

• a three-beat pattern (6:32-34) containing an identical pattern of conditional protasis, rhetorical question, and subjoined reason;

• a three-beat pattern (6:35abc, containing three imperatives, and 35def, an explanatory expansion in three clauses) with an arhythmic summary rule (6:36).

In this scheme, then, 6:36 concludes the third "strophe" just as 6:31 concludes the first. The imitation of God in 6:36 clearly resumes the Children of God title in 6:35e, since it names God πατήρ. Then 6:35, resuming all the imperatives of 6:27-30 and linked by the motif of Child of God to 6:36, serves with 6:36 as climax and summary rule for all three preceding strophes (6:27-35), giving the largest sense underlying the Christian ethic of the love command. Sonship, then, accounts for the intent and source of the radical ethic of love.[67]

(b) Thematically, "Children of the Most High" occurs in an explicit contrast between the (mediocre) good actions of sinners (6:32-34) and the

---

[66] In Daly, ed., *Christian Biblical Ethics* 188–89.

[67] Further, the imitation of the Father's compassion leads into the theme of not judging in 6:37-38. The image of sonship is, then, structurally central not only as the climax of 6:27-35 but also as the hinge introducing 6:37-38, as Schürmann and others saw clearly.

extraordinary self-giving conduct of the Christian who hears Jesus' words (6:27-31, 35). Thus it directly responds to our question about the radical nature of the Sermon's ethic.

Since both structurally and thematically "Children of the Most High" is the image by which Luke conveys the underlying relationships that ground his Christian ethic, we now explore the depths of what we have previously seen of the Lukan usage of "Sons of God" in Chapter 5.

(c) The existential depths of "Son of God": Appendix E shows that "Son of God" applied to Jesus means not only the eschatological Messiah exalted to God's right hand, but also Jesus' more-than-human status, his special relationship to God that flowed from his divine conception. The question "Son of God" raised about Jesus could be answered only in metaphysical terms, and the Christian community had to wait three centuries for the metaphysical answer.[68] But we have seen that a preconceptual glimpse of the answer already lies in Luke's tantalizing use of the title "Son of God" to describe Jesus' divine status and his power over evil.

Luke, however, did not explicitly connect Christians' being "sons of God" with Jesus' own sonship, the way Paul or John did.[69] Nevertheless, Luke's use of the correlative of Son (πατήρ) demonstrates the link between the disciples' sonship of God and that of Jesus. Luke has Jesus call God his Father in ways that bespeak his intimate personal relationship as Son in eleven of his fifty-six gospel uses of πατήρ: 2:49; 10:21-22 (5x); 22:29, 43; 23:34, 46; 24:49.[70] Of particular importance are Jesus' use of the vocative πάτερ[71] in prayer, where the usage reflects Jesus' original Aramaic ʾAbba, expressing his unique relationship to God as Father: 10:21; 22:42; 23:34, 46.[72] In the only remaining uses where πατήρ denotes God, Jesus refers to the disciples' God as their own Father in 6:36; 11:13;

---

[68] John Courtney Murray, *The Problem of God, Yesterday and Today* (New Haven: Yale University Press, 1964) 31–60.

[69] John 1:12 speaks of those receiving the Word (in faith) as getting the power to be τέκνα θεοῦ. Paul speaks of Christians as being baptized into Christ (Rom 6:3) and so being members of the Son's body (1 Cor 12:13); Christians are not sons in the same way as Jesus, but τέκνα by adoption (υἱοθεσία), Rom 8:15.

[70] Chapter 1 remarked on the genetic significance of Jesus' referring to God as his Father in the presence of Joseph. Luke 10:21-22 highlights the exclusive intimacy of Father and Son, not only in their mutual personal knowledge but in the absolute use of both πατήρ and υἱός.

[71] The nominative ὁ πατὴρ in 10:21 is a substitute vocative; cf. BDF §147 (3).

[72] Luke 22:42 omits the ʾAbba of the parallel Mark 14:36 because Luke omits Semitic expressions and repetitions (Henry J. Cadbury, *The Style and Literary Method of Luke* [Cambridge, Mass.: Harvard University Press, 1920] 156); the πάτερ nevertheless reflects the original intimate term, here and in all the vocatives (Joachim Jeremias, *Abba* [Göttingen: Vandenhoeck & Ruprecht, 1966], especially 56–58).

12:30, 32. Indeed, he gives them this intimate term used in the vocative for their own prayer in 11:2. Thus the disciples who believe and receive the Kingdom from Jesus, just as Jesus received it from his Father (22:29), enter into something of Jesus' own sonship of his Father now, in their present life on earth. And so the disciples' calling God Father means that their sonship is like that of Jesus, one that empowers them to act as Jesus did and live a radically different way of life out of trust in their Father, as he did. This means that they are *now* eschatological sons of God, known by their actions as such, thus fulfilling what their Jewish background had meant by "sons of God."

The last two uses of πατήρ referring to the disciples' God occur in Jesus' injunction to a faith-filled trust in God in 12:22-34, which summarizes everything we have been saying about the disciples' empowerment to live the radical call of the Sermon. The passage is set in a literary context (12:13-21) of greedily hoarding one's possessions to prolong one's life and for this-worldly pleasure (12:19). In contrast (διὰ τοῦτο, 12:22) Jesus tells his *disciples* not to be anxious about food and clothing—precisely those worries that prevent people from living the Sermon's commands to give away one's coat and shirt (6:29), and to experience the hunger (6:20) and poverty (6:20) of those who give everything away (6:30). These are the anxieties of the Gentiles (12:30) who live by calculating reason, and so do not have faith in a provident Father who values them more than he does crows and lilies (12:24-28). Such anxieties in the disciples spring from a lack of *faith* (ὀλιγόπιστοι, 12:28). Rather, the disciples, as *sons and daughters,* have a God who is their *Father* (12:30), and so of course will provide for them. Consequently they need seek only the eschatological *Reign of God* (12:31), which will include (now) their bodily needs. Nor do they need to worry whether their Father will send them this *Reign,* since he has already decided to do so (12:32). This confidence frees them from the cares for their own survival (12:30-32) and so enables them to sell all and give alms (12:33; cf. 6:20, 30, 35). Living these actions of the Sermon wins them eschatological treasure in heaven, and fixing this *treasure* in their *hearts* empowers these actions (12:33-34).

Thus the good treasure of the heart (6:45), fed by faith in the provident love of their Father, empowers Jesus' disciples as sons of God to live out of the power of the eschatological Reign of God, to do the commands of the Sermon on the Plain. Only the Holy Spirit is missing from this summary, and yet that Holy Spirit is central to what we have seen of the empowerment of Jesus' disciples. And so we must make the last step of probing beneath the surface of these literary expressions toward a deeper world-view that locates and interprets these factors.

e. *Conclusion:* We have seen three ways in which the disciples are enabled to do the work of Jesus: faith in Jesus, acceptance of the Reign of God, and reception of the Holy Spirit. These three factors create a new existential relationship to God that empowers the Christian. Luke does not seem to have consciously connected them in any way, but he summarizes their ethical effect by expecting disciples to be compassionate as their Father is compassionate. Since God is their Father, they are now daughters and sons of this compassionate God. I suggest that in this image, "Children of God," Luke unconsciously points to the underlying world-view holding these three factors together. Christians become existentially Children of God through the Holy Spirit they have received in faith, and which is in them the power of the Reign of God. Since Jesus became Son of God through the Holy Spirit, both in his conception (1:35) and in his ministry (3:21-22), and celebrated that sonship through the Holy Spirit (10:21-22), Luke probably, without saying so, conceived of the disciples' baptism in the Spirit and fire (Acts 2:3) as the event that made them children of God, empowered as such to do the works of his Kingdom in the world he leaves them. Besides the persistent parallel between the careers of Jesus and his disciples, the only other argument that can be advanced for this connection is that it makes sense of the unconnected data that do lie within the text.[73]

An Authentic Human Ethic

If Jesus' disciples, as children of their compassionate Father, are animated by the Holy Spirit to do the works of the Sermon, how does that address the seeming "irrationality" of its commands? To answer this question we must delve into contemporary psychology and theology, of which neither Jesus nor Luke and his readers would have had any inkling.

1. *The Psychology of Moral Development:* In 1932 the Swiss child psychologist Jean Piaget theorized that children's moral judgment matured from accepting the rules of others as "given" (heteronomy) to affirming the rules in order to reap maximum benefits from social interaction (autonomy).[74] In 1958 Lawrence Kohlberg grounded his theory of stages of moral judgment on these findings of Piaget. By 1974 he had laid out a six-stage

---

[73] That both Paul and John make this connection symbolically does not argue that Luke did, but only that it could be potentially in his preconscious thought. The theoretical formulation of the existential relationship of the Christian to God through the Spirit occurs in medieval theologians.

[74] Jean Piaget, *The Moral Judgment of the Child* (London: Kegan Paul, Trench, Trubner, 1932).

schema of human moral development, in which the first three stages corresponded to Piaget's heteronomy and the latter three to his autonomy.[75]

Of particular interest is Kohlberg's highest stage, the level of universal ethical principles, such as the absolute autonomy of human beings (Kant's "Treat each person as an end, not a means") and the equality of all humans. Persons at this stage are willing to lay down their lives heroically for the vindication of these rights for all. This is indeed noble, but Kohlberg's method of stage analysis is so focused on rule making that it ignores the underlying experience of the Other as an appeal to my compassion and concern. As a result, Kohlberg's Stage 6 person cannot get out of his autonomy into a genuine altruism, an ethic of caring.[76] In short, his ethic seems to have, at root, the same self-interest as that of the Hellenistic ethical thinkers; indeed, he thinks that Socrates is the parade example of the very few who attain to this Stage 6.

As early as 1973 Kohlberg had asked whether there was a Stage 7 in which a cosmic perspective rooted in a kind of natural law might resolve the questions that Stage 6 had provoked. As a response to James Fowler's investigation of the stages of faith development,[77] he began to investigate whether faith could evoke a further stage of moral reasoning.[78] But his limitation to rule-forming rational modes of inquiry precluded his ability to conceive of moral reasoning that arises from experience of intersubjective and altruistic love that pushes one beyond schemes of autonomous enlightened self-interest.[79]

---

[75] Lawrence Kohlberg, "Moral Stages and Moralization: the Cognitive-Developmental Approach," in Thomas Lickona, ed., *Moral Development: Theory, Research, and Social Issues* (New York: Holt, Rinehart & Winston, 1976). Kohlberg developed the theory in a series of essays collected in two volumes of *Essays on Moral Development* (San Francisco: Harper & Row, 1981, 1984). His most systematic expression of his theory is in vol. 2, *The Psychology of Moral Development* (San Francisco: Harper & Row, 1984).

[76] This is precisely the charge that his disciple Carol Gilligan, leveled against his system (*In a Different Voice* [Cambridge, Mass.: Harvard University Press, 1982])—it cannot account for the ethic of caring in which girls are reared, which forms women's ethical consciousness. This impulse to care for the Other is irreduceably part of human experience. Walter E. Conn sees self-transcendence at work, but not accounted for, in the schemes of Jean Piaget, Erik Erikson, and Lawrence Kohlberg in ch. 2 of his *Conscience: Development and Self-Transcendence* (Birmingham, Ala.: Religious Education Press, 1981).

[77] James Fowler, "Stages in Faith: the Structural Developmental Approach," in Thomas C. Hennessy, ed., *Values and Moral Development* (New York: Paulist, 1976) 173–211.

[78] His classic articulation of this investigation is in "Moral Development, Religious Thinking, and the Question of a Seventh Stage," ch. 9 of his *The Philosophy of Moral Development: Moral Stages and the Idea of Justice* (New York: Harper & Row, 1981) 311–72.

[79] Although Kohlberg is open to meta-ethical theories, he rejects a Stage 7 in principle because he does not see it as capable of arguing morally without using the rational principles of Stage 6. He chooses as examples of Stage 7 thinking not Jesus or Christian saints,

2. *Developmental Moral Theology:* These schemes ignore the inborn drive that Bernard Lonergan identified as spontaneous intersubjectivity. Prior to any moral reflection, one seeing a child about to be hit by a car will spontaneously risk her life to push the child out of harm's way. Phenomenological analysis of this spontaneity reveals that humans are linked to one another by bonds of affection that condition the individual's independence.[80] This drive to help, or even be in communion with, the Other is every bit as natural to humans as are the drives for autonomy and security made ultimate values by the psychologists and philosophers of enlightened self-interest.

But in a world of sinfully distorted self-interest such spontaneity will wither unless it is cultivated and reinforced by a family, a tribe, or a community that values bonding and care for the Other. For such spontaneous intersubjectivity to become dominant in one's actions, it must be developed into virtue, such as trust or compassion. Then this compassion brings one to take the ultimate risk of falling in love and committing oneself to the good of another as the goal of one's life. Ultimately, the drive terminates in falling in love unrestrictedly, in love of God.

In the Christian community, stories of Jesus set the example of an altruistic life. By reading these stories in faith as a personal invitation the Christian experiences herself as the object of an infinitely compassionate love and finds herself transformed by that love into membership in the Body of Christ, bound to others in a common identity of loving concern. This new identity is the gift of God, raising to an unimagined level of divinely inspired compassion the drive to love the other that is natural to us all.

This experience shapes and extends a Christian moral theologian's readings of the stages of moral development. Louis Monden elaborated a three-stage theory in which his first two levels corresponded to Piaget's heteronomy and autonomy, but his third broke entirely new ground.[81] In his scheme the elements of conversion take on new meanings at each stage of development.

---

or mystics of world religions, but a Stoic philosopher (Marcus Aurelius) and a Unitarian turned Quaker whose conversion does not flow from experience of divine love (Andrea Simpson). Even when he later considers a Christian mystic such as Teilhard de Chardin, the divine love at the center of Chardin's system is reduced purely to a metaphysical principle driving evolution.

[80] Such phenomenological analyses ultimately ground Lévinas's Face of the Other in his *Totality and Infinity* (see n. 6 above) and *Otherwise than Being: or, Beyond Essence*. Translated by Alphonso Lingis (The Hague: Martinus Nijhoff, 1981).

[81] *Sin, Liberty, and Law*. Translated by Joseph Donceel (New York: Sheed and Ward, 1965) ch. 1.

a. *The instinctual level:* Children cannot reason for themselves what is good for them, and so society, through parents and institutions, rears children with taboos and commands sanctioned by physical punishments and rewards. Then *law* comes not from within, but from outside the child, who assumes this pressure from society and turns it in to a feeling of *obligation.* But the obligation is experienced as alien, and so, increasingly, is observed with ambivalence.[82] At this level *guilt* and *sin* reside in the material transgression of some taboo, producing a blind feeling of having offended some order.[83] *Contrition,* then, is not a desire to reform, but a desire to escape punishment as consequence of the transgression, usually through a system of formulas or, in religion, magical rites.

b. *At the moral level* we begin to recognize our autonomy as subjects who by reason and will can actualize ourselves as free spirits in the world. Our dignity resides in our achieving free and authentic *self*-development in communion with others.[84] Actions are now seen as right because they contribute to self-development in community.[85] *Law* now is not extrinsic, but the interior law of personal growth, and *obligation* is what a person's freedom owes itself in fidelity to the drive for authentic self-development. *Conscience* emerges as the power to judge what will promote development.[86] *Sin* is infidelity to our authentic unfolding, and *guilt* is the realization of sin. *Contrition* and *confession* are now conversion to further development and the fixing of resolution through communal ritual and reinforcement.

c. *The personal (religious) level* occurs when a You summons me to aid him or share communion in her life. One enters this level not through self-development, but through self-gift from and to the lover, especially

[82] This is Kohlberg's preconventional level, where moral values reside in some quasi-physical order of bad acts and physical needs rather than in intentions and relationships.

[83] This is not conscience, but what Freud called the superego. Here occurs that Catholic neurosis, the scrupulous conscience, which prescinds from personal freedom and intention and is harassed by always falling short of the perfect fulfillment of the physical act by which salvation is secured.

[84] Kohlberg divides this autonomy into (1) the conventional level, where children between seven and twelve begin to orient themselves to the expectations of others expressed in laws, and (2) the post-conventional level, where morality resides in shared rights and values, as these are attained and affirmed by one's free conscience.

[85] Here one could even obey a law that impedes one's interests because it is subsumed into a larger web of society's order, and being a member of society promotes personal development.

[86] One must follow one's conscience, even if it is wrong, for only so can one eventually learn what is bad, and so reform the conscience toward the objectively good, which subjectively is authentic personal development.

the Absolutely Personal Lover who is God. Development comes not from within by a calculated process, but by a risky leap of faith in which one commits oneself to the beloved and finds wholeness in communion. Development is not of two individuals, but of a mutual union that enriches the partners beyond their abilities to achieve alone. Now *law* is an invitation to yield in love, to "let go" to persons and to God, which results in the divinization of persons. *Obligation* becomes vocation. *Conscience* is discernment of what the Spirit urges subtly, in a choice among diverse goods. *Guilt* and *sin* are saying no to love. *Contrition* and *confession* are the redirection of desire to reenter dialogue and communion with God and other persons.

Let me offer some observations about Monden's developmental scheme:

(1) Like the psychologists' stages, these moral levels are not watertight compartments: one can be at one stage in sexual morality and another in socioeconomic morality, and one can jump forward or lapse over time in one's mode of acting and thinking in any one area.

(2) Ordinarily (but not always) one moves through these stages sequentially, from the socially constructed "me" to the freely chosen "I" to the fulfilling gift of the interpersonal "we"—from heteronomy to autonomy to koinonomy. What motivates one to move is the inadequacy of the previous framework to satisfy one's developing hunger for self-transcendence.

(3) One moves to altruistic koinonomy not by a rational development of one's autonomy but by risking it to transcend it, by decentering one's ego to center it in another person as the meaning of one's life. The grounds for such a move cannot be secured by calculating reason, but are found through an act of trust, a leap of faith.[87] This is the morality of the lover, whose altruistic love drives her to self-sacrifice (or even death) so that the beloved might live.

(4) An authentic religious tradition will address people at all three stages, to evoke the most authentic response that one can make at whatever level in which one reads its scripture. Thus one can find in the Bible taboos and threats that address the reader stuck at the instinctual level, reasoned persuasion for those operating out of the rational level, and summons to holiness for those loved into the religious level of morality. Likewise, the wise minister will discern at which level a questioner is living so as to help him arrive at that mode of acting that is the best he can

---

[87] The roots of this self-transcendence lie in being created in the λόγος of John 1:1-18, and its achievement is the gratuitous justification by faith described in Paul's letters to the Romans and the Galatians.

do, and that will nevertheless lead him to seek for the highest level to which Jesus is summoning him, perhaps over a lifetime of slow growth.

Now it is clear that Monden's third stage describes an entirely different kind of morality than that of the calculating reason that passes for ethics in psychological and philosophical discourse. In a religious person this love is urged and made possible by the experience of God's unconditional love. For the Christian it is an experience of Jesus' personal love and his summons to receive it. That it is the highest form of human morality is not a calculated motive of the lover, but a subsequent realization. This is the moral stage elicited by Jesus' Sermon.

The Good News of Jesus' Sermon on the Plain

Jesus' Sermon fulfills the anticipations built up by the Prologue and the inception of his ministry. His teaching is new and astonishing (Luke 2:47; 5:33-39) making him a sign of contradiction (2:34) to all-too-human culture. Its root lies in the Son of God's unique and intimate awareness that God is not primarily lawgiver and judge, but provident and unconditionally loving Father (10:21-22; 12:22-32). The Spirit's work making Jesus Son of God in his conception (1:32, 35) and in his ministry (3:22–4:22) introduces the eschatological reign of God (4:43; 11:20; Acts 2:17) in which disciples are empowered to live a truly human life as sons and daughters of such a Father. All of this is not only possible but also mandatory, because as Messiah, prophet, Son of God, and savior Jesus authoritatively articulates the authentic orientation of each human.

Jesus addresses his Sermon primarily to his disciples (6:12-17, 20), Luke's Christian audience who had been catechized (1:4), had accepted in faith the call to discipleship, and had been baptized in the Spirit who made them sons and daughters of their compassionate Father. They were empowered to hear and respond to Jesus' message at the religious stage of morality.

The center of the Sermon on the Plain is the love commandment (6:27-36), and the heart of the love commandment is the Golden Rule (6:31) and its specification as imitation of the divine compassion (6:36). In the Golden Rule Jesus asks his disciples to attend to the totality (καθὼς θέλετε) of their desires. The disciples know their desire for food and clothing; for shelter, security, law, and order; for the opportunity to grow in achievement and mastery, and so to independence and freedom; for a concomitant status, honor, glory; for the development of their talents, creativity, and contemplative peace; for friendship, intimacy, the family and community to which they commit themselves and in which they find their ultimate thirst for union with God as the supreme Lover found in all.[88] Jesus' Golden Rule "traps" his disciples (as his parables trap his hearers) into affirmation of others' needs by experiencing the integrity of their own range of desires, stretching to, and terminating in, the Reign of their loving Father. The spring of that trap is their spontaneous intersubjectivity, which implicitly recognizes kinship in being with the Other, and so the Other's correlative thirst to fill the same needs and achieve the same goals.[89] In short, Jesus asks his disciples to settle for nothing less in their own lives than the exacting fulfillment of the Reign of God, and to settle for nothing less for the Other, who must, then, be considered not enemies, but potentially or actually what they are, children of God. Clearly, Jesus is talking about a level of altruism that cannot be contemplated by human reason, still less codified in an ethical system.

Jesus makes compassion the disciple's response to all the Other's desires.[90] Οἰκτίρμονες expresses the passionate depths of the spontaneous intersubjectivity that reaches out to save and heal our broken fellow humans (and other creatures with whom we experience kinship). Primarily in the Bible God has compassion on the little ones, those oppressed by the powerful and marginalized by society. Jesus also asks for compassion on those who beg (6:30a), but in the love commandment he focuses compassion on the oppressors themselves—the enemies who hate the disciples, curse them, maltreat them (6:67-68), strike them on the cheek and take their clothing and other possessions (6:29-30).[91] They are to love their oppressors as God loves the useless and even those rightly called evil (6:35). The reason is that even those oppressors at their core want a world of justice and peace in community; it is the sinful world in which they came to power that has distorted their deepest desires into fear-based greed for

---

[88] These needs occur in a different hierarchy in Abraham Maslow, *Motivation and Personality* (New York: Harper & Row, 1970) 35–53, who betrays his own *egological* bias for autonomy by placing the esteem needs and need for self-actualization higher than love needs. The needs as I have articulated them move from the lower to the religious levels of moral development.

[89] The disciples presume that their thirst for God's justice, which they recognize as God's gift, is somehow operative in the Other. The thirst to be in a communion of love with the infinite God is natural to all humans, even if its attainment depends on God's gracious gift. This theorem can be vindicated only in systematic theology; see Karl Rahner, *Hearers of the Word* (New York: Continuum, 1994 [1941]) and its adumbration in his article on "Man" in his *Encyclopoedia of Theology* (New York: Seabury, 1975), especially 891–92.

[90] The English translation "compassion" (feeling with) articulates spontaneous intersubjectivity better than does the Greek οἰκτίρμων, which indicates the depth of the passion.

[91] Jesus does not commend compassion for one's well-off benefactors (6:32-34); instead he erects a counter-cultural dynamic of unconditional love for the unfortunate, which may come to include also one's benefactors.

wealth and power as the way to security or anger-based revenge on those who have opposed them. As Paulo Freire has pointed out, they in their own ways are victims of the sinful social situation.[92] Unconsciously they want to be resisted, prevented, corrected so as to become what their depths cry out to be: the sons and daughters of the compassionate God in whose image and likeness they are created. They are the non-disciples who have come to hear and be healed (6:17b-19; 7:1). They must be challenged by turning the other cheek, or surrendering one's shirt, so that they become aware of the dehumanization that has imprisoned them and keeps them from fulfillment of their deepest desires to love all others as their compassionate Father loves them. Only in this way can power be subverted without its being replaced by just another dehumanizing power structure. Conceiving of the enemy as the You who is to be part of the "We" is not "rational," judged by the self-protecting standards of autonomy, but is super-rational, operating out of the Spirit-driven koinonomous level of morality. The compassionate intersubjective love for the Other that Jesus demands of his disciples is the outreach of the Reign of God in a sinful world.

This compassion implies forgiveness (6:37-42) not only of the oppressors, but also of the oppressed's own passive acceptance of the sinful structures of power, their impotence to challenge and resist those powers creatively and humanely. This forgiveness is especially important in a community that includes the rich, the satisfied, and the carefree (6:24-26) and those who prefer the more "reasonable" standards of the world (6:32-34) to Jesus' radical ethics. Not condemnation, but forgiving love will move them forward.

Again, the disciples are summoned to a divine generosity that exceeds all human reason and expectation (6:38). This means that the poor, the hungry, the wailers, and the persecuted will be liberated now (6:20b-23) because their tormentors will be converted. The rich, the sated, the mirthful are challenged to be converted to the deepest levels of human authenticity, inborn and graced (6:24-26). Their dispossession and sharing is the material grounds for the human community of the Reign coming to be. If they become poor by such generosity, they too will be fed by other rich people caught by the disciples' contagious love. And in all cases they will be sharing their lives in the Reign of God with their Lord who "for your sake . . . became poor although he was rich, so that by his poverty you might become rich" (2 Cor 8:9).

[92] Paulo Freire, *The Pedagogy of the Oppressed* (New York: Continuum, 1982) 40–46. Freire's strategy for their liberation is for the oppressed to neutralize the power of the oppressors and so restore them to their own humanity.

The exemplar of this ethic is Jesus' own fidelity to his prophetic challenge, even to the death in which he forgave those who killed him (23:34). Accepting in faith this foundation (6:48b) implies falling in love with the infinite love of the compassionate God, who by the action of his Holy Spirit in the eschatological Reign of God transforms his sons and daughters into true "chips off the old block," so that those who see them see God in human space and time.

Living this way is building one's home on the solid rock of Jesus' commands (6:46-49), which saves the disciples from neurotic acquisitiveness to secure their life, from dependence on honor ascribed by a sinful world, from the loneliness of competitive individualism, from hatred of their oppressors and of themselves as complicit in systems of oppression. It leads them into the peace and joy of Christ's present reign and hope for the perfect Reign of God. Such, finally, is the way hungered for by the outsiders, not only for those who draw near to hear and be healed (6:17c-18a) but also for those who reject the message and even persecute those who follow it, for they too are created to be children of a compassionate God, desiring to be touched by an outreach of altruistic love drawing them into community in God's everlasting Reign.[93]

Such is the sketch of one theory about the unconscious existential anthropology that underlies the commands of the Sermon on the Plain. The truth of this construction lies in its ability to interpret the demands of the Sermon as the authentic fulfillment of humans created in God's image and likeness and sanctified as God's sons and daughters. But this construction can also be tested by its ability to make sense of Jesus' hard sayings (Luke 14:33; 16:14) and other seemingly incongruous passages (Luke 18:18-22), and even of his death and resurrection. Demonstrating that would require yet another book; in the meantime, the faith-filled reader can confirm this hypothesis in her own experience of discipleship.

---

[93] A fuller sketch of this liberation is given in L. John Topel, *The Way to Peace: Liberation Through the Bible* (Maryknoll, N.Y.: Orbis, 1979), especially 138–45.

Scholarly Discussion of *'Anāwîm*

Scholarly investigation of the meaning of *'anāwîm* falls into three stages:

1. In 1893 Isidore Loeb postulated that the poor of the Psalms were pious Israelites of the post-exilic period who came together as "the party of the poor." He held that the pious formed brotherhoods called "the Humble," "the Poor," etc., who took vows of humility or poverty.[1] In the same year Alfred Rahlfs theorized that the *'anāwîm* of the Psalms began at the time of the exile to conceive of all Israel as the Poor under God's judgment. The Servant of God in Deutero-Isaiah would have been the literary personification of this party.[2]

2. In the first third of the twentieth century, however, scholars moved away from the concreteness of "party" and increasingly spoke of a spiritual movement behind the Psalms.[3] The French sociologist Antonin Causse held that the roots of the poor of Israel were in its nomadic beginnings. The height of Israel's identity as the poor came during the Persian epoch,

---

[1] *La littérature des Pauvres dans le Bible* (Paris: Cerf, 1892). After the destruction of the Temple this community would have entered the Pharisaic party, and eventually the Jewish nation became the *hasidim* or *'anāyyîm*.

[2] *'Ani und 'anaw in den Psalmen* (Göttingen: Dieterische Verlagsbuchhandlung, 1892). Rahlfs, still less than Loeb, conceived of this party as a political party. Norbert Lohfink, "Von der 'Anawim-partei' zur 'Kirche der Armen,'" *Bib* 67 (1986) 153–76 makes a brilliant analogy between the socialist worker movement at the time of Loeb and Rahlfs and the "Greens" of our era, who had to decide whether to stay a clearly defined "movement" or enter the power struggle as a political party.

[3] Wolf W. F. Baudissin, "Die alttestamentliche Religion und die Armen," *Preussische Jahrbücher* 149 (1912) 193–231; Rudolf Kittel, "Exkurs: Die Armen und Elenden im Psalter," in his *Die Psalmen Israels, nach dem Versmass der Urschrift* (Leipzig: A. Deichertsche Verlagsbuchhandlung W. Scholl, 1915) 314–18; Antonin Causse, *Les "Pauvres" d'Israël* (Strasbourg: Librairie Istra, 1922); Harris Birkeland, *'Ani und 'anaw in den Psalmen*. SNVAO 4 (Oslo: J. Dybwad, 1932). All held that the *'anāwîm* are a religious movement or tendency within the population, and all see the experience of exile as intensifying or originating the movement.

when the Psalter was written by the poor and for the poor. These were socio-economically poor people whose laments in the Psalms expressed their protest against the selfishness of their society. This protest, however, issued in a spiritual movement that led to a religion of humility whose faithful put their hope in God's eschatological action to free them.

3. After World War II Albert Gelin completed the spiritualization of the poor.[4] Words for poverty, which originally described a social reality, came to carry (only) an intense spiritual meaning. He located the origins of this transformation in the prophet Zephaniah, just before the Babylonian exile. The *'anāwîm* of the Psalms became the humble, ready to suffer for the sake of God and to wait in joyful practice of the Temple cult for YHWH's eschatological vindication.

Still, there was always a counter-movement against this spiritualizing tendency. Already in 1924 Hans Bruppacher, even while he was contending that the Bible provides no clear sociological picture of an organized party of the poor in Israel, sharply criticized the emerging link between poverty and piety in contemporary scholarship.[5] In 1933 Harris Birkeland modified his prior position (mostly by a reexamination of the term *'ānî,* not *'ānāw*) to admit that the poor might be a continuing group, or even the designation of a class.[6] In 1936 P. Munch, influenced by class analysis, reassessing the socioeconomic situation of *'ānî* (not *'ānāw*) turned both into "the class of the oppressed."[7] Finally, in 1950, in sharp response to the spiritualizing tendencies of French exegesis after Causse, Jan van der Ploeg[8] investigated *'ānî, 'ebyôn,* and *dāl* and concluded that the prophetic descriptions of these are so concrete that the poverty about which they spoke was social and economic, and not some spiritual phenomenon. Further, the Bible never romanticizes poverty or holds it up as a religious ideal. It never asserts that the poor are especially pious or that poverty evokes special religious concepts; the poor are the objects of God's special concern not because of their piety but because they are the victims of

---

[4] *The Poor of Yahweh* (Collegeville: The Liturgical Press, 1964 [1953]).

[5] *Die Beurteilung der Armut im Alten Testament* (Zürich: Seldwyla, 1924). Bruppacher found no place in the Bible where poverty was idealized, exalted into the status of a virtue.

[6] *Die Feinde des Individuums in der israelitischen Psalmenliteratur* (Oslo: Grøndahl & Sons, 1933).

[7] "Einige Bemerkungen zu den *'anāwîm* und den *resa'im* in den Psalmen," *Le Monde Oriental* 30 (1936) 13–26. Along this same line was Arnulf Kuschke's "Arm und reich im Alten Testament mit besonderer Berücksichtigung der nachexilischen Zeit," *ZAW* 57 (1939) 31–57, which rooted two different conceptions of the poor in two different social milieux of the biblical authors.

[8] "Les pauvres d'Israel et leur pieté," *OTS* 7 (1950) 236–70.

unjust oppression. Finally, he suggests that *'anāwîm* refers to religious humility, the virtue of submitting to God no matter what one's social or economic situation.

Although this article has never been refuted, the notion of the poor of Israel as a spiritual group continues as common coin in much exegetical literature.

4. Finally, a contemporary literary approach considers πτωχεία/-πλοῦτος a rhetorical *topos*. Among the Hellenistic moralists (the Stoics, the Cynics, the middle Platonists) πτωχός denoted not so much socioeconomic status as a type for the virtuous, while πλούσιος denoted the vicious.[9] A number of monographs have investigated this literary significance of rich/poor in Luke-Acts. Luke T. Johnson's study of the community of goods in Acts 4:32-36 as a Hellenistic *topos* on friendship (Aristotle, *Nicomachean Ethics* IX, 8, 2) concluded that (1) the πτωχός was an economically poor person, (2) generally described as a type, in combination with other types of powerless people, (3) ordinarily referring metaphorically to the people who fear God and recognize the prophet Jesus; (4) the disposition of possessions is the disposition of self; (5) thus Acts 4:32-36 symbolizes the people's acceptance of the apostles as authorities whose word delivers the prophet Jesus in mission now to the Gentiles.[10]

David P. Seccombe's attempt to reconcile the gospel condemnation of the rich with Jesus' own favor to them and their reception of faith in the early church concludes that (1) "poor" is a traditional characterization of Israel suffering and humiliated; (2) Lukan texts on renunciation of goods are interpreted as the Christian ethic of sharing, to which all are *invited;* (3) there is no choosing of poverty for ascetic reasons in Luke-Acts; (4) the rich are therefore not automatically excluded from the Reign, and so show up as holders and sharers of possessions in the early church.[11]

S. John Roth's attempt to understand why the blind, lame, and poor are so prominent in Luke and absent in Acts concludes that (1) the poor are not pious, but character types for the anonymous, powerless, vulnerable, and a-responsible, conventional recipients of God's eschatological

---

[9] See Hans-Dieter Betz, *The Sermon on the Mount: A Commentary on the Sermon on the Mount, Including the Sermon on the Plain (Matthew 5:3–7:27 and Luke 6:20-49).* Edited by Adela Yarbro Collins. Hermeneia (Minneapolis: Fortress, 1995) 572–73, excursus "Poor and Rich," and the abundant bibliography cited there. Heinz Schürmann was the first to introduce this consideration into his exegesis of Luke.

[10] Luke T. Johnson, *The Literary Function of Possessions in Luke-Acts.* SBLDS 39 (Missoula: Scholars Press, 1977).

[11] David P. Seccombe, *Possessions and the Poor in Luke-Acts.* SNTU Series B, 6 (Linz; A. Fuchs, 1983).

agent of salvation; (2) because Jesus' acceptance of sinners contradicted the Jews' expectation of God's eschatological judgment on them, his care for the poor, etc., is necessary to prove that he is nevertheless God's eschatological agent of salvation; (3) these types disappear from Acts because the ascended Lord no longer needs such signs of his eschatological early ministry.[12]

Although both Johnson and Roth affirm that πτωχός means economically poor, their emphasis on the symbolic function of these types obscures the social message of Jesus in Luke and Acts. While I can agree that any such types carry symbolic weight, it is clear to me that Luke's primary intention is to show that the generous donation of one's goods to the poor is intended to create a church (and a world) without needy, the fulfillment of the promise in Deut 15:4 that when YHWH's commands are perfectly fulfilled there will be no need in the land.

---

[12] S. John Roth, *The Blind, the Lame, and the Poor: Character Types in Luke-Acts.* JSNT.SS 144 (Sheffield: Sheffield Academic Press, 1997).

Pre-industrial Agrarian Societies*

Class	Population	Wealth
1. The Ruler	1 family	25%
2. Governing Class	1%	25%
3. Retainer Class	5%	10%
4. Merchant Class	5%	15%
5. Priestly Class	1%	10%
totals for upper class	**12%**	**85%**
6. Peasant Class	60%	10%
7. Artisan Class	10%	5%
8. Unclean, Degraded	8%	—
9. Expendable Class	10%	—
	100%	**100%**

The ruler

Governing class

Power and privilege

Governing Class

Retainers and priests

Merchants

Peasants

Artisans

Unclean and degraded

Expendables

Numbers

* This diagram is adapted from Gerhard Lenski, *Power and Privilege: A Theory of Social Stratification* (Chapel Hill: University of North Carolina Press, 1984) 189–290. The figures and percentages are my approximations, built off the analysis given by John Dominic Crossan in *The Historical Jesus: The Life of a Mediterranean Jewish Peasant* (San Francisco: HarperSan Francisco, 1991) 44–46.

Interpretation of the Reign of God

I. For one hundred years the historical Jesus has been considered the eschatological prophet who came preaching the imminence of the Reign of God.[1] Johannes Weiss in *Jesus' Proclamation of the Kingdom of God* (Philadelphia: Fortress, 1971 [1892]) rooted Jesus' preaching in the Jewish apocalyptic vision of the Reign of God. In 1906 this perspective became dominant as *konsequente Eschatologie* in Albert Schweitzer's *The Quest of the Historical Jesus* (New York: Macmillan, 1968 [1906]). In both of these treatments Jesus' "Kingdom of God" referred to God's apocalyptic reign, which was to arrive imminently as the consequence of Jesus' calls for *metanoia* and decision.

II. This view remained practically unchallenged until 1935,[2] when C. H. Dodd published *The Parables of the Kingdom*.[3] Dodd articulated the opposite view, a realized eschatology in which "Kingdom of God" referred to the presence of God's reign in Jesus' preaching and works. For Dodd any reference to a future Reign of God was metaphorical, stressing the ultimacy of Jesus' message.

III. In the years 1935–1955 C. J. Cadoux, A. M. Hunter, and Vincent Taylor all concluded that Jesus' various statements about the Reign of God referred to both his present ministry and a future consummation of God's reign. This period of interpretation came to a climax in 1947 with Joachim

---

[1] For two excellent summaries of the direction of scholarship for these one hundred years see Norman Perrin, *The Kingdom of God in the Teaching of Jesus* (Philadelphia: Westminster, 1963) and Bruce D. Chilton, *The Kingdom of God* (Philadelphia: Fortress, 1989), and the bibliographies cited there.

[2] One notable exception in the English-speaking world was T. W. Manson, *The Teaching of Jesus* (Cambridge: Cambridge University Press, 1931), which maintained that Peter's confession was the acknowledgment that made the Kingdom become a *de facto* kingdom that could be presently entered. Manson nevertheless maintained that this Reign of God was still moving toward a final consummation.

[3] New York: Charles Scribner's Sons, 1961.

Jeremias's *The Parables of Jesus* (London: S.C.M., 1963). Jeremias held that Jesus expected a crisis subsequent to his own ministry. One series of his parables (the *Kontrastgleichnisse* of the Mustard Seed, the Leaven, the Sower, and the Patient Husbandman) looks for future fulfillment of what has already begun in his work, but other series of parables (the Rich Fool, the Fig Tree, the Ten Virgins, the Great Supper) look for an imminent catastrophe in the future that makes the present a time of decision.[4] Jeremias concluded to a *sich realisierende Eschatologie* in which Kingdom language refers to an eschatological process that began with Jesus' Word but would be completed by the apocalyptic Reign of God at the end of time. Also in 1947 Oscar Cullman, in *Christ and Time*,[5] proposed a view of salvation history in which Jesus preached a Kingdom that was present in his ministry, still imminent, and also to be fulfilled at the end of time. Thus the future sayings refer to an immediate inbreaking of the Kingdom and also to some passage of time between Jesus' ministry and the final consummation.

IV. A distinctive treatment of Jesus' eschatology was the enormously influential work of Rudolf Bultmann, which spanned the time of the previous two stages.[6] Bultmann's first achievement was to identify the work of the early Christian community in the development of the oral traditions that underlie the synoptic gospels. Although he was skeptical about finding in these traditions the sayings and deeds of the historical Jesus, he throughout his work considered Jesus an apocalyptic preacher, summoning humans to decision in the light of the coming eschatological crisis.[7] Developments of the synoptic tradition that dealt with the delay of the *parousia* and a more distant appearance of God's Reign would be secondary formulations of the early community. Bultmann's second influential position was a disparagement of those elements of the synoptic tradition that had lost the sharp edge of this apocalyptic summons.[8]

---

[4] Note that the first series is found mainly in Mark 4, while the second series derives primarily from Q.

[5] Philadelphia: Westminster, 1960.

[6] In one way or another most of Bultmann's enormous output dealt obliquely with this issue; for our purposes his views can be drawn from *The History of the Synoptic Tradition* (New York: Harper & Row, 1963 [1919]); *Jesus and the Word* (New York: Scribner's, 1958 [1926]); *Theology of the New Testament* (New York: Scribner's, 1951, 1955 [1948]).

[7] Both of these developments can be rooted in Bultmann's profound Lutheran reverence for the Word of God summoning sinful humans to repentance and a faith incapable of being grounded in human reason's research into history.

[8] This element of his theology can also be traced to the hermeneutic he drew from Heidegger's *Daseinsanalyse* in *Sein und Zeit* (1927). In this view, the future that is coming determines the human present through the existential decision to which it summons one.

Consequently, when his students shifted the locus of interpretation from the oral tradition to the work of the evangelists in the *Redaktionsgeschichte* movement of the 1950s they brought with them a disparagement of those elements of an evangelist's theology that de-emphasized the apocalyptic preaching of the Reign of God. When in 1956 Hans Conzelmann, in *Die Mitte der Zeit* (translated into English as *The Theology of Saint Luke* [New York: Harper & Row, 1960]) saw Luke as an attempt to deal with his community's problem with the delay of the *parousia,* he viewed the Lukan preaching of God's Reign as embodying an inferior theology. In place of the arrival of the eschatological Kingdom of God Luke has substituted in the time of the Church the non-eschatological gift of the Spirit, which lacks an urgent summons to decision and so constitutes an inferior presentation of the NT summons to conversion in the Reign of God.

This thesis of Conzelmann set the questions for Lukan exegesis for a good twenty years. It provoked some attempts to reestablish the preaching of an imminent Kingdom in Luke.[9] Others agreed that the apocalyptic edge of many Kingdom preachings was dulled, but that imminent expectation still played a role. Still others tried to find the preaching for conversion in places in Luke other than in Kingdom preachings. But the net effect was a reticence to take up the Lukan perspective on the Reign of God until the ice was broken in 1973.[10]

V. A recent movement sees the historical Jesus not as an apocalyptic preacher but as a sage, teaching a radical new way of human existence that overturns the injustices of his own time (and ours).[11] This understanding provokes our investigation of the Reign of God in Luke-Acts as a rich new vision that Luke had to work out for his community.

---

[9] A. J. Mattill, *"Naherwartung, Fernerwartung,* and the Purpose of Luke-Acts: Weymouth Reconsidered," *CBQ* 34 (1972) 276–93; Eric Franklin, *Christ the Lord: A Study in the Purpose and Theology of Luke-Acts* (London: S.P.C.K., 1975), especially 9–47. These attempts have been largely unsuccessful.

[10] Stephen S. Smalley, "Spirit, Kingdom and Prayer in Luke-Acts," *NovT* 15 (1973) 59–71; Martin Völkel, "Zur Deutung des 'Reiches Gottes' bei Lukas," *ZNW* 65 (1974) 57–70; Otto Merk, "Das Reich Gottes in den lukanischen Schriften," in E. Earle Ellis and Erich Grässer, eds., *Jesus und Paulus. Festschrift für Werner Georg Kümmel zum 70. Geburtstag* (Göttingen: Vandenhoeck & Ruprecht, 1975) 201–20.

[11] Marcus Borg, *Jesus: A New Vision* (San Francisco: Harper, 1987) is not only a survey of the movement, but a brilliant exposition of it.

Persecution Terminology
in Luke-Acts and the NT

"Persecution" can be official (sanctioned by an ordinance from legitimate authority, Jewish or Gentile, against all Christians), unofficial (using official prisons and courts against "disturbers of the peace"), or personal (using various means of harassment, ranging from stoning to chasing one out of town, but without any process or even connivance by authorities). There seems to be no instance of official persecution of Christians in the NT.[1]

Luke 21:12-19, Jesus' prediction of his disciples' persecution before the destruction of Jerusalem (21:20-24), is Luke's most formal description of persecution: ἐπιβαλοῦσιν ἐφ᾽ ὑμᾶς τὰς χεῖρας αὐτῶν καὶ διώξουσιν, παραδιδόντες εἰς τὰς συναγωγὰς καὶ φυλακάς, ἀπαγομένους ἐπὶ βασιλεῖς καὶ ἡγεμόνας, ἕνεκα τοῦ ὀνόματός μου. All of this will bring them to witness, μαρτύριον. They will be betrayed by parents, family, friends, and be put to death. All of this, then, is summarized by the only word that had also occurred in Luke 6:22, μισούμενοι. Thus this hatred, when it issues in a persecution sanctioned by authorities (kings and governors), will include imprisonment and punishment extending even to the death penalty.[2]

---

[1] Not until the second century does Christianity become illegal and membership a capital crime; see the excellent summaries of the scholarly consensus on this issue by A. N. Sherwin-White, "Appendix V: The Early Persecutions and Roman Law," in his *The Letters of Pliny* (Oxford: Clarendon Press, 1966) 772–87, and by Gerhard Krodel, "Persecution and Toleration of Christianity until Hadrian," in Stephen Benko and John J. O'Rourke, eds., *The Catacombs and the Colosseum* (Valley Forge, Pa.: Judson Press, 1971) 255–67. For further discussion and bibliography see W. H. C. Frend, *Martyrdom and Persecution in the Early Church* (Oxford: Blackwell and Mott, 1967) and the more focused study in John H. Elliott, *A Home for the Homeless: A Sociological Exegesis of 1 Peter* (Philadelphia: Fortress, 1981) 78–84, 88–90.

[2] Disciples put to death in Acts include Stephen (Acts 7), but not by a formal process, and James (Acts 12:2), at least without mention of any judicial process.

Luke 12:8-12 includes similar terminology in which the disciples must profess Jesus (v. 12) when they are brought before synagogues, rulers, and authorities (v. 11).[3] What this means for the readers of Luke is probably best portrayed in Acts. The most widespread (διωγμὸς μέγας ἐπὶ τὴν ἐκκλησίαν) seems to be the Jewish persecution of the Church in Acts 8:1b–9:30, but this was short-lived and now seems to have affected only Jewish Christians. Luke says the church was scattered and uses διώκω of Paul's breaking and entering houses, dragging out Christians and throwing them into prison.[4] The rest of Acts' "persecutions" seem to be Jewish attacks on individuals for disrupting the peace of the Jewish community. Διωγμός[5] is used only once more (Acts 13:50), this time of a Jewish effort to drive just Paul and Barnabas out of Antioch of Pisidia.

Words describing unofficial and personal "persecutions" of Christians in the rest of Acts include "seizing," "laying hands on" (ἐπιβάλλειν χεῖρας) (4:3; 5:18; 6:12; 12:1,[6] 3-4; 21:30, 33); "throwing (τιθῆναι, παραδιδόναι) into prison (τήρησις, φυλακή)" (4:3; 5:18; 8:3; 12:4-5; 16:22; 22:4; 26:10), and chains (9:2, 14; 16:24; 20:24); forcing them to answer charges (4:9; 5:27; 6:12-13; 24:2; 25:7);[7] beating or whipping them (5:40; 16:22-23; 22:24), or killing them by stoning (7:58).

Outside of any quasi-official or unofficial *process,* they were slandered (κακολογεῖν, 19:9),[8] insulted (βλασφημεῖν, 13:45; 18:6); (7:58; 14:5,19; 21:30),[9] and slain (12:2).

---

[3] Matthew has this Q material is two different places in Jesus' missionary discourse to the Twelve (10:26-33//Luke 12:2-9 and 10:19-20//Luke 12:11-12). Luke 12:2-12 is a general warning to all disciples in a section strongly marked by eschatology (12:2-3, 5, 20-21, 33, 35-59).

[4] Acts 9:4-5; 22:4, 7-8; 26:14-15, all in descriptions of Paul's conversion. Acts 7:52 speaks of the sometimes personal, usually unofficial Jewish persecution of the prophets. Presumably the prisons referred to here were associated with the synagogues, a penal system parallel to the Greco-Roman prisons.

[5] In both cases the noun seems to mean little more than the abstract θλίψις (Acts 11:19, describing the same procedure; 14:22; Rom 8:35; 2 Thess 1:40); Gerhard Schneider, *Die Apostelgeschichte.* HTKNT 5 (Freiburg: Herder, 1980) 478 n. 62.

[6] It appears that even this act of King Herod Antipas was done without any official decree or public edict.

[7] The town clerk in Ephesus says that the public courts stand open to the accusers of Christians (19:38).

[8] In 25:7, as part of a formal charge Paul is described as a (virulent) "pest" (λοιμόν).

[9] Actually, the stoning of Stephen follows something like the formal process against blasphemy later found in *b. Sanh.* 6–7, with a hearing, the condemned taken outside the court (*b. Sanh.* 6:1=Lev 24:14) to be stoned (*b. Sanh.*7:4) by the witnesses (*b. Sanh.* 6:4). But the actions in 14:5, 19 do not presume these niceties.

Consequently, all of Jesus' predictions of persecution have come true for the community described in Acts. We did not, however, see the words of the beatitude in 6:22 (μισεῖν, ἀφορίζειν, ὀνειδίζειν, ἐκβάλλειν τὸ ὄνομα ὡς πονηρόν).

The "Son of God"

I. *Pre-Lukan Christian Use of the Title*[1]

"Son of God" is applied to Jesus twenty-six times in the gospel tradition and fifteen times in the Pauline writings, and the theological ideas of imitation of Jesus and incorporation into Christ were strong enough to have influenced the Christian use of "sons of God." So we must see what resonances the title may have had as it came to Luke.

A. *The Development of the Notion:* The earliest Christian tradition probably developed "Son of God" along the lines suggested by Raymond E. Brown's "christological moments."[2] Two principal witnesses to this pre-Lukan tradition may have influenced Luke's conception of Jesus and Christians as Sons of God.

1. *Paul's Notion of Son of God:*[3] Paul's earliest writings see Jesus as the eschatological son of God whom Paul expects to return from heaven as royal messiah (1 Thess 1:10).[4] Paul witnesses, in his adoption of a pre-Pauline

---

[1] The Jewish use of the title is already given on pp. 170–71.

[2] In *The Birth of the Messiah* (Garden City, N.Y.: Doubleday, 1977) 29–32. Brown postulates four stages of development: (a) Jesus was first understood as Son of God when he was exalted to God's right hand (= royal enthronement) through the resurrection (Rom 1:3-4; Acts 13:32-33); (b) Jesus was then understood to have been Son of God throughout his ministry, and so was identified as Son of God at his baptism (Mark 1:11); (c) still later Jesus is understood as Son of God in his conception (Matt 1:18-25 and especially in Luke 1:32-35); (d) Jesus was seen as always Son of God in a preexistent state (John 1:1-18).

[3] Whatever position one takes on the personal relationship of Paul and Luke (I find Philipp Vielhauer's thesis exaggerated), or on the lack of explicit knowledge of Paul's letters in Acts, one cannot exclude the possibility that by the 80s Paul's thought had circulated beyond the ambit of his churches. Further, pre-Pauline traditions probably circulated much more widely than the letters themselves.

[4] Possibly the exaltation of the Messiah through resurrection and ascension makes Jesus like the angelic sons of God as possessors of eternal life; Jarl E. Fossum, "Son of God," *ABD* 6:134.

creedal formula in Rom 1:3-4, to the earliest stage of christological development, the exaltation sonship. However, contrary to the expectations of our developmental hypothesis, he had already accepted a tradition of preexistence christology (2 Cor 8:9)![5] This preexistent sonship is already synthesized with risen sonship in (pre-Pauline!) Phil 2:6-11:[6] the preexistent Son, not clinging to the immortal mode of being he shared with God,[7] took the slave's mode of existence in which humans were, and therefore passed through death to that exalted state of the resurrection in which all creation acknowledges his name.[8] Thus the Son received back in the resurrection precisely the immortal life that the OT tradition had seen as the essence of the (angelic) Son of God. His preexistence is presumed by the choices he makes in 2 Cor 8:9 and Phil 2:7-8. This preexistence underlies "Son of God" in the "sending of the Son" formula of Gal 4:4-5; Rom 8:3.[9]

This view of Christ grounds Paul's view of Christians as "sons of God." Romans 6:8-9 shows that Christians, now justified by faith, are sons through faith and baptism. But their status is also hidden, attested only by the Spirit in whom they cry *"Abba,"* in conscious imitation of the earthly Jesus in Mark 14:36. They must still die, to be conformed to Christ in his sufferings (Rom 8:17), but the Spirit is the first installment and guarantee

[5] Brendan Byrne, in *"Sons of God"—"Seed of Abraham" : The Sonship of God of all Christians in Paul Against the Jewish Background.* AnBib 83 (Rome: Biblical Institute Press, 1979) 197–205, and even more in "Christ's Pre-Existence in Pauline Soteriology," *TS* 58 (1997) 308–30 mounts a convincing refutation of the superficial exegetical consensus that there is no preexistence christology in Paul. Byrne not only demonstrates that Phil 2:6-11 describes a preexistent Christ, but also demonstrates that such preexistence is central to Paul's soteriology.

[6] Jerome Murphy-O'Connor's thesis that Paul is not speaking of preexistence in "Christological Anthropology: Phil II, 6-11," *RB* 83 (1976) 25–50 is unconvincing because it does not explain the entrance into human existence in v. 7. This pre-Pauline hymn witnesses to a preexistence christology older than any NT writing, as old as the pre-Pauline resurrection christology found in Rom 1:3-4 and Acts 13:32-33.

[7] See Byrne's judicious analysis of the literature on ἴσα and ἁρπαγμός, 201–202. Μορφή is not a merely external likeness, but refers to the Son's *Daseinsweise* (Ernst Käsemann, "A Critical Analysis of Philippians 3:2-11," in Robert W. Funk, ed., *God and Christ: Existence and Province* [Tübingen: Mohr; New York: Harper, 1968] 59–63), implying a non-philosophical analysis that still attends to ontological realities.

[8] Servant humility had obscured Jesus' glory during his ministry, so that the risen glory is only the manifestation of the glory that had always been his as Son.

[9] "God sends him who is already Son, and so Christ is Son of God at all three stages of his personal career—pre-existent, earthly, and risen;" Byrne, *"Sons"* 199. Byrne accepts Werner R. Kramer's argument that the "giving up of the Son" formula of Gal 2:20; Rom 8:32 also refers to the preexistent Son's being given up to incarnation, not death. Although in 1 Cor 8:6 Jesus plays a mediatorial role in creation, and in 1 Cor 10:4 he is the "spiritual rock" in the Israelite camp, these provide shaky foundations for the kind of personal preexistence of a son (Byrne, "Pre-Existence," 314. n. 26).

of the coming revelation of their sonship in the resurrection, when they will share the immortal life of the first fruits (1 Cor 15:20; Rom 8:29).[10]

How could such a notion of "sons of God" have influenced Luke 6:35c?

a. Christ's status as Son is not effected primarily by his ethical imitation of the Father, but by an almost ontological relationship, which he has always had.[11]

b. Christians who share Christ's risen life (Rom 6:4; 8:9-17) share in something of that ontological relationship,[12] expressed symbolically by the vital relationships "in Christ" and "the Body of Christ" and the use of συμ–compounds.

c. Their sonship is presently hidden, but nonetheless real. Its orientation to full realization in the final restoration (Rom 8:25) does not deny the fact that we are presently changed and empowered for a new life (Rom 6:1-14; 8:12-17), and that the Spirit helps us now in our weakness (Rom 8:26), enabling us to pray now to our Abba (Rom 8:14-16). This "already/not-yet" eschatology may obviate a choice in Luke 6:35 between eschatological sonship and one presently effecting divine action in us (6:36). But this is to be investigated in Luke's own usage.

2. *The Pre-Lukan Synoptic Tradition:*[13] The understandings most likely to have affected Luke's thought-world are his synoptic sources. There Jesus as Son of God is ordinarily found in contexts that stress the Judaic roots of the title in royal messiahship and the filial relation of the pious Israelite.

At his trial the high priest asks Jesus if he is the Messiah, the "Son of the Blessed" (Mark 14:61). The pre-Lukan gospel tradition then advanced this christological title to Jesus' baptism, conceived as a royal installation,[14] and even to his conception.[15] The Markan tradition made "Son of the Most

---

[10] This is my summary of Byrne's thesis, which is an analysis of Christians' sonship mostly in Romans 8–9; cf. his own summary in *"Sons"* 213–14.

[11] Paul's use of ἐν μορφῇ θεοῦ, ἁρπαγμός, ἴσα θεῷ in Phil 2:6-11 makes explicit the kind of existential relationship that is implied throughout Paul's writings (2 Cor 8:9; Gal 2:20; 4:4-5; Rom 8:32) and now seen also in Rom 5:15-17; Byrne, "Pre-Existence," 3.

[12] Paul differentiates Christ's sonship from the Christians' by υἱοθεσία (Gal 4:5; Rom 8:15, 23; 9:4) and by calling Christians τέκνα (Phil 2:5; Rom 8:16-17, 21; 9:8).

[13] I mean what is clearly from Q or pre-Lukan Mark. Because of the uncertainties regarding hypotheses of *Urmarkus* and the difficulties in separating pre-Markan tradition from Markan redaction I am going to consider as *possible* influences on Luke anything in Mark that is not judged almost unanimously to be part of a final Markan redaction.

[14] The use of Ps 22:7 by the heavenly voice marks this quite clearly, but for other elements of the royal enthronement see Fossum, "Son," 134.

[15] Matthew 1:18-25 *implies* divine sonship by its virgin birth story; Luke 1:26-38 *proclaims* it, as we have seen in Chapter 1. Although the diversity of these presentations

High" the demons' title for Jesus as wonderworker during his ministry (6:7//Luke 8:28).[16]

"The Son" manifests its pre-synoptic development by appearing in both Markan (Mark 12:6//Matt 21:37//Luke 20:13; Mark 13:32//Matt 24:36) and Q (Matt 11:27//Luke 10:22) traditions.[17] The allegorical parable of the tenant farmers (Mark 12:1-12 and parallels) gives the traditional understanding of Jesus' role as Son of God: he comes as a climax to the series of prophets, as one with full authority to receive the fruits of the vineyard because he is the Lord's son.[18] "The Son" appears as a title in Jesus' surprising assertion that not even the Son knows the hour of the Son of Man's return (Mark 13:32//Matt 24:36).[19] This subordination of the Son to the Father (who *does* know) corresponds to Paul's use of "Son of God": the Son's divine power and glory are hidden in this state of servitude, to be revealed only in the resurrection, when sonship is established in power. Thus the Markan "the Son" correlates with "Son of God."

At the other end of the spectrum, Q's "the Son" affirms the mutual and exclusive personal knowledge of the Father and the Son (Matt 11:27//Luke 10:22).[20] This exclusive reciprocity, augmented by the Son's unknowability,[21] demands a status like the ontologically divine.[22]

---

negates a written source (such as Q), still their agreement in eleven points suggests a tradition that antedates the writing of Matthew and Luke (Brown, *Birth of the Messiah* 34–35).

[16] The pre-Markan tradition may have made a transition from ὁ ἅγιος θεοῦ (Mark 1:24) to υἱὸς θεοῦ by analogy with θειός ἀνήρ (Eduard Schweizer, *TDNT* 8:377). Possibly this usage lay behind the demons' use of "Son of God" (cf. the Q tradition behind Luke 4:3, 9, in which Satan tempts Jesus to work miracles).

[17] J. M. McDermott, "Jesus and the Son of God Title," *Greg* 62 (1981) 277–317 argues that Jesus' authentic use of "the Son" provides the earliest historical stage of the "Son of God" tradition.

[18] Even if one sees the allegorical elements of the parable as deriving from the early church, the core of the parable proper identifies Jesus as God's Son and may go back to the historical Jesus. He is subordinate to, but the personal agent of the Father. The following pericope's application of Ps 118:22-23 to the Son refers to the Father's establishment of the Son in power through the resurrection.

[19] Since it speaks of human lowliness, some exegetes thought the church derived this title from its lowly Son of Man sayings; McDermott, "Jesus and the Son of God Title," 283 has disproved this provenance. The admission of ignorance in the Son manifests a provenance earlier than the Church's increasing desire to divinize Jesus.

[20] The intimacy is represented by Jesus' unique use of *'Abba* in Mark 14:36, but the vocative may be Markan redaction.

[21] Indeed, the Son seems more unknowable than the Father, since he can reveal the Father to others but is himself known only to the Father!

[22] It was so understood in the development of christological dogma, where "everything has been given me by my Father" (Luke 10:22) became a scriptural foundation for the Father and Son's community of being and substance. This underlying notion of divine status accounts

The title "sons of God" occurs only in Matt 5:45//Luke 6:35 in the pre-Lukan synoptic tradition.[23] In the Matthaean redaction it refers to a relationship constituted by ethical conduct in the lifetime of the disciples.

How could these early synoptic traditions have influenced Luke's notion of "sons of God?"

a. Jesus as Son of God is the royal Messiah, so demonstrated and constituted by his resurrection and ascension to heaven;

b. Jesus is the Son of God from the time of his conception through the Holy Spirit, and this Sonship is recognized by the spirit world though his miraculous acts of healing;

c. The absolute title "the Son" witnesses to a unique and climactic role in salvation history (Mark 12:6 and parallels), as well as to a unique personal relationship that strongly implies a relationship approaching equality with God his Father.

d. But the pre-synoptic tradition does not connect this sonship of Jesus with sonship in the disciples; their sonship seems to be that of ethical imitation of their Father, rather more like the Jewish notion of eschatological sonship.

Conclusions: By the time Luke came to write his gospel Christian communities not only had begun to proclaim Jesus as Messiah and Son of God but, doubtless under the experience of his resurrection and powerful presence to them in the Spirit, had begun to ask what could have been the grounds for such powerful action on the world. In the twenty years before Luke wrote, Paul and the Markan tradition had begun to move from a merely functional notion of "Son of God" to a use of the title that began to probe at the existential status of Jesus' sonship. Other communities, represented by the epistle to the Hebrews and the gospel and epistles of John, had already begun before Luke's writing to explore the existential status of a Son of God who had created the world (Heb 1:1-4; John 1:1-5) and had a kind of dynamic equivalence with his Father (John 1:14, 18; 8:21-59).[24] Although we have not argued for the influence of these latter communities on Luke, it now seems unlikely that his own community could have burked these same questions. Thus Luke comes to his literary task of

---

for earlier exegetes' desire to transfer this "meteorite from a Johannine heaven" to a gospel whose prologue has a divine preexistent Word.

[23] I take Matt 5:9 to be redaction.

[24] Against J. D. G. Dunn's attempt to prove that the preexistence in Heb 1:1-4 was that of an idea or purpose in God's mind, see John P. Meier, "Symmetry and Theology in the Old Testament Citations of Heb 1,5-14," *Bib* 66 (1985) 504–33.

creating his gospel at the least with background notions of "Son of God" derived from the pre-synoptic traditions and Paul:

1. Jesus is "Son of God" as the eschatological royal Messiah,

(a) exalted to heaven but coming again as ruler and judge, and

(b) wonderworker and liberating king in conception and in earthly ministry;

2. Jesus is unique (and pre-existent) divine Son;

3. Christians are "sons of God" through their eschatologically purified living of the ethical demands of their covenantal relationship with their heavenly Father.[25]

II. Lukan Use of the Title

Luke himself uses as titles for Jesus υἱὸς ὑψίστου (only in 1:32) and υἱὸς θεοῦ (eight times in Luke: 1:35; 3:22; 4:3, 9, 41; 8:28; 9:35; 22:70, and twice in Acts: 9:20; 13:33). Further, two uses of the Father/Son relationship between God and Jesus (10:21-22; 11:2-4) are also important for understanding the title.

1:26-38: Luke does not give titles for Jesus at the beginning of his gospel, preferring rather to have them proclaimed in narrative.[26] In 1:32a Gabriel gives him the title υἱὸς ὑψίστου, which is joined to the notions of receiving the throne of his father David (1:32b) and eternal rule over the house of Israel (1:33). Thus "Son of the Most High" indicates a royal Messiah.[27] But Mary's consequent question arising from her virginity (1:34) is the literary springboard to deeper aspects of this sonship. The Spirit will descend not on Jesus to anoint him king, but on Mary, as the locus of Jesus' conception as Son of God (1:35bc).[28] Luke, then, is the first Christian writer to link the virgin birth explicitly (διό, 1:35d) with the conception of the Son

---

[25] It is just possible that something of Jesus' sonship may have influenced Luke's notion of Christians' sonship, because such a move had already occurred in Paul.

[26] Contrast Mark 1:1; Matt 1:1. Chapter 1 already discussed the context and form of Luke's programmatic announcement of Jesus' identity and mission in 1:32-35. Chapters 1 and 2 provide the basic argumentation for much that is asserted in this survey of Son of God usage prior to the Sermon.

[27] The clear allusions to 2 Sam 7:12-14 reinforce Luke's linking of these notions here. This does not mean that "Son of God" is a messianic title, but that it has messianic resonances for a first-century Jew (n. 175 on p. 171).

[28] Luke has depicted the conceptional Son of God with the same triad of elements (Holy Spirit, power, Son of God) that earlier tradition has ascribed to the resurrectional Son of God (Rom 1:3-4) and the baptismal Son of God (Luke 3:22; 4:14 with Acts 10:37); see the convincing exposition in Brown, *Birth of the Messiah* 312–13.

of God, so that what is born of the virgin Mary is God's uniquely gener-ated Son (1:35).[29] What could birth from a virgin without a human father mean?[30] "Son" denotes one generated by a father of the same species; it is doubtful that the term could be reduced to such a dead metaphor as to lose totally its original meaning of conception from the same nature. Luke will reemphasize this direct divine generation by his parenthetical comment denying Joseph's fatherhood in the genealogy of the Son of God in 3:23b.[31] Luke does not answer our question here, but he has placed in his Prologue this special sonship, described in terms that seem more deeply rooted in Jesus' person than the "ascribed" sonship of the baptism or the resurrection, to color and lend a special dimension to the traditional uses of "Son of God" throughout Luke-Acts.[32]

In **2:41-52** Mary and Joseph's expectation that Jesus should be with his (human) father, their surprise when they find him in the Temple, and Mary's pondering of his words reveal that they understand him as the tra-ditional Jewish son. But the boy Jesus, in the face of his putative father, pro-claims his Father to be God.[33] At the end of the Prologue these first words

[29] The δύναμις ὑψίστου links the subsequent appositional title, υἱὸς θεοῦ, to the origi-nal title υἱὸς ὑψίστου; they are synonyms.

[30] Adam is called Son of God without a human father in 3:38. Does Luke mean the race is being founded on a new Adam? Though J. D. G. Dunn, *Christology in the Making* (Philadelphia: Westminster, 1980) has found evidences of an Adamic christology behind the NT, it does not seem to be conscious in Luke.

[31] That this is the genealogy of the Son of God is indicated by his descent from Adam as Son of God (3:37); Marshall D. Johnson, *The Purpose of the Biblical Genealogies with Special Reference to the Setting of the Genealogies of Jesus.* MSSNTS 8 (Cambridge: Cam-bridge University Press, 1969) 237 points out that no other known biblical or rabbinic ge-nealogy ends in the Son of God. But its position as a comment on Jesus' baptismal anointing (4:18) as the Son of God in 3:22 marks it even more strongly as the genealogy of the Son of God.

[32] Besides the already-mentioned parenthetical comment of 3:28, the "divine" identity of Jesus comes to expression in places where Jesus is not called Son of God. In 1:43 when Elizabeth calls Jesus her Lord, κύριος has already begun to take on resonances of the Chris-tian proclamation of Jesus as Lord, and, in view of Palestinian practice of referring to YHWH as *'adon* or *mare'*, the title seems to raise Jesus to the same level as YHWH; Joseph A. Fitzmyer, "New Testament *Kyrios* and *Maranatha* and their Aramaic Background," in idem, *To Advance the Gospel: New Testament Studies* (New York: Crossroad, 1981) 218–35, and his discussion of the Lukan retrojection of Christian meaning into κύριος throughout Luke-Acts in *The Gospel According to Luke*. 2 vols. AB 28, 28A (Garden City, N.Y.: Doubleday, 1981, 1985) 202–203. Therefore when Zechariah prophesies that John will "go before the Lord to prepare his ways" (1:71; 3:4-6, 16-17; 7:24-27) Jesus is identified with the God of justice come for final vindication of his people (Mal 2:17; 3:1; 4:5). Indeed, Jesus is this Lord come to his Temple in 2:22-38 (Mal 3:1).

[33] Jesus' first words are as programmatic for Luke as those of Matt 3:15 are for Matthew.

of Jesus reinforce the opposition between natural human sonship and Jesus' special sonship of God enunciated at the beginning of the prologue.

In **3:1-4:13** Jesus' preparation for ministry reflects the general synoptic christology of Jesus' sonship manifested at the beginning of his ministry (Brown's second christological moment). In **3:21-22** the conflated allusion to Ps 2:7, σὺ εἶ ὁ υἱός μου, and Isa 42:1, ὁ ἀγαπητός, ἐν σοὶ εὐδόκησα, identifies Jesus as God's enthroned royal Son, anointed by the Spirit as his Servant. That even this ascribed sonship is colored by the earlier conception-sonship is demonstrated by two facts we have just considered: (1) the same combination of "Son of God," "power," and "Holy Spirit" that had conceived Jesus as the Son in 1:32-35 operate again in this manifestation of his Sonship; 2) the ὡς ἐνομίζετο in the very next verse (3:23) refers to the divine conception without Joseph in 1:32-35.

The devil's use of "Son of God" in **4:3, 9** is both retrospective, referring to the proclamation of Jesus as Son of God in 3:22,[34] and prospective, referring to the demonic name for him as wonderworker (4:41). A. B. Taylor and Birger Gerhardsson have demonstrated that already in Q Jesus is the obedient son in the desert, as opposed to Israel as the disobedient son in the desert.[35] Luke weaves this concept into his larger theology that only in full humanity can Jesus be the divine Son, so that he can be the Son of God only by living out the servant role of Deutero-Isaiah. Although the echoes of divinity in the conception-sonship are carried into this passage through the baptismal proclamation, the servant-sonship theme here puts them in the background.

Luke 4:14-44: In 4:16-30 Jesus articulates his mission, again in terms of the prophetic Servant of YHWH and not as Son of God. But the Nazarenes' programmatic rejection of Jesus, though obscure,[36] seems to arise from their misunderstanding of who Jesus is. "Isn't this Joseph's son?" contradicts what the reader already knows: Jesus is not Joseph's son (3:23), but the Son of God (1:32, 35). First the Nazarenes do not understand Jesus as the Servant/royal Son of God of the baptism from which the Spirit has brought him and which accounts for his identity just proclaimed in the synagogue (4:18). Second, they miss the deeper sonship of 3:23 as a resonance of 1:32-35.[37]

[34] "Son of God" in 3:22, 23, 38; 4:3, 9 formally links 3:21-22 to 4:1-13 as a unit.

[35] A. B. Taylor, "Decision in the Desert: The Temptations of Jesus in the Light of Deuteronomy," *Int* 14 (1960) 300–309, and Birger Gerhardsson in *The Testing of God's Son (Matt 4:1-11 & Par). An Analysis of an Early Christian Midrash* (Lund: Gleerup, 1966).

[36] For a survey of opinions about the cause of this rejection see David Hill, "The Rejection of Jesus at Nazareth (Luke iv, 16-30)," *NovT* 13 (1971) 161–80.

[37] Thus the rejection springs from ignorance, unlike that of the high priests and scribes of Luke 20:1-19 who, in the parable, know he is the Son.

In 4:41 Luke has inserted σὺ εἶ ὁ υἱὸς τοῦ θεοῦ in the demons' mouths (contrast Mark 1:34//Matt 8:16). In the context of Lukan christology thus far this redactional insertion is a demonic witness to the divine power at work in Jesus (4:33-41; cf. 8:28).[38] But Luke gives it a messianic interpretation when he redactionally gives the reason for Jesus' silencing them: "they knew that he was the Christ." Thus "Son of God" explicitly refers to the Messiah's role as king of Israel.

In Jesus' subsequent ministry there are three references to the Son of God.

Luke 9:28-36: Although the transfiguration continues the synoptic view of Jesus' sonship during his ministry it is more closely related than the baptism to a christology of full sonship at the resurrection.[39] Still, the heavenly voice not only reveals the Son in his risen glory but does so in vindication of his present teaching of the necessity of the disciples' taking up the cross daily (9:23, 35).[40] Thus Jesus is the divine son in the synoptic tradition and in Luke not only as a healer and exorcist, but also as a teacher of God's way.

Luke 10:1-24 describes the transmission of these two functions to the seventy-two disciples.[41] The disciples return in triumph and Jesus in the following pericope (10:21-24) gives the reason for the triumph:[42] as simple ones they have received the revelation of the Father that comes from the intimate, exclusive, reciprocal knowledge of the Father and the Son. At a minimum the passage speaks of the mutual knowledge of personal identity that only a father and son can possess of each other through intimate personal observation and self-revelation. That Jesus claims a special relationship to God as Son to Father is indicated by (1) the remote context of special (conception) sonship running through Luke; (2) the special address to his Father (*"Abba"*) in the Spirit (v. 21); (3) the identification of this Father as his Father (πατρός μου, v. 22a); (4) the claim that this knowledge gives unique authority to Jesus' revelation and works of healing

---

[38] Jewish literature does not associate "Son of God" with miraculous power over demons, but Luke 8:28//Mark 5:7 again associates the title with just such power.

[39] This is indicated by (1) the synoptic context, following the first prediction of the Passion and resurrection and the prediction that the Reign of God will come in the lifetime of the present generation, and (2) three redactional touches of Luke (the two men in 9:30 foreshadow the two in 24:4; Acts 1:10; the addition of glory [cf. 24:46], and the *exodus* in Jerusalem in 9:31-32).

[40] Jesus' teaching of the radical ethics of the Sermon carries that same authority, demonstrated by the destruction that attends nonobservance (Luke 6:49).

[41] Jesus sends them out to exorcise and to preach that the Reign is at hand (10:9-11, 17-18), and assures them that those who hear them hear himself (10:16).

[42] Arguing from the proximate context; construing from the immediate context (10:20), Jesus gives the reason why their names are written in heaven.

(10:23-24). This revelation to those whom Jesus calls blessed (the makarism in 10:24) confers something of that mutual knowledge peculiar to Father and Son, and so brings the recipients of the revelation into their own relationship of sonship to the Father. This consequence is not explicit here, but does become so at the beginning of the next chapter (11:2-4).

Luke 11:2b-4: Here most clearly in the synoptic tradition Jesus invites his disciples to address God with his own intimate term of relationship, *"Abba."* By receiving Jesus' revelation of God they have become special children. Such revelation empowers them not only to preach and heal, but also to do the works of God, such as forgiving sins (cf. μόνος in Luke 5:21). However one takes the condition expresssed in καὶ γὰρ (11:4b),[43] the disciples are already exercising a power of forgiveness that signals the work of the Father (Luke 5:21; 15:7, 10; 18:14; 23:34), the work of the Son (5:24, 32; [9:55?]; 15:1-32; 19:1-10; [22:61-62?]; 23:34, 43), and so the work signalizing the arrival of the eschatological salvation (1:77-79; 3:1-6; 17:4; 19:7-10; 23:43; 24:47; Acts 2:38, etc.).

This empowerment to do the works of Father and Son because one already is a son or daughter is ascribed to the Holy Spirit in the following pericope. At the end of a passage on a father's providence for his children (11:11-12) Jesus argues *a fortiori* that the heavenly Father will give his children the Spirit (11:13). This Spirit made Jesus the Son (1:35; 3:21-22), empowered him for his eschatological work (4:18-21), and enabled him to rejoice in calling God *"Abba"* (10:21). If this Spirit is now given to the disciples, they too will be able to call God *"Abba"* (11:2b; cf. Gal 4:6; Rom 8:15-16) and do the eschatological work of forgiving sins (11:4).[44] If

[43] Jean Carmignac, *Recherches sur le "Nôtre Père"* (Paris: Letouzey et Ané, 1969) 230–35, takes it not as the condition that forces God to forgive us, but as the condition that enables us to ask. I go further: it is because God has already given us the gift of sonship that our ability to forgive as God forgives is the condition for our asking and receiving a child's forgiveness from her father.

[44] That this empowerment in the Spirit is already present in Jesus' work is the burden of the next passage (11:20). Luke links two phases of the Spirit's work: Jesus' mission was to baptize his disciples in the Holy Spirit and fire (3:16). Such a baptism is promised in 24:29; Acts 1:4-5 and occurs in Acts 2:3-4, and designated a phenomenon of the last days in Acts 2:17. The disciples go out to do the very works that Jesus had done in the Spirit: curing a cripple (Luke 5:25; 7:22; Acts 3:1-20; 9:32-35; 14:8-10); raising the dead (Luke 7:11-17; 8:49-56; Acts 9:3-42; 20:7-10). This wonderworking power in which Peter and Paul parallel the works of the Lord manifests that the Spirit, which had already signalized the presence of the Reign of God in Jesus' ministry (Luke 11:20), is now making that Reign present in the life of the church (Luke 9:27). The Spirit is also a gift for the historical time of persecution already broken out against Luke's community (Luke 12:12). Luke's conscious editing of the synoptic apocalypse clearly separates the time of persecution (21:12-19; cf. the similarity of 21:14-15 to 12:11-12) from that of the parousial eschaton (21:25-28).

the Spirit can empower disciples to be children of God, do Jesus' works, and resist persecution, it can enable them to live the divine ethics of the Sermon.

Luke 22:70-71 is the one place in Luke-Acts where Jesus allows himself to be called Son of God. Possibly he means the (messianic) royal Son (22:67), qualified by his reinterpretation of "Son of God" by the destiny of the Son of Man (cf. 9:20-22), just as he describes the destiny of Christ in terms of the Servant (24:26, 46). However, Luke's removal of his source's explicit identification of Christ with Son of God (cf. Mark 14:61//Matt 26:63) warns against too simple an identification.[45]

In **Acts 9:20** Paul, immediately after his conversion, proclaims Jesus in Damascus in terms of the Christian kerygma: Jesus is the Son of God. The parallel proclamation that Jesus is the Christ in v. 22 indicates that at this stage of the proclamation "Son of God" means the royal Messiah. This is confirmed by Paul's usage in Acts 13:33, where the risen Jesus is proclaimed the Son of God as fulfillment of the psalm of royal enthronement (2:7).

Conclusions

1. *For Jesus as Son of God.*

a. There is in Luke-Acts a traditional theology of sonship by the power of the Spirit in the resurrection (Acts 2:34-36; 13:33), which Luke highlights redactionally (Luke 9:21-36).

b. Luke more fully presents the synoptic christology in which Jesus is Son of God in his ministry (Luke 3:21-22)—indeed, he intensifies this christology by making Jesus Son of God in his whole human life (1:32-35). In general this sonship is of the royal adoption type, but stretched out of such a clearly definable category by reinterpretation in terms of the Servant of YHWH (3:22; 4:18-22; 9:21-36; 22:67-71).[46]

c. This sonship in all cases is effected and empowered by the Spirit of God, whether in Jesus' conception (1:32-35), or in his baptism (3:21-22, with 4:1, 14), or in his ministry of preaching (4:18), or of exorcising (11:20).

---

[45] However, by omitting the charge of blasphemy (22:71 in comparison with Mark 14:64//Matt 26:65) Luke is not stressing the special Sonship to the Father that derives from his miraculous conception.

[46] Emphasis on a historical sonship does not de-eschatologize the notion of Son of God, since Lukan theology considers the historical time of Jesus and the church to be eschatological reality now moved into time (Luke 11:20; Acts 2:3-4, 7).

d. Luke specially emphasizes Jesus' conception as Son of God. It is prominent in the Prologue's foreshadowing of Jesus' career and destiny, and from that preeminent position it influences subsequent uses of the title (3:22, 23, 38; 4:3, 9, 22, 41) or of other titles (1:43, 76, etc.). Conception as Son of God grounds Q's unique sonship (Luke 10:22, the intimate, exclusive, reciprocal knowledge of Father and Son; Luke 11:2, the address of God as *"Abba"* — cf. 22:42; 23:34). Indeed, sonship by conception, by the very nature of the symbol of sonship, implies a deeper metaphysical relationship to a Father of the same species than do some forms of preexistence christology (e.g., a preexistent Wisdom christology).[47]

2. *For Disciples as sons of God the evidence in Luke-Acts is exceedingly sparse.*

a. Luke's one clear use of the term (Luke 20:36) speaks of eschatological sons of God. The resurrection will transform the disciples so that they neither marry nor die, but approach the angelic possession of eternal life.

b. But if "sons of God" in any way derives its meaning from the use of the title for Jesus it is not because they are, like him, sons from the moment of their conception. If they are, like the Jews, sons of God because they act like God (cf. Matt 5:45; Luke 6:35c), it is because God has made them his sons and daughters. This seems to be intimated in Luke-Acts in three ways:

(1) As Jesus' baptism in the Spirit made him Son of God (3:22; Acts 13:33), his mission is to baptize his disciples in the Spirit (3:16), presumably making them sons of God, so that they can call God *"Abba"* (11:2b; 8:21; 10:22).

(2) This enables them to do Jesus' works (10:9, 16), as evidenced in the healing works of Peter and Paul in Acts, which parallel Jesus' own. In short, their actions in the Spirit are those of Jesus the Son.

(3) Thus Christians as special sons and daughters of God will not only be so in a new way (angelic sons of God in the resurrection, 22:70-71), but now enjoy this new relationship in their present (eschatological) existence. Therefore they can act in the radically new imitation of the Father that is the basis of Jesus' ethic of forgiveness (11:4; 15:1-32, etc.) and compassion (6:35d-36).

---

[47] I have already justified this intimation of the metphysical in the figurative language of the Bible in my essay in Robert J. Daly, ed., *Christian Biblical Ethics* (New York: Paulist, 1984) 49–54, as well as in ch. 6 above.

Narrative Asides
in Lukan Discourse Material

The narrative aside of Luke 6:39a, which breaks into the continuous speech of Jesus in Luke 6:20b-49, has not been adequately explained. For source critics it reveals a shift in sources;[1] for rhetorical critics it marks a new unit of the Sermon.[2] But neither group has proved its position.[3] Steven Sheeley's study of narrative asides in Luke does not deal with 6:39a because his work is focused entirely on narrative asides *within narrative material*.[4] Hence we still need a study of such a narrative aside in the midst of speech material.[5]

Since Luke is the conscious author of εἶπεν δὲ καὶ παραβολὴν αὐτοῖς,[6] close literary study of his use of verbs of saying with παραβολὴν in

---

[1] Among commentators on Luke, Paul Schanz, H. J. Holtzmann, Erich Klostermann, Alfred Loisy, J. M. Creed, Friedrich Hauck, and Walter Schmithals. Heinz Schürmann (*Das Lukasevangelium* [Freiburg: Herder, 1969] 367 n. 164) finds 6:39a a slight Lukan retouching of a clause that already stood in his source; similarly I. Howard Marshall.

[2] Among commentators, Georg L. Hahn, Bernhard Weiss, Alfred Plummer, Marie-Joseph Lagrange, Karl H. Rengstorf, Alfred R. Leaney, Walter Grundmann, Heinz Schürmann, David L. Tiede, and John Nolland.

[3] C. F. Georg Heinrici, *Die Berpredigt (Matth 5–7. Luk 6,20-49)* (Leipzig: Dürr, 1900), asserts that the aside in Luke 6:39a opens a new rhetorical section of the Sermon, marked by figurative language. But he does not argue the point from Lukan usage; indeed, figurative language in Luke 6:38 had preceded the aside. Yet this division has dominated rhetorical analysis of the Sermon for a century.

[4] *Narrative Asides in Luke-Acts.* JSNT.SS 72 (Sheffield: Sheffield Academic Press, 1992) 98–119 shows that seventy per cent of the asides provide material necessary to understand the story.

[5] Robert C. Tannehill, *The Narrative Unity of Luke-Acts: A Literary Interpretation.* 2 vols. (Minneapolis: Fortress, 1986) 1:174 notes Luke's use of such asides with parables, but the discussion is brief.

[6] Εἶπεν (58x in Luke; 14 in Acts) and δὲ καὶ are Lukan; Henry J. Cadbury, *The Style and Literary Method of Luke* (Cambridge, Mass.: Harvard University Press, 1920) 169,

narrative asides may help. For this investigation I define a narrative aside operationally, in terms of Luke 6:39a. The narrator breaks into the speech of a character without advancing the narrative; the aside does not show a change of speaker or addressees, nor does it introduce a new topic or set a new scene, or indicate an action that reacts to the preceding speech or elicits a further speech act by the present speaker. These asides contain no information, but advert to figurative language about to be used, something the reader could figure out for herself. In short, there is so little content in such a narrative aside that it could easily be omitted.

I. The Data

A. λέγειν or εἰπεῖν παραβολήν: Luke uses λέγειν or εἰπεῖν παραβολὴν as a narrative aside in speech material nine times in the gospel: 5:36; 6:39; 12:16; 13:6; 18:1, 9; 19:11; 20:9; 21:29.[7] The aside marks a change of source only twice (18:1; 19:11); thus that is not a function of the Lukan aside. Luke 5:36; 12:16; 13:6; 18:1; 21:29 perfectly fit the pattern we modeled on 6:39: they do not change the audience or the topic, nor do they introduce a new rhetorical unit.[8] Twice (18:9; 20:9) the narrative aside changes the audience but leaves the topic and the rhetorical unit intact. Only 19:11 does not fit our pattern, for it changes both the audience and the topic, and introduces a new rhetorical unit, the appearance of the judge in the Reign of God.[9] Thus of the nine narrative asides introducing a parable,

---

146. Except for Mark 12:12, εἶπεν παραβολὴν is only Lukan in the gospels; Alfred Plummer, *A Critical and Exegetical Commentary on the Gospel according to St. Luke* (Edinburgh: T & T Clark, 1896) 190 and Schürmann, *Lukasevangelium* 367 n. 161. Schürmann points out that, with the exception of Mark 13:33, only Luke uses verbs of saying with παραβολὴν in the accusative.

[7] Six other uses of λέγειν or εἰπεῖν with παραβολὴν are not narrative asides in Jesus' speech. Three times the clause follows upon narrative, so these do not interrupt speech material (8:4; 14:7; 15:3). Once it is integral to Jesus' speech, not an aside (4:23), and twice (12:41; 20:19) others use the clause in reaction to Jesus' usage of parables.

[8] In 18:1 the topic (the coming of the Reign of God) remains the same throughout 17:22-37. Luke interrupts Jesus' long speech to add a parable on the necessity of prayer while awaiting the Son of Man. The parable refocuses the topic of eschatological judgment by illustrating its surety, but this refocusing does not introduce a new rhetorical section, any more than the paired parable in 18:9 introduces a new rhetorical section.

[9] Six other Lukan uses of verbs of saying with παραβολὴν do not fit the pattern of an aside interrupting one's speech. Three times the clause follows other narrative settings of scene, so that there is no speech of Jesus to be interrupted (8:4; 14:7; 15:3). Once Jesus himself uses the clause in his own speech (4:23). Once a new speaker (Peter) uses the clause in speaking to Jesus (12:41). Finally, 20:19 is not an aside but a narrative reaction of the addressees to Jesus' parable, followed by more narration.

six occur in our narrowly defined pattern (5:36; 6:39; 12:16; 13:6; 18:1; 21:29). Two other narrative interruptions that change the audience (18:9; 20:9), and one (19:11) that not only changes the audience but also sets a new topic, exceed the pattern of 6:39. However, in eight of the nine cases the parable illustrates material Jesus had been discussing, and so it is too retrospective to introduce a new rhetorical unit.[10]

B. *Other Narrative Asides within Speeches:* Once the pattern emerges one can identify four other such asides in Luke. Curiously, three of them introduce parabolic language. Luke 11:5 καὶ εἶπεν πρὸς αὐτοὺς introduces the similitude of the friend at midnight; 13:20 καὶ πάλιν ἔλεγεν introduces the similitude of yeast; 15:11 εἶπεν δὲ introduces the parable of the Prodigal Son. The last one, 21:10 τότε ἔλεγεν αὐτοῖς, clears up the confusion of expecting an imminent *parousia* or of identifying its imminence with the Temple's destruction. None of these changes audience, topic, rhetorical unit, or source. They are as "contentless" as the preceding nine asides.

Thus we have in Luke a total of ten narrative asides (Luke 5:36; 6:39a; 11:5; 12:16; 13:6, 20; 15:11; 18:1; 21:10, 29) that break into a speech without changing speaker, audience, or topic, and so seem otiose.

II. Interpretation of the Data

What might be Luke's rhetorical purpose for such seemingly useless asides?[11]

They may break up long speeches, providing a breather, or variation: 5:36 occurs in 5:34-39 (105 words); 6:39a in 6:20-49 (573 words); 11:5 in 11:2-13 (197 words); 12:16 in 12:15-40 (431 words); 13:6 in 13:2b-9 (139 words); 13:20 in 13:18-21 (59 words); 15:11 in 15:4–16:13 (788 words); 18:1 in 17:20–18:14 (483 words); 21:10 and 29 in 21:8-36 (443 words)

More obviously and significantly, they introduce either figurative language or an attempt to clear up a complex confusion on the part of the community. We have seen that six of the asides explicitly introduce a parable (5:36; 6:39a; 12:16; 13:6; 18:1; 18:9; 21:29) and three additional narrative asides in speech material (11:5; 13:20; 15:11) introduce similitudes

---

[10] When 19:11 introduces a new topic and 18:1, 9 refocus the topic, Luke adds supplementary clauses to guide the reader to the new focus on the topic at hand. Thus if 6:39 were a change of topic Luke would spell that out for the reader.

[11] I exclude the possibility that they are a Lukan pattern of oral speech, rather like the colloquial "He said . . . and then he said . . . ." These long speeches show no evidence of such a pattern.

or a parable. Luke 21:10 clarifies eschatological material that confused the early Christian community (and has bedeviled forty-five years of Lukan scholarship).

This connection of narrative asides with figurative language and confusing predictions shows that Luke thinks of parables as subtle and mysterious, and so lets his audience know that Jesus is using figurative language. Luke clearly thinks the parables are not easy to understand, even for disciples (8:9). Further, Luke has nothing similar to Mark 4:33, where Mark points out that parables were adapted to the listeners' learning style, or to 4:34, where he shows Jesus clarifying the meaning of the parables to his disciples in private.[12] Because his parables embody a mysterious message, Luke, more than the other evangelists, carefully gives the setting of a parable and often adds an application to facilitate its interpretation.[13]

In short, just before Jesus talks about matter that is subtle or confusing, Luke alerts his readers that something subtle is coming. This interpretation coheres with Sheeley's finding that narrative asides in narrative material are principally used to explain material necessary to understand the story. In the narrative asides in speech material, Luke has Jesus warn his readers to watch out for the mysterious meaning of figurative language and other materials misunderstood by his disciples.

III. Conclusions

In interpreting 6:39a, this investigation has revealed that the narrative aside introducing a parable into Jesus' speech

> (1) is part of Luke's art in giving the reader a breather in a long speech (the Sermon is, with 475 words of Jesus, the third longest of Jesus' speeches in Luke);

> (2) calls attention to the intricate and mysterious meaning of the figurative language of the parable that follows;[14]

---

[12] Also omitted, whether Luke knew of the passage or not, is anything similar to Matt 13:35's assertion that Jesus shouted out what had been hidden from the world's foundation.

[13] One can see the careful setting of the scene that guides interpretation of the parable in Lukan redaction of traditional material, as in 15:1-3 (πρὸς αὐτοὺς). The effort to supply applications is especially clear in the parables that derive from Lukan SG (7:43; 10:36-37; 11:8, 13; 12:21; 13:28-30; 14:11, 33; 15:10; 17:10; 18:8cd, 14). Even those without specific applications are set in contexts that interpret them (13:6-9; 15:11-32; 16:19-31). Even when the parable's mysterious meaning escapes secure interpretation Luke does his best to give his readers hints (16:9-13).

[14] As our exegesis points out, the "parable" in 6:39a actually describes three different figures and the relationship between them is extremely confusing.

(3) does not begin a new rhetorical section of the speech, but rather connects what follows with what went before. In all of the cases of pure narrative asides, none introduces a new topic, still less a new rhetorical section. Thus those who argue on the basis of the narrative aside that a new section begins in 6:39 must have other arguments to support their division.

Lukan Anthropology

In Luke's gospel Jesus, no less than his disciples, is fully embodied, from conception to resurrection, and so senses with his eyes, ears, and hands, thinks and loves, eats, drinks, and dies. Our concern is with how the various organs and powers of these human beings function in ethical actions.

In general the Hebrew language does not have the range of words that the Greeks had for mind or will as the source of human action.[1] In the NT, besides καρδία, these are the faculties/organs that generate human thought and action:

αἴσθησις (perception), 1x (in Paul)
διάνοια (mind, imagination), 12x (evenly distributed among NT authors)
θέλημα (human will as source of one's own action), 8x
νοῦς (the [speculative] mind), 24x (21 in Paul)
σάρξ (the flesh), 147x (91x in Paul)
σπλάγχνα (the guts as source of compassionate action), 11x (8x in Paul)
συνείδησις (consciousness, conscience, conscientiousness), 30x (20x in Paul)
σύνησις (the faculty of understanding, intelligence, insight), 7x (5x in Paul)
σῶμα (the body), 142x (91x in Paul)
φρήν (the breast, heart, mind), 2x (both in Paul)
φρόνημα (aim, aspiration), 4x (all in Paul)
φρόνησις (way of thinking, understanding), 2x
πνεῦμα (the human spirit), 30x (20 in Paul)
ψυχή (the soul as principle of life, heart, mind), 101x (evenly distributed).

[1] The main Greek words are ψυχή (soul), νοῦς, θυμός, φρήν, φρόνημα, διάνοια, φρόντις, σύνησις, συνείδησις (mind), νόημα (intellect), βούλημα, θέλημα (will), φαντασία (imagination), σῶμα (body), αἴσθησις, αἴσθημα (sensation), καρδία, κῆρ, ἦτορ (heart), σπλάγχνα (guts). Of these the LXX uses διάνοια (90x), θυμός (4.5 columns of Hatch and Redpath's concordance), καρδία (13 columns), σάρξ (3 columns), σύνησις (2 columns), and σῶμα (2 columns), to cover most of these uses. The rest of the words do not occur at all, or occur less than 45 times, mostly in the Hellenistic books. The classic work for the Hebrew terms is Hans-Walter Wolff's *Anthropology of the Old Testament* (Philadelphia: Fortress, 1974).

This rough table suggests that Paul is the NT author who has the most developed anthropology. Further analysis would reveal that the synoptics have a quite undeveloped psychological and anthropological analysis of human behavior.

Luke shares the general synoptic lack of interest in the internal structures of human behavior. His principal articulation of this structure is Jesus' citation of the commandment leading to eternal life (Deut 6:5): ἀγαπήσεις Κύριον τὸν θεόν σου ἐξ ὅλης καρδίας σου καὶ ἐν ὅλῃ τῇ ψυχῇ σου καὶ ἐν ὅλῃ τῇ ἰσχύϊ σου, καὶ ἐν ὅλῃ τῇ διάνοιᾳ σου (Luke 10:27). Although due allowance must be made for the Semitic piling up of parallel expressions, it is possible that both Deuteronomy and Luke intended to articulate four discrete human faculties as the totality of undivided human dedication to God. In that case, καρδία would refer to the emotional depths of human decision, ψυχή to the Jew's vitality and consciousness, ἰσχύς (for δύναμις) to energy and executive power, and διάνοια to one's intelligence and planning capabilities.[2] Again, the angel distinguishes between καρδία and φρόνησις (understanding, mind) when he gives the Baptist's role as converting the καρδίας of fathers toward their children and the disobedient toward φρονήσει δικαίων (Luke 1:17). Such parallel usage might signal a distinction between a person's commitment rooted in emotion and an intellectual understanding triggering conversion. Elsewhere, however, Luke is not so clear: in 1:51 he puts διάνοια καρδίας together,[3] so that intelligent planning may be part of the heart's function, or perhaps the phrase may refer to the effect of perverse desires on the mind.

The clearest word for this faculty of intelligence is νοῦς in Luke 24:45, where it refers to the speculative understanding of the Scriptures.[4] Luke uses σύνησις in 2:47 to describe the boy Jesus' intelligence or intellectual grasp of the law. Finally, in Acts 23:1; 24:16 συνείδησις describes Paul's conscience, i.e., his understanding and decision about how to act as a moral agent. Thus it is clear that Luke conceives of the human person as having an ability to grasp the world and relations such that one can live a moral life, but he has no consecrated terms for these powers and rarely

---

[2] Joseph A. Fitzmyer, *The Gospel According to Luke*. 2 vols. AB 28, 28A (Garden City, N.Y.: Doubleday, 1981, 1985) 878–80, opposed to I. Howard Marshall, *The Gospel of Luke* (Exeter: Paternoster, 1978) 444. That all the synoptics include διάνοια, although it is not in the OT text, may indicate that the tradition made some distinctions between these powers.

[3] Again this usage comes from Luke's source (in this case the canticles), and so we cannot ascribe it to Luke's conscious artistic intention.

[4] The conjunction of νοῦς with συνιέναι emphasizes this speculative function. Here the fact that νοῦς is *hapax* in the gospels and occurs in Luke's *Sondergut* indicates a more conscious and more proper Lukan conception.

refers to them. Like any dramatic writer, he shows such a faculty in the action of his characters.

We have already seen in Chapter 7 that καρδία is the most important anthropological term in the OT and in the NT (where it is used 156x). Luke uses it (42x) in its Hebrew sense as an organ of thinking, but he regularly emphasizes its role in decision-making leading to moral (or sinful) action.

Luke uses πνεῦμα only four times in Luke-Acts to indicate an intrinsic principle of human activity.[5] In Luke 8:55 and 23:46 it refers to the principle of life, its meaning as *rûaḥ* throughout the Hebrew Bible (Gen 7:22).[6] In 1:47 Mary's spirit rejoices in God her savior; in 1:80 the Baptist becomes strong in spirit. In both these uses πνεῦμα refers to the seat of the intellect and will as they orient one to God. Consequently, in Luke it can refer to the source of conscious human acts of praising God or following God's will.

Much more common is Luke's use of ψυχή, soul, as the source of conscious human activity. Ordinarily Luke takes it to mean the soul as principle of physical life (Luke 6:9; 12:20, 22; 14:26; Acts 20:10, 24; 27:10, 22).[7] Sometimes, however, one and the same ψυχή stands for both the physical life and one's eternal life (Luke 9:24 twice; 12:23; 17:33). From there it comes to mean the principle of eternal life (Luke 9:56; 21:19; Acts 2:27). In Acts "souls" comes to mean discrete persons (2:41, 43; 3:23; 7:14; 27:37). In Acts 4:32 the community is of one heart and soul, as if it were one person.[8] Corresponding to our inquiry here, the soul is the conscious center of human action: striving for the necessities of life and enjoying them (Luke 12:19), the seat of loving and sorrow pierced by a sword (2:35), the mind that does not function properly when poisoned (Acts 14:2) or upset (15:24), the seat of resolution and endurance (Acts 14:22). Finally,

---

[5] The Baptist's mission "in the spirit and power of Elijah" probably means "after the model of," "inspired by," and not driven by Elijah's personal spirit. In 4:33 πνεῦμα δαιμονίου ἀκαθάρτου should mean the spirit as a faculty of the unclean spirit, but the language really means "an unclean diabolical spirit," as is indicated by 4:35b where the demon acts, not the demon's spirit.

[6] For the Hebrew notion of the conjunction of breath and life see Erik Sjöberg, "πνεῦμα," *TDNT* 6:375–77; Wolff, *Anthropology* 34–36.

[7] This is the fundamental meaning of the word in both Greek and Hebrew thought; Edmond Jacob, "ψυχή," *TDNT* 9:608–31. In a related use Barnabas and Paul devoted their souls (lives, careers) to (spreading) the name of Jesus (Acts 15:26).

[8] In Acts 2:43-47; 4:32-37 Luke consciously employs the Hellenistic *topos* of friendship, in which friends have all things in common (2:44; 4:32) and are of one soul (4:32). Luke may have added καρδία to give a biblical flavor to the Hellenistic commonplace, as Luke T. Johnson suggests in *The Acts of the Apostles*. SP 5 (Collegeville: The Liturgical Press, 1992) 86.

ψυχή is used in synthetic parallelism with πνεῦμα to describe the center of praising and magnifying God (Luke 1:46).

Although θέλημα, the will, is almost always used of God's will in the NT, Luke uses it three times of the human faculty of deciding and executing action. In the parable of the stewards the untrustworthy steward knows his master's will and does not act in accordance with it (12:47). In Luke 22:42 Jesus sets aside his own will not to have to suffer in favor of God's will. In 23:25 Pilate gives Jesus over to the will of the crowd. This is the clearest description in Luke-Acts of a human faculty that determines action.

Luke uses σάρξ (flesh) in Luke 3:6; Acts 2:17, 26, 31 as his OT citations (Isa 40:5; Joel 3:1; Ps 15:9-10) do—to indicate a human being or all humanity. In Luke 24:39 σάρξ is contrasted with πνεῦμα (here a ghost) to indicate a physical body, as it does in Acts 2:31, and this usage probably colors all of his uses. Σῶμα, the body, means the embodiment of the human person as mortal. In fact, four of Luke's thirteen gospel uses refer to a dead body, a corpse (17:37; 23:52, 55; 24:3, 23). In 12:4 σῶμα refers to the part of human existence bound for temporal death; in 12:22-23 it is associated with such trivialities as clothing, although the body, as human, is (destined for) more than clothing. Yet when Jesus gives his body to his disciples in 22:19 he means his whole person, including all his thinking and loving faculties. But in none of these passages does Luke use σάρξ or σῶμα to indicate an active role in moral agency. Even in 11:33-36, where the eye communicates light to the whole body in such a way as to make the whole person light in accepting Jesus' message, it is the eye (probably as a symbol of the open heart and mind) that is the active agent in getting the person to receive Jesus' word.[9]

Σπλάγχνα (guts, heart) indicates an emotional response that triggers compassionate action in 1:78 (cf. the verbal form in 7:13; 10:33; 15:20).

Summary: In Chapter 7 we saw that καρδία, Luke's favorite word for the intrinsic principle of human activity, means the center of emotionally engaged thinking that leads to decision and action (moral conduct). Indeed, Luke's words for a more theoretical reasoning faculty (νοῦς, διάνοια, σύνησις) are rare and always susceptible of moving in the direction of συνείδησις, conscience. Πνεῦμα, like ψυχή (but much more rarely), refers to the principle of life. Twice in Luke 1–2 πνεῦμα means a principle of human thinking and acting oriented toward God. Ψυχή more often refers to the human center of thought and will, but it too does not clearly distinguish these two activities. Σάρξ and σῶμα usually refer to human physical existence, and never describe a principle of human activity.

---

[9] Fitzmyer, *Luke* 939–40.

In short, Luke's work does not contain an articulated biblical anthropology such as one finds in Paul's use of σάρξ, ψυχή, and πνεῦμα. Luke uses these terms and others, but he does not distinguish them clearly or articulate how they ground or issue in human thought and action.

Selected Bibliography

I. Modern Commentaries on Luke

Bovon, François. *Das Evangelium nach Lukas.* EKK 3/1-2. Neukirchen-Vluyn: Neukirchener Verlag; Zürich: Benziger, 1989, 1996.

Caird, George B. *The Gospel of Saint Luke.* Harmondsworth: Penguin, 1963.

Creed, John Martin. *The Gospel according to St. Luke.* London: Macmillan, 1930.

Danker, Frederick W. *Jesus and the New Age.* Rev. ed. Philadelphia: Fortress, 1988.

Ellis, E. Earle. *The Gospel of Luke.* London: Nelson, 1966.

Ernst, Josef. *Das Evangelium nach Lukas übersetzt und erklärt.* Regensburg: Pustet, 1977.

Evans, Christopher F. *Saint Luke.* Philadelphia: Trinity Press International, 1990.

Fitzmyer, Joseph A. *The Gospel According to Luke.* 2 vols. AB 28, 28A. Garden City, N.Y.: Doubleday, 1981, 1985.

Goulder, Michael D. *Luke: A New Paradigm.* 2 vols. JSOT.SS 20. Sheffield: Sheffield Academic Press, 1989.

Grundmann, Walter. *Das Evangelium nach Lukas.* Berlin: Evangelische Verlaganstalt, 1961.

Hahn, Georg L. *Das Evangelium nach Lukas erklärt.* 2 vols. Breslau: Morgenstern, 1892, 1894.

Hauck, Friedrich. *Das Evangelium nach Lukas.* Leipzig: Deichert, 1934.

Johnson, Luke Timothy. *The Gospel of Luke.* SP 3. Collegeville: The Liturgical Press, 1991.

Klostermann, Erich. *Das Lukasevangelium.* HNT 2:1. Tübingen: J.C.B. Mohr (Paul Siebeck), 1919.

Lagrange, Marie-Joseph. *Evangile selon Saint Luc.* Paris: Gabalda, 1921.

LaVerdiere, Eugene. *Luke.* Wilmington, Del.: Michael Glazier, 1980.

Leaney, Alfred R. C. *The Gospel according to St. Luke.* London: A. and C. Black, 1966.

Loisy, Alfred. *L'Evangile selon Luc.* Paris: E. Noury, 1924.

Manson, Thomas W. *The Gospel of Luke.* London: Hodder and Stoughton, 1930.

Marshall, I. Howard. *The Gospel of Luke.* NIGTC. Exeter: Paternoster, 1978.

Nolland, John. *Luke 1–9:20. Luke 9:21–18:34. Luke 18:35-24:53.* 3 vols. WBC 35A, B, C. Dallas: Word Books, 1989.

Plummer, Alfred. *A Critical and Exegetical Commentary on the Gospel according to St. Luke*. ICC Edinburgh: T & T Clark, 1896.

Rengstorf, Karl H. *Das Evangelium nach Lukas*. Göttingen: Vandenhoeck & Ruprecht, 1962.

Rigaux, Béda. *Témoignage de l'Evangile de Luc*. Bruges: Desclée de Brouwer, 1970.

Schanz, Paul. *Commentar über das Evangelium des heiligen Lukas*. Tübingen: Franz Fues, 1883.

Schlatter, Adolf. *Das Evangelium des Lukas: aus seinen Quellen erklärt*. Stuttgart: Calwer, 1960.

Schmid, Josef. *Das Evangelium nach Lukas*. Regensburg: Pustet, 1955.

Schmithals, Walter. *Das Evangelium nach Lukas*. Zürich: Theologischer Verlag, 1980.

Schürmann, Heinz. *Das Lukasevangelium*. HTKNT 3. Freiburg: Herder, 1969.

Tannehill, Robert C. *The Narrative Unity of Luke-Acts: A Literary Interpretation*. 2 vols. Philadelphia: Fortress, 1986.

Tiede, David L. *Luke*. Minneapolis: Augsburg: 1988.

Tinsley, Ernest J. *The Gospel according to Luke*. Cambridge: Cambridge University Press, 1965.

Weiss, Bernhard, and Johannes Weiss. *Die Evangelien des Markus und Lukas*. 8th ed. Göttingen: Vandenhoeck & Ruprecht, 1892.

Wellhausen, Julius. *Das Evangelium Lucae übersetzt und erklärt*. Berlin: G. Reimer, 1904.

Zahn, Theodor. *Das Evangelium des Lucas*. Leipzig: Deichert, 1930.

II. Other Works Cited

Achtemeier, Paul J. "The Lukan Perspective on the Miracles of Jesus: A Preliminary Sketch." *JBL* 94 (1975) 550–59.

_____. *1 Peter: A Commentary on First Peter*. Hermeneia. Minneapolis: Fortress, 1996.

Adamson, James B. *James: the Man and His Message*. Grand Rapids: Eerdmans, 1989.

Adkins, Arthur W. H. *Moral Values and Political Behaviour in Ancient Greece; from Homer to the End of the Fifth Century*. New York: Norton, 1972.

Albertz, Rainer. "Die 'Antrittspredigt' im Lukasevangelium auf ihrem alttestamentlichen Hintergrund," *ZNW* 74 (1983) 182–206.

Alexander, Loveday. "Luke's Preface in the Context of Greek Preface-writing," *NovT* 28 (1986) 48–74.

Allison, Dale C. "The Pauline Epistles and the Synoptic Gospels. The Pattern of the Parallels," *NTS* 28 (1982) 1–32.

Aune, David E. *Prophecy in Early Christianity and the Ancient Mediterranean World*. Grand Rapids: Eerdmans, 1983.

Barbiero, Gianni. *L'Asino del Nemico: Rinuncia alla vendetta e amore del nemico nella legislazione dell'Antico Testamento (Ex 23,4-5; Dt 22:1-4; Lv 19:17-18)*. Rome: Biblical Institute Press, 1991.

Barrett, Charles Kingsley. *A Commentary on the Epistle to the Romans.* New York: Harper, 1957.

Barrosse, Thomas. "The Relationship of Love and Faith in St. John," *TS* 18 (1957) 538–59.

Barton, John. "Postexilic Hebrew Prophecy," *ABD* 5:489–95.

Bartsch, Hans-Werner. "Feldrede und Bergpredigt: Redaktionsarbeit in Luk. 6," *TZ* 16 (1960) 5–18.

Bauer, Johannes B. "Sin," *EBT* 849–62.

Baudissin, Wolf W. F. "Die alttestamentliche Religion und die Armen," *Preussische Jahrbücher* 149 (1912) 193–231.

Baumann, Arnulf. "*ʾabal*," *TDOT* 1:44-48.

Beck, Brian E. *Christian Character in the Gospel of Luke.* London: Epworth, 1989.

Becker, Ernest. *The Denial of Death.* New York: Free Press, 1973.

Becker, Jürgen. "Feindesliebe—Nächstenliebe, Bruderliebe. Exegetische Betrachtungen als Anfrage an ein ethisches Problemfeld," *ZEE* 25 (1981) 5–18.

Behm, Johannes. "καρδία," *TDNT* 3:608–14.

Bellet, P. "Estructura i forma: annunciació de naixement i forma d'eleccio profètica (Lc 1,26-38)," *RevCatTeol* 7 (1982) 91–130.

Benson, John. "Making Friends: Aristotle's Doctrine of the Friend as Another Self," in Andros Loizou and Harry Lesser, eds., *Polis and Politics: Essays in Greek Moral and Political Philosophy.* Aldershot: Avebury, 1990.

Berger, Klaus. *Die Gesetzesauslegung Jesu; ihr historischer Hintergrund im Judentum und im Alten Testament.* WMANT 40. Neukirchen-Vluyn: Neukirchener Verlag, 1972.

Betz, Hans-Dieter. *Lukian von Samosata und das Neue Testament; religionsgeschichtliche und paranetische Parallelen. Ein Beitrag zum Corpus Hellenisticum Novi Testamenti.* Berlin: Akademie-Verlag, 1961.

_____. *Nachfolge und Nachahmung Jesu Christi im Neuen Testament.* Tübingen: J.C.B. Mohr (Paul Siebeck), 1967.

_____. *The Sermon on the Mount: A Commentary on the Sermon on the Mount, Including the Sermon on the Plain (Matthew 5:3–7:27 and Luke 6:20-49).* Hermeneia. Minneapolis: Fortress, 1995.

Beutler, Johannes. "Lk 6,16: Punkt oder Komma?" *BZ* 35 (1991) 231–33.

Bietenhard, Hans. "ὄνομα," *TDNT* 5:242–83.

Birkeland, Harris. *ʿAni und ʿanaw in den Psalmen.* Oslo: J. Dybwad, 1932.

_____. *Die Feinde des Individuums in der israelitischen Psalmenliteratur; ein Beitrag zur Kenntnis der semitischen Literatur- und Religionsgeschichte.* Oslo: Grøndahl & Sons, 1933.

Black, Matthew. *An Aramaic Approach to the Gospels and Acts.* London: Oxford, 1967.

Bock, Darrell L. *Proclamation from Prophecy and Pattern: Lucan Old Testament Christology.* Sheffield: Sheffield Academic Press, 1987.

Bolkestein, Hendrick. *Wohltätigkeit und Armenpflege im vorchristlichen Altertum.* Utrecht: A. Oosthoek, 1939.

Borg, Marcus. *Conflict, Holiness and Politics in the Teaching of Jesus*. Lewiston, N.Y.: Mellen, 1984.

_____. *Jesus: A New Vision*. San Francisco: HarperSan Francisco, 1987.

Borgen, Peder. "The Golden Rule with Emphasis on its Usage in the Gospels," in idem, *Paul Preaches Circumcision and Pleases Men, and Other Essays on Christian Origins*. Trondheim: TAPIR, 1983.

Bousset, Wilhelm. *Kyrios Christos*. Nashville: Abingdon, 1970 [1913].

Brawley, Robert L. *Luke-Acts and the Jews: Conflict, Apology, and Conciliation*. Atlanta: Scholars, 1987.

Broer, Ingo. "Plädierte Jesus für Gewaltlosigkeit?" *BiKi* 37 (1982) 61–69.

Brouwer, Steve. *Sharing the Pie*. New York: Holt, 1998.

Brown, Raymond E. *The Birth of the Messiah*. Garden City, N.Y.: Doubleday, 1977.

Bruppacher, Hans. *Die Beurteilung der Armut im Alten Testament*. Zürich: Seldwyla, 1924.

Büchsel, Friedrich. "κρίνω," *TDNT* 3:935–40.

Bultmann, Rudolf. "ἀπελπίζω," *TDNT* 2:534.

_____. "Aimer son prochain, commandement de Dieu," *RHPR* 10 (1930) 222–41.

_____. *Jesus and the Word*. New York: Scribner, 1958 [1926].

_____. "οἰκτίρω," *TDNT* 5:159.

_____. *Primitive Christianity in its Contemporary Setting*. New York: Meridian, 1956 [1949].

_____. *The History of the Synoptic Tradition*. New York: Harper & Row, 1963 [1919].

_____. *Theology of the New Testament*. London: S.C.M., 1955 [1948].

Burggraeve, Roger. *From Self-Development to Solidarity: An Ethical Reading of Human Desire in its Socio-Political Relevance According to Emmanuel Lévinas*. Leuven: Peeters, 1985.

Busse, Ulrich. *Die Wunder des Propheten Jesus: Die Rezeption, Komposition und Interpretation der Wundertradition im Evangelium des Lukas*. Stuttgart: Katholisches Bibelwerk, 1979.

_____. *Das Nazareth-Manifest Jesu.*. Stuttgart: Katholisches Bibelwerk, 1978.

Byrne, Brendan. "Christ's Pre-Existence in Pauline Soteriology," *TS* 58 (1997) 308–30.

_____. *"Sons of God"—"Seed of Abraham" : The Sonship of God of all Christians in Paul Against the Jewish Background*. AnBib 83. Rome: Biblical Institute Press, 1979.

Cadbury, Henry J. *The Style and Literary Method of Luke*. Cambridge, Mass.: Harvard University Press, 1920.

_____. "Commentary on the Preface of Luke," in Foakes Jackson and Kirsopp Lake, eds., *The Beginnings of Christianity* 2. London: Macmillan, 1926.

Carmignac, Jean. *Recherches sur le "Nôtre Père"* Paris: Letouzey et Ané, 1969.

Cassidy, Richard J. *Jesus, Politics, and Society: A Study of Luke's Gospel*. Maryknoll, N.Y.: Orbis, 1978.

Causse, Antonin. *Les "Pauvres" d'Israël*. Strasbourg: Librairie Istra, 1922.

Cerfaux, Lucien. "La section des pains (Mc VI,31–VIII,26; Mt XIV,13–XVI,12)." in Josef Schmid and Anton Vögtle, eds., *Synoptische Studien: Alfred Wikenhauser zum siebzigsten Geburtstag*. Munich: Zink, 1953.

Chilton, Bruce D. *The Kingdom of God in the Teaching of Jesus.* Philadelphia: Fortress, 1989.

Chirico, Peter. *Infallibility: The Crossroads of Doctrine.* Kansas City, Kan.: Sheed, Andrews, and McMeel, 1977.

Coleridge, Mark. *The Birth of the Lukan Narrative: Narrative as Christology in Luke 1–2.* JSNT.SS 88. Sheffield: JSOT Press, 1993.

Collins, Raymond F. "Beatitudes," *ABD* 1:629–31.

_____. "Twelve, The," *ABD* 6:67–71.

Colpe, Carsten. "ὁ υἱὸς τοῦ ἀνθρωποῦ," *TDNT* 8:400–477.

Conn, Walter E. *Conscience: Development and Self-Transcendence.* Birmingham, Ala.: Religious Education Press, 1981.

Conzelmann, Hans. *The Theology of Saint Luke.* New York: Harper & Row, 1960.

Copeland, M. Shawn. "Reconsidering the Idea of the Common Good," in Oliver Williams and John Houck, eds., *Catholic Social Thought and the New World Order.* Notre Dame, Ind.: University of Notre Dame Press, 1993.

Cosgrove, Charles H. "The Divine ΔEI in Luke-Acts: Investigations into the Understandings of God's Providence," *NovT* 26 (1984) 168–90.

Couroyer, Bernard. "De la mesure dont vous mesurez, il vous sera mesuré," *RB* 77 (1970) 366–70.

Cullman, Oscar. *Christ and Time.* Philadelphia: Westminster, 1960.

_____. *The Christology of the New Testament.* Philadelphia: Westminster, 1959.

Culpepper, R. Alan. "The Pivot of John's Prologue," *NTS* 27 (1980) 1–31.

Daly, Robert J., ed. *Christian Biblical Ethics.* New York: Paulist, 1984.

Davies, J. K. "Wealth, attitudes to," in Simon Hornblower and Antony Spawforth, eds., *The Oxford Classical Dictionary.* Oxford: Oxford University Press, 1996.

Davies, W. D. *The Setting of the Sermon on the Mount.* Cambridge: Cambridge University Press, 1964.

Day, Peggy L. *An Adversary in Heaven: Satan in the Hebrew Bible.* Atlanta: Scholars, 1988.

Delorme, Jean. "Luc v. 1-11: Analyse Structurale et Histoire de la Redaction," *NTS* 18 (1972) 331–50.

Dillon, Richard J. "Easter Revelation and Mission Program in Luke 24:46-48," in Daniel Durken, ed., *Sin, Salvation, and the Spirit.* Collegeville: The Liturgical Press, 1979.

_____. *From Eye-witnesses to Ministers of the Word: Tradition and Composition in Luke 24.* AnBib 82. Rome: Biblical Institute Press, 1978.

_____. "Previewing Luke's Project from His Prologue (Luke 1:1-4)," *CBQ* 43 (1981) 205–27.

Dodd, Charles Harold. "The Kingdom of God has Come," *ExpT* 48 (1936–37) 138–42.

_____. *The Parables of the Kingdom.* New York: Charles Scribner's Sons, 1961.

Dömer, Michael. *Das Heil Gottes. Studien zur Theologie des lukanischen Doppelwerkes.* Cologne: P. Hanstein, 1978.

Donahue, John R. "Tax Collector," *ABD* 6:337–38.

_____. *The Gospel in Parable.* Philadelphia: Fortress, 1988.

Doran, Robert M. *Theology and the Dialectics of History.* Toronto: University of Toronto Press, 1992.

Dover, Kenneth James. *Greek Popular Morality in the time of Plato and Aristotle.* Berkeley: University of California Press, 1974.

Duling, Dennis R. "Kingdom of God, Kingdom of Heaven," *ABD* 4:49–69.

Dunn, J. D. G. *Christology in the Making.* Philadelphia: Westminster, 1980.

_____. "Paul's Knowledge of the Jesus Tradition: the Evidence of Romans," in Karl Kertelge et al., eds., *Christus Bezeugen: Für Wolfgang Trilling.* ETS 59. Leipzig: St. Benno-Verlag, 1990.

Duplacy, Jean. "Le Veritable Disciple," *RSR* 69 (1981) 71–86.

Dupont, Jacques. "L'Appel à imiter Dieu en Matthieu 5,48 et Luc 6,36," *RivBib* 14 (1966) 137–58.

_____. *Les Béatitudes.* 2 vols. Paris: Gabalda, 1969.

_____. *Les tentations de Jésus au desert.* Bruges: Desclée de Brouwer, 1968.

_____. "Le salut des gentiles et la signification théologique du livre des Actes," *NTS* 6 (1959–60) 132–55.

_____. "Le Magnificat comme discours sur Dieu," *NRT* 102 (1980) 321–43.

_____. "The Poor and Poverty in the Gospel and Acts," in Augustin George, et al., *Gospel Poverty: Essays in Biblical Theology.* Chicago: Franciscan Herald Press, 1977.

Eisenman, Robert H., and Michael Wise. *The Dead Sea Scrolls Uncovered.* Rockport, Mass.: Element, 1992.

Elliott, John H. *A Home for the Homeless: A Sociological Exegesis of 1 Peter.* Philadelphia: Fortress, 1981.

_____. *What is Social Scientific Criticism?* Minneapolis: Fortress, 1993.

Ellis, E. Earle. "Present and Future Eschatology in Luke," *NTS* 12 (1965–66) 27–41.

_____. *Eschatology in Luke.* Philadelphia: Fortress, 1972.

Erdmann, Gottfried. *Die Vorgeschichten des Lukas- und Matthäus-Evangeliums und Vergils vierte Ekloge.* Göttingen: Vandenhoeck & Ruperecht, 1932.

Feuillet, André. "Vocation et mission des prophètes. Baptême et mission de Jesus," *NovVet* 54 (1979) 22–40.

Fichtner, Johannes. "πλησίον," *TDNT* 5:312–15.

Fishbane, Michael. "The Treaty Background of Amos 1:11 and Related Matters," *JBL* 89 (1970) 313–18.

Fitzmyer, Joseph A. "New Testament *Kyrios* and *Maranatha* and their Aramaic Background," in idem, *To Advance The Gospel: New Testament Studies.* New York: Crossroad, 1981.

_____. "The Composition of Luke, Chapter 9," in Charles H. Talbert, ed., *Perspectives on Luke-Acts.* Edinburgh: T & T Clark, 1978, 139–52.

_____. "The Contribution of Qumran Aramaic to the Study of the New Testament," *NTS* 20 (1973–74) 382–407.

_____. "The Semitic Background of the New Testament *Kyrios*-Title," in idem, *A Wandering Aramean: Collected Aramaic Essays* Missoula: Scholars, 1979.

_____. *Essays on the Semitic Background of the New Testament.* Atlanta: Scholars, 1974.

Flender, Helmut. *St. Luke, Theologian of Redemptive History.* London: S.P.C.K., 1967.

Foakes-Jackson, F. J., and Kirsopp Lake. *The Beginnings of Christianity.* 5 vols. London: Macmillan, 1920–1933.

Focke, Friedrich, "Synkrisis," *Hermes* 58 (1923) 327–68.

Foerster, Werner, and Gerhard von Rad. "διαβάλλω, διάβολος," *TDNT* 2:71–81.

Foerster, Werner. "ἔχθρος," *TDNT* 2:11–14.

_____. "κύριος," *TDNT* 3:1081–89.

Forsyth, Neil. *The Old Enemy: Satan and the Combat Myth.* Princeton: Princeton University Press, 1987.

Fossum, Jarl E. "Son of God," *ABD* 6:128–37.

Fowler, James. "Stages in Faith: the Structural Developmental Approach," in Thomas Hennessey, ed., *Values and Moral Development.* New York: Paulist, 1976.

Francis, Fred O. "Eschatology and History in Luke-Acts," *JAAR* 37 (1969) 49–63.

Franklin, Eric. *Christ the Lord: A Study in the Purpose and Theology of Luke-Acts.* London: S.P.C.K., 1975.

Frein, B. C. "Narrative Predictions, Old Testament Prophecies and Luke's Sense of Fulfilment," *NTS* 40 (1994) 22–37.

Frend, W. H. C. *Martyrdom and Persecution in the Early Church.* Oxford: Blackwell and Mott, 1965.

Freire, Paulo. *The Pedagogy of the Oppressed.* New York: Continuum, 1982.

Fuller, Reginald H. *The Foundations of New Testament Christology.* New York: Scribner, 1965.

Furnish, Victor P. *The Love Command in the New Testament.* Nashville: Abingdon, 1972.

Gager, John. *Kingdom and Community.* Englewood Cliffs, N.J.: Prentice-Hall, 1975.

Garrett, Susan R. *The Demise of the Devil: Magic and the Demonic in Luke's Writings.* Minneapolis: Fortress, 1989.

Gaventa, Beverly Roberts. "The Eschatology of Luke-Acts Revisited," *Encounter* 43 (1982) 27–42.

Gelin, Albert. *The Poor of Yahweh.* Collegeville: The Liturgical Press, 1964 [1953].

George, Augustin. "Le disciple fraternel et efficace. Lc 6 39-45," *Assemblées du Seigneur* 39 (1972) 68–77.

Gerhardsson, Birger. *The Testing of God's Son (Matt 4:1-11 & Par). An Analysis of an Early Christian Midrash.* Lund: Gleerup, 1966.

Gerstenberger, Erhard. "The Woe-Oracles of the Prophets," *JBL* 81 (1962) 249–63.

Gibson, Jeffrey B. "A Turn on 'Turning Stones to Bread.' A New Understanding of the Devil's Intentions in Q4:3," *BibRes* 41 (1996) 37–57.

Gilligan, Carol. *In a Different Voice.* Cambridge, Mass.: Harvard University Press, 1982.

Glöckner, Richard. *Die Verkündigung des Heils beim Evangelisten Lukas.* Walberger Studien 9. Mainz: Matthias Grünewald, 1975.

Goppelt, Leonhard, "πεινάω," *TDNT* 6:12–22.

Grässer, Erich. "Zum Verständnis des Gottesherrschaft," *ZNW* 65 (1974) 3–26.

Green, Joel B. "Jesus and a Daughter of Abraham (Luke 13:10-17): Test Case for a Lukan Perspective on Jesus' Miracles," *CBQ* 51 (1989) 643–54.

Greeven, Heinrich, "Erwägungen zur synoptischen textkritik," *NTS* 6 (1959–60) 281–96.

Gregson, Vernon, ed. *The Desires of the Human Heart: An Introduction to the Theology of Bernard Lonergan.* New York: Paulist, 1988.

Grundmann, Walter. "ἀγαθός," *TDNT* 1:10–18.

_____. "ἁμαρτάνω," *TDNT* 1:302–303.

_____. "καλός," *TDNT* 3:536–50.

Guillet, Jacques. "Blessing," *DBT* 47–51.

Hahn, Ferdinand. *The Titles of Jesus in Christology.* London: Lutterworth, 1969.

Hahn, P. *Structure in Rhetorical Criticism and the Structure of the Sermon on the Plain: Luke 6:20-49.* Milwaukee: Marquette University diss., 1990.

Hamm, M. Dennis. "Luke 19:8 Once Again: Does Zacchaeus Defend or Resolve?" *JBL* 107 (1988) 431–37.

_____. *The Beatitudes in Context.* Wilmington, Del.: Michael Glazier, 1990.

_____. "Zacchaeus Revisited Once More: A Story of Vindication or of Conversion?" *Bib* 72 (1991) 249–52.

Hamp, Vinzenz. "*bākāh*," *TDOT* 2:116–20.

Hanson, K. C., and Douglas Oakman. *Palestine in the Time of Jesus.* Minneapolis: Fortress, 1998.

Hanson, Paul D. *The Dawn of Apocalyptic: The Historical and Sociological Roots of Jewish Apocalyptic Eschatology.* Philadephia: Fortress, 1975.

Harder, Günther. "πονηρός," *TDNT* 6:546–48.

Hardie, William F. R. *Aristotle's Ethical Theory.* Oxford: Clarendon Press, 1980.

Hare, Douglas R. A. *The Theme of Jewish Persecution of Christians in the Gospel according to St. Matthew.* Cambridge: Cambridge University Press, 1967.

Hasel, Gerhard. "Sabbath," *ABD* 5:849–56.

Hauck, Friedrich. "καρπός," *TDNT* 3:614–15.

_____. "θησαυρός," *TDNT* 3:136.

Hauck, Friedrich, and Georg Bertram, "μακάριος," *TDNT* 4:362–70.

Haught, John F. *Religion and Self-Acceptance.* New York: Paulist, 1976.

Heck, E. "Krippenkind—Schmerzensmann. Eine bibeltheologische Betrachtung zu Lukas 2,1-20," *GL* 61 (1988) 451–59.

Heinrici, C. F. Georg. *Die Bergpredigt (Matth 5–7. Luk 6,20-49)* Leipzig: Dürr, 1900.

Hellmann, Marie-Christine. "Caves et sous-sols dans l'habitat grec antique," *Bulletin de correspondence hellénique* 116 (1992) 132–55.

Herntrich, Volkmar. "κρίνω," *TDNT* 3:923–26.

Herrmann, Johannes. "εὔχομαι," *TDNT* 2:785–800.

Highet, Gilbert. "Reciprocity," in Simon Hornblower and Antony Spawforth, eds., *The Oxford Classical Dictionary.* Oxford: Oxford University Press, 1996.

Hill, David. "The Rejection of Jesus at Nazareth (Luke iv, 16-30)," *NovT* 13 (1971) 161–80.

Holladay, John S., Jr. "House, Israelite," *ABD* 3:308–10.

Horbury, William. "The Benediction of the Minim and Early Jewish-Christian Controversy," *JTS* 33 (1982) 19–61.

Humbert, Paul. "'Laetari et exultare' dans le vocabulaire religieux de l'Ancien Testament," *RHPR* 22 (1942) 185–214.

Jacob, Edmond. "ψυχή," *TDNT* 9:608–31.

Jaeger, Werner W. *Paideia: The Ideals of Greek Culture.* Translated by Gilbert Highet. 3 vols. New York: Oxford University Press, 1943–45.

Jeremias, Joachim. *Die Sprache des Lukasevangeliums.* Göttingen: Vandenhoeck & Ruprecht, 1980.

_____. *Jesus' Promise to the Nations.* London: S.C.M., 1958.

_____. *New Testament Theology.* New York: Scribner, 1971.

_____. *The Eucharistic Words of Jesus.* London: S.C.M., 1966.

_____. *The Parables of Jesus.* London: S.C.M., 1963.

_____. *The Sermon on the Mount.* Philadelphia: Fortress, 1963.

Jervell, Jacob. *Luke and the People of God.* Minneapolis: Augsburg, 1972.

Johnson, Luke Timothy. *The Acts of the Apostles.* SP 5. Collegeville: The Liturgical Press, 1992.

_____. "On Finding the Lukan Community, A Cautious Cautionary Essay," *SBL Seminar Papers* 16/1 (1979) 87–100.

_____. *Sharing Possessions: Mandate and Symbol of Faith.* Philadelphia: Fortress, 1981.

_____. *The Literary Function of Possessions in Luke-Acts.* SBLDS 39. Missoula: Scholars, 1977.

Johnson, Marshall D. *The Purpose of the Biblical Genealogies with Special Reference to the Setting of the Genealogies of Jesus.* Cambridge: Cambridge University Press, 1969.

Jones, D. L. "The Title Κύριος in Luke-Acts," in George W. MacRae, ed., *SBL 1974 Seminar Papers* 2 vols. (Cambridge, Mass.: Society of Biblical Literature, 1974) 2:85–101.

Jonge, Marinus de. "Sonship, Wisdom, Infancy: Luke ii.41-51a," *NTS* 24 (1978) 317–54.

Kahlefeld, Heinrich. *Der Jünger: eine Auslegung der Rede Lk 6,20-49.* Frankfurt: J. Knecht, 1962.

Karris, Robert J. "Missionary Communities: A New Paradigm for the Study of Luke-Acts," *CBQ* 41 (1979) 80–97.

_____. "Poor and Rich: the Lukan *Sitz im Leben,*" in Charles Talbert, ed., *Perspectives on Luke-Acts* 112–25.

Käsemann, Ernst. "A Critical Analysis of Philippians 2:5-11," in Herbert Braun, et al., *God and Christ: Existence and Providence.* Tübingen: Mohr; New York: Harper, 1968.

Kennedy, George A. *New Testament Interpretation through Rhetorical Criticism.* Chapel Hill: University of North Carolina Press, 1984.

Kerans, Patrick. *Sinful Social Structures.* New York: Paulist, 1974.

Kilgallen, John J. "Luke 2.41-50: Foreshadowing of Jesus, Teacher," *Bib* 66 (1985) 553–59.

_____. "The Conception of Jesus (Luke 1,35)," *Bib* 78 (1997) 225–46.

Kimelman, Ronald R. "*Birkat Ha-Minim* and the Lack of Evidence for an Anti-Christian Jewish Prayer in Late Antiquity," in E. P. Sanders, ed., *Jewish and Christian Self-Definition*. Vol. 2, *Aspects of Judaism in the Graeco-Roman Period*. Philadelphia: Fortress, 1981.

Kingsbury, Jack Dean. *Conflict in Luke*. Minneapolis: Fortress, 1991.

Kissinger, Warren S. *The Sermon on the Mount: A History of Interpretation and Bibliography*. Metuchen, N.J.: Scarecrow Press, 1975.

Kittel, Gerhard. "Die Bergpredigt und die Ethik des Judentums," *ZST* 2 (1924–25) 555–94.

Kittel, Rudolf. "Exkurs: Die Armen und Elenden im Psalter," in idem, *Die Psalmen Israels, nach dem Versmass der Urschrift*. Leipzig: A. Deichertsche Verlagsbuchhandlung W. Scholl, 1915, 314–18.

Kohlberg, Lawrence. "Moral Development, Religious Thinking, and the Question of a Seventh Stage," in idem, *The Philosophy of Moral Development*. New York: Harper & Row, 1981.

_____. "Moral Stages and Moralization: the Cognitive-Developmental Approach," in T. Lickona, ed., *Moral Development and Behavior: Theory, Research, and Social Issues*. New York: Holt, Rinehart & Winston, 1976.

_____. *The Psychology of Moral Development*. San Francisco: Harper & Row, 1984.

Koninck, Charles de. *De la Primauté du Bien Commun*. Quebec: Université Laval, 1943.

Kramer, Werner R. *Christ, Lord, Son of God*. Translated by Brian Hardy. Naperville, Ill.: A. R. Allenson, 1966.

Krodel, Gerhard. "Persecution and Toleration of Christianity until Hadrian," in Stephen Benko and John J. O'Rourke, eds., *The Catacombs and the Colosseum: The Roman Empire as the Setting of Primitive Christianity*. Valley Forge, Pa.: Judson Press, 1971.

Kümmel, Werner G. "Lukas in der Anklage der heutigen Theologie," *ZNW* 63 (1972) 149–65.

_____. *Promise and Fulfilment, The Eschatological Message of Jesus*. Translated by Dorothea M. Barton. London: S.C.M., 1961.

Kunz, George. *The Paradox of Power and Weakness: Lévinas and an Alternative Paradigm for Psychology*. Albany: S.U.N.Y. Press, 1998.

Kuschke, Arnulf. "Arm und reich im Alten Testament mit besonderer Berücksichtigung der nachexilischen Zeit," *ZAW* 57 (1939) 31–57.

Kyo-Seon Shin, Gabriel. *Die Ausrufung des endgültigen Jubeljahres durch Jesus in Nazareth*. Frankfurt: Peter Lang, 1989.

Lambrecht, Jan. "The Sayings of Jesus on Non-Violence," *Louvain Studies* 12 (1987) 291–305.

Legrand, Lucien. "The Angel Gabriel and Politics. Messianism and Christology," *IndThSt* 26 (1989) 1–21.

Leivestad, Ragnar. "*tapeinos-tapeinophron*," *NovT* 8 (1966) 36–47.

Lenski, Gerhard E. *Power and Privilege: A Theory of Social Statification*. Chapel Hill: University of North Carolina Press, 1984.

Lévinas, Emmanuel. *Ethics and Infinity.* Translated by Richard A. Cohen. Pittsburgh: Duquesne University Press, 1985.

_____. *Otherwise than Being: or, Beyond Essence.* Translated by Alphonso Lingis. The Hague: Martinus Nijhoff, 1981.

_____. *Totality and Infinity: An Essay on Exteriority.* Pittsburgh: Duquesne University Press, 1969.

Lifton, Robert Jay. *The Protean Self: Human Resilience in an Age of Fragmentation.* New York: Basic Books, 1993.

_____. *Revolutionary Immortality; Mao Tse-tung and the Chinese Cultural Revolution.* London: Heidenfeld & Nicholson, 1969.

Loeb, Isidore. *La littérature des Pauvres dans le Bible.* Paris: Cerf, 1892.

Lohfink, Gerhard. "Der ekklesiale Sitz im Leben der Aufforderung Jesu zum Gewaltverzicht (Mt 5,39b-42/Lk 6,29f)," *ThQ* 162 (1982) 237–53.

_____. *Die Sammlung Israels. Eine Untersuchung zur lukanischen Ekklesiologie.* Munich: Kösel, 1975.

Lohfink, Norbert. "The Laws of Deuteronomy: A Utopian Project for a World without any Poor," *ScrBull* 26 (1996) 2–19.

_____. "Poverty in the Laws of the Ancient Near East and of the Bible," *TS* 52 (1991) 34–50.

_____. "Von der 'Anawim-partei' zur 'Kirche der Armen,'" *Bib* 67 (1986) 153–76.

Lonergan, Bernard. *Insight; A Study of Human Understanding.* New York: Philosophical Library, 1956.

_____. *Method in Theology.* New York: Herder and Herder, 1972.

Lorenzmeier, Theodor. "Zum Logion Mt 12;18; Lk 11:20," in Hans-Dieter Betz and Luise Schottroff, eds., *Neues Testament und Christliche Existenz.* Tübingen: Mohr, 1973.

Luck, Ulrich. "Kerygma, Tradition und Geschichte bei Lukas," *ZTK* 57 (1960) 51–66.

Lührmann, Dieter. "Liebet eure Feinde (Lk 6,27-36/Mt 5:39-48)," *ZTK* 69 (1972) 412–38.

Luz, Ulrich. *Matthew 1–7.* Minneapolis: Augsburg, 1992.

Mack, Burton L. "The Kingdom Sayings in Mark," in *Foundations and Facets Forum* 3 (1987) 3–47.

_____. *Rhetoric and the New Testament.* Minneapolis: Fortress, 1990.

Maddox, Robert. *The Purpose of Luke-Acts.* Edinburgh: T & T Clark, 1982.

Malina, Bruce J. *The New Testament World: Insights from Cultural Anthropology.* Atlanta: John Knox, 1981 [rev. ed., 1993].

Malina, Bruce J., and Richard L. Rohrbaugh. *Social-Science Commentary on the Synoptic Gospels.* Minneapolis: Fortress, 1992.

Manson, Thomas W. *The Teaching of Jesus.* Cambridge: Cambridge University Press, 1931.

_____. *The Sayings of Jesus.* London: S.C.M., 1937.

Maritain, Jacques. *The Person and the Common Good.* Translated by John J. Fitzgerald. New York: Charles Scribner's Sons, 1947.

Marshall, I. Howard. "The Synoptic Son of Man Sayings in Recent Discussion," *NTS* 12 (1964) 327–51.

Maslow, Abraham. *Motivation and Personality.* New York: Harper & Row, 1970.

Massaux, Edouard. *Influence de l'Évangile de St. Matthieu sur la littérature chrétienne avant St. Irénée.* Louvain: Gembloux, 1950. English: *The Influence of the Gospel of Saint Matthew on Christian Literature before Saint Irenaeus.* Translated by Norman J. Belval and Suzanne Hecht; edited and with an introduction and addenda by Arthur J. Bellinzoni. Leuven: Peeters; Macon, Ga.: Mercer University Press, 1990.

_____. "Le texte du sermon sur la montagne de Mattieu utilisé par saint Justin," *ETL* 28 (1952) 411–48.

Mattill, Andrew J. "*Naherwartung, Fernerwartung,* and the Purpose of Luke-Acts: Weymouth Reconsidered," *CBQ* 34 (1972) 276–93.

_____. "The Jesus-Paul Parallels and the Purpose of Luke-Acts: H. H. Evans Reconsidered," *NovT* 17 (1975) 15–46.

McArthur, Harvey K. *Understanding the Sermon on the Mount.* New York: Harper, 1960.

McDermott, J. M. "Jesus and the Son of God Title," *Greg* 62 (1981) 277–317.

McEleney, Neil J. "Peter's Denials—How Many? To Whom?" *CBQ* 52 (1990) 467–472.

McKenzie, John L. *Second Isaiah.* Garden City, N.Y.: Doubleday, 1968.

Meier, John P. *A Marginal Jew: Rethinking the Historical Jesus.* 2 vols. to date. New York: Doubleday, 1991, 1994.

_____. "The Circle of the Twelve: Did it Exist during Jesus' Public Ministry?" *JBL* 116 (1997) 635–72.

_____. "Symmetry and Theology in the Old Testament Citations of Heb 1,5-14," *Bib* 66 (1985) 504–33.

Merk, Otto. "Das Reich Gottes in den lukanischen Schriften," in E. Earle Ellis and Erich Grässer, eds., *Jesus und Paulus. Festschrift für Werner Georg Kümmel zum 70. Geburtstag.* Göttingen: Vandenhoeck & Ruprecht, 1975.

Merx, Adalbert. *Die vier kanonischen Evangelien nach ihrem ältesten bekannten texte. Uebersetzung und erläuterung der syrischen im Sinaikloster gefundenen palimpsesthandschrift.* 2 vols. in 4. Berlin, G. Reimer, 1897–1911.

Meyer, Rudolf. "προφήτης," *TDNT* 6:812–28.

Minear, Paul S. "Jesus' Audiences according to Luke," *NovT* 16 (1974) 103–109.

_____. "Luke's Use of 'the Birth Stories,'" in Leander Keck and J. Louis Martyn, eds., *Studies in Luke-Acts.* Nashville: Abingdon, 1966, 111–30.

Mitchell, Alan C. "Zacchaeus Revisited: Luke 19,8 as a Defense." *Bib* 71 (1990) 153–76.

Mitsis, Phillip. *Epicurus' Ethical Theory: The Pleasures of Invulnerability.* Ithaca: Cornell University Press, 1988.

Monden, Louis. *Sin, Liberty, and Law.* Translated by Joseph Donceel. New York: Sheed and Ward, 1965.

Moore, Stephen D. "Doing Gospel Criticism as/with a Reader," *BTB* 19 (1989) 85–93.

Moran, William L. "The Ancient Near Eastern Background of the Love of God in Deuteronomy." *CBQ* 25 (1963) 77–87.

Morgenthaler, Robert. *Die lukanische Geschichtsschreibung als Zeugnis. Gestalt und Gehalt der Kunst des Lukas.* 2 vols. ATANT 14, 15. Zürich: Zwingli, 1949.

Moulder, James. "Who are my Enemies?" *JTSA* 25 (1978) 41–49.

Moxnes, Halvor. *The Economy of the Kingdom.* Philadelphia: Fortress, 1988.

Munch, P. "Einige Bemerkungen zu den *ʿanawîm* und den *resaʿim* in den Psalmen," *Le Monde Oriental* 30 (1936) 13–26.

Murphy-O'Connor, Jerome. "Christological Anthropology: Phil II, 6-11," *RB* 83 (1976) 25–50.

Murray, John Courtney. *The Problem of God.* New Haven: Yale University Press, 1964.

Nauck, Wolfgang. "Freude im Leiden: Zum Problem in der urchristlichen Verfolgungstradition," *ZNW* 46 (1955) 73–76.

Nissen, Andreas. *Gott und der Nächste im antiken Judentum: Untersuchungen zur Doppelgebot der Liebe.* WUNT 15. Tübingen: Mohr, 1974.

Noack, Bent. *Das Gottesreich bei Lukas. Eine Studie zu Luk 17,20-24.* Lund: Gleerup, 1948.

_____. *Satanás und Sotería: Untersuchungen zur neutestamentlichen Dämonologie.* Copenhagen: Gads, 1948.

ó Fearghail, Fearghus. *The Introduction to Luke-Acts: A Study of the Role of Lk 1, 1–4, 44 in the Composition of Luke's Two-Volume Work.* AnBib 126. Rome: Biblical Institute Press, 1991.

_____. "The Literary Forms of Luke 1,5-25 and 1,26-38," *Marianum* 43 (1981) 321–44.

O'Toole, Robert F. *The Unity of Luke's Theology.* Wilmington, Del.: Michael Glazier, 1984.

Osiek, Carolyn. *What are They Saying about the Social Setting of the New Testament?* New York: Paulist, 1992.

Ott, Wilhelm. *Gebet und Heil: Die Bedeutung der Gebetsparänese in der lukanischen Theologie.* SANT 12. Munich: Kosel, 1965.

Palmer, Richard E. *Hermeneutics; Interpretation Theory in Schleiermacher, Dilthey, Heidegger, and Gadamer.* Evanston: Northwestern University Press, 1969.

Perkins, Pheme. *Love Commands in the New Testament.* New York: Paulist, 1982.

Perrin, Norman. *Jesus and the Language of the Kingdom.* Philadelphia: Fortress, 1976.

_____. *The Kingdom of God in the Teaching of Jesus.* Philadelphia: Westminster, 1963.

Piaget, Jean. *The Moral Judgment of the Child.* London: Routledge & Kegan Paul, 1932.

Pilgrim, Walter E. *Good News to the Poor: Wealth and Poverty in Luke-Acts.* Minneapolis: Augsburg, 1981.

Piper, John. *"Love Your Enemies": Jesus' Love Command in the Synoptic Gospels and in the Early Christian Paraenesis: A History of the Tradition and Interpretation of its Uses* MSSNTS 38. London: Cambridge University Press, 1979.

Pleins, J. David. "Poor, Poverty," *ABD* 5:402–414.

Ploeg, Jan van der. "Les pauvres d'Israel et leur piete," *OTS* 7 (1950) 236–70.

Pope, Stephen J. "Knowability of the Natural Law: A Foundation for Ethics of the Common Good," in James Donahue and Mary Teresa Moser, eds., *Religion,*

Ethics, and the Common Good. CTS 41. Mystic, Conn.: Twenty-Third Publications, 1996.

Pottérie, Ignace de la, "Le titre κύριος appliqué à Jésus dans l'évangile de Luc," in Albert Descamps and André de Halleux, eds., *Mélanges bibliques en hommage au R. P. Béda Rigaux.* Gembloux: Duculot, 1970.

Puech, Emile. "4Q525 et les pericopes des beatitudes en Ben Sira et Matthieu," *RB* 98 (1991) 80–106.

Quell, Gottfried. "ἀγαπάω," *TDNT* 1:21–35.

_____. "κύριος," *TDNT* 3:1058–81.

_____. "πατήρ," *TDNT* 5:959–74.

Quesnell, Quentin. *The Mind of Mark.* AnBib 38. Rome: Biblical Institute Press, 1969.

Rad, Gerhard von, et al. "βασιλεύς," *TDNT* 1:565–93.

Rahlfs, Alfred. *'Ani und 'anaw in den Psalmen.* Göttingen: Dietrich, 1892.

Rahner, Karl. *Foundations of Christian Faith.* New York: Seabury, 1978.

_____. *Hearers of the Word.* New York: Continuum, 1994 [1941].

Rank, Otto. *Beyond Psychology.* New York: Dover, 1958.

Rasco, Emilio. *La Teología de Lucas: origen, desarrollo, orientaciones.* Rome: Gregorian University Press, 1975.

Reese, David G. "Demons, New Testament," *ABD* 2:140–42.

Resseguie, James L. "Reader-Response Criticism and the Synoptic Gospels," *JAAR* 52 (1984) 307–24.

Rehkopf, Friedrich. *Die lukanische Sonderquelle.* Tübingen: Mohr, 1959.

Rengstorf, Karl H. "ἁμαρτωλός," *TDNT* 1:317–25.

_____. "διδάσκαλος," *TDNT* 2:140–60.

_____. "μαθητής," *TDNT* 4, 400–61.

Rice, George E. "Luke 4:31-44: Release for the Captives." *AUSS* 20 (1982) 23–28.

Ricoeur, Paul. *Freud and Philosophy: An Essay on Interpretation.* New Haven: Yale University Press, 1970.

_____. "The Golden Rule: Exegetical and Theological Perplexities," *NTS* 36 (1990) 392–97.

Rider, Bertha Carr. *The Greek House; Its History and Development from the Neolithic Period to the Hellenistic Age.* Cambridge: Cambridge University Press, 1965 [1916].

Rimmon-Kenan, Shlomith. *Narrative Fiction: Contemporary Poetics.* London and New York: Methuen, 1983.

Ringe, Sharon H. *Jesus, Liberation, and the Biblical Jubilee: Images for Ethics and Christology.* Philadelphia: Fortress, 1985.

Rondet, Henri. *Original Sin: The Patristic and Theological Background.* Translated by Cajetan Finegan. New York: Alba House, 1972.

Roth, S. John. *The Blind, the Lame, and the Poor: Character Types in Luke-Acts.* Sheffield: Sheffield Academic Press, 1997.

Rücker, H. von. "Warum wird *'ahab* (lieben) im Alten Testament selten zur Bezeichnung für Nächstenliebe gebraucht?" in Joseph Reindl and Georg Hentschel, eds., *Dein Wort Beachten: Alttestamentliche Aufsätze.* Leipzig: St. Benno-Verlag, 1981.

Rüger, Hans-Peter. "Mit welchem Mass ihr meßt, wird euch gemessen werden," *ZNW* 69 (1960) 174–82.

Sagne, Jean Claude. *Conflit, changement, conversion. Vers une éthique de la réciprocité.* Paris: Cerf-Desclée, 1974.

Sahlins, Marshall D. *Stone Age Economics.* Chicago: Aldine-Atherton, 1972.

Sakenfeld, Katherine Doob. "Love (OT)," *ABD* 4:375–81.

Saldarini, Anthony J. "Pharisees," *ABD* 5:289–303.

_____. *Pharisees, Scribes, and Sadduccees in Palestinian Society.* Wilmington, Del.: Michael Glazier, 1988.

Sand, Alexander. "ἄνθρωπος," *EDNT* 1:100–104.

Sanders, James A. "From Isaiah 61 to Luke 4," in Jacob Neusner, ed., *Christianity, Judaism and Other Greco-Roman Cults: Studies for Morton Smith at Sixty.* Leiden: Brill, 1975.

Sauer, Jürgen. "Traditionsgeschichtliche Erwägungen zu den synoptischen und paulinischen Aussagen über Feindesliebe und Wiedervergeltungsverzicht," *ZNW* 76 (1985) 1–28.

Scharbert, Josef. "Blessing," *EBT* 69–75.

Schmid, Josef. "Der Lohngedanke im Judentum und in der Lehre Jesu" in idem, *Das Evangelium nach Matthäus.* Regensburg: Pustet, 1959.

Schnackenburg, Rudolf. *God's Rule and Kingdom.* Translated by John Murray. New York: Herder & Herder, 1963.

Schneider, Gerhard. "Imitatio Dei als Motiv der 'Ethik Jesu,'" in Helmut Merklein, ed., *Neues Testament und Ethik.* Freiburg: Herder, 1989.

_____. *Die Apostelgeschichte.* HTKNT 5. Freiburg: Herder, 1980.

Schneiders, Sandra M. *The Revelatory Text.* San Francisco: HarperSan Francisco, 1991.

Schoonenberg, Piet. *Man and Sin; A Theological View.* Notre Dame: University of Notre Dame Press, 1965.

Schottroff, Luise. "Das Magnificat und die älteste Tradition über Jesus von Nazareth," *EvTh* 38 (1978) 298–313.

_____. "Non-Violence and the Love of One's Enemies," in Reginald H. Fuller, ed., *Essays on the Love Commandment.* Philadelphia: Fortress, 1978.

Schottroff, Luise, and Wolfgang Stegemann. *Jesus von Nazareth: Hoffnung der Armen.* Stuttgart: Kohlhammer, 1978.

Schrage, Wolfgang. "τυφλός," *TDNT* 8:270–94.

Schrenk, Gottlob. "πατήρ," *TDNT* 5:945–59.

Schubert, Paul. "The Structure and Significance of Luke 24," in Walter Eltester, ed., *Neutestamentliche Studien für Rudolph Bultmann zu seinem 70. Geburtstag am 20. August 1954.* BZNW 21. Berlin: Töpelmann, 1957.

Schweitzer, Albert. *The Quest of the Historical Jesus.* New York: Macmillan, 1968 [1906].

Schweitzer, Wolfgang. *Gotteskindschaft, Wiedergeburt und Erneuerung im Neuen Testament und in seiner Umwelt.* Unpublished Dissertation at Tübingen, 1943.

Schweizer, Eduard. "Formgeschichtliches zu den Seligpreisungen Jesu," *NTS* 19 (1972–73) 121–26.

Scott, Bernard Brandon. *Hear then the Parable: A Commentary on the Parables of Jesus.* Minneapolis: Fortress, 1989.

Seccombe, David P. *Possessions and the Poor in Luke-Acts.* SUNT Series B/6. Linz: A. Fuchs, 1983.

Seitz, Oscar. "Love Your Enemies," *NTS* 16 (1969–70) 39–54.

Selwyn, Edward Gordon. *The First Epistle of St. Peter.* London: Macmillan, 1947.

Serra, Aristide M. "'Fecit mihi magna' (Lc 1,49a). Una formula communitaria?" *Marianum* 40 (1978) 305–43.

Sheeley, Steven M. *Narrative Asides in Luke-Acts.* JSNT.SS 72. Sheffield: Sheffield Academic Press, 1992.

Sherwin-White, A. N. "Appendix V: The Early Persecutions and Roman Law" in idem, ed., *The Letters of Pliny; A Historical and Social Commentary.* Oxford: Clarendon Press, 1966.

Sjöberg, Erik. "πνεῦμα," *TDNT* 6:375–77.

Sloan, Robert Bryan, Jr. *The Favorable Year of the Lord: A Study of Jubilary Theology in the Gospel of Luke.* Austin: Schola Press, 1977.

Smalley, Stephen S. "Spirit, Kingdom and Prayer in Luke-Acts," *NovT* 15 (1973) 59–71.

Smith, Charles Forster. *Thucydides* 4 vols. LCL. Cambridge, Mass.: Harvard University Press, 1919–23.

Smith, Dennis E. "Messianic Banquet," *ABD* 4:788–91.

_____. "Table Fellowship," *ABD* 6:302–304.

Smith, Morton. *Tannaitic Parallels to the Gospels.* JBLMS 6. Philadelphia: Fortress, 1968.

Smith, Robert H. "History and Eschatology in Luke-Acts," *CurTM* 29 (1958) 881–901.

Soggin, J. Alberto. *Das Königtum in Israel.* Berlin: A. Töpelmann, 1967.

Sperling, S. David. "Blood, Avenger of," *ABD* 1:763–64.

Staerk, Willy. *Das Deuteronomium: sein Inhalt und seine literarische Form.* Leipzig: J. C. Hinrich, 1894.

Stählin, Gustav. "τύπτειν," *TDNT* 8:263.

Stange, Carl. "Zur Ethik der Bergpredigt," *ZST* 2 (1924–25) 37–74.

Stark, Rodney. *The Rise of Christianity: A Sociologist Reconsiders History.* Princeton: Princeton University Press, 1996.

Steck, Odil Hannes. *Israel und das gewaltsame Geschick der Propheten.* Neukirchen-Vluyn: Neukirchener Verlag, 1967.

Stegemann, Wolfgang. *The Gospel and the Poor.* Philadelphia: Fortress, 1984.

Stendahl, Krister. "Hate, Non-retaliation, and Love," *HTR* 55 (1962) 343–55.

Sternberg, Meier. *The Poetics of Biblical Narrative.* Bloomington, Ind.: Indiana University Press, 1985.

Stock, Klemens. "Die Berufung Marias (Lk 1,26-38)," *Bib* 61 (1980) 461–65.

Strachey, James, et al., eds. *The Standard Edition of the Complete Psychological Works of Sigmund Freud.* London: Hogarth, 1963.

Strecker, Georg. "Die Makarismen der Bergpredigt," *NTS* (1970–71) 255–75.

_____. *Die Bergpredigt: ein exegetischer Kommentar.* Göttingen: Vandenhoeck & Ruprecht, 1985. English: *The Sermon on the Mount : an exegetical commentary.* Translated by O. C. Dean, Jr. Nashville: Abingdon, 1988.

Stuhlmacher, Peter. "Jesustradition im Römerbrief? Eine Skizze," *TBei* 14 (1983) 140–50.

Suchocki, Marjorie Hewitt. *The Fall to Violence: Original Sin in Relational Theology.* New York: Continuum, 1994.

Talbert, Charles H. "Tradition and Redaction in Romans xii, 9-21," *NTS* 16 (1969–70) 83–94.

_____. *Reading Luke: A Literary and Theological Commentary on the Third Gospel.* New York: Crossroad, 1982.

_____. *Perspectives on Luke-Acts.* Edinburgh: T & T Clark, 1978.

_____. *Literary Patterns, Theological Themes, and the Genre of Luke-Acts.* SBLMS 20. Missoula: Scholars, 1974.

Tannehill, Robert C. *The Narrative Unity of Luke-Acts: A Literary Interpretation.* 2 vols. Philadelphia: Fortress, 1986.

_____. *The Sword of His Mouth.* Philadelphia: Fortress, 1975.

Taylor, A. B. "Decision in the Desert: The Temptations of Jesus in the Light of Deuteronomy," *Int* 14 (1960) 300–309.

Theissen, Gerd. *Sociology of Early Palestinian Christianity.* Translated by John Bowden. Philadelphia: Fortress, 1978.

Theobald, Christoph. "La regle d'or chez Paul Ricoeur. Une Interrogation théologique." *RechSciRel* 83 (1995) 43–59.

Thompson, William G. *Matthew's Advice to a Divided Community.* AnBib 44. Rome: Biblical Institute Press, 1970.

Topel, L. John. "On the Injustice of the Unjust Steward: Lk 16:1-13," *CBQ* 37 (1975) 216–27.

_____. "The Lukan Version of the Lord's Sermon," *BTB* 11 (1981) 48–49.

_____. "The Tarnished Golden Rule (Luke 6:31): The Inescapable Radicalness of Christian Ethics," *TS* 59 (1998) 475–85.

_____. *The Way to Peace.* Maryknoll, N.Y.: Orbis, 1979.

Trèves, M. "Le magnificat et la Benedictus," *CCER* 27 (1979) 105–110.

Tyson, Joseph B. "Source Criticism of the Gospel of Luke," in Charles H. Talbert, *Perspectives on Luke Acts* 24–39.

_____. "The Birth Narratives and the Beginning of Luke's Gospel," *Semeia* 52 (1990) 103–20.

Unnik, W. C. van. "Die Motivierung der Feindesliebe in Lukas VI 32-35," *NovT* 8 (1966) 287–88.

Vandervelde, George. *Original Sin: Two Major Trends in Contemporary Roman-Catholic Reinterpretation.* Amsterdam: Rodopi, 1975.

Vaux, Roland de. *Ancient Israel: Its Life and Institutions.* New York: McGraw-Hill, 1961.

Vögtle, Anton. "Das Zwiegespräch der Liebe zwischen Gott und dem Menschen," *WuW* 44 (1981) 143–53.

Völkel, M. "Zur Deutung des 'Reiches Gottes' bei Lukas," *ZNW* 65 (1974) 57–70.

Watson, Francis. *Text, Church and World: Biblical Interpretation in Theological Perspective.* Grand Rapids: Eerdmans, 1994.

Weiss, Johannes. *Die Schriften des Neuen Testaments.* Vol. 1. Göttingen: Vandenhoeck & Ruprecht, 1917.

_____. *Jesus' Proclamation of the Kingdom of God.* Translated, edited, and with an introduction by Richard Hyde Hiers and David Larrimore Holland. Philadelphia: Fortress, 1971 [1900].

Weiss, Karl. "χρηστός," *TDNT* 9:483–87.

Wenham, David. "Paul's Use of the Jesus Tradition: Three Samples," in idem ed., *The Jesus Tradition Outside the Gospels.* Sheffield: JSOT Press, 1985.

Westbrook, Raymond. "Punishments and Crimes," *ABD* 5:546–56.

Westermann, Claus. *Basic Forms of Prophetic Speech.* Translated by Hugh Clayton White. Philadelphia: Westminster, 1967.

_____. *Isaiah 40–66; A Commentary.* Translated by David M. G. Stalker. Philadelphia: Westminster, 1966.

Wettstein, Johann Jakob. Ἡ Καινὴ Διαθήκη: *Novum Testamentum Graecum: editionis receptae cum lectionibus variantibus codicum mss., editionum aliarum, versionum et patrum nec non commentario pleniore ex scriptoribus veteribus hebraeis, graecis et latinis historiam et vim verborum illustrante.* 2 vols. Amsterdam: Dommer, 1751–52.

Wilckens, Ulrich. "ὑποκρίνομαι," *TDNT* 8:559–65.

Willis, Wendell, ed. *The Kingdom of God in 20th-Century Interpretation.* Peabody, Mass.: Hendrickson, 1987.

Winandy, Jacques. "Le signe de la mangeoire et des langes," *NTS* 43 (1997) 140–46.

Windisch, Hans. *The Meaning of the Sermon on the Mount.* Philadelphia: Westminster, 1951 [1929].

Wink, Walter. "Beyond Just War and Pacifism: Jesus' Nonviolent Way," *RExp* 89 (1992) 197–214.

_____. "Jesus and the Non-Violent Struggle of our Time," *Louvain Studies* 18 (1993) 3–20.

_____. *John the Baptist in the Gospel Tradition.* Cambridge: Cambridge University Press, 1968.

Wolbert, Werner. "Die Goldene Regel und das ius talionis," *TTZ* 95 (1986) 170–72.

_____. "Die Liebe zum Nächsten, zum Feind und zum Sünder," *ThGl* 74 (1984) 262–82.

Wolff, Hans-Walter. *Anthropology of the Old Testament.* Translated by Margaret Kohl. Philadelphia: Fortress, 1974.

Wrege, Hans-Theo. *Die Überlieferungsgeschichte der Bergpredigt.* WUNT 9. Tübingen: Mohr, 1968.

Wren, Malcolm. "Sonship in Luke: The Advantage of a Literary Approach," *SJT* 37 (1984) 301–11.

Wright, Christopher J. H. "Jubilee, Year of," *ABD* 3:1025–1030.

Wulfing-von Martitz, Peter. "υἱός," *TDNT* 8:338–40.

Zimmerli, Walter. "χάρις," *TDNT* 9:376–87.

Zmijewski, Josef. *Die Eschatologiereden des Lukas-Evangeliums; eine traditions- und redaktionsgeschichtliche Untersuchung zu Lk 21, 5-36 und Lk 17, 20-37.* BBB 40. Bonn: P. Hanstein, 1972.

Biblical Index